FIVE
VIEWS
ON **BIBLICAL INERRANCY**

FIVE VIEWS ON BIBLICAL INERRANCY

R. Albert Mohler Jr.

Peter Enns

Michael F. Bird

Kevin J. Vanhoozer

John R. Franke

J. Merrick, Stephen M. Garrett, general editors
Stanley N. Gundry, series editor

COUNTERPOINTS
▶ BIBLE & THEOLOGY ◀

ZONDERVAN®

ZONDERVAN

Five Views on Biblical Inerrancy
Copyright © 2013 by James R. A. Merrick, Stephen M. Garrett, R. Albert Mohler Jr.,
Kevin J. Vanhoozer, Michael F. Bird, Peter E. Enns, and John R. Franke

This title is also available as a Zondervan ebook. Visit www.zondervan.com/ebooks.

Requests for information should be addressed to:

Zondervan, *Grand Rapids, Michigan* 49530

Library of Congress Cataloging-in-Publication Data

Five views on Biblical inerrancy / R. Albert Mohler Jr., Peter Enns, Michael F. Bird,
    Kevin J. Vanhoozer, John R. Franke.
        pages cm. — (Counterpoints: Bible and theology)
    ISBN 978-0-310-33136-0 (softcover) 1. Bible—Evidences, authority, etc. 2.
    Evangelicalism.
    BS480.F58 2013
    220.1'32—dc23   2013017952

Published in association with the literary agency of Wolgemuth & Associates Inc.

Cover design: Tammy Johnson
Cover photography: FogStock LLC / SuperStock
Interior design: Matthew Van Zomeren

Printed in the United States of America

---

13 14 15 16 17 18 19 20 21 22 /QVS/ 20 19 18 17 16 15 14 13 12 11 10 9 8 7 6 5 4 3 2

CONTENTS

INTRODUCTION: ON DEBATING INERRANCY
J. MERRICK WITH STEPHEN M. GARRETT

The Bible is central to evangelical faith and witness, and, for many evangelicals, inerrancy is crucial to securing the centrality of the Bible. Inerrancy has been commonly viewed as *the* doctrine upon which evangelicalism stands or falls.[1] Perhaps the most obvious example is the doctrinal basis of the Evangelical Theological Society, which, until relatively recently, was just the doctrine of inerrancy (the doctrine of the Trinity was added in 1990). The assumption seemed to be that there was a direct correlation between believing in the accuracy of Scripture and reading Scripture accurately. When we approach Scripture in faith, we are motivated to harmonize apparent discrepancies and persist into historical or scientific data to see the vindication of the Bible. Challenges raised by critical scholarship are products not of the text but of suspicious scholars dissatisfied with or hostile to Scripture or Christianity.

Inerrancy, then, is not a mere statement about Scripture for evangelicals. Since Scripture is the source of evangelical faith, and since inerrancy is ultimately a matter of reading Scripture faithfully, inerrancy is often regarded as of the essence of genuine Christian faith. It should come as no surprise that inerrancy is resurfacing as evangelicalism is increasingly fragmented and contested, submerged between "emergence" and "resurgence."[2] All indications are that evangelicalism is once more poised to "battle over the Bible" and focus afresh on the

---

1. Examples from decades ago abound, but more recent examples include John Woodbridge, "Evangelical Self-Identity and the Doctrine of Biblical Inerrancy," in *Understanding the Times: New Testament Studies in the 21st Century*, ed. Andreas Köstenberger and Robert Yarbrough (Wheaton, Ill.: Crossway, 2011); Gregory Beale, *The Erosion of Inerrancy in Evangelicalism: Responding to New Challenges to Biblical Authority* (Wheaton, Ill.: Crossway, 2008); and Norman Geisler and William Roach, *Defending Inerrancy: Affirming the Accuracy of Scripture for a New Generation* (Grand Rapids, Mich.: Baker, 2012).

2. Referring to the emerging/emergent church movement and the so-called restless Reformed or new Calvinist movement, respectively.

doctrine of inerrancy. This time, however, evangelicals are not battling mainline Protestants; they are debating *themselves*.[3]

Our project is concerned that this link between inerrancy and evangelical identity can obscure the meaning of inerrancy and frustrate the vitality of evangelical faith. Because inerrancy is seen as the guarantor of evangelical identity, many of the conversations about it are negative in thrust, focusing more on what could be lost if inerrancy, or at least a certain version of inerrancy, is not maintained. Moreover, inerrancy is not simply a stand-alone doctrine; it is interconnected with others. Unfortunately, the electricity of the debate obscures these other doctrines, limiting the conversation and diminishing evangelical faith. There is great risk, then, that inerrancy may become the only cipher for a certain account of what it means to be an evangelical.

Accordingly, for the sake of the health of evangelicalism and the vibrancy of its faith, this book aims to concentrate not only on the doctrine of inerrancy but also on the key doctrines that inform what it means to say that Scripture is inerrant. In other words, we want to encourage conversation on the doctrinal rationale of inerrancy and its Scriptural warrant rather than on why it may or may not be detrimental to evangelicalism. For in the final analysis, our beliefs should be motivated by theological and biblical reasons rather than by sociological ones. Said simply, we should hold to inerrancy not because it secures evangelicalism but because it teaches evangelicals about God and how to put faith in him.

On Inerrancy as a Doctrine

It might be helpful to begin by reflecting on what inerrancy means as a "doctrine." In a scientific age such as ours, doctrines are often viewed as facts or as theories about biblical facts. As the scientist examines nature and formulates theories to explain its consistent behavior, so the

---

3. Three works by evangelical authors, one of whom is a contributor to this volume, are worth mentioning: Peter Enns, *Inspiration and Incarnation: Evangelicals and the Problem of the Old Testament* (Grand Rapids, Mich.: Baker Academic, 2005); A. T. B. McGowan, *The Divine Authenticity of Scripture: Recovering an Evangelical Heritage* (Downers Grove, Ill.: InterVarsity, 2008); Kenton Sparks, *God's Word in Human Words: An Evangelical Appropriation of Critical Biblical Scholarship* (Grand Rapids, Mich.: Baker Academic, 2008). The latter two are taken to task by Robert W. Yarbrough in a review essay with a telling title: "The Embattled Bible: Four More Books," *Themelios* 34, no. 1 (April 2009), http://thegospelcoalition.org/themelios/article/the_embattled_bible_four_more_books/ (March 2, 2013).

theologian formulates doctrine that explains the data of Scripture. Yet, as we have already intimated, inerrancy is not merely a statement of fact but also a posture toward the Bible—a way of reading the Bible, a criterion for what counts as faithful interpretation. Critical interpretations are often ruled out by inerrancy not always because the evidence to the contrary is compelling but also because such interpretations seem to exhibit a lack of confidence in God and the Bible.

This can be illustrated by recourse to one of perhaps the most prominent debates about inerrancy *inside* evangelicalism, the resignation of Robert Gundry from ETS in 1983.[4] Gundry's commentary on Matthew argued that certain portions of the infancy narratives were midrash. This did not contradict inerrancy, he said, because being midrash, these portions of Scripture were never intended to be factual reports. Norman Geisler headed the campaign calling for Gundry's resignation or dismissal. He never contested the details of Gundry's interpretation. Instead, on the basis of the meaning of inerrancy, he routinely returned to the point that biblical events must be factual.[5] Yet Gundry's consistent claim was that the portions of Matthew in question were never intended to be factual reports. As he explained in his surrejoinder to Geisler: "I do not deny that events reported in the Bible actually happened, but only that the Biblical authors meant to report events, or historical details in connection with events, at points where Geisler and others think they did so mean. I deny in some texts what would be the literal, normal meaning for a reader who assumes a modern standard of history-writing, but not what I believe to be the literal, normal meaning for the original audience, or even for a modern audience that is homiletically oriented."[6]

---

4. For a discussion of Gundry's ouster, see Leslie R. Keylock, "Evangelical Scholars Remove Robert Gundry for His Views on Matthew," *www.christianitytoday.com/ct/2003/novemberweb-only/11-17-42.0.html* (March 2, 2013).

5. Geisler twice insists that "a 'report' of an 'event' must be factually true, especially an inspired report" (Norman Geisler, "Is There Madness in the Method? A Rejoinder to Robert H. Gundry," *Journal of the Evangelical Theological Society* 26, no. 1 [March 1983], 102). A telling instance of Geisler's refusal is when he declared, "This is precisely what Gundry does—namely, he claims that some events reported in Matthew did not actually occur but were invented by the gospel writer" ("Methodological Unorthodoxy," *Journal of the Evangelical Theological Society* 26, no. 1 [March 1983], 91).

6. Robert Gundry, "A Surrejoinder to Norman L. Geisler," *Journal of Evangelical Theological Society* 26, no. 1 (March 1983): 113–14.

Geisler's refusal to concede this point could be viewed as an act of stubbornness. However, it must be understood that Geisler thought the meaning of inerrancy itself disallowed the possibility of midrash in the Bible. In other words, Geisler believed midrash was incommensurate with the kind of truth inerrancy claims of Scripture. It is simply inappropriate for God to reveal himself in midrashic forms. Gundry, of course, felt that Geisler was insensitive to premodern forms of communication. For Geisler, inerrancy is an axiom — a necessary truth that follows upon belief in God's truthfulness. Here inerrancy is not a conclusion drawn from exhaustive investigation into the veracity of Scripture's claims but a *rule* for reading Scripture in ways consistent with the conviction that God is truthful. Inerrancy establishes both a set of expectations about the text and the condition of sound readings of the text. Geisler never disputed the details of Gundry's interpretation but instead spoke of how interpretations espouse a philosophy.[7] Thus, in the following way, Geisler's theological intuition was correct: inerrancy bears more than just a statement about Scripture. It bears several theological convictions, convictions about who God is and how God relates to and communicates in and through the text of Scripture.

It is important therefore to recognize from the Gundry-Geisler example that, as a doctrine, inerrancy communicates far more than simply an attribute of Scripture. It communicates a way of understanding God and a way of understanding ourselves before Scripture. It is therefore bound up with the whole of Christian teaching and cannot be properly understood apart from some discussion of its doctrinal setting. Such being the case, this book hopes to generate conversations on the doctrinal commitments that determine inerrancy.

On the Doctrinal Location of Inerrancy

We will have more to say about the doctrinal commitments and the nature of this book below. Before doing so, it is important to recognize the way in which inerrancy functions as doctrine and thus speak to the issue of where inerrancy should occur in a doctrinal system. It is not at all uncommon to find the confession of inerrancy at the head of the doctrinal statements

---

7. See, for example, Geisler, "Methodological Unorthodoxy," 92; and Geisler, "Is There Madness in the Method?" 105.

of evangelical churches, ministries, and organizations. This of course has the benefit of declaring that what follows is reliable information, not merely the opinions of the people involved in the institution. Certainly, believers should be confident in their faith. But the question is, what kind of confidence, and what or who is the source of that confidence?

We wonder if there are some unintended consequences to misplacing the doctrine of inerrancy, that is, extracting it from its context of teaching about Holy Scripture and locating it at the beginning of a doctrinal statement. Placing inerrancy at the fount of doctrine can suggest things about the nature of doctrine itself. It can indicate that doctrines are merely facts or theories. Doctrine of course accords with reality, but it is not a mere fact.

The events which Christians proclaim are not events simply comparable to other historical events. They happen in history, but they are not merely historical. This is because the agent involved is not created but the Creator. Hence, the New Testament often describes events of our salvation as events of new creation (for example, John 1:1ff). The transformation effected in the events of Christian faith is rather different from a mere alteration of the general course of human history. What happens in Jesus Christ is nothing short of a reconstitution of the created order and the human being. Therefore, knowing the reality of Christ is not like knowing how the colonies won the Revolutionary War or the meaning of the Constitution of the United States. We can assimilate these truths into our repository of knowledge without much modification of ourselves or even our understanding of the world. Indeed, any aspect that may be challenging can be relativized: that was then; this is now.

But as Christians have recognized for two millennia, coming into contact with Christ involves repentance, a deep turning away from self and toward God. It involves abandoning some of our most commonsensical assumptions about what kind of place the world is, who we are, and what makes for a good life. The cross is a stumbling block (1 Cor. 1:23) and a cornerstone for a new form of humanity (Eph. 2:20) in which human enmity against one another and God is resolved (Gal. 3:28). To believe in Christ, in a certain sense, requires that we cease being "realistic," for it requires us to see beyond the so-called necessities or realities of life in a fallen world and to let our faith in Christ ground a new way of life that takes seriously the presence of the kingdom of God.

While inerrancy helpfully insists upon the factuality of Christianity, extracting it from its context in the doctrine of revelation and placing it at the head of Christian doctrine can ironically lead to a diminishment of Christian truth. Placing inerrancy at the outset of doctrinal statements seems to teach that Christian beliefs are of the order of facts. As we have suggested, facts can usually be assimilated into the self without much modification of the self, without a deep existential and moral reordering. Consequently, the Christian is taught that becoming a Christian is about learning the right information rather than submitting to the regeneration of the Holy Spirit.

What is at stake here is the existential dimensions of Christian faith.[8] Take the doctrine of justification as an example. Taken as a fact, the doctrine merely teaches that it is the work of Christ, not our own works, that makes us righteous before God. Notice how if the doctrine is seen as a mere fact rather than an existential reality, it could allow the Christian to continue in his or her life unaltered. In fact, acceptance of such a fact could be seen as something to be proud of (and some of the debates within evangelicalism about justification do tempt people to be prideful about their view of justification). Because justification is viewed as just a fact, people who believe in it are not forced to behold its true depth as a fundamentally self-shattering reality. Because justification is more than a fact, because it is a reality performed by the Creator of the world and so constitutes human identity, knowledge of justification must be more than mere acknowledgement and understanding of the mechanics of a person's relationship to Christ. Knowing justification means knowing ourselves as unrighteous, knowing ourselves as having no right to claim our justification, knowing that Christ is the only righteous one. In this way, the factuality of the doctrine is secondary to its existentiality.[9]

---

8. Use of the term *existential* should not be understood in a way that means the authors are committed to existentialist philosophy. Rather the term is being used in a less technical sense to capture the way in which Christian teaching penetrates to the deepest core of a person's identity and self-perception.

9. The great English Reformer Richard Hooker, in his "Learned Discourse on Justification" (*www.ccel.org/ccel/hooker/just.toc.html* [March 2, 2013]), recognized that the doctrine of justification itself demands that it is possible for some Catholics to have been justified by faith without believing in the doctrine of justification by faith, simply by their own self-understanding.

Furthermore, when we consider the order of Christian teaching, inerrancy is a function of the larger doctrine of revelation. Yet when inerrancy is removed from this doctrinal context, it could prove distortive of the doctrine of revelation. Specifically, it could pit revelation found in Scripture against all other human knowledge and thereby foster retreat from intellectual engagement.[10] Because we have access to indubitable truth and because secular fields of inquiry reject that source, or at least rely primarily on other data for the formulation of their views, secular fields are not as trustworthy as the simple teaching of Scripture. Hence, a misplaced doctrine of inerrancy leads to overinflated perceptions of our knowledge of truth when this doctrine is not bracketed by larger considerations of general and special revelation as well as of the relationship between revelation and reason, all of which are typically treated in the doctrine of revelation. It is best, then, to understand inerrancy within its proper doctrinal context, yet only in light of doctrinal convictions that are more fundamental. To these we now turn.

On the Doctrine of Inerrancy

Key definitions of inerrancy such as the Chicago Statement on Biblical Inerrancy (CSBI) show that inerrancy is not an isolated idea that floats free from Christian conviction. Rather inerrancy is at the very least bound up with convictions about Scripture's inspiration, reliability, and authority as well as convictions about the character of God (especially the attribute of truthfulness). The CSBI claims that inerrancy is crucial for maintaining the evangelical conviction that when the Bible speaks, God speaks. Yet inerrancy on its own does not necessarily imply anything about God's speech. It could simply be that the humans who wrote the Bible were very careful or very lucky. Moreover, divine authorship of Scripture is surely more complicated than this evangelical conviction suggests, for the relationship between divine speech and the speech of the human authors would have to be explained, at the very least, which is why verbal plenary inspiration has gone hand in hand with inerrancy in evangelicalism. There is a

---

10. On this phenomenon, see Mark Noll, *The Scandal of the Evangelical Mind* (Grand Rapids, Mich.: Eerdmans, 1995).

complex of issues that must be elucidated before inerrancy can function. What follows therefore will be a sketch of the doctrinal nexus in which inerrancy occurs.

Inerrancy is located within the doctrine of Holy Scripture. It takes place amidst a series of claims about the nature and function of Scripture, among which are the sufficiency, authority, and primacy of Scripture. These claims about Holy Scripture can be made only by first discussing the inspiration of Scripture, and thus inspiration qualifies inerrancy. Of course, the doctrine of Holy Scripture itself is a subset of the doctrine of revelation, and the doctrine of revelation is a subsidiary of the doctrine of the Holy Spirit, Christology, and ultimately the triune God. Furthermore, we must also consider revelation's reception, which must be shaped by the prior doctrines of salvation, Christ, sin, humanity, and creation.

Let's begin with the doctrine of Scripture. As we said, inerrancy must be developed in dialogue with other claims about the Bible, such as its authority and sufficiency. We'll take the latter first. Sufficiency is an interesting qualifier because it speaks to the scope of Scripture's meaning. On the one hand, the sufficiency of Scripture means that Scripture is self-interpreting. In the Reformation context, this meant that Scripture was so coherent and plain that the commoner could read it in the local vernacular and gain the knowledge necessary for salvation. Does this mean that on things not pertaining to salvation, Scripture is insufficient? Thus we might be permitted to engage in science and historiography in order to understand other matters that do not immediately pertain to our faith in Christ. Or is what is meant that all things in Scripture pertain to salvation? On the other hand, what is the meaning of sufficient? Does it mean that what Scripture says is adequate for us to have true faith but that such knowledge could be expanded by engagement with other sources so long as such expansion does not compromise the knowledge gained in Scripture? Answers to these questions will help assess the scope of inerrancy.

As we observed above, in modern scientific culture the only ideas that have authority (or rationality) are those rooted in fact, and thus if the factuality of Scripture is demonstrated, Scripture is made an authority. This is where some theologians would want to argue that inerrancy should be developed within a larger conception of divine authority rather than be determinative for authority. The Bible's authority must be understood according to the authority of God and thus should not be reduced to the authority of fact.[11] Far more than just a reliable repository of information, Scripture has intense meaning and purpose that must be engaged, and its authority is not fully regarded until the Bible is brought into conversation with contemporary realities, since God is the creator of all things. That is to say, we have not heeded the authority of Scripture as divine authority until we have heard Scripture address us utterly and obeyed.

The doctrine of revelation in which the doctrine of Scripture occurs is relevant here. One of the major questions has to do with the relationship between revelation and reason. How does reason function in relation to revelation? Are there things knowable by bare human reason on which we do not require revelation? Once more, we run into the question of the scope of Scripture's claims. There has been a tradition of saying that reason is adequate to gaining certain metaphysical and scientific truths but incapable of the higher truths of salvation and God.[12] Thomas Aquinas, for example, claimed that human reason can attain some knowledge of the being of God naturally but could never recognize that the being of God is triune.[13] What does this mean for Scripture? Does it mean that Scripture is concerned with imparting the knowledge beyond human reason, and so unconcerned with knowledge attainable by human reason? If so, does this mean that Christians can defer to science on physical or historical matters and heed Scripture only when it touches on higher truths?[14] Here the scope of revelation and its relationship to natural knowledge is important for understanding the scope of inerrancy.

---

11. For an exemplar of this perspective, see N. T. Wright, *Scripture and the Authority of God: How to Read the Bible Today* (New York: HarperOne, 2011).

12. Thomas Aquinas, Richard Hooker, and John Calvin are just three examples.

13. Note Gilles Emery, the foremost scholar of Aquinas's Trinitarian theology: "St Thomas was vigorously opposed to this apologetic project in Trinitarian theology. Neither the goodness nor the happiness of God, nor his intelligence, are arguments capable of proving that the existence of a plurality of divine persons imposes itself by rational necessity. Only the 'truth of faith', to the exclusion of any other reason, leads us to acknowledge God's tripersonality" (Gilles Emery, *The Trinitarian Theology of St Thomas Aquinas*, trans. Francesca Murphy [New York: Oxford Univ. Press, 2007], 25).

14. An interesting example of this can be found in Augustine's discussion of the relationship between science and the book of Genesis in his "The Literal Meaning of Genesis," in Augustine, *On Genesis* (New York: New City Press, 2002), 185–86.

Indeed, the doctrine of revelation should be determined, in part, by the doctrine of salvation, for revelation is not an end in itself but serves the larger end of salvation. What constitutes saving knowledge of God? Is it perfectly accurate understanding of historical events, physical laws, biology, and so on, or is it a moral and spiritual relationship with God? And what is the goal of salvation and so of saving knowledge? Here we must consider how salvation is a history and indeed is often referred to as the "history of salvation" or "history of redemption." Everyone recognizes that God works differently at different times in the course of his redemption of humankind. Dispensationalists recognize several dispensations (for example, Adam and Eve, Noah, Abraham, Moses, David, Jesus Christ, the church), while covenant theologians admit two covenants, the covenant of works and the covenant of grace. In the latter, it is usually suggested that God had to convince humanity of its sin, especially since the essence of sin is a kind of divinizing of humanity, and thus God had to first work through law in order to make way for grace, to demoralize humanity, as it were, so that humanity had no choice but to rest in the grace of God. But this seems to admit that God does not exhaustively reveal himself or his salvation in any one moment, but revelation develops over time. Some versions of inerrancy can suggest an almost exhaustive and complete account of events and divine intent. How does this square with progressive salvation/revelation? It seems inerrancy must be developed in conversation with the specificity of salvation and revelation in history. We look at the Bible as completed, but it was not always so. How, then, do we appropriately engage those earlier moments? Issues of the relationship between the two Testaments are thus important, which is why we have asked our contributors to comment on one possible discrepancy between Old and New Testaments, to be described below.

These questions of the nature and purpose of the text are further complicated by the doctrine of inspiration. As the Gundry-Geisler debate demonstrated, this doctrine was a source of divergence. Geisler disallowed Gundry's hermeneutics which saw authorial intent as the locus of meaning or at least a clue to meaning. He wrote, "Gundry fails to recognize that the locus of meaning (and truth) for an evangelical is in the text, not in the mind of the author behind the text. It is the *graphai* that are inspired, not the author's intentions behind them."[15] Geisler believed that inerrancy implied verbal plenary inspiration. Verbal plenary inspiration means that the text we have is verbatim the text God inspired, down to the very terminology and syntax. It is not that God gave human authors a general impression or message that they then communicated in their own words and according to their own understanding. Rather God accommodated his message to each author's style and understanding, even as such did not interfere with the content.

However, many have argued that verbal plenary inspiration is destructive of human agency and reduces inspiration to dictation. The doctrine of inspiration should be determined by the doctrine of the Holy Spirit, which specifies the Spirit as the mediator of communion, the divine agent who unites distinct agents. In the immanent life of the Trinity, the Spirit is the bond of love, the one in whom Father and Son commune. In the economy, the Spirit is the one in and by whom believers are united to Christ. It is the Spirit's peculiar ministry to unite that which is different, and it is essential that the Spirit preserves the integrity of the different parties he unites. In this regard, any doctrine of inspiration must show how the biblical authors retain their faculties. Some have argued that if humanity is preserved from the limitations of culture and perspective, then the integrity of the human nature is compromised.[16] And what if hermeneutics shows us that authorial intent is the locus of meaning? Does a doctrine of inspiration which locates meaning in the text rather than the author destroy the normal human conventions of communication? Does it mean that the reader of Scripture does not need to engage God in order to understand the text, to gain the meaning of the text? Inerrancy should not control the mode of inspiration but should be understood as a consequence of it. But here much work needs to be done on how God secures an inerrant text without diminishing or displacing human agency.

Like all doctrines, inerrancy has its deepest mooring in the doctrine of God. For Geisler and many other inerrantists, including the authors of the CSBI, inerrancy is a consequence of the truthfulness

---

15. Geisler, "Is There Madness in the Method?" 105.
16. For example, Enns, *Incarnation and Inspiration*; Sparks, *God's Word in Human Words.*

of God, not immediately of the text itself. But as we have seen, such a quick move from divine truthfulness to inerrancy breezes over or, at the very least, abbreviates some major doctrinal issues. In the final analysis, such a quick transition ignores God's relationship to time. Classically, God's eternality meant that human language, being temporally structured or constrained, was incapable of simple reference to God's reality. Scriptural language tended to be read contemplatively and allegorically; divine illumination was necessary for finite language to be effective.[17] Later, in the Middle Ages, language was conceived of as analogical, sufficient for communicating knowledge but not technically precise.[18] The difference between God and creatures meant that human language and predication were adequate but not exhaustive of divine truth.

While there are good theological reasons for divine truthfulness, there seem to be equally good reasons for recognizing a difference between created and uncreated being as well.[19] And if there is distance, as it were (analogical language!), between our reality and God's, then perhaps it is not so simple to call God's truthfulness into question if there is a supposed error in Scripture. For example, if God's eternality means that his historical presence exceeds any temporal event, and indeed that the human relationship to God always strains human language, then the reporting of an event by a biblical author seems to involve more than mere historical accuracy. And there is possibly a sense in which factual accuracy may need to be subordinated to a more poetic rendering of an event so that its significance is grasped. How does the historical circumscription of human language fit within inerrancy? Thus God's relationship to time is important for any discussion of God's truthfulness in history.

---

17. On the issues of language, knowledge, and biblical interpretation, see Marcia Colish, *The Mirror of Language: A Study of the Medieval Theory of Knowledge* (New Haven: Yale Univ. Press, 1968); G. R. Evans, *The Language and Logic of the Bible: The Earlier Middle Ages* (Cambridge: Cambridge Univ. Press, 1991); R. P. C. Hanson, *Allegory and Event: A Study of the Sources and Significance of Origen's Interpretation of Scripture* (Louisville: Westminster John Knox, 2003); Michael Cameron, *Christ Meets Me Everywhere: Augustine's Early Figurative Exegesis* (New York: Oxford Univ. Press, 2012).

18. See, for example, Thomas Aquinas, *Summa Contra Gentiles*, bk. 1, chap. 34, *www.ccel.org/ccel/aquinas/gentiles.iv.xxxi.html*.

19. See, for example, John Wippel, *The Metaphysical Thought of Thomas Aquinas: From Finite Being to Uncreated Being* (New York: Catholic Univ. Press of America, 2000).

The above is but a sketch of the doctrinal nexus by which inerrancy must be explicated and understood. But there is also what may be called a meta-issue that inerrancy raises, namely, the nature of truth. One of the interesting issues here is the relationship between the truth of inerrancy and the truth inerrancy claims of the Bible. As intimated above, inerrancy is often viewed as an axiom, a necessary truth that follows upon divine truthfulness. Again, the Gundry-Geisler debate is illustrative. Geisler claimed that inerrancy meant factual accuracy.[20] Yet his argumentation for inerrancy turned not on the facts—again, he never disputed the details of Gundry's interpretation—but on the philosophical warrants for inerrancy. Geisler accordingly disallowed the facts of Gundry's interpretation. But here is a curious issue in the nature of truth: if inerrancy claims that the Bible is factually accurate and yet inerrancy itself is not a fact but an axiom, what ultimately do facts have to do with inerrancy? There seem to be two different standards of truth here: truth as metaphysical necessity and truth as historical factuality. How does a theory of the factual accuracy of Scripture relate to the facts of Scripture? The larger issue of truth, therefore, needs to be discussed in any account of inerrancy.

On This Book

Mindful of the complexity of inerrancy, this book hopes to generate conversation from a variety of diverse quarters on the doctrinal framework that surrounds inerrancy. As mentioned above, discussions of inerrancy too often produce more heat than light, being polemical rather than constructive. One of the aims of this book is to restore focus on these doctrinal issues so that debates about inerrancy enrich evangelical theology and faith, facilitating deeper understanding. Yet in a volume like ours, in which different perspectives are being expressed and responses are given, it would be impossible to have contributors develop and defend a full doctrinal framework while also treating some of the issues that accompany discussions of inerrancy. We have

---

20. See, for example, Geisler, "Methodological Unorthodoxy," 91–92, and Geisler, "Is There Madness in the Method?" 101–3. Also, note his comment in his resignation announcement: "What is more, I love the organization and that for which it once firmly stood—the total factual inerrancy of the written Word of God" (Geisler, "Why I Resigned," http://www.normgeisler.com/articles/Bible/Inspiration-Inerrancy/ETS/2003-WhyIResigned-FromTheETS.htm).

accordingly narrowed our focus to what seem to be the most significant issues, asking our contributors to treat four topics: (1) God and his relationship to his creatures, (2) the doctrine of inspiration, (3) the nature of Scripture, and (4) the nature of truth. Contributors have been asked to develop their position on these in reference to the CSBI, given its historical prominence as the standard definition of inerrancy, and in relation to three case studies that might pose challenges to inerrancy.

One of the first requests the editors made of the contributors was that they submit three texts they believed constituted a potential challenge to inerrancy and by which they would have to test their view of inerrancy. We instructed contributors to supply suggestions for texts for three categories: (1) the factuality of Scripture, (2) canonical coherence, and (3) theological coherence. From the submissions, the editors chose two passages which were common to the submissions and one which we felt was the best of the possibilities.

For the first, we chose Joshua 6, since current archaeological and historiographical evidence calls into question the details of the text's account. Obviously, those who maintain a strictly factual account of inerrancy must defend the Bible's factuality. But for those who have a broader or different understanding of truth, or for those whose understanding of inspiration does not extend to factual accuracy, we wanted to see how Joshua 6 could still function as Scripture without being factually correct. For the second, we chose the discrepancy between Acts 9:7 and Acts 22:9. Both texts describe Saul's conversion. The former says that his travel companions "heard the voice but saw no one," while the latter says that they "saw the light but did not hear the voice of the one who was speaking" (NRSV).[21] For questions of theological coherence, we asked authors to consider Deuteronomy 20 in relation to Matthew 5. Deuteronomy is of course a portion of the Law of Israel, while many scholars believe that the Sermon on the Mount in Matthew 5 is Jesus acting as a new Moses bringing the new Law of God. Jesus himself claims that his instructions constitute the fulfillment of the Law (Matt. 5:17–20). But this is where the question of theological coherence is pressing. How is it that Deuteronomy 20

---

21. It is true that both the ESV and the NIV translate the word for "hear" as "understand" in the latter passage in order to get around this discrepancy. But both translations admit that this is a debatable decision.

instructs Israel that the complete extermination of Yahweh's enemies is a matter of Israel's purity before and obedience to Yahweh, while Jesus subsequently says that faithfulness to God requires nonretaliation and sacrificial love of enemies (Matt. 5:38–48)? If, as in some views of inerrancy, new revelation cannot be seen to correct or alter previous revelation, then how can these passages be understood? While all of our choices raise the issue of truth and inspiration, this one particularly raises the extent of inspiration. How could our knowledge of God be said to be accurate if the human relationship to God varies over time?

As you might imagine, with a doctrine as controversial as inerrancy, where what is at stake is not just the legitimacy of the view but also the very integrity and identity of evangelicalism, it was not easy to establish who should be involved, what views should be represented, and what issues should see discussion in the essays. Most basically, we wanted major voices within the evangelical community who represented both the diversity of theological disciplines and the current spectrum of evangelical opinion. We landed on two systematic theologians (John Franke and Kevin Vanhoozer), two biblical scholars (Michael Bird and Peter Enns), and one historical theologian (Albert Mohler).

After identifying authors, the most difficult issue the editors faced was trying to shape the conversation along the lines sketched above while allowing authors to develop their essays in accordance with their own personal concerns and disciplinary interests. Yet, as the contributors will likely verify, we were eager to force the conversation to take place upon the theological and biblical grounds discussed above. And this leads us to the peculiar organization of this volume. We had originally intended to follow the usual practice of volumes in the Counterpoints series and label each view in a way that captured something of the essence of its perspective. However, as the contributions came in, we realized that the conversations were happening at different levels and that there was no meaningful or fair way of categorizing them.

What we observed, and what we regard as one of this book's main contributions to the conversation, is that discussions of inerrancy are very much determined by a person's theological sensibilities and particular location within evangelicalism. Specifically, a person's understanding of inerrancy is dependent upon their sense of its function in evangelicalism and upon their diagnosis of what is needed at the present hour. We take this as further proof of the aforementioned deep connection between inerrancy and the identity of evangelicalism, which is one of the main concerns of all the authors. Our project thus must be regarded as a first step toward disentangling inerrancy as the primary link to evangelical identity.

As we reflected on the contributions, we observed that two essays seemed to be driven by a sense of evangelicalism's past. They were sensitive to the way inerrancy has functioned in previous decades. Here we slotted Mohler and Enns. Not only did their essays have noticeable and interesting lines of divergence, but also both were concerned with how inerrancy has functioned in evangelical history. Mohler is very pleased with the achievements of evangelical forebears like Warfield and Henry and is content with the CSBI. He sees little need to update previous evangelical positions on inerrancy. Enns, however, believes that evangelicalism has been hindered and deformed by older views of inerrancy. Because inerrancy carries with it some destructive baggage, he is not optimistic about the project of refreshing inerrancy for today. Moreover, both seem to hold to a more factual view of truth, with Mohler thinking the Bible must be factually accurate in every detail and Enns thinking the Bible is empirically false at times and so cannot be regarded as inerrant. Thus we place Mohler's and Enns's essays in a section titled "Perspectives on Inerrancy and the Past."

It made sense to have Bird's essay follow in part 2, "Inerrancy from an International Perspective," since much of Bird's essay represents those evangelicals outside the U.S. who feel that inerrancy is possibly too constrictive or too determined by American developments. While he finds much value in inerrancy and its articulation in the CSBI, he believes that evangelicals should not break fellowship over it and should be open to revising it so that it does not force unhelpful constraints upon Scripture. Bird's essay also brings other important textual considerations to the fore and provides a logical bridge to part 3.

In our third section, "Perspectives on Renewing and Recasting Inerrancy Today," Vanhoozer and Franke are both concerned with how inerrancy has been received and perceived within contemporary evangelicalism. Yet both address the situation differently, with Vanhoozer seeking to renew inerrancy by recovering Christian tradition and Franke desiring to recast inerrancy in light of our plural context. Unlike Mohler and Enns, Vanhoozer and Franke also think inerrancy needs to be reexpressed or rethought so that evangelicalism can meet the challenges of today and speak into current academic debates — linguistics for Vanhoozer, and concerns of colonialism and missiology for Franke.

The obvious disadvantage to this approach is that it might suggest that conversation across different sensibilities is impossible. We do not think conversations are impossible; we think they are just more complicated than what we and likely many of our readers expected. Moreover, grouping the contributions in this manner *does not* mean that the conversations are only between two authors. Rather this arrangement should be viewed as an open conversation with crisscrossing lines between all the essays. Hence, we believe this is an advantage that calls attention to where the debate lies at present; and, as mentioned above, we think this is one of the key contributions of this volume and one of the ways it can move the conversation forward to include more diverse voices from both within and without North America.

At the same time, readers are encouraged to examine the conclusion, where we will continue the conversation started here about the doctrinal dimensions of inerrancy by making plain the lines of continuity and discontinuity between the authors, which will particularly emerge in the response sections. Consequently, readers should be able to see the kinds of theological and hermeneutical decisions necessary to constructing a doctrine of inerrancy. We believe this will generate new conversations about inerrancy that consider previous questions as well as new ones, enriching the lives and faith of evangelicals. Furthermore, we will call attention to those matters that are insufficiently developed and thus require more attention in future conversations.

This book is not an end in itself but a means to an end, that end being a charitable, fruitful conversation designed to enrich the life and faith of evangelicals. Our hope is that its readers will gain a sense for the theological and hermeneutical decisions on which fresh conversations need to take place, for the health and vitality of evangelical faith.

PERSPECTIVES ON
INERRANCY AND THE PAST

WHEN THE BIBLE SPEAKS, GOD SPEAKS:
THE CLASSIC DOCTRINE OF BIBLICAL INERRANCY

R. ALBERT MOHLER JR.

An affirmation of the divine inspiration and authority of the Bible has stood at the center of evangelical faith as long as there have been Christians known as evangelicals. The Reformation itself was born out of a declaration of the supreme authority of the Bible and absolute confidence in its truthfulness. In affirming that the Bible, as a whole and in its parts, contains nothing but God-breathed truth, evangelicals have simply affirmed what the church universal had affirmed for well over a millennium — *when the Bible speaks, God speaks.*

The centrality of inerrancy has been a core affirmation of evangelical Christianity as a movement, as evidenced by consensus documents such as the Chicago Statement on Biblical Inerrancy and the fact that the Evangelical Theological Society has required an affirmation of the Bible's inerrancy from the society's inception. The society's statement expresses the affirmation clearly and succinctly: "The Bible alone, and the Bible in its entirety, is the Word of God written and is therefore inerrant in the autographs."

Nevertheless, the inerrancy of Scripture has not been universally accepted by all who would call themselves evangelical and who would function within the evangelical movement. Even an inerrantist of the stature of Carl F. H. Henry would argue that inerrancy should be seen as a requirement of evangelical consistency rather than as a test of evangelical integrity.[1] Some, such as Clark Pinnock, would write clear-minded

---

1. Carl F. H. Henry, "Evangelicals in Search of Identity," *Christianity Today* (January 16, 1976), 32–33.

affirmations of the classical evangelical statement of inerrancy, only to turn years later and write manifestoes calling for evangelicals to abandon the doctrine.[2]

In more recent times, some have warned that an affirmation of Scripture's inerrancy would lead to intellectual disaster for the evangelical movement. Still others complain that the concept is bothersome at best and inherently divisive. Roger Olson of Truett Theological Seminary at Baylor University has argued that inerrancy "has become a shibboleth — a gate-keeping word used to exclude people rather than to draw authentic Christians together for worship and witness."[3]

To the contrary, I believe that the affirmation of the Bible's inerrancy has never been more essential to evangelicalism as a movement and as a living theological and spiritual tradition. Furthermore, I believe that the inerrancy of Scripture is crucial to the project of perpetuating a distinctively evangelical witness into the future. Without inerrancy, the evangelical movement will inevitably become dissolute and indistinct in its faith and doctrines and increasingly confused about the very nature and authority of its message.

The issue remains as clear as it was when evangelicals first sought to define a theological and spiritual trajectory that would simultaneously avoid the liberalism and theological accommodationism of mainline Protestantism and the intellectual separatism of fundamentalism. Those who would affirm the divine inspiration and authority of the Bible must make clear the extent of that affirmation. Do we really believe that God breathed out and inspired every word of the Bible? Do we believe that the Bible, as the Word of God written, shares God's own perfection and truthfulness? Do we believe that when the Bible speaks, God speaks? If so, we affirm the inerrancy of Scripture without reservation or hesitation.

If we do not make these affirmations, then we have set ourselves upon a project of determining which texts of the Bible share those perfections, if any. We will use a human criterion of judgment to decide

2. See Clark Pinnock, *A Defense of Biblical Infallibility* (Phillipsburg, N.J.: P&R, 1967); Pinnock, *Biblical Revelation: The Foundation of Christian Theology* (Chicago: Moody, 1971); cf. Pinnock, *The Scripture Principle* (New York: Harper & Row, 1984).

3. Roger Olson, "Why 'Inerrancy' Doesn't Matter," *The Baptist Standard* (February 3, 2006).

which texts bear divine authority and which texts can be trusted. We will decide, one way or another, which texts we believe to be God speaking to us.

I will make my position plain. I do not believe that evangelicalism can survive without the explicit and complete assertion of biblical inerrancy. Given the pressures of late modernity, growing ever more hostile to theological truth claims, there is little basis for any hope that evangelicals will remain distinctively evangelical without the principled and explicit commitment to the inerrancy of the Bible.

Beyond this, inerrancy must be understood as necessary and integral to the life of the church, the authority of preaching, and the integrity of the Christian life. Without a total commitment to the trustworthiness and truthfulness of the Bible, the church is left without its defining authority, lacking confidence in its ability to hear God's voice. Preachers will lack confidence in the authority and truthfulness of the very Word they are commissioned to preach and teach. This is not an issue of homiletical theory but a life-and-death question of whether the preacher has a distinctive and authoritative Word to preach to people desperately in need of direction and guidance. Individual Christians will be left without either the confidence to trust the Bible or the ability to understand the Bible as something less than totally true.

The way out of hermeneutical nihilism and metaphysical antirealism is the doctrine of revelation. It is indeed the evangelical, biblical doctrine of revelation that breaks this epistemological impasse and becomes the foundation for a revelatory epistemology. This is not foundationalism in a modernist sense. It is not rationalism. It is the understanding that God has spoken to us in a reasonable way, in language we can understand, and has given us the gift of revelation, which is his willful disclosure of himself, the forfeiture of his personal privacy.

Though many efforts have been made to suggest that the issue of inerrancy is too complex to be reduced to simple alternatives, the simple alternatives steadfastly remain: we will either affirm the total truthfulness of the Bible in whole and in part, or we will concede that at least some parts, if not the whole, are something less than totally truthful and trustworthy. There are indeed complex and complicated issues to consider, but the stark alternatives remain.

J. I. Packer has described a "thirty years' war" over inerrancy within evangelicalism, spanning the years 1955–85.[4] This very discussion is evidence that this issue is not yet fully settled and that the struggle to maintain a full embrace of inerrancy is ongoing, now fifty years and more after the issue arose with new vigor.

Packer expressed his concern this way: "I see biblical authority as methodologically the most basic of theological issues. And I have fought not just for the sake of confessional orthodoxy or theological certainty or evangelical integrity or epistemological sanity or to counter dehumanizing rationalisms. Rather, my affirmation and defense of Holy Scripture has been first and foremost for the sake of pastoral and evangelistic ministry, lay godliness, the maturing of the church, and spiritual revival."[5]

The Evangelical Theological Society made the affirmation of inerrancy a requirement for membership when the group was founded in 1949. At that time, the denominations and institutions of mainline Protestantism were moving quickly into a mode of theological liberalism, and many had abandoned or explicitly denied biblical inerrancy long before then. Evangelicals understood themselves to be, as a movement, distinct from mainline Protestantism precisely because of the theological affirmations evangelicals were determined to maintain. As in the Reformation, the foundational affirmation, even the formal principle of evangelicalism, was the full affirmation of biblical authority.

But did that affirmation of biblical authority require inerrancy? A private gathering of evangelical theologians from several nations in 1966 in Wenham, Massachusetts, set the stage for the debate within evangelicalism that rages even today. At that meeting, it became clear that at least some evangelical scholars present had serious reservations about inerrancy.[6]

---

4. J. I. Packer, "The Thirty Years' War: The Doctrine of Holy Scripture," in *Practical Theology and the Ministry of the Church, 1952–1984: Essays in Honor of Edmund P. Clowney*, ed. Harvie M. Conn (Phillipsburg, N.J.: P&R, 1990), 25–46.

5. Packer, "The Thirty Years' War," 25.

6. Packer would later reflect, "Those who organized and funded Wenham wanted it to be a peace conference, either resolving the differences or showing that all were already agreed deep down. But not all were agreed, and peace was impossible, although a friendly communiqué was issued at the end. Division continued." (Packer, "The Thirty Years' War," 31.)

Writing years later, Carl Henry recalled, "None of the participants in the 1966 Wenham Conference on Scripture either affirmed the errancy of Scripture or contended that scriptural errancy is the historic view of the church; in other words, those who did not champion inerrancy did not on that account automatically express commitments to errancy. They were simply noncommittal on the question of the errorlessness of Scripture."[7] And yet, Henry observed, the failure to commit to biblical inerrancy opened the door to concessions that were, in truth, made almost inevitable by this failure.

Henry observed, "To say that biblical inerrancy is not the first thing to be declared is not to deny its importance; it is integral to a Christian apologetic that presents evangelical theology in its totality. The search for a biblical authority that accommodates errancy has tragically eroded theological energies, and has been as fruitless and even more so than has a fixation on inerrancy."[8]

On the other side of the Atlantic, the debate emerged even earlier. In 1957, Gabriel Hebert threw down a gauntlet of sorts with his book *Fundamentalism and the Church of God*.[9] In that book, Hebert accused British evangelicals of holding, in effect, to a view of scriptural truth and authority that is tantamount to idolatry. He rejected not only inerrancy but also any affirmation, however qualified, of the Bible's total truthfulness. In response, Packer delivered a series of addresses that were published the very next year as *"Fundamentalism" and the Word of God*.[10] Packer's position was clear, and it represented the mainstream of British evangelicalism.

The Bible, Packer asserted, "is word for word God-given; its message is an organic unity, the infallible Word of an infallible God, a web of revealed truths centered upon Christ; it must be interpreted in its natural sense, on the assumption of its inner harmony; and its meaning can be grasped only by those who humbly seek and gladly receive the help of the Holy Spirit."[11]

---

7. Carl F. H. Henry, *God Who Speaks and Shows*, God, Revelation and Authority, vol. 4, 2nd ed. (Wheaton, Ill.: Crossway, 1999), 367.

8. Ibid., 366.

9. Gabriel Hebert, *Fundamentalism and the Church of God* (London: SCM Press, 1957).

10. J. I. Packer, *"Fundamentalism" and the Word of God* (Leicester: Inter-Varsity Fellowship, 1958).

11. Ibid., 113–14.

Back in the United States, Fuller Theological Seminary, a flagship institution of what had been known as the "New Evangelicalism," revised its confessional statement in the early 1970s after more than a decade of intense debate among the school's faculty, trustees, and alumni. In its earlier version, the confession stated, "The books which form the canon of the Old and New Testaments as originally given are plenarily inspired and free from all error in the whole and in the part. These books constitute the written Word of God, the only infallible rule of faith and practice."[12]

In 1972, Fuller adopted a new statement that read very differently: "Scripture is an essential part and trustworthy record of this divine self-disclosure. All the books of the Old and New Testaments, given by divine inspiration, are the written word of God, the only infallible rule of faith and practice. They are to be interpreted according to their context and purpose in reverent obedience to the Lord who speaks through them in living power."[13]

Clearly, the new statement was written in order to accommodate positions that would not affirm the total inerrancy of the Bible. Plenary verbal inspiration and inerrancy were no longer required of Fuller's faculty.

The issue of inerrancy reached a fever pitch in the year 1976, declared by *Newsweek* magazine to be the "Year of the Evangelical." Harold Lindsell, a former Fuller faculty member and editor of *Christianity Today*, leveled a broadside critique at Fuller Theological Seminary, the Southern Baptist Convention, and other evangelical institutions that had abandoned or compromised the full inerrancy of Scripture. Lindsell's attack was journalistic and controversial, but his point has been made. As Carl Henry would affirm, "Lindsell is certainly right when he says, 'The doctrine of biblical inerrancy has been normative since the days of the Apostles. It was not until the last century and a half that the opponents of inerrancy ... have become a dominant force in Christianity.'"[14] Henry would affirm Lindsell's

---

12. George M. Marsden, *Reforming Fundamentalism: Fuller Seminary and the New Evangelicalism* (Grand Rapids, Mich.: Eerdmans, 1987), 113.

13. Fuller Theological Seminary, "Statement of Faith," *www.fuller.edu/about-fuller/mission-and-history/statement-of-faith.aspx* (January 12, 2013).

14. Henry, *God Who Speaks and Shows*, 367.

point: "Inerrancy is the evangelical heritage, the historic commitment of the Christian church."[15]

The issue only grew in significance throughout the 1970s, and the great crystalizing event came with the establishment of the International Council on Biblical Inerrancy and its greatest achievement, the Chicago Statement on Biblical Inerrancy, adopted in 1978.

The aims of the ICBI were clear from the outset. The group aimed to establish that plenary inerrancy has been and remains a central evangelical distinctive. The leaders of the ICBI sought "to counter the drift from this important doctrinal foundation by significant segments of evangelicalism and the outright denial of it by other movements."[16]

To do this, the leaders of the movement invited prominent evangelicals to meet near Chicago's O'Hare International Airport, October 26–28, 1978. Of the 268 delegates present, 240 voted to approve what became known as the Chicago Statement on Biblical Inerrancy (CSBI). The 240, representing an overwhelming majority of participants, affirmed a clear definition of the Bible's total inerrancy: "Being wholly and verbally God-given, Scripture is without error or fault in all its teaching, no less in what it states about God's acts in creation, about the events of world history, and about its own literary origins under God, than in its witness to God's saving grace in individual lives."[17]

Properly speaking, the Chicago Statement on Biblical Inerrancy includes an introductory statement, a short statement of the doctrine, and then a set of nineteen articles of affirmation and denial.

In the preface to the statement, the ICBI warned, "To stray from Scripture in faith or conduct is disloyalty to our Master. Recognition of the total truth and trustworthiness of Holy Scripture is essential to a full grasp and adequate confession of its authority."[18] They then declared that the CSBI "affirms this inerrancy of Scripture afresh, making clear our understanding of it and warning against its denial."[19]

---

15. Ibid.

16. From the preface to *Forever Settled: Various Documents of the International Council on Biblical Inerrancy* (Philadelphia: International Council on Biblical Inerrancy, 1979).

17. *Forever Settled*, 22.

18. Ibid., 193.

19. Ibid.

The section titled "A Short Statement" set forth the main thrust of the CSBI:

1. God, who is Himself Truth and speaks truth only, has inspired Holy Scripture in order thereby to reveal Himself to lost mankind through Jesus Christ as Creator and Lord, Redeemer and Judge. Holy Scripture is God's witness to Himself.

2. Holy Scripture, being God's own Word, written by men, prepared and superintended by His Spirit, is of infallible divine authority in all matters upon which it touches: it is to be believed, as God's instruction, in all that it affirms; obeyed, as God's command, in all that it requires; embraced, as God's pledge, in all that it promises.

3. The Holy Spirit, Scripture's divine Author, both authenticates it to us by His inward witness and opens our minds to understand its meaning.

4. Being wholly and verbally God-given, Scripture is without error or fault in all its teaching, no less in what it states about God's acts in creation, about the events of world history, and about its own literary origins under God, than in its witness to God's saving grace in individual lives.

5. The authority of Scripture is inescapably impaired if this total divine inerrancy is in any way limited or disregarded, or made relative to a view of truth contrary to the Bible's own; and such lapses bring serious loss to both the individual and the Church.

Those five definitional points establish the classical doctrine of the Bible's inerrancy, and the final point establishes the urgency. The CSBI makes the claim that the authority of Scripture is "inescapably impaired" if the total truthfulness of the Bible "is in any way limited or disregarded, or made relative to a view of truth contrary to the Bible's own." I believe that the CSBI remains the quintessential statement of biblical inerrancy and that its clearly defined language remains essential to the health of evangelicalism and the integrity of the Christian church.

There was particular wisdom in the section titled "Articles of Affirmation and Denial," to which I will make further reference. The council understood that, like every important doctrinal affirmation, biblical inerrancy had to be carefully and continually defined and redefined and that a statement of any vital doctrine required both positive and negative clarifications of meaning and intent.

The Case For Inerrancy

The argument for the total inerrancy of Scripture flows from three major sources—the Bible itself, the tradition of the church, and the function of the Bible within the church. Each source is important, and the case for inerrancy is a cumulative argument that begins and ends with the obvious point that if the Bible is not inerrant, it is something far less.

Inerrancy and the Bible's Testimony to Itself

The first point to be made is that the Bible consistently and relentlessly claims to be nothing less than the perfect Word of the perfect God who breathed its very words. The Bible is pervasively concerned with truth and, contrary to many current arguments, speaks directly to its own truthfulness in a way that cannot be relativized by modern or postmodern (or post-postmodern) theories of truth, language, and meaning.

Second Peter 1:21 makes this assertion clear: "No prophecy was ever produced by the will of man, but men spoke from God as they were carried along by the Holy Spirit."[20] Peter's point is that the Scripture is to be trusted at every point, and he defines its inspiration as being directly from God, through the agency of human authors, by means of the direct work of the Holy Spirit.

Here it is necessary to make the point that the inerrancy of the Bible is inextricably linked to a specific understanding of its inspiration. Inerrancy requires and defines verbal inspiration—the fact that God determined the very words of the Bible in the original text. A rejection of biblical inerrancy usually contains a rejection of verbal inspiration as well. This is why article 6 of the CSBI states, "We affirm that the whole of Scripture and all its parts, down to the very words of the original, were given by divine inspiration."

---

20. All Scripture quotations are from the English Standard Version unless otherwise indicated.

Note carefully that this view of inspiration does not imply divine dictation, with the human authors limited to the role of secretaries. To the contrary, verbal inspiration (specifically, a verbal plenary understanding of inspiration) affirms that God, through the Holy Spirit, sovereignly superintended the lives of the human authors and made intentional use of their own individuality. Through the work of the Holy Spirit, the human authors of Scripture freely wrote what the Holy Spirit divinely inspired, so that when the Scripture speaks, God speaks.[21] The actual mode of divine inspiration, the CSBI notes, "remains largely a mystery to us" (article 7).

In 2 Timothy 3:16, Paul asserts that all Scripture is "breathed out by God." The careful translation of this text reveals that the Bible was not merely "inspired" in the sense that the eventual product was recognized to represent a superior wisdom; the text was specifically breathed out by God.

B. B. Warfield helpfully defined this aspect of the Bible's origin and nature by insisting that the Bible is "an oracular book." As Warfield argued, the Bible is "the Word of God in such a sense that whatever it says God says — not a book, then, in which one may, by searching, find some word of God, but a book which may be frankly appealed to at any point with assurance that whatever it may be found to say, that is the Word of God."[22]

The writer of the book of Hebrews, citing Psalm 95:7–11, introduces the text with "as the Holy Spirit says" (Heb. 3:7). In Acts 4:25, a citation from Psalm 2 is described as "said by the Holy Spirit." The direct identification of the words of Scripture as said by God is found

---

21. Anything approaching a full discussion of the many issues related to the relation of the divine and human wills in the inspiration of the Bible is beyond the limitations of this essay. Suffice it here to say that the doctrine of verbal inspiration and the affirmation of biblical inerrancy require an understanding of the concursive operation of the divine and human wills in which there is divine superintendence without any violation of the human will. This flows from a natural reading of the relevant scriptural texts, and it explains the actual text of the Bible, which bears all the marks of numerous human authors and their own style, language, and context while remaining, in whole and in all its parts, nothing less than the Word of God.

22. Benjamin B. Warfield, *The Inspiration and Authority of the Bible*, ed. Samuel G. Craig (Philadelphia: Presbyterian and Reformed, 1948), 119. A helpful corrective to many misunderstandings and misrepresentations of Warfield's position is found in Michael D. Williams, "The Church, a Pillar of Truth: B. B. Warfield's Church Doctrine of Inspiration," in *Did God Really Say? Affirming the Truthfulness and Trustworthiness of Scripture*, ed. David B. Garner (Phillipsburg, N.J.: P&R, 2012), 23–47.

here and elsewhere in the Bible as both asserted and assumed. No defense of the claim is considered necessary. In Romans 9:17, Paul writes, "the Scripture says to Pharoah," referring back to Exodus 9:16. In Romans 9:15, Paul writes, "[God] says to Moses," referring to Exodus 33:19. Clearly, Paul believed that the voice of the biblical text and the voice of God are one and the same, interchangeable in his argument. As his letters reveal, he expected the churches under his care to believe that Scripture is nothing other and nothing else than the Word of God.

In 1 Thessalonians 2:13, Paul expressed appreciation for the way that the church in Thessalonica received this message: "We also thank God constantly for this, that when you received the word of God, which you heard from us, you accepted it not as the word of men but as what it really is, the word of God, which is at work in you believers."

As the Word of God, Scripture bears God's own authority and shares in his perfection. God cannot lie (Heb. 6:18), and he establishes the perfect character of his own truthfulness (Num. 23:19). If the Scriptures are the very breath of God, their perfect inspiration implies and requires that they are without error.

In an unbroken sequence of direct assertions, the Bible claims to possess God's own authority, to be directly and supernaturally inspired of God, to be unbreakable and irrefutable, and to be God's perfectly revealed Word. Inerrancy and infallibility are nothing more than summary affirmations of what Scripture claims for itself. To affirm the inerrancy of the Bible is to claim nothing more than what the Bible asserts in its consistent and pluriform attestation.

Referring to the Old Testament, Jesus affirms that the Scripture cannot be broken and that not even the smallest part will pass away. Heaven and earth will pass away, but until then, not the Word of God, in part or in whole (see John 10:34–35; Matt. 5:17–20).

Inerrancy and the Faith of the Church

The second major source for the affirmation of the Bible's inerrancy comes from the history of the church. In truth, inerrancy was the affirmation and theological reflex of the church until the most recent centuries. Earlier generations argued about the proper interpretation of the Bible, the relative authority of the Bible, and such issues as the translation of Scripture, but not about the question of the Bible containing errors. The patristic fathers employed allegorical exegesis but never claimed to find the slightest error in Scripture. The Reformers and the Roman Catholic Church debated the authority and the right to interpret the Scripture, but Protestants and Catholics were agreed that the Bible is wholly without error of any kind.

In the midst of the inerrancy controversy at Fuller Theological Seminary in the 1970s, Jack B. Rogers and Donald K. McKim argued that inerrancy is a recent development, which came about largely in response to the anti-supernaturalism of modernity. Rogers and McKim claimed that the mainstream of Christian theology through the centuries claimed the infallibility of the Bible without requiring inerrancy. Their argument gained a great deal of traction among evangelicals seeking historical argumentation to buttress their intention to reject inerrancy. But that effort was decisively refuted by John D. Woodbridge, who demonstrated that inerrancy was not merely implied but required when the historical record of the church is thoroughly explored.[23]

A decade after the Rogers and McKim thesis appeared, two leading Anglican scholars sought to dispense, once and for all, with any claim of the Bible's divine inspiration. Anthony Hanson and Richard Hanson were identical twin brothers, and both were ordained as ministers in the Church of England. Anthony would teach theology at the University of Hull, and Richard would become a bishop of the church before retiring to teach theology at the University of Manchester. In *The Bible without Illusions*, the Hanson brothers were unsparing in their rejection of any claim that the Bible was divinely inspired, much less inerrant.

Nevertheless, in making their argument for approaching the Bible "without illusions," the Hansons acknowledged, quite clearly, that the rejection of inerrancy is a very modern development in the church and that Christians throughout the centuries had both assumed and asserted the complete and total inerrancy of the Bible. In their words:

---

23. Jack B. Rogers and Donald K. McKim, *The Authority and Interpretation of the Bible: An Historical Approach* (New York: Harper and Row, 1979); John D. Woodbridge, *Biblical Authority: A Critique of the Rogers/McKim Proposal* (Grand Rapids, Mich.: Zondervan, 1982).

Again, as we have seen, the writers of the New Testament certainly believed in the inerrancy of the Old Testament, which constituted for them the scriptures. The Christian Fathers and the medieval tradition continued this belief, and the Reformation did nothing to weaken it. On the contrary, since for many reformed theologians the authority of the Bible took the place which the Pope had held in the medieval scheme of things, the inerrancy of the Bible came to be more firmly maintained and explicitly defined among some reformed theologians that it had ever been before. Only since the very end of the seventeenth century, with the rise of biblical criticism, has this belief in the inerrancy of Scripture been widely challenged among Christians.[24]

Taking their argument further, the Hanson brothers explained that any widespread rejection of the Bible's inerrancy is a very recent development. With rare honesty, they acknowledged, "The beliefs here denied [inerrancy] have been held by all Christians from the very beginning until about a hundred and fifty years ago. They are still held by a great many Christians."[25]

B. B. Warfield helpfully reminds us that inerrancy is essential to what he rightly called "the church doctrine of inspiration." In this way, Warfield asserted that inspiration and inerrancy were central affirmations of the church, not merely of individual Christians. "The church has always believed her Scriptures to be the book of God, of which God was in such a sense the author that every one of its affirmations of whatever kind is to be esteemed as the utterance of God, of infallible truth and authority."[26]

Further, Warfield stated that "in every way possible, the church has borne her testimony from the beginning, and still to our day, to her faith in the divine trustworthiness of her Scriptures, in all their affirmations of whatever kind."[27]

In a conclusive paragraph, Warfield makes the quintessential argument from the history of the church and the church doctrine of

---

24. R. P. C. Hanson and A. T. Hanson, *The Bible without Illusions* (London: SCM Press, 1989), 51–52.

25. Ibid., 13.

26. Warfield, *Inspiration and Authority of the Bible*, 112.

27. Ibid., 111–12.

inspiration. Does inerrancy entail difficulties of understanding? Warfield acknowledged that inerrancy, like every doctrinal assertion, entails certain intellectual difficulties. The real issue is whether the denial of inerrancy brings fewer difficulties. As Warfield argues, it is the rejection of inerrancy that entails the greater difficulties by far:

> The question is not, whether the doctrine of plenary inspiration has difficulties to face. The question is, whether these difficulties are greater than the difficulty of believing that the whole church of God from the beginning has been deceived in her estimate of the Scriptures committed to her charge—are greater than the difficulty of believing that the whole college of the apostles, yes and Christ himself at their head, were themselves deceived as to the nature of those Scriptures which they gave the church as its precious possession, and have deceived with them twenty Christian centuries, and are likely to deceive twenty more before our boasted advancing light has corrected their error—are greater than the difficulty of believing that we have no sure foundation for our faith and no certain warrant in our trust in Christ for salvation. We believe this doctrine of the plenary inspiration of the Scriptures primarily because it is the doctrine which Christ and his apostles believed, and which they have taught us. It may sometimes seem difficult to take our stand frankly by the side of Christ and his apostles. It will always be found safe.[28]

Warfield's nineteenth-century language may seem quaint to us, but his logic is irrefutable. The rejection of inerrancy is a modern development in the church, brought about by the rejection of specific biblical texts as inspired and authoritative and by the rejection of the very idea of divine inspiration. Inerrancy has been what the church has believed, based upon the Bible's own testimony to itself. It is what those who would affirm the full authority and verbal inspiration of the Bible must affirm even now.

Inerrancy and the Needs of the Church

The final source of the doctrine of inerrancy is the practical needs of the church. The church must live by the Word of God, or it will depend upon some human authority as a substitute for God's Word.

---

28. Ibid., 128.

Without the Bible as the supreme and final authority in the church, we are left in what can only be described as a debilitating epistemological crisis. Put bluntly, if the Bible is not the very Word of God, bearing his full authority and trustworthiness, we do not know what Christianity is, nor do we know how to live as followers of Christ.

The framers of the CSBI pointed to the pastoral needs of the church as one of the most important reasons for the importance of inerrancy. As James M. Boice explained, faithful preaching depends on the truthfulness and trustworthiness of every word of the Bible. "If the Bible contains errors," he wrote, "it is not God's Word itself, however reliable it may be. And if it is not God's Word, it cannot be preached with authority."[29]

What are Christians to believe, and how are we to live? Without a fundamental and complete trust in the whole Bible as the Word of God, we are cast adrift. Just consider the radical confusion of our day over the issue of human sexuality. Are we bound by the authority of the Bible as the authority of God himself, or is the Bible merely a sourcebook of privileged writings from which we draw some level of wisdom? The answer to that question determines what the church will teach and how Christians will live.

The same is true of what the church believes about the gospel of Christ and the entire scope of Christian theology. If the Bible is merely a collection of Jewish and Christian wisdom, it will serve only as a literary voice from the past. Any adequate understanding of the Christian faith requires a confidence that the Bible is nothing less than the living Word of the living God.

The Trustworthiness of God and His Word

In recent years, the apologetic importance of God's trustworthiness has come into clearer view. If God is trustworthy, we are saved. If he is not, we are doomed. But can God be truly trustworthy if what he presents as his own Word is not trustworthy?

Put positively, our confidence in the total truthfulness of the Bible is rooted in our confidence that God himself is completely and totally trustworthy. Paul Helm and Carl R. Trueman offer a most helpful approach in their book *The Trustworthiness of God: Perspectives on the*

---

29. *Forever Settled*, 18.

Nature of Scripture.[30] As Trueman explains, "Scripture is trustworthy because the God behind Scripture is trustworthy; and faith depends upon being convicted of the revelatory and epistemological implications of this divine trustworthiness."[31]

The focus on God's trustworthiness underlines the personal nature of God's gift of his own self-revelation. God intended not merely to give the church a collection of infallible and inerrant facts but also to reveal himself—and to do so in a manner that is completely trustworthy. Our trust in the Scriptures is entirely dependent upon our trust in God. In the same way, a lack of confidence in the truthfulness and trustworthiness of the Bible reveals a lack of confidence in either God's ability or his intention—or both—to give his people a trustworthy revelation. But, as Helm and Trueman affirm, "God has both the ability and the intention to act in a manner consistent with his goodness; he is, therefore, trustworthy."[32]

Paul Helm rightly argues that "responsible Christian interpretation of Scripture, hermeneutics, exegesis, or whatever can only be carried on against a background in which the Scriptures themselves, understood as the revelation of an utterly faithful God, exercise a regulative influence."[33] Taking full account of the responsibilities and challenges of faithful exegesis, Helm continues: "Whatever the difficulties and intricacies of exegesis, and however often our initial expectations may be overturned by our second and subsequent thoughts as interpreters, we can be confident that behind these efforts stands the authentic word of a faithful God."[34]

That phrase, *the authentic word of a faithful God*, is another way of expressing what the inerrancy, authority, inspiration, infallibility, and total perfection of Scripture claim and assure.

Truth, Trust, and Theology: Inerrancy in View

No doctrinal formulation or truth claim stands alone. The affirmation of biblical inerrancy requires prior affirmations and entails theological

---

30. Paul Helm and Carl R. Trueman, eds., *The Trustworthiness of God: Perspectives on the Nature of Scripture* (Grand Rapids, Mich.: Eerdmans, 2002).

31. Trueman, "The God of Unconditional Promise," in *The Trustworthiness of God*, 178.

32. *The Trustworthiness of God*, ix.

33. Helm, "The Perfect Trustworthiness of God," in *The Trustworthiness of God*, 250–51.

34. Ibid., 251.

consequences. To claim that the Bible is inerrant is to assume a conception of truth that affirms, in the first place, theological realism.

In other words, inerrancy is set within a theological context in which we claim to be speaking of a God who really exists and who really speaks. Christian theological realism affirms the irreducible ontological reality of the God of the Bible. This God who really exists is truly knowable, but only because he has freely revealed himself to his human creatures. God's ultimate and saving self-revelation is Jesus Christ, God's own Son. The Bible is God's written and verbal self-revelation, which finds its fulfillment in Christ and testifies of him. Without the Scriptures, we would be left with nothing more than an oral tradition concerning Christ and the comprehensive whole of God's message to us. But God, rich in mercy to his people, has given us a written Word.

In other words, God wrote a book. He did so through human authors he selected and prepared. By the Holy Spirit, the human authors of Scripture were guided into truth and protected from all error. Making full use of their human faculties and personalities, the Holy Spirit breathed the very words of Scripture through them so that the canonical writings are the product of human authors and, at the same time, are the very Word of God.

Inerrancy affirms that language is adequate to convey truth and that the actual words of Scripture were divinely inspired. The Bible is an oracular book, through which the living God speaks. The language of the Bible is, generally speaking, ordinary language. The words of Scripture include propositional statements that are meant to be believed and affirmed with full propositional force. Scripture claims to be totally true, and its truthfulness is essential to its other perfections, even as its divine inspiration is essential to its truthfulness. The God who is completely trustworthy has given his people a book that is equally trustworthy.

Words such as *infallible* and *inerrant* are meant to affirm precisely what the Bible claims for itself, and a rejection of inerrancy entails a rejection of the total truthfulness and trustworthiness of the Bible. John Frame explains, "I could wish to be done with all the extrabiblical technical terms such as *infallible* and *inerrant* and simply say that the Bible is true. But in the contexts of historical and contemporary theological discussion, that alternative is not open to us. Theologians are too inclined to distort the word *truth* into some big theological construct that has nothing to do with simple propositional correctness."[35]

Thus, I argue not only that the inerrancy of the Bible is true but also that it is necessary. Without it, we are left with the unavoidable admission that it is something less than, or other than, inerrant. And that concession would mean that the Bible contains at least some texts that are not fully trustworthy and authoritative. In the wake of that recognition, the church is left with the task of determining which texts, if any, are true and trustworthy and authoritative—and to what extent. The consequences of that confusion would be disastrous to the church and to individual Christians. Furthermore, this confusion would unavoidably reach the very heart of the church's message—the gospel of Jesus Christ.

The Chicago Statement on Biblical Inerrancy

Without reservation, I affirm the Chicago Statement on Biblical Inerrancy. I affirm the document and agree with its assertions in whole and in part. To be true to the Scriptures, I believe, evangelicals must affirm its stated affirmations and join in its stated denials.

Included in these affirmations and denials is the assertion that the Bible is "to be received as the authoritative Word of God" (article 1), and the denial that the Scriptures derive their authority from the church or from any human source. The Scriptures are "the supreme written norm by which God binds the conscience" (article 2). The church is subordinate to the Scriptures, and all creeds, councils, and confessions are normed by the Scriptures. The Bible is God's written Word "in its entirety" (article 3) and not merely a witness to revelation.

The God who made us in his image "has used language as a means of revelation" (article 4). Therefore it is denied "that human language is so limited by our creatureliness that it is rendered inadequate as a vehicle for divine revelation" (article 4). Human sin does not thwart God's inspiration of the Bible.

God's revelation in the Bible is progressive. Nevertheless, later revelation never corrects or contradicts previous revelation. The whole of

---

35. John Frame, *The Doctrine of the Word of God*, A Theology of Lordship, vol. 4 (Phillipsburg, N.J.: P&R, 2010), 170–71.

Scripture and every part, "down to the very words of the original, were given by divine inspiration" (article 6). The perfections of Scripture cannot be affirmed of the whole without including every part.

The origin of Scripture is divine, but "the mode of divine inspiration remains largely a mystery to us" (article 7). Nevertheless, the Scripture's divine inspiration cannot be "reduced to human insight, or to heightened states of consciousness of any kind" (article 7).

God used the personalities of the chosen human authors and did not override their personalities in choosing the very words of his Word. The Holy Spirit gave the human authors of Scripture "true and trustworthy utterance" (article 9) in all they wrote. Their genuine humanity did not allow falsehood of any sort to be introduced into God's Word.

The inspiration of Scripture, "strictly speaking, applies only to the autographic text of Scripture" (article 10). Translations are accurate insofar as "they faithfully represent the original" (article 10). The church is not impaired in faith or witness by the absence of the autographic texts. The Bible is both infallible and inerrant, and it cannot be one without the other. Inerrancy and infallibility "may be distinguished, but not separated" (article 11). Every word of the Bible is inerrant, not just texts limited to redemptive themes. "We further deny that scientific hypotheses about earth history may properly be used to overturn the teaching of Scripture on creation and the flood" (article 12).

Inerrancy is a necessary term, but it is not to be used "to evaluate Scripture according to standards of truth and error that are alien to its usage or purpose" (article 13). The Scriptures are a unity and are internally consistent. "Alleged errors and discrepancies" not yet resolved do not "vitiate the truth claims of the Bible" (article 14).

The Bible's own teaching affirms its inerrancy, and Jesus' own teachings about Scripture cannot be dismissed due "to accommodation or to any natural limitation of His humanity" (article 15). The doctrine of inerrancy "has been integral to the Church's faith throughout its history" and is not a recent innovation "postulated in response to negative higher criticism" (article 16).

The Holy Spirit bears witness to the Scriptures and does not act in isolation from or in opposition to the Scriptures. The proper interpretation of the Bible comes by grammatical-historical interpretation, "taking account of its literary forms and devices" (article 18) as Scripture is interpreted by Scripture. No legitimate treatment of any biblical text can lead to "relativizing, dehistoricizing, or discounting its teaching, or rejecting its claims to authorship" (article 18).

Finally, "a confession of the full authority, infallibility, and inerrancy of Scripture is vital to a sound understanding of the whole of the Christian faith," which should "lead to increasing conformity to the image of Christ" (article 19). The affirmation of inerrancy is not necessary for salvation, but a rejection of inerrancy will produce "grave consequences, both to the individual and to the Church" (article 19).

I affirm every affirmation and join in all of the CSBI's denials. There is much more to be said and confessed about the Bible, but not less. Like every doctrinal statement, the CSBI was developed at a particular moment in the life of the church, and in a particular social, historical, and cultural context. Since 1978, new challenges to the truthfulness and authority of the Scriptures have emerged, but every one of the challenges addressed by the CSBI remains relevant.

As already stated, from its inception the Evangelical Theological Society has required its members to sign a doctrinal affirmation: "The Bible alone, and the Bible in its entirety, is the Word of God written and is therefore inerrant in the autographs." In 2004, the ETS adopted the CSBI as its definition of inerrancy. Why? Because the affirmation of inerrancy is necessary for evangelical consistency, and a definition of inerrancy is integral to its affirmation.

Contested Issues: Test Cases

Each contributor to this volume has been asked to address three specific test cases. The texts in these cases have been identified as "problematic" with respect to the affirmation of biblical inerrancy. In truth, I do not believe that these texts are more inherently problematic than any other text of Scripture, but the discussion of these texts and the issues they entail will reveal how our views of the authority, inspiration, truthfulness, and trustworthiness of the Bible operate at the level of interpretation.

The Question of Historical Accuracy (Josh. 6)

The sixth chapter of Joshua contains the narrative of Israel's conquest of the city of Jericho. Many modern scholars dispute the biblical account of the fall of Jericho and argue that archaeological evidence contradicts the narrative as found in Joshua. In the words of archaeologist Bryant G. Wood, "Jericho has become the parade example of the difficulties encountered in attempting to correlate the findings of archaeology with the biblical account of a military conquest of Canaan."[36]

Jericho (Tell es-Sultan) may well be the world's most ancient city. It is also considered the lowest city in the world, situated 670 feet below sea level. Its water supply and strategic location made Jericho a most important city for the Israelite conquest of Canaan.

According to Joshua 6, the inhabitants of Jericho had shut their city in order to prevent capture by the Israelites. The Lord told Joshua to march around the walls of the city with all of his men of war once a day for six days, with seven priests blowing trumpets of rams' horns before the ark of the covenant. On the seventh day, they were to march around the city seven times, with the priests blowing the trumpets. The priests were then to blow a great blast and the people were to give a great shout, and the walls were promised to fall. Joshua 6:15–21 provides the historical detail of that plan obediently put into action by Joshua, his men of war, the priests, and the people. After final instructions from Joshua, the people shouted and the walls came down. Joshua 6:20 states, "The people shouted, and the trumpets were blown. As soon as the people heard the sound of the trumpet, the people shouted a great shout, and the wall fell down flat, so that the people went up into the city, every man straight before him, and they captured the city."

The text makes an unambiguous historical claim. Furthermore, Joshua 6 is situated within a book that consistently makes historical claims and is included within the canon as revealed sacred history. Until recent times, there existed an unbroken consensus within the church that Joshua as a whole, certainly including chapter 6, reveals true history as written by an ancient chronicler inspired by the Holy Spirit.

In more recent times, archaeological research has cast doubt on the historical veracity of Joshua 6, as well as many other biblical passages.

---

36. Bryant G. Wood, "Did the Israelites Conquer Jericho? A New Look at the Archaeological Evidence," *Biblical Archaeology Review* (March-April 1990), 49.

As recently as the 1930s, British archaeologist John Garstang declared the archaeological evidence to be perfectly consistent with a conquest of Jericho around 1400 BC, but the archaeological consensus changed when Kathleen Kenyon later concluded that Jericho had been destroyed about 1550 BC and that no city existed at Tell es-Sultan at any time that would be consistent with the account in Joshua. Archaeologists have also argued that the claim in Joshua 6:24 that the Israelites "burned the city with fire" is inconsistent with the evidence.

In sum, a considerable body of archaeological evidence has been brought forth to argue that the evidence at Tell es-Sultan contradicts the claims of Joshua 6. Furthermore, biblical scholars committed to higher criticism now argue that Joshua, along with other historical books of the Old Testament, was written centuries after any historical events and take the form of invented history designed to serve theological, cultic, and political agendas.

What are we to do with this? The CSBI says, in its short statement, that a commitment to the full truthfulness of the Bible requires us to affirm that Scripture is without fault or error "in all its teaching," specifically including "the events of world history." According to article 18, texts making historical claims are to be believed as historically true, and no effort to dehistoricize or to deny the full truthfulness of the text is legitimate.

Defenders of biblical inerrancy face the undeniable reality that serious historical claims are made against the Bible and specific biblical texts. Various lines of argument from fields of scholarship including biblical criticism, paleontology, and archaeology have been used to deny the truth status of biblical texts such as Joshua 6. The existence of these lines of argument should not be denied or discounted. At the same time, I do not believe they represent any insurmountable challenge to the inerrancy of the Bible.

Why? First, to assert the ultimate authority of the Bible is to affirm, a priori, the truthfulness of the text in part and in whole and all that the Bible affirms. This assertion is grounded in the status of the Bible as the oracular Word of God, verbally inspired and thus without error. This is an inescapably supernatural claim that is consistent with a scriptural a priori. Every field of inquiry or scholarship begins with some fundamental assumptions, plausibility structures, and axioms of thought. This is as true of the naturalistic assumptions of modern science (including the dominant field of archaeology) as of the supernatural assumptions of Christian theology.

Second, as John M. Monson has argued, "archaeology is a relatively young field of study, and its relationship to other disciplines is still very much in flux."[37] Young or old, scholarly fields demonstrate a striking degree of change, often revolutionary change, in terms of scholarly consensus. The shift from the assumption that the archaeological evidence is consistent with Joshua 6 (Garstang) to the belief that the evidence contradicts Joshua (Kenyon) came within the span of a single generation. Long after Kathleen Kenyon conducted her research, her theory of a destruction of Jericho in 1550 BC by the Hyskos has been largely discounted. Wood concludes, "When we compare the archaeological evidence at Jericho with the biblical narrative describing the Israelite destruction of Jericho, we find a quite remarkable agreement."[38] Monson states, "The Bible's account of Joshua's entry into the land is far more compelling and in line with the available evidence than are the stale verdicts of historical criticism."[39]

Archaeologists will disagree among themselves. I am not an archaeologist, and I am not qualified to render any adequate archaeological argument. The point is that I do not allow *any* line of evidence from outside the Bible to nullify to the slightest degree the truthfulness of any text in all that the text asserts and claims. That statement may appear radical to some readers, but it is the only position that is fully compatible with the claim that every word of Scripture is fully inspired and thus fully true and trustworthy. Any theological or hermeneutical method that allows extrabiblical sources of knowledge to nullify the truthfulness of any biblical text assumes, a priori, that the Bible is something less than the oracular Word of God.

Third, I would argue that evangelicals should keep in mind the phenomenological nature of modern secular scholarship. Starting

37. John M. Monson, "Enter Joshua: The 'Mother of Current Debates' in Biblical Archaeology," in James K. Hoffmeier and Dennis R. Magary, eds., *Do Historical Matters Matter to Faith? A Critical Appraisal of Modern and Postmodern Approaches to Scripture* (Wheaton, Ill.: Crossway, 2012), 435.

38. Wood, "Did the Israelites Conquer Jericho?" 53.

39. Monson, "Enter Joshua," 456.

with a secular set of assumptions, secular fields of inquiry and scholarship seek to understand the materials and theoretical frameworks of their interest, in general, by looking at the phenomena at face value. There is value in this approach, of course, and it has produced great goods for humanity, including everything from antibiotics to air travel. At the same time, this phenomenological approach (which is used as an intellectual tool by many Christian scholars) is necessarily embedded in its own metaphysical claims and metanarrative. These claims and narratives may well contradict the Bible (as in the prevailing consensus of evolutionary biology), and at this point the Christian must make clear a primary and unqualified affirmation of the Bible and the biblical worldview. Secular fields of study may yield rich insights, but none can trump the authority of the Bible as the Word of God.

The Question of Intracanonical Accuracy (Acts 9:7; 22:9)

Can the Bible contradict itself? Inerrancy requires an affirmation that the Bible is a consistent and progressive unfolding of divine revelation. Later texts may and do fulfill earlier texts, but no text contradicts any other canonical text. The CSBI states, "We affirm the unity and internal consistency of Scripture. We deny that alleged errors and discrepancies that have not yet been resolved vitiate the truth claims of the Bible" (article 14). Any apparent contradictions are to be considered in light of this affirmation.

A contradiction, in this sense, is a conflicting truth claim — not merely a difference in perspective or aspect. In this light, does Acts 9:7 contradict Acts 22:9? I am sure that these texts do not contradict each other, and this question is rather easily resolved. Both texts have to do with Paul's vision of Christ on the road to Damascus.

Acts 9:7 states, "The men who were traveling with him stood speechless, hearing the voice but seeing no one."

Acts 22:9 states, "Those who were with me saw the light but did not understand the voice of the one who was speaking to me."

Did the associates of Paul hear anything or not? Did they see the light, or did they not?

Some scholars suggest that these two verses reveal an inherent contradiction. In order to overcome an apparent lexical contradiction, some scholars have pointed out that the verb used of hearing in these texts is used in two different tenses. Others have simply accepted the contradiction, explaining it in terms of Paul's faulty memory or Luke's faulty account. Neither approach is necessary.

First, I would simply and straightforwardly assert that any problem with our understanding of these two verses lies in our interpretation and not in the texts themselves. Once again, this is an unapologetic a priori argument.

Second, we must remember that Luke is the inspired author of the book of Acts and that he was fully aware of the different aspects of the event as recorded in Acts 9 and Acts 22. The very fact that he left us with both accounts is evidence that he saw no contradiction and intended his readers to see none.

Third, the best and most honest reading of the texts from the viewpoint of the Bible's plenary inspiration and inerrancy is to see, quite clearly, the difference of aspect in the texts and Luke's very careful use of language. In Acts 9:7, Paul's associates are said to hear the voice but to see no one. In Acts 22:9, they see the light but do not understand the voice. Given the point of both passages, these texts are perfectly complementary. Putting the two texts together, both affirm that Paul, and Paul alone, saw Christ and both heard and understood his voice. Paul's associates heard the voice without understanding and saw the light without seeing the appearance of Christ. In both passages, the point is that Paul, and Paul alone, received the content of the vision and the theophany of Christ. Paul's associates witnessed the supernatural character of the event, seeing light and hearing a voice, but they neither saw Christ nor understood his words.

Darrell L. Bock gets it just right when he explains, "It is over-interpretation to suggest that Acts 9:7 says that they did not see the light whereas here [Acts 22:9] it says they did. All that is said here is that they did not see anyone. For those with Saul, there was neither an appearance nor revelation. The point is that the others knew something happened and that Saul did not have a merely inner, psychological experience. Those with Paul, however, did not know exactly what took place."[40]

---

40. Darrell L. Bock, *Acts*, Baker Exegetical Commentary on the New Testament (Grand Rapids, Mich.: Baker Academic, 2007), 660.

Defenders of biblical inerrancy should acknowledge the presence of apparent contradictions more difficult to resolve than this alleged problem in Acts. I state this in order to make the point that, even when we cannot resolve the question as easily as in this test case, the affirmation of the unity and consistency of Scripture must rule. Otherwise the Bible is not the Word of God in every word and every respect.

The Question of Theological Plurality (Deut. 20:16 - 17; Matt. 5:43 - 48)

Does the Bible contain contradictory or changing depictions of God's own character? That is the real question asked here. Is the God who ordered massive death in Israel's conquest of Canaan the same God who, in Christ, commands that we are to love our enemies, to pray for people who persecute us, to walk the extra mile, and to turn the cheek?

This is the most serious and significant question raised in this series, for it calls into question the very possibility of our knowledge of God. If we cannot trust the Bible, in all its parts, to reveal God with perfect truthfulness, how can we know him at all?

Deuteronomy 20:16–18 reads, "In the cities of these peoples that the LORD your God is giving you for an inheritance, you shall save alive nothing that breathes, but you shall devote them to complete destruction, the Hittites and the Amorites, the Canaanites and the Perizzites, the Hivites and the Jebusites, as the LORD your God has commanded, that they may not teach you to do according to all their abominable practices that they have done for their gods, and so you sin against the LORD your God."

Matthew 5:43–48 reads, "You have heard that it was said, 'You shall love your neighbor and hate your enemy.' But I say to you, Love your enemies and pray for those who persecute you, so that you may be sons of your Father who is in heaven. For he makes his sun rise on the evil and on the good, and sends rain on the just and on the unjust. For if you love those who love you, what reward do you have? Do not even the tax collectors do the same? And if you greet only your brothers, what more are you doing than others? Do not even the Gentiles do the same? You therefore must be perfect, as your heavenly Father is perfect."

Some argue that these two passages, one from the Old Testament and one from the New Testament, reveal two different theologies, two contradictory moral codes, and two irreconcilable renderings of God. This is hardly new. Marcion, whose father was a bishop in the second century, was excommunicated for claiming this very thing—that the God of the Old Testament and the God of the New Testament are irreconcilable. Marcion thus rejected the Old Testament (and much of the New Testament) and nullified any notion of promise and fulfillment in Scripture.

More recently, Kenton L. Sparks has argued that the Bible reveals a trajectory in which the New Testament (and the Gospels specifically) corrects the primitive and erroneous theology of the Old Testament. He argues that the Bible "does not contain a single coherent theology but rather numerous theologies that sometimes stand in tension or even in contradiction with one another."[41] We are, he argues, "to take a theological step beyond the written word by listening to God's living voice, which includes not only Scripture but also the voices of creation, tradition, and the Spirit."[42]

The Old Testament, Sparks argues, contains "outright literary fabrications" and "propaganda."[43] Sparks calls for evangelicals to appropriate biblical criticism in order to choose among and between what he says are fully incompatible theologies and moralities within the Bible. Getting to the heart of the issue, he asserts, "Biblical criticism suggests that the Bible does not speak with one divine voice but offers instead a range of human voices with different judgments and opinions on the same subjects."[44] He explicitly rejects divine inspiration and affirms a range of human voices as the contents of Scripture. Accordingly, Sparks specifically rejects the inerrancy of the biblical text.

A similar approach at the popular level is taken by Brian McLaren, who has argued that the Bible should be seen as a "community library"

---

41. Kenton L. Sparks, *God's Word in Human Words: An Evangelical Appropriation of Critical Biblical Scholarship* (Grand Rapids, Mich.: Baker Academic, 2008), 301. Sparks continues, "This being so, it is no longer possible to envision biblical theology in the way that conservative evangelicals construe it."

42. Ibid., 299.

43. Ibid., 120–21.

44. Ibid., 121.

of books to be consulted rather than as a canon of perfectly inspired Scriptures.[45] He rejects the divinely inspired nature of the Bible as a whole, arguing that many passages are flatly and dangerously wrong in their depiction of God. Pointing to the account of the flood in Genesis 6, McLaren asserts that "a god who mandates an intentional supernatural disaster leading to unparalleled genocide is hardly worthy of belief, much less worship."[46]

Speaking directly of texts such as Deuteronomy 20, Eric A. Seibert has stated, "I discovered that the Bible sometimes promotes values that are objectionable, encourages behaviors that are unethical, and portrays God in ways that are unacceptable."[47] Seibert's proposal amounts to a form of postmodern deconstructionism in which alternative readings of the Old Testament are developed in order to correct its violent and "unethical" passages. "Old Testament texts," he asserts, "especially those that are morally questionable, need to be ethically critiqued rather than uncritically approved. We must weigh and evaluate the claims such texts make in order to determine whether they should be accepted or rejected."[48]

Are Deuteronomy and Matthew offering two different and irreconcilable revelations of God's character and moral expectations? A responsible answer to that question must begin, once again, with the affirmation that every word of the Bible, in the Old Testament no less than the New Testament, is fully inspired by God and completely true and trustworthy. We trust Deuteronomy to be as true as Matthew. At the same time, we recognize the pattern of promise and fulfillment that explains the relation between the two Testaments. As article 5 of the CSBI states, "We affirm that God's revelation in the Holy Scriptures was progressive. We deny that later revelation, which may fulfill earlier revelation, ever corrects or contradicts it."

The command in Deuteronomy was given to Israel as God's elect nation, sent to conquer a land of promise that was inhabited by idolaters who, according to God himself, had to be put to death, young and

---

45. Brian McLaren, *A New Kind of Christianity* (San Francisco: HarperOne, 2010).
46. Ibid., 109–10.
47. Eric A. Seibert, *The Violence of Scripture: Overcoming the Old Testament's Troubling Legacy* (Minneapolis: Fortress Press, 2012), 5.
48. Ibid., 65.

old, in order to fulfill his saving purpose. Christopher Wright makes this point clearly:

> This is the way in which God in his sovereignty chose to work within human history to accomplish his saving purpose for humanity and for creation, including me. I may not understand why it had to be this way.... But at some point I have to stand back from my questions, criticisms, or complaints and receive the Bible's own word on the matter. What the Bible unequivocally tells me is that this was an act of God that took place within an overarching narrative through which the only hope for the world's salvation was constituted.[49]

Matthew 5:43–48 is found within the Sermon on the Mount, which is addressed to the church as the people of God in the new covenant of Christ. The church is sent into the world to bear witness to the gospel, not to conquer territory. Our land of promise is an eschatological kingdom, not territory within this earth, bearing the curse of sin. Nevertheless, the divine ordering of death for the Canaanites is a stark reminder of the divine verdict of death upon all humanity, apart from Christ. In this sense, the concluding chapters of Revelation reveal the fulfillment of God's righteous judgment in a comprehensive display that goes far beyond anything found in Deuteronomy 6, or any other Old Testament passage, for that matter. Those who would use their human judgment to reject the inspired status of Deuteronomy 6 must, if consistent, reject Revelation 19 and 20 and a host of other passages.

Once an interpreter of Scripture begins to use human standards of moral judgment to evaluate the truth status and authority of the Bible, in whole or in part, the authority of the Bible is immediately denied. The real standard of judgment is now to be human moral reason and sensitivity. A commitment to biblical inerrancy requires a commitment to the responsible interpretation of Scripture and to the development of a mature biblical theology. The abandonment of inerrancy renders every biblical text suspect until it passes or fails some test of human reason. Those who would deny the divine inspiration of Deuteronomy 6 will not, if consistent, stop there.

49. Christopher J. H. Wright, *The God I Don't Understand: Reflections on Tough Questions of Faith* (Grand Rapids, Mich.: Zondervan, 2008), 106–107.

In Conclusion: When the Bible Speaks, God Speaks

The affirmation of biblical inerrancy is necessary for the health of the church and for our obedience to the Scriptures. Though necessary, it is not sufficient, taken by itself, to constitute an evangelical doctrine of Scripture. Evangelicals must embrace a comprehensive affirmation of the Bible as the Word of God written. In the end, inspiration requires inerrancy, and inerrancy affirms the Bible's plenary authority. The Bible is not inerrant, and thus the Word of God; it is the Word of God, and thus inerrant.

The affirmation of biblical inerrancy means nothing more, and nothing less, than this: *When the Bible speaks, God speaks.*

PETER ENNS

Though my response to Mohler's essay will be largely critical, I want to begin by acknowledging where there is some agreement between us. I agree with Mohler that "no doctrinal formulation or truth claim stands alone" (p. 44); God is knowable; God speaks; and human language is adequate for revelation and for speaking of God. We also share a deep concern about the health of the church and how followers of Jesus negotiate life's path, though we differ significantly on the diagnosis and prescription. This concern no doubt contributes to our passionate expositions of our positions.

Nevertheless, while agreeing on these sorts of general issues, Mohler's essay is deeply problematic both in terms of its content and tone: he does not actually deal with the nature of Scripture on anything beyond a simplistic level, and he wields his view as a sword against those who disagree. I had hoped that perhaps we might see here a shift towards greater nuance and some acknowledgment that his inerrantist position is neither self-evident nor the only viable alternative for accounting for the phenomena of Scripture and giving it due respect, and that knowledgeable and no less committed Christian scholars hold different views and have very good reasons for doing so. Unfortunately, however, Mohler continues to promulgate an alarmist view of the nature of Scripture that does not bear up under the scrutiny of the biblical data or biblical scholarship.

In my estimation, what I read here is more of an attempt to control the discussion than engage an issue within a context of collaboration and charity. It is a rhetorical tour de force that leads to one and only one conclusion: there is no other acceptable option — for either evangelicalism or true Christianity (which are to be equated) — than to accept with uncompromising zeal the view that the Bible is inerrant in the manner in which Mohler sees it, which, we are told, is also the view of Jesus, the Bible's self-witness, and the entire history of the church until quite recently. To arrive at another conclusion is to be seduced by secular academic thinking, to compromise God's truth, which is to put oneself in the place of judgment over Scripture (and therefore God), to lead the church astray, and to aid and abet the collapse of the Christian faith. I wish I were exaggerating.

I have a good number of dear friends who, when pushed, would articulate a view of inerrancy somewhat close to Mohler's. We get along just fine and I lose no sleep over what they believe. My primary concern is not with those who hold this type of view but rather with those in positions of power in the church (I will let that unhappy contradiction slide for the sake of discussion) who prefer coercion to reason and demonization to reflection. Mohler's position is in my view intellectually untenable, but when wielded as a weapon, it becomes spiritually dangerous. (I am happy that both Bird and Franke in their essays echo these concerns in addressing the "ethics of inerrancy.") And when seen to speak publicly for a significant number of others, or for American evangelicalism as a whole, it is disconcerting and embarrassing.

Mohler's essay is on one level difficult to respond to because it is largely devoid of argumentation, resting rather on a collation of unexamined assertions. These assertions appear often as premises that, if uncritically accepted, would lock the reader into a train of thought toward an inevitable conclusion. These premises include the following: the evangelical/Reformation tradition is the true iteration of Christianity; inerrancy has always been the view of the true church, beginning with Jesus and the apostles; either inerrantism or liberalism are one's only options; the entire discussion of the nature of Scripture rests solely on one's "metaphysical claims and metanarrative" (p. 52); to reject inerrancy is to replace the Bible with some other authority (discerning the *nature* of biblical authority is a simple matter of accepting propositions); without inerrancy the church will have no basis upon which to preach.

As I see it, this rhetorical strategy is designed to insulate Mohler and his views from criticism—details and other complexities don't matter, for it all comes down to having the right a priori commitments that Mohler claims are clearly derived from Scripture's "teaching" about itself. Thus, he gives himself license to escape the complexities of the serious study of Scripture by referring all challenges to his unexamined, though apparently, self-evident, godly, and unimpeachable philosophical precommitments. At each crucial juncture of his handling of the three passages, Mohler simply asserts how Scripture *must* behave, leaving counterevidence to the side and then fearlessly, without compromise or apology, obeying God. To be clear, I am not criticizing Mohler simply for *having* philosophical precommitments — we all do. I am criticizing him for treating them as self-evident and beyond dispute, not open to scrutiny or refinement, even when they can be shown to be inadequate and obscurantist.

With respect to the archaeological evidence concerning Jericho, Mohler's defense of literalist inerrancy begins to falter on the second sentence, where he states that "*many* modern scholars dispute the biblical account" (p. 48). Not to split hairs, but "many" understates the dilemma for Mohler, and I am not sure whether this is part of Mohler's rhetoric or if he is not aware of the state of the discipline. There is, in fact, *no* serious dispute among archaeologists about whether Joshua 6 gives what we would call an "accurate" historical account of Jericho (let alone inerrant). Those who see some historical echo in the story nevertheless consider it legendary. Dissenting voices are limited to archaeologists committed to aligning the archaeological portrait with inerrancy of whatever flavor.

To be clear, yes indeed, archaeological evidence needs to be interpreted, but this is exactly what mainstream archaeologists do; they are not fools incapable of discerning their own thought patterns, mindlessly subject to their own biases. I also happily acknowledge that dissenting voices should not be ignored without due cause, and there is always more to be discovered. But the archaeology of Jericho is now more than one hundred years old, and there is an overwhelming consensus that, whatever history there may be behind the biblical story, Joshua 6 does not represent "history" in a way amenable to inerrantist expectations. I would rather Mohler simply acknowledge that, though the archaeology concerning the historicity of Jericho is not in serious dispute, he chooses to ignore that consensus and appeal only to those archaeologists whose views are (somewhat) compatible with his own predetermined conclusions, and in doing so imply that the only archaeologists capable of doing competent field work are those who know the proper conclusions to reach.

That is the heart of Mohler's view on Jericho, which is not open for discussion. Filtered throughout are various rhetorical remarks along the lines of what I mention above. He sets up the discussion by pointing out that Joshua 6 "provides historical details" and "makes unambiguous historical claims" (p. 49), thus implying that to dissent is to miss the obvious and disrespect Scripture. Mohler does not consider that fictional narratives regularly make "historical claims," but that alone doesn't make them any more historical. Needless to say, Mohler would counter that a book written *by God* would never "deceive" us by making "false" historical claims, since God is "trustworthy." I would counter that Mohler continues to evade the entire discussion of what historiography and trustworthiness mean in an ancient text, not only because of his a priori commitments but also because of his latent commitments to a modernist understanding of history.

It seems that Mohler would have little patience for such an exchange. Scholars who question the Bible's "historical claims" simply show how they are "committed to higher criticism," have as their starting point "a secular set of assumptions," and "use" archaeology "to deny the truth status" (p. 50) of Joshua 6 — as if they are out to discredit the Bible, blinded by sin or incompetence. Mohler needs to spend some time with these enemies of the faith to see that they are passionately committed to truth, are no more biased than the archaeologists he favors, and are actually competent to assess evidence prudently and draw conclusions. But such would not enter Mohler's mind: "I do not allow *any* line of evidence from outside the Bible to nullify to the slightest degree the truthfulness of any text in all that the text asserts and claims" (p. 51). Such self-assurance to discern truth, Mohler concedes, "may appear radical to some readers" (p. 51), but I simply see it as an unhealthy and unrealistic assessment of one's own abilities.

With respect to the second passage, Mohler makes the usual claim made by those trying to harmonize contradictions that, however contradictory the two conversion accounts might appear, their very presence in Luke's work must indicate they are not contradictory, since Luke never would have allowed such a contradiction to stand. Luke, in other words, is on Mohler's side. Most would call this a circular argument. Worth noting is that Mohler has misconstrued the contradictory element in Acts 9 and 22. It is not about who did or did not *see* (which is hardly a problem by any standard), but who did or did not *hear*. I am not sure how Mohler would handle that actual contradiction, but judging from his rhetoric thus far, he would simply label it an "apparent contradiction," awaiting future resolution (if not in this life then the next). But to call the "hearing" problem in Acts 9 and 22 an "apparent contradiction" would, ironically, in an effort to defend inerrancy, call into question one's basic competence in reading comprehension and promote a reading strategy applicable only to Scripture and no other piece of literature ever written.

Mohler's treatment of Canaanite extermination is also inadequate. Note his alarmist strategy for setting up the discussion, claiming that "the very possibility of our knowledge of God" (p. 54) is at stake in how we address the difference between Deuteronomy 20:16–18 and Matthew 5:43–48. He continues, "If we cannot *trust* the Bible, in all its parts, to reveal God with *perfect truthfulness*, how can we know him at all?" (p. 54, my emphasis). By frontloading the discussion in this manner, that our very knowledge of God rests on addressing this issue (in the manner in which he lays out), Mohler is already steering the discussion toward his desired end. This is a common debate tactic, and one should not be taken in by it. Note too that Mohler's assertions here effectively blunt *any* attempt to reconcile these passages that do not treat them first and foremost as propositions, rather than, for example, culturally embedded statements (my view) or a demonstration of progressive revelation.

What gives me greater concern here is how quickly Mohler is willing to trot out a litany of heretics to neutralize counterproposals to his assertions. He allows two options: his and that of the well-known second century go-to heretic Marcion, who saw in the Old Testament a different God. Of course, who wants to be on the side of Marcion? Then Mohler traverses all of church history to link Marcion to Kent Sparks, Brian McLaren, and Eric Seibert, with the obligatory nod to the dangers of postmodernism. The fact that none of these men are Marcionite but are voicing the theological tensions between the testaments recognized by the earliest church fathers does not faze Mohler. He has created a guilt by association. I see no purpose for such a tactic other than to demonize a point of view he wishes to, well, demonize.

Mohler, without argumentation or support, offers his own solution in passing: the death of the Canaanites is a "stark reminder of the divine verdict of death upon all humanity, apart from Christ" (p. 57). This is a common solution of Christian apologists, but it is arbitrary to the Bible's own statements. As I lay out in my essay, Scripture states clearly why the Canaanites were singled out for extermination, and a preview of final judgment is not one of them, no matter how theologically convenient that view would be. Failure to address the Bible's own stated reasons for Canaanite extermination is, ironically, a failure to be truly biblical in addressing the problem.

MICHAEL F. BIRD

I have a deep appreciation for President Al Mohler, particularly because I know how dear this important topic is to his heart, as it is to mine. Furthermore, he writes with great conviction, which is precisely what the subject calls for, as it does for charity and humility as we reason about Scripture together.

Let me preface my criticisms by saying that I broadly identify with Mohler's model of a "confessional evangelicalism," even if I might confess it differently.[50] I agree too that the trustworthiness of Scripture is ultimately anchored in the faithfulness of God. I likewise concur with Mohler that inspiration and authority are at the center of evangelical faith, and when the Bible speaks, God speaks. I even agree for the most part with his summary about what Scripture says regarding its own origin and authority, though I would heavily nuance his inferences to verbal inspiration and inerrancy. Finally, I concur with his statement that "Those who would affirm the divine inspiration and authority of the Bible must make clear the extent of that affirmation" (p. 30). Yes, we need a thick description of biblical veracity, but I would hasten to add that the American inerrancy tradition (AIT) and the Chicago Statement on Biblical Inerrancy (CSBI) is only one way of doing that, not the only way, and it's a way beset with many pros and cons.

To get down to business, Mohler believes that inerrancy is a "core affirmation," "essential to evangelicalism." He does not believe that "evangelicalism can survive without the explicit and complete assertion of biblical inerrancy," and he states that inerrancy is "necessary and integral to the life of the church, the authority of preaching, and the

---

50. R. Albert Mohler, "Confessional Evangelicalism," in *Four Views on the Spectrum of Evangelicalism*, ed. A. Naselli and C. Hansen (Grand Rapids, Mich: Zondervan, 2011), 68–96.

integrity of the Christian life" (p. 31). Strong assertions, but what is astounding to me is Mohler's remark that the CSBI is "the quintessential statement of biblical inerrancy and that its clearly defined language remains essential to the health of evangelicalism and the integrity of the Christian church" (p. 36). This statement is patently false, for two reasons:

(1) *Historically* there were evangelicals before the CSBI (1978), before ETS (1949), and before Old Princeton (1812–1920) who had a high view of Scripture's inspiration and authority but did not operate with the same grammar and conceptualization of inerrancy. Our forefathers of the faith were probably operating with an idea of Scripture that was analogous to inerrancy, but in no way was it strictly identical. The reason for this was that the contours and context of North American Christianity changed in the twentieth century, and the debates about Scripture were shaped by arguments in American denominations that had only recently emerged. In fact, proof that AIT was contingent upon its American context is given by Mohler when he says that mature statements of inerrancy emerged when "evangelicals first sought to define a theological and spiritual trajectory that would simultaneously avoid the liberalism and theological accommodationism of mainline Protestantism and the intellectual separatism of fundamentalism" (p. 30). That tells me that the AIT was both a *retrieval* of a confessional heritage that asserted Scripture's infallibility and authority and also a *reaction* formed out of debates transpiring in American churches.

When Mohler says, "In truth, inerrancy was the affirmation and theological reflex of the church until the most recent centuries" (p. 39), this is only a half-truth. If by inerrancy he means something like inspired, authoritative, and trustworthy, then yes, definitely so! The church catholic and reformed has always regarded Scripture as God's Word in its totality, and true and trustworthy in all that it affirms. However, if by inerrancy Mohler means what is stated in the CSBI, then the answer is no. A survey of Origen, Chrysostom, Augustine, and Calvin shows that they could handle the challenges of Scripture rather differently from the way that modern defenders of biblical authority proceed in their task. Although none of them would consider themselves to be advocating "errancy," I find it impossible to identify them as proto-American inerrantists in a strict sense.

(2) *Geographically*, there are churches around the world—Oceania, Asia, Africa, South America—that have never heard about Old Princeton, the CSBI, and inerrancy and yet have a vibrant evangelical faith. To give an analogy, if Mohler was to state something like "Churches cannot maintain a credible evangelical witness without an ESV study Bible," and if you just happened to visit some wonderful Christ-believing churches in Lebanon or Liberia who don't have ESV Study Bibles, then you would have to infer that Mohler was wrong and that you do not really *need* an ESV Study Bible to be a healthy evangelical church.[51]

I think I can sink Mohler's bibliological battleship simply by pointing out that his version of inerrancy has not existed for all time and in every place where the evangelical churches have confessed that Jesus is Lord. The AIT has some good value, things which people outside of North America can consider when it comes to configuring a doctrine of Scripture, but you cannot make it an essential item of the evangelical faith when it does not command the assent of global evangelical churches and when some of its precise statements lack roots in the traditions of the Reformers and the church fathers (e.g., "Science and Scripture"; "Inspiration and Autographs"). Thus, the biggest problem I have with the AIT and CSBI are their lack of catholicity. What Christians have said about Scripture in the past might have been similar to the AIT and CSBI, but they were never absolutely the same!

To take up another issue, I don't understand how Mohler can claim to be a confessional evangelical and yet criticize Fuller Seminary for a doctrinal statement on Scripture that looks remarkably like what the Westminster Confession of Faith (WCF) and London Baptist Confession (LBC) say about Scripture. If Fuller was so reprehensible for changing "free from all error" to "trustworthy record," then what are we to say about the WCF and LBC, which do not ever say that Scripture is "without error"? I cannot figure out what is so villainous

---

51. Let me say that I do not own an ESV Study Bible, that several of my friends and students use it and speak of it warmly, and that if the lovely people at Crossway Publishers would like to send me one, I would seriously reconsider my position about the necessity of owning an ESV Study Bible.

about Fuller's doctrinal statement when it looks like most doctrinal statements I've seen about Scripture in most churches and institutions around the world. What is more, Mohler seems to think that the line in the sand that separates the good guys from the bad guys is drawn between those who say "infallible" and those who say "inerrancy" as if there were somehow a galaxy of difference between the two terms. Well, where I live, the big challenge is among those who say that Scripture is authoritative and normative (i.e., the evangelicals) and those who say that Scripture is antiquated and negotiable (i.e., the liberals). As a global evangelical, I could not find the enthusiasm to denounce as dangerous to the evangelical faith a person whose doctrine of Scripture is at its essence the same as my own.[52]

I also reject the dichotomy that Mohler sets up between "errancy" and "inerrancy" as if they were the only games in town. As a pastoral necessity, he seems to think that unless *his* version of inerrancy is affirmed, then the whole idea of Christianity as based on revelation is thrown out the door. This is pastorally dangerous. It means that if some young Christian comes across a passage of Scripture that is historically or ethically challenging, then they are faced with the choice between belief and unbelief. I submit that this kind of "my way or the highway" approach to a doctrine of Scripture is why we have so many ex-evangelicals like Bart Ehrman and Rob Bell running around making all kinds of howling protests against the Bible. In their theological training, they were given shallow and terse multiple-choice answers to deep questions and were never equipped with a proper hermeneutical tool kit to deal with the ambiguity or complexity that they can be confronted with in scriptural study and application. Mohler's approach is not helpful because it is reductionistic and adversarial. It

---

52. For a case in point, a group of Anglican scholars in my native city of Brisbane, Australia, have recently put together a collection of essays arguing that Scripture's role in Christian faith is purely aesthetic and not authoritative (Gregory C. Jenks, ed., *The Once and Future Scriptures: Exploring the Role of the Bible in the Contemporary Church* [Salem, Ore.: Polebridge, 2013]). For those of us who don't live in the mega-church mecca of North American evangelicalism, this is what we are up against. I'm trying to fight the good fight of the faith against people who deny that God even speaks in Scripture and who advocate that Scripture is not and should not be our authority. So when I look at the American evangelical scene, where people want to divide denominations over "infallible" versus "inerrancy," the whole thing looks kind of piddly and pathetic in comparison. It's like I'm fighting the barbarians at the gate while some of you guys back in your mega-seminary sanctuaries are engaging in a ferocious fratricide over the proper length of church candles.

produces not a faith seeking understanding but a rationalism seeking certainty.

In regards to the problem of the contested texts, Mohler and I reach similar conclusions for the most part, but usually by a different route. The biggest problem I have in this section is that Mohler treats the CSBI like it is a kind of evangelical magisterium. The inerrancy of Scripture is anchored in the infallibility of the CSBI. If the claims of the CSBI are not true, then the entire edifice of Scripture crumbles into ruin. I would surmise that Mohler has turned the CSBI into a type of *horcrux* upon which Scripture's own life depends.

For instance, Mohler says that "I do not allow *any* line of evidence from outside the Bible to nullify to the slightest degree the truthfulness of any text in all that the text asserts and claims" (p. 51). There are three problems here. First, Mohler does not distinguish between the text and his interpretation of it; he conflates them. The result is that he preaches the inerrancy of the text but practices the inerrancy of his interpretation.[53] Second, Mohler's unyielding commitment to the Bible turns out to be a type of extreme fideism, and in practice it means a closed-mindedness to examining all the evidence, pro and con, concerning the Bible and his interpretation of it. Third, Mohler has a faulty view of revelation. He forgets that God's *Word* comes to us in God's *world* so that God's revelation of himself in Scripture (i.e., special revelation) is taken in tandem with God's revelation of himself in nature and history (i.e., general revelation). The problem is that Mohler wants to interpret nature and history in light of Scripture, but not Scripture in light of history or nature. That means that whenever there is a dissonance between the claims of special revelation and those

---

53. In fairness to Mohler, in his discussion of the differences between Acts 9:7 and 22:9, he does recognize that problems can rest "in our interpretation and not in the texts themselves," but he does not apply such a view to other interpretive problems. For example, some time ago, Mohler accused Michael Licona of denying inerrancy by claiming in his book *The Resurrection of Jesus: A New Historiographical Approach* that Matt. 27:51–54 is a poetic metaphor and not a literal narration of saints of old coming back to life (see Mohler's post at *http://www.albertmohler.com/2011/09/14/the-devil-is-in-the-details-biblical-inerrancy-and-the-licona-controversy/*). Mohler lambasted Licona not because he said that Matthew was wrong or that we know that dead people don't come back to life but because Licona used a hermeneutical approach that Mohler rejected. This is the problem with AIT and its advocates. They merge their interpretation with the text so that to disagree with their interpretation is to deny the inerrancy of the text. This alone is enough to turn many Christians off the doctrine of inerrancy.

of general revelation, Mohler will always find the error to be in *secular interpretation* of general revelation, whereas the error might just as well reside in *his interpretation of special revelation!*[54]

At the end of the day, I want to eat the same fish that Mohler has on the menu. My point is that the fish can be skinned and cooked a few different ways. I want to cook it slower, and, rather than rely on American ingredients like grits and southern fried chicken, I want to add in a few exotic spices from distant places like Antioch, Lausanne, Alexandria, and Westminster. But in the end, we will still have a nutritious dish that Mohler and I can both enjoy as we sip on either a Shirley Temple (for Southern Baptist Al) or on a Pinot Grigio (for Anglican Mike). Then perhaps the Scripture will be fulfilled: "They saw God, and did eat and drink" (Exod. 24:11 KJV).

---

54. For case in point, I disagree with Mohler that Genesis 1 teaches a literal six-day creation and a young earth, because (a) I think there is overwhelming scientific evidence for an old earth; (b) The notion of an old earth is entirely consistent with what is stated and affirmed in Genesis 1; and (c) great theological minds like Augustine and Calvin do not appear to have believed in a literal six-day creation.

RESPONSE TO R. ALBERT MOHLER JR.

KEVIN J. VANHOOZER

Al Mohler's chapter title rightly emphasizes the primary raison d'être for the doctrine of inerrancy—namely, to acknowledge that when we have to do with Scripture, we have to do with the personal communication from God to us in human language, and hence with a message that is as trustworthy as its sender. Mohler and I agree with what John Frame calls the "personal-word" model: the Bible is not simply a record of God's past speaking but also a means of God's speaking today: "when the Bible speaks, God speaks."[55] Strictly speaking, of course, the Bible does not speak, but rather God speaks in and through the Bible. Even more strictly speaking: God speaks in and through the written discourse of its human authors. Discourse is language in use: what someone says to someone about something in some way. Mohler and I agree that the Bible is verbally inspired, which is to say that it is an instance of dual-author (i.e., divine-human) discourse. I have developed and defended accounts of Scripture as divine communicative action on repeated occasions, and written a book on the importance of taking divine authorship with the utmost seriousness.[56]

Although I frame some of these points differently than Mohler—for example, I want to say more about the Bible not only as divine but also specifically *triune* discourse—we are staring at the same picture: the Bible as God's word written. I therefore found myself agreeing with much of the substance of Mohler's position on divine trustworthiness, biblical authority, and their centrality for a vital Christian faith and healthy

---

55. See John Frame, *The Doctrine of the Word of God* (Phillipsburg, N.J.: P&R Publishing, 2010), 3.

56. See, for example, my *Remythologizing Theology: Divine Action, Passion, and Authorship* (Cambridge: Cambridge Univ. Press) and "Triune Discourse: Theological Reflections on the Claim That God Speaks," in *Trinitarian Theology for the Church: Scripture, Community, Worship*, Daniel J. Treier and David Lauber, eds. (Downers Grove, Ill.: InterVarsity, 2009), 25–78.

church. Indeed, I found myself affirming virtually all of the positive things Mohler says about God and the importance of biblical truth. In many respects, Mohler and I are allies in the book on these matters, even if we weigh them differently. Still, I find his chapter somewhat troubling, not because of what he explicitly says but rather because of how he says it, and in particular because of what he does not say. Most of my critical remarks, then, have to do with these latter sins of omission (so to speak).

Though the subtitle of his essay is "The Classic Doctrine of Inerrancy," the bulk of Mohler's chapter is given over to tracing the development of the doctrine of inerrancy in North American evangelicalism. Although he mentions the apostles, the Reformation (but not the Reformers themselves!), and the historical Christian tradition, the essay really focuses only on the mid-twentieth century and onward, giving the impression that the "classic" view of inerrancy may actually be of more recent vintage than Dr. John Pemberton's recipe for Classic Coke. In general, my impression is that Mohler is a better storyteller than conceptual analyst. The failure to more thoroughly examine the sense in which the doctrine of inerrancy is "classic" is, to my mind, the most serious problem with the chapter.

The problem is not with Mohler's claim that the assertion of the Bible's truth is classic (because Christians from ancient to modern times affirmed it). It is rather that the doctrine of inerrancy now enshrined in the Chicago statement is not quite the same proposition that the early church affirmed — and I can prove it. Before I do, however, let me mention my own title. I was careful to use the adjective *Augustinian* (rather than *Augustine's*) precisely to signal that I was not trying to replicate his position as much as continue on in the same spirit. What I miss in Mohler's chapter is a sense that the doctrine of the Bible's truthfulness has developed.[57]

The point I'm trying to make is rather subtle. I affirm, with Mohler, that the church has, from the start, affirmed the entire truthfulness of the Bible in the strongest of terms. Indeed, this is one reason why I call my own position Augustinian. Some of the best quotes from

---

57. I am using the term *developed* in a neutral sense. Some developments, like the doctrine of the Trinity, were good because they made explicit what was already implicit in Scripture; other developments, like the doctrine of the immaculate conception of Mary, are less salutary because (in my opinion) they go beyond the limits of what we can rightly deduce or infer from Scripture.

the patristic era about the truthfulness of Scripture come from Augustine. To take but one example: "For it seems to me that most disastrous consequences must follow upon our believing that anything false is found in the sacred books."[58]

Mohler approvingly cites Carl F. H. Henry, who approvingly cites Harold Lindsell: "The doctrine of biblical inerrancy has been normative since the days of the Apostles" (p. 34). But hang on: what exactly is the apostolic doctrine of biblical inerrancy? Where are its earliest formulations? Show me the money!

In a nutshell: Mohler's "classic" rubric does not sufficiently take into account the difference that some perceive between "original" and "modernist/rationalist" versions of inerrancy.[59] "Original" inerrancy refers to the church's traditional understanding that the Bible is true and trustworthy because God is its ultimate author. On this view, the Bible's authoritative domain extends to matters of nature and history as well as faith and practice, but not in a way that concedes anything to modern scholarship, including the notion of what counts as an error.

By way of contrast, the proponents of "modernist/rationalist" inerrancy are much more concerned with showing that biblical truths comport with and are confirmed by modern science, *or* that the Bible shows how far modern science has strayed from the truth, as is the wont of scientific creationists: "Part of the reason why rationalistic inerrantists produce false dilemmas is that they read Scripture with a modern mindset. In doing so they read the concerns of contemporary science into Scripture and then declare the resultant interpretation inerrant."[60] Interestingly enough, Warfield, a proponent of original inerrancy, distanced himself from this rationalist understanding of inerrancy over the matter of evolution.[61]

---

58. Augustine, *Letter 28* (to Jerome). Augustine is referring not to "scientific" errors but rather to Jerome's implication that Paul might have said something false (when in Gal. 2:11–14 he reproaches Peter for his inconsistency in dealing with Jews and Gentiles) in order to soothe troublesome opponents, as if falsehood or deceit could ever be expedient for an apostle.

59. I am here indebted to Jitse M. van der Meer, "Infallibility and Inerrancy in the Canadian and American Reformed Churches" (available at *http://www.scribd.com/doc/143020052/Infallibility-and-Inerrancy-in-the-CanRC-by-Jitse-van-der-Meer*, accessed June 6, 2013).

60. Van der Meer, "Infallibility and Inerrancy," 8.

61. See Mark A. Noll and David N. Livingstone, eds., *B. B. Warfield: Evolution, Science, and Scripture; Selected Writings* (Grand Rapids, Mich.: Baker, 2000), 16–25.

Mohler seems oblivious to the varied meanings of *inerrancy* currently in circulation. He quotes the ICBI definition ("without error or fault in all its teaching"), but he does not say what counts as an error or whether Scripture intends to teach (modern) science. In his case study on Joshua 6, however, he does say this: "I do not allow *any* line of evidence from outside the Bible to nullify in the slightest degree the truthfulness of any text in all that the text asserts and claims" (p. 51). Neither do I. The relevant question, however, is whether he allows any line of evidence from outside the Bible to nullify, or rather *modify*, in the slightest degree the truthfulness of any *interpretation* of the biblical text. I'm willing to be radical about the truthfulness of Scripture too, but this radicalism or boldness must be tempered with humility as concerns my interpretations. Humility does not mean that I give up without a fight for traditional interpretations; it only means that I do not summarily rule out readings that challenge traditional interpretations, especially if they claim to make better sense of the text as it stands. After all, what is inerrant is the text, not our interpretation.

As I see it, then, one of the chief challenges facing evangelical theology today is the deep confusion over just what inerrancy means and entails. In my opinion, one reason why some evangelicals today find inerrancy implausible is because they have encountered either poor definitions or poor applications of the notion. Instead of insisting that every sentence has to correspond to historical fact the way a modern empiricist does, we must ask what meaning God intends to convey in using just these words in just this way in just this context.

And this brings me to the most important difference between original and modernist/rationalist inerrancy. The former focuses on the communicative intention of the divine author: what Scripture says, God says, and says truly. In contrast, the modernist/rationalist view takes the text as history and science without error in the modern scholarly sense of error. It is this move that turns the wine of biblical meaning into the water of literalistic interpretations. Rationalist inerrancy insists that the Bible speaks truly *on our terms* rather than those of the divine author's. In short, original inerrancy is about God's authorial intentions; rationalist inerrancy is about the interpreter's modern presuppositions.

Mohler appeals to J. I. Packer at several points in his essay—always an appropriate thing for an evangelical theologian to do. (I'll do so

in a moment myself.) However, he would have done well to mention
Packer's attempt to distinguish between original inerrancy (what he
intended to endorse in signing the Chicago statement) and mistaken
uses and applications of rationalist inerrancy. Packer is clear that it is
a mistake to think that inerrancy requires us to read Genesis 1 "as if it
were answering the same questions as today's scientific textbooks aim
to answer."[62] Packer also makes, more eloquently and concisely, the
point that I was trying to make above and in my own chapter about the
importance of not confusing literal truth with its modern, literalistic
counterpart: "it does not follow that because Scripture records matters
of fact, therefore it does so in what we should call matter-of-fact language."[63] Packer rightly reminds us that confessing inerrancy "implies
nothing at all about the literary character of particular passages."[64]
These cannot be decided in advance but must rather be determined
by carefully attending to each passage's language, genre, and context.
Evangelical exegetes must make every effort to hear what God is saying
in the biblical text rather than what we would like God to be saying.

Because Mohler does not mention the abuses of inerrancy that
have given the term a bad name in some quarters, I am somewhat
ambivalent about his insistence that inerrancy "has never been more
essential to evangelicalism" (p. 30). I think he means "original" inerrancy, but I can't be absolutely sure. Nevertheless, he is onto something
vitally important. Evangelicals must affirm Scripture as the supremely
authoritative source, criterion, and norm for faith, life, and theology—
indeed, for all domains that Scripture addresses. I agree that, without
confidence in the truth of Scripture, evangelicalism "will inevitably
become dissolute and indistinct in its faith and doctrines" (p. 30). In
no way, then, should the critical points I make above be thought to
cast aspersions on Scripture's entire truthfulness, or Mohler's good
intentions.

The questions I've raised about Mohler's "classic" doctrine of inerrancy are not questions about the truthfulness of Scripture. They are

---

62. J. I. Packer, "Encountering Present-Day Views of Scripture," in *The Foundation of
Biblical Authority*, James Montgomery Boice, ed. (London and Glasgow: Pickering and Ing-
lis, 1979), 78.
63. Ibid.
64. Ibid.

rather about the adequacy of the category "classic doctrine of inerrancy" and the overconfident conflation of affirming inerrancy with certain types of interpretation. Yet what concerns I have must be read in light of my own positive proposal not to reject but to redeem the concept of inerrancy. However, given the widespread confusion over the concept and its implications for biblical interpretation, I think that we must do more than call people to hold onto inerrancy: we must first define it, and then distance ourselves from its interpretive abuses.

I can summarize my response to Mohler's chapter with three cheers (minus one):

As to the Bible's being the wholly true and trustworthy word of God: hooray!

As to the necessity of evangelical theology's maintaining the above: huzzah!

As to the "classic" doctrine of inerrancy: say what?

RESPONSE TO R. ALBERT MOHLER JR.

JOHN R. FRANKE

The essay by Al Mohler articulates what he takes to be the classic doctrine of biblical inerrancy. He argues that the case for this view of inerrancy flows from three major sources: the Bible itself, the tradition of the church, and the function of the Bible within the church. He couples this with an articulation of the Chicago Statement on Biblical Inerrancy, which he affirms without reservation, stating that in order to be true to the Scriptures "evangelicals must affirm its stated affirmations and join in its stated denials" (p. 46). The difficulty I have with this position is that it takes a particular notion of inerrancy and biblical authority, that of the CSBI, and asserts that it is a universal ideal that must be affirmed by all who would seek to be faithful to the Bible.

It is fair enough for Mohler to assert that "inerrancy was the affirmation and theological reflex of the church until the most recent centuries" (p. 000). However, the sort of inerrancy that was affirmed was not that of historical-grammatical interpretation, a literal reading of the Bible, and the CSBI. For instance, Origen of Alexandria affirmed the inerrancy of Scripture but was able to do so because of his commitment to spiritual and allegorical interpretation. In his response to Gnostic communities that rejected the Old Testament on the grounds that it taught a different God than the one revealed in Christ (because they believed that the deity of the Old Testament was vengeful, jealous, capricious, and often directly responsible for sin and evil), Origen asserted the necessity of spiritual exegesis. He believed that their conclusions were unavoidable if the biblical texts were to be accepted as literal and, hence, he asserted that they must be understood allegorically. In fact, he argues that in many cases the texts are intentionally obscure and incoherent in order to coax and compel the reader to seek their true, spiritual meaning.

Likewise, Augustine of Hippo, prior to his conversion, was persuaded by the arguments against Christianity because of a literal reading of the Bible, particularly the Old Testament. As with many who shared his Platonist mind-set, he found much that he believed to be unworthy of God. It was not until he discovered the spiritual, allegorical, and figurative interpretation of Scripture in the preaching of Ambrose that he was able to affirm Christian teaching and the truth of Scripture. In this context, the Hellenistic appreciation of myth and symbol became an essential part of Augustine's approach to biblical interpretation, in which allegory served as a powerful and important means of conveying religious and philosophical truth. Origen and Augustine were hardly alone in this regard as many, even most, early Christian teachers made use of spiritual and allegorical interpretation to defend the divine origin of the Bible and explain away some of its literal teachings in the face of cultural assumptions and challenges.

These early Christian teachers developed interpretive approaches that enabled them to effectively relate the Scriptures to particular settings without denying their truthfulness as the Word of God. The dualistic outlook of Hellenism, with its assumptions about the superiority of the spiritual world, compelled Christian teachers such as Origen and Augustine to employ an allegorical approach to biblical interpretation in order to justify their commitment that the Bible was inspired and without error. To assert that it could not or should not be interpreted in such a fashion would be tantamount to denying its inspired character. Affirming the Bible as the Word of God entailed the assumption that its form and teaching were consistent with the cultural standards of the time. Throughout the history of the church, the affirmation of inerrancy has been coupled with a varied and flexible hermeneutic that allowed the biblical texts to be appropriated in a culturally relevant fashion. It seems to me that if Mohler wants to appeal to the history of the church as a basis for the affirmation of biblical inerrancy, he needs to be willing to accept the diversity of interpretive approaches that have enabled and shaped this commitment.

However, what Mohler does in his essay is tie the confession of inerrancy to a specific hermeneutic, that of the CSBI. His reasoning would seem to be that without such a connection, the commitment to inerrancy is rendered meaningless. I suspect that is what he would say to me regarding my pluralist account of inerrancy. But I believe that such a pluralist approach is necessary in order to do justice to the actual contents of the Bible. The interesting point from my perspective is that, with appropriate nuances, I share Mohler's basic outlook: the Bible is divinely inspired and, as such, is a form of the Word of God. Hence, when the Bible speaks, God speaks. Where we differ is on the question of what God has spoken, is speaking, and will speak in and through the texts of Scripture. It is precisely because I believe that Scripture is the Word of God that I am concerned about the attempt to tie the confession of inerrancy to a particular cultural and hermeneutical outlook.

Historians and theologians have routinely pointed out the ways in which figures of the past such as Origen and Augustine provide us with object lessons in the dangers of cultural accommodation, the practice of too closely associating the Bible and Christian faith with the values and presuppositions of a particular social, cultural, or philosophical outlook. While it is important to remember that all human forms of thought are situated and embedded in social contexts, it is also important to resist the temptation of promoting a form of cultural Christianity that simply mirrors and affirms the norms of the surrounding society. From this perspective, Origen and Augustine are perhaps most guilty of the assumption that the Bible, as the Word of God, must be interpreted in conformity with the standards and aspirations of their Hellenistic setting. In making this assumption, they run the risk of domesticating the Bible by insisting that it conform to a particular set of social outlooks and customs, thus limiting its ability to speak beyond those settings and circumstances.

It seems to me that in binding the notion of inerrancy to the hermeneutic of the CSBI, Mohler is moving in a similar direction. He is asserting that if the Bible is really the inerrant Word of God, it must be interpreted according to modern assumptions concerning the writing of history and the communication of fact which place little value on literary devices, such as myth and saga, which are part of the landscape of the ancient world. The difficulty with this assumption is that he might actually be hindering the reception of Scripture by demanding interpretive assumptions that are alien to its context. Of course, to raise this challenge poses questions to all of us. Have we too readily assumed our own conceptions of the Bible and its interpretation? Do we demand that the diverse contents of Scripture fit comfortably into our contemporary assumptions about language and history? And further, given our participation in our culture, on what basis are we able to make such an assessment? In short, how do we develop doctrines and teachings that are not simply accommodated to our own cultural assumptions and aspirations?

Missionary theologian Lesslie Newbigin has addressed this question by observing that while the ultimate commitment of the Christian theologian is to the biblical story, such a person is also a participant in a particular social setting whose whole way of thinking is shaped by the cultural model of that society in ways that are both conscious and unconscious. These cultural models cannot be absolutized without impairing the ability to properly discern the teachings and implications of the biblical narrative. Yet as participants in a particular culture, we are not able to see many of the numerous ways in which we take for granted and absolutize our own socially constructed cultural models. Given this state of affairs, Newbigin maintains that the unending task of theology is to be wholly open to the biblical narrative in such a way that the assumptions and aspirations of a culture are viewed in its light in order to find ways of expressing the biblical story in terms that make use of particular cultural models without being controlled by them. He concludes with the assertion that this can only be done if Christian theologians are "continuously open to the witness of Christians in other cultures who are seeking to practice the same kind of theology."[65]

Mohler says that he affirms the CSBI "without reservation," agrees with its assertions "in whole and in part," and believes that all evangelicals must affirm "its stated affirmations and join in its stated denials" (p. 46). For him a mutual commitment to inerrancy and the CSBI appears to be inseparable because, as he says, "the affirmation of inerrancy is necessary for evangelical consistency, and a definition of inerrancy is integral to its affirmation" (p. 48). From my perspective, the difficulty with Mohler's position is that in making the prescriptions of

65. Lesslie Newbigin, "Theological Education in a World Perspective," *Churchman* 93 (1979): 114–15.

inerrancy as interpreted by the CSBI absolute, he has cut off conversation with those who raise questions and concerns about it. Might it be that the CSBI is more reflective of a particular set of North American hermeneutical and theological assumptions than is appropriate in light of the biblical narrative? How does he account for differences among evangelicals who are committed to inerrancy but not the CSBI? Is it possible that people who represent other traditions of evangelicalism might perceive legitimate difficulties that ought to be corrected? Is it possible that the CSBI is mistaken on some matters and that, because of his participation in a particular community of discourse, Mohler is not able to perceive these shortcomings? If this is possible, how will he become aware of it if the model he proposes is made absolute in his mind?

While I appreciate his commitment to truth, my major concern with Mohler's outlook is that he seems to construe doctrinal formulations such as the CSBI more as first-order language rather than second-order. I would view only the contents of Scripture as first-order language and all exegetical, theological, and doctrinal interpretations as second-order statements, meaning that they are always subject to critical scrutiny and the possibility of correction. It does not appear to me that Mohler would say this of the CSBI. He seems to think that it would be appropriate to put an equal sign between it and the teaching of the Bible. From my perspective, the primacy of Scripture as the norming norm for Christian thought and practice means that all doctrinal statements must be understood as provisional and subordinate. Where we fail to do this we run the risk of transforming them into *de facto* substitutes for Scripture.

INERRANCY, HOWEVER DEFINED, DOES NOT DESCRIBE WHAT THE BIBLE DOES

PETER ENNS

Some Thoughts on the Current Evangelical Disharmony over Inerrancy[1]

The Bible is the book of God for the people of God. It reveals and conceals, is clear yet complex, open to all but impossible to master. Its message clearly reflects the cultural settings of the authors, yet it still comforts and convicts across cultures and across time. The Bible is a book that tells one grand narrative, but by means of divergent viewpoints and different theologies. It tells of God's acts but also reports some events that either may not have happened or have been significantly reshaped and transformed by centuries of tradition. It presents us with portraits of God and of his people that at times comfort and confirm our faith while at other times challenge and stretch our faith to its breaking point. This is the Bible we have, the Bible God gave us.

Redefining or nuancing inerrancy to account for these properties can be of some value, and some are no doubt content to do so. The core issue, however, is how inerrancy functions in contemporary evangelical theological discourse. This too varies, but when all is said and done, I do not think inerrancy can capture the Bible's varied character and complex dynamics. Though intended to protect the Bible, inerrancy

---

1. Numerous friends and colleagues read portions or all of this essay and provided valuable insight: Steve Bohannon, Art Boulet, Sam Boyd, Rob Kashow, Nathan Mastnjak, John Oliff, Tony Stiff, and Stephen Young.

actually sells it short by placing on it expectations it is not designed to bear—as evidenced by the need for generations of continued publications and debates to defend it.

On a deeper and ultimately more important level, inerrancy sells God short. Inerrancy is routinely propounded as the logical entailment of God's truthfulness, which for many inerrantists leads to the necessary expectation of the Bible's historical accuracy. The premise that such an inerrant Bible is the only kind of book God would be able to produce, or the only effective means of divine communication, strikes me as assuming that God shares our modern interest in accuracy and scientific precision, rather than allowing the phenomena of Scripture to shape our theological expectations. As I see it, the recurring tensions over inerrancy in evangelicalism are largely a byproduct of the *distance* between a priori theological assertions about God and about how his book should behave and the Bible we meet once we get down to the uncooperative details of the text itself. When the Bible needs so much careful, persistent tending in order to preserve a particular doctrine of Scripture, we might wonder whether the doctrine is the solution or the very source of the problem. Put another way, inerrancy is a theory. The question before us is whether this theory can explain the phenomena of the text. If not, then inerrancy should be amended accordingly or, in my view, scrapped altogether.

The stark reality, however, faced by evangelicals who are critical of inerrancy is that inerrancy has been a central component of evangelicalism for its entire history, a response to the challenges of biblical higher criticism of the eighteenth and nineteenth centuries. Inerrancy is encoded into the evangelical DNA, and conversations, however discreet, concerning its continued usefulness are rarely valued. In fact, considerable personal and professional fallout are well documented, and examples are not difficult to find. Inerrancy's definitive—and nonnegotiable—role in forming evangelical identity in the face of modern challenges reached a defining moment in the framing of the Chicago Statement on Biblical Inerrancy (1978).

The Chicago Statement on Biblical Inerrancy Preempts Needed Dialogue

Inerrancy has traditionally functioned in evangelicalism as a theological boundary marker against faulty exegetical conclusions or misguided hermeneutical approaches. The history of American evangelicalism readily attests to this prescriptive role, showcased in the Chicago Statement on Biblical Inerrancy (CSBI), which has enjoyed a quasi-authoritative boundary-marking role. However helpful some might find the formulations continued in the CSBI, when given prescriptive force, it obstructs the kind of critical dialogue clearly surfacing within evangelicalism, and therefore threatens to neutralize self-criticism, a necessary quality of any healthy intellectual pursuit. At such times, evangelicalism appears intellectually dishonest, thus forfeiting intellectual witness to our culture and creating spiritual stumbling blocks for its own members.[2]

The implied premise of the CSBI is that God as God would necessarily produce an inerrant Bible, and this premise is the very point coming under increasing scrutiny within evangelicalism. To the minds of many, maintaining inerrancy requires that perennially nagging counterevidence from inside and outside of the Bible must be adjusted to support that premise rather than allowing that evidence to call the premise into question. In my opinion, the distance between what the Bible is and the theological hedge placed around the Bible by the CSBI has been and continues to be a source of considerable cognitive dissonance.

The problem surfaces already in the reasoning found in the preface to the CSBI, which makes four discernable assertions: (1) The authority of Scripture is a key issue for each generation of believers and in every age, for to stray from Scripture is to stray from Christ himself. Inerrancy guards against this slippery slope. (2) In fact, since inerrancy is Jesus' own view of the Bible, to set inerrancy aside is to set aside "the witness of Jesus Christ and of the Holy Spirit." (3) Though it is claimed that the CSBI has no "creedal weight," the writers hope that their efforts will bring on a "new reformation of the Church in its faith,

---

2. For a focused critique of the CSBI (and its later sister document the Chicago Statement on Biblical Hermeneutics 1982), see Iain Provan, "'How Can I Understand, Unless Someone Explains It to Me?' (Acts 8:30–31): Evangelicals and Biblical Hermeneutics," *BBR* 17.1 (2007): 1–36. See also Carlos Bovell, *Rehabilitating Inerrancy in a Culture of Fear* (Eugene, Ore.: Wipf & Stock, 2012), 44–65; Kevin J. Vanhoozer, "Lost in Interpretation? Truth, Scripture, and Hermeneutics," *JETS* 48, no. 1 (March 2005): 89–114. For an appeal for a more prominent role the Chicago statements should play in evangelicalism today, see Jason Sexton, "How Far beyond Chicago? Assessing Recent Attempts to Reframe the Inerrancy Debate," *Themelios* 34 (2009): 26–49.

life, and mission." (4) The CSBI is offered in "humility and love" and in a spirit of dialogue, acknowledging that people who deny inerrancy do not necessarily "display the consequences of this denial in the rest of their belief and behavior," and that people who uphold inerrancy do not always reflect that faith in their lives.

Several observations come to mind. First, note that in numbers 1 and 2, biblical authority, Christ's (and the Spirit's) authority, and inerrancy are inseparably linked, if not equated, without indicating that such linkage might need to be demonstrated and defended. Second, no attempt is made to define just what kind of authority is envisioned for the Bible (number 1) and on what basis such a view of authority can rightly be justified. The type of authority implicitly signaled here (which the CSBI demonstrates throughout) can be described as a "legal" authority—that is, the Bible, as God's Word, provides information from God, through human writers, that prescribes interpretive conclusions on every matter Scripture touches. Third, the content of the word *inerrancy* is not yet given; we are only assured that it is Jesus' own view. That content will be supplied in the articles that follow, and we are apparently expected to agree at that point that Jesus' brand of inerrancy (assuming the term has any resonance with a first-century figure) matches that of the CSBI. Finally, introducing an allegedly noncreedal document (number 3) offered in a dialogical spirit (number 4) by saying, in effect, "Like us, Jesus was an inerrantist (and so should you be)" will hardly encourage critical reflection on what is to follow. I genuinely wonder whether discouraging critical interaction was precisely the task of these opening statements.

In a similar vein, following the preface is a section titled "A Short Statement," consisting of five assertions intended to set parameters for what follows. The first assertion speaks of God "who is Himself Truth and speaks truth only" (that is, in the Bible). Here we see explicitly the linking of inerrancy to the very nature of God, as I mentioned above. This is a critical premise of the rhetoric of the CSBI, but again, whether such linkage is warranted and how the nature of that linkage would be defined are precisely what needs to be brought to the table. This premise of the CSBI should not be given a free ride, for to leave it as is implies that people who wish to critique inerrancy on exegetical and theological grounds *stand in opposition to God himself.* In a nutshell, this explains the theological confidence expressed by some inerrantists and why objections to inerrancy are met with such force.

What is regrettably missing here at the outset of the CSBI — where it is most needed — is a display of hermeneutical self-consciousness on the part of the framers, which would encourage needed reflection on the nature of truth that God speaks in ancient texts. That the CSBI does not give even a nod here to the hermeneutical and theological complexities inherent in this discussion is more than just a gaping hole; it is a factor that cripples the document's usefulness.[3] What should be brought explicitly to the forefront here is the manner in which God speaks truth, namely, *through the idioms, attitudes, assumptions, and general worldviews of the ancient authors.* When speaking of the nature of Scripture, a valid definition of the word *truth* must address as a first order of business the energetic interplay of the Spirit of God working in and through ancient human authors, thus ensuring that our cultural assumptions are held in check and revised through engaging this dynamic. Otherwise our cultural assumptions become petrified and immune to criticism.

In evangelical disputes over the nature of Scripture, I continue to be somewhat perplexed at how immune those discussions seem to be from the real, live historical particularities within which God has spoken. The Christian faith is a historical faith, yet when it comes to articulating how the Bible — a record of that historical faith — operates, we seem to find ourselves quickly in abstractions and other sorts of discussions that claim to have some immediate access to the very mind of God. For this reason, I continue to see an incarnation model of Scripture as helpful, not in providing the only model or last word on the subject but as a corrective for moving the evangelical discussion forward so that Scripture's historically conditioned behavior ceases being a problem to be solved, marginalized, or ignored and becomes the very stuff of evangelical bibliology.[4] It seems to me that C. S. Lewis's warning seventy years

---

3. The inescapable hermeneutical dimension of inerrancy is positively articulated in Harvie Conn, ed., *Inerrancy and Hermeneutics: A Tradition, a Challenge, a Debate* (Grand Rapids, Mich.: Baker, 1988).

4. Peter Enns, *Inspiration and Incarnation: Evangelicals and the Problem of the Old Testament* (Grand Rapids, Mich.: Baker, 2005); "Preliminary Observations on an Incarnational Model of Scripture: Its Viability and Usefulness," *Calvin Theological Journal* 42, no. 2 (2007): 219–36; "Bible in Context: The Continuing Vitality of Reformed Biblical Scholarship," *Westminster Theological Journal* 68 (2006): 203–18.

ago remains apt. Christians must come to terms with the "irreverent doctrine" of the incarnation if they wish to see Scripture as it really is.[5] In fact, the Christian faith itself, according to Lewis, is an "incurably irreverent religion" in that incarnation is the central, principle operative (though differently so) in both Christ and Scripture. When seen in this light, exploring what "God speaks truth" means cannot and must not be undertaken apart from a warm embrace of the idioms, attitudes, assumptions, and general worldviews of the ancient authors.

The CSBI, however, illustrates repeatedly the dilemma of defining the word *truth* apart from Scripture's historical framework. One example is article 12, which deals with the creation story and historicity. We read that "Scripture in its entirety is inerrant, being free from falsehood, fraud, or deceit," including in "the fields of history and science." The article mentions specifically that no "scientific hypotheses about earth history may properly be used to overturn the teaching of Scripture on creation and the flood." The implication is self-evident: inerrancy means, first of all, that literalism is the default hermeneutic of the CSBI, and second, that no appeal to the study of ancient history or scientific discoveries can be allowed to overturn what the Bible so plainly (that is, literally, dehistoricized) says about creation and the flood. Taken at face value, this means that any comparison of Genesis with other ancient Near Eastern origins stories *that results in drawing non – CSBI-style-inerrantist conclusions about how to interpret Genesis* is ruled out of bounds. Likewise, scientific knowledge concerning the vast age of the universe and of the earth and the antiquity of humanity are not to be brought into biblical interpretation. Hermeneutical reflection on how to read Genesis 1 – 11 is unnecessary—and, by virtue of what we saw in the preface (points 1 and 2), potentially *unfaithful to Christ and the Spirit*. For those evangelicals, however, who see the pressing need to bring ancient Scripture and our present world into more careful conversation, it is precisely this sort of reasoning that is both discouraging and frustrating.

The fourth assertion found in the short statement of the CSBI compounds the problem by expanding inerrancy to the entirety of the Bible's "teaching, no less in what it states about God's acts in *creation*,

---

5. C. S. Lewis, introduction to J. B. Phillips, *Letters to Young Churches: A Translation of the New Testament Epistles* (New York: Macmillan, 1953), vii–viii.

about the *events of world history*, and about its own *literary origins* under God, than in its witness to *God's saving grace* in individual lives" (my emphasis). This statement is striking. Taken at face value, it rules out of bounds, as a matter of principle, any true conversation between science and faith and any historical investigation prompted by archaeological findings or by probes into the time and place of the biblical books that would question inerrantist claims. We have here a preemptive strike against those very factors that prompt reevaluation of the theological assertions made in the CSBI.

And even more concerning to me is the final element mentioned in the citation above: God's saving grace. It is a bit unsettling to see the matter of salvation conjoined to the three legitimate and pressing academic/scholarly issues. Although one can sense the urgency of the framers for maintaining an inerrantist stance, this linkage borders on emotional blackmail. The logic seems to be that if the teaching of Scripture on creation, history, and authorship is wrong, then we have no reason to trust what Scripture says about salvation. Hence, to give ground on any of the first three points removes any reason for not giving ground on the fourth.

This familiar slippery slope argument should be rejected by thoughtful evangelicals. Arguing for a position on the basis of what you might lose if that position is not retained is not an argument but an expression of fear, which when allowed to reign leads to anger, either directly or indirectly by means of manipulation, passive-aggressiveness, and — as seen above — emotional blackmail.[6] Moreover, this slippery slope argument is, as already discussed above, rooted in the assumption that God as truth-teller requires a text that is only superficially, if at all, circumscribed by the idiom of the day. In order for Christians today to be able to trust what God says about salvation, he *must* at all costs avoid any hint of the Bible's mingling with ancient ways of thinking about where the cosmos comes from and with ancient conventions of history writing. God *must* keep his distance from the human drama, and Scripture must bear witness to how well he transcends the fragile landscape of antiquity.

---

6. On the role of the slippery slope argument in evangelicalism, see Harriet A. Harris, *Fundamentalism and Evangelicalism* (New York: Oxford Univ. Press, 2008).

Of course, on the surface, few would simply deny the Bible's historical rootedness, but in practice it is muted in an inerrantist apologetic. The "true" message is somehow lifted off the unfortunate restrictions of the historical page and made to abide in a world of detached dogmatic "universals." I wonder too if there is not some sort of gnosticism inherent in at least some forms of inerrancy, in which a God "up there" saves us from a finite world too mundane to warrant God's attention. To acknowledge Scripture's historical dimension in principle but then lay it aside when making dogmatic assertions — particularly when history challenges dogma — fails to grapple with why God, in his wisdom (which is not our wisdom), spoke truth in a world where such things as myth and tribal cultural norms were ubiquitous.

The CSBI has certainly played a role in helping some move out of more restrictive views on the Bible and land in a "safe" place. But too often it serves as a conversation stopper and a means by which people are judged safe or dangerous, which prevents evangelicalism from honestly considering developments in modern biblical studies and other fields. In my view, this is a hindrance to the health of evangelicalism and the integrity of its witness. In recent years, I have seen firsthand, again and again, the spiritual and emotional fallout of holding scholarship at bay in order to protect, by force if necessary, evangelical views of inerrancy. I have had many conversations with trained, experienced, and practicing biblical scholars, young, middle-aged, and near retirement, working in evangelical institutions, under inhuman personal and professional stress, trying to negotiate the line between institutional inerrantist expectations (willfully isolated from contrary data) and academic integrity. Not only does this squander the potential of holy camaraderie and true progress within evangelicalism, but it also leaves informed scholars who are outside of evangelicalism scratching their heads at times.

To be sure, I am aware that historical-critical biblical scholars have made grand claims or otherwise exhibited a self-assurance that goes beyond what the data warrant. But that charge can be leveled just as appropriately, and should be leveled, against any ideologically driven approach to biblical interpretation, including an evangelical approach. Further, as much as there is to criticize within the diverse discipline of modern biblical scholarship, few evangelical biblical scholars (including some inerrantists) would deny that critical biblical scholarship has done much to clarify such things as the historical contexts of the biblical writings, the time frames when various portions of the Bible were written, and the reasons they were created. At the very least, enough evangelicals agree to inspire a volume such as this.

To summarize, I do not think inerrancy can be effectively nuanced to account for the Bible's own behavior as a text produced in ancient cultures. In my view, inerrancy regularly functions to short-circuit rather than spark our knowledge of the Bible. Contrary to its intention to preserve the truthfulness of Scripture and the truth-telling God behind it, inerrancy prematurely shuts down rigorous inquiry into what the Bible's "truthfulness" means, and so interrupts rather than fosters careful reading of Scripture. When inerrancy asks us to override the best historical and scientific inquiry with (what is taken to be) the plain teaching of Scripture, it also hinders us from addressing the more interesting, spiritually edifying, and lovely topic of what kind of a God we have, one who is willing to speak within the limitations of his audience. Indeed, despite its apparent interest in seeing God as so powerful that he can overrule ancient human error and ignorance, inerrancy portrays a weak view of God. It fails to be constrained by the Bible's own witness of God's pattern of working—that God's power is made known in weakness, he reigns amidst human error and suffering, and he lovingly condescends to finite human culture. Ironically, inerrancy prevents us from grappling with the God of the Bible.

Inerrancy also prevents us from coming to terms with ourselves. There are lessons to be learned in the canonical growth and development of God's people, namely, how little current precisionist views of truth come into play when speaking of the Bible. Inerrancy paints us into a corner of thinking that biblical statements are by default timeless and therefore as applicable to us in the modern world as it was to people in the ancient world. By obscuring the finitude of the text, inerrancy obscures the finitude of our own contemporary context, which ironically concedes to the modern mindset that many inerrantists fear is present in modern historical criticism.

Three Biblical Test Cases

The three test cases on which we have been asked to comment illustrate the inadequacies of an inerrantist paradigm. They represent challenges

to inerrancy—from outside the Bible and from within the Bible itself—
that evangelicals are quickly introduced to when they open their Bibles
and try to be faithful, responsible, and informed readers. Despite some
protestations, the fall of Jericho in Joshua 6 is significantly at odds with
archaeological data pored over for more than a century. The book of
Acts gives no fewer than two accounts of Paul's encounter with the
risen Christ on the way to Damascus, one in which his companions
heard the voice of Christ and the other in which they did not. God's
command to exterminate the Canaanites is, like the fall of Jericho, at
odds with the archaeological evidence. It also represents the perennial
and difficult moral issue of the "violence of God" in the Old Testament,
a problem made all the more difficult in view of Jesus' admonition to
love one's enemies rather than kill them to take their land.

These issues cannot be reconciled with how inerrancy functions in
evangelicalism as articulated in the CSBI. To be clear, this assertion
does not rest on simply citing three "problems" in the Bible. Rather the
three test cases are illustrative of a pervasive problem for inerrantist
apologetics, perhaps *the* problem: the oftentimes troubling relationship
between the text and the event about which the text speaks. Maintaining a strong connection between the two has been the raison d'être of
intellectual evangelical bibliology. What makes the evangelical apologetic all the more urgent is that the problem of history does not simply
affect incidental events here and there; it affects those that sit at the
very core of Israel's story—such as the conquest of Canaan, which is
directly relevant to the first and third passages discussed below. The
example chosen from the book of Acts, though the importance of its
content is less central, nevertheless exerts its own pressure on the inerrantist paradigm: contradiction in the reporting of events, in this case
within the same book by the same author.

As the lone Old Testament scholar in the group, I felt it would be
irresponsible of me not to spend a little less time developing the philosophical and theological issues that are the topic of this volume, and
spend a bit more time than do my coauthors in laying out more clearly
why these three passages, especially the first and third (though, as we
will see, an Old Testament motif is also relevant for Acts), are problematic for inerrancy. After looking at each of these, I will conclude
with some brief summative comments.

The Fall of Jericho: Inerrancy and the "Possibility" of Historicity

A central—if not *the* central—and perennial concern of inerrancy is the essential historical reliability of the Bible where it clearly speaks to historical matters: "[T]he Bible's historical narratives are trustworthy. The narratives correspond to what happened in real time and in real places."[7] Though "trustworthy" and "correspond to" leave some wiggle room, few will doubt that for inerrancy in evangelicalism to have any teeth, historical narratives in the Bible need to correspond in some meaningful and concrete way to actual events, even if they are not literalistic accounts of events, since God is a God of truth, not historical inaccuracy. If the Bible indeed claims that Jericho's walls fell, then there were actual walls that actually fell. The archaeological record of the fall of Jericho in Joshua 6, however, is a well-known problem for this assertion, since the overwhelmingly dominant scholarly position is that the city of Jericho was at most a *small settlement* and *without walls* during the time of Joshua.

The archaeological period relevant to Jericho is the Late Bronze Age (1550–1200 BC). If one accepts the late date for the exodus (around 1260 BC), the fall of Jericho would have happened sometime around 1220 BC (after the forty years in the wilderness).[8] If one follows the traditional date of the exodus, 1446 BC, the fall of Jericho would be dated closer to 1400 BC.[9] In the 1930s, John Garstang claimed to have found remains of a walled city corresponding to the traditional date and of sufficient size to support the biblical story. Kathleen Kenyon's excavations of the 1950s led to a significant reevaluation of Garstang's

---

7. John D. Woodbridge, foreword to James K. Hoffmeier and Dennis R. Magary, eds., *Do Historical Matters Matter to Faith? A Critical Appraisal of Modern and Postmodern Approaches to Scripture* (Wheaton, Ill.: Crossway, 2012), 13.

8. The date of 1260 BC is derived from two dates documented by outside corroboration. Rameses II of Egypt took the throne in 1275, and he is the pharaoh credited with building the storehouses of Pithom and Rameses mentioned in Exodus 1. In the Egyptian Merneptah Stele of 1208 BC, "Israel" is mentioned as a distinct group of nomadic (not settled) people defeated by Pharaoh Merneptah in or near the land of Canaan. For "Israel" to be present in this part of the world, the exodus would have needed to happen sometime between these two dates, and at least forty years before 1208.

9. 1446 BC is the traditional date of the exodus, calculated on the basis of a literal reading of 1 Kings 6:1: Solomon built the temple in 966 BC, which we are told was in "the four hundred and eightieth year after the Israelites came out of Egypt." Many, if not most, trained inerrantist evangelical scholars either accept or are sympathetic to the later date in view of some of the data we are discussing in this section.

interpretation of the material remains. She argued that Garstang's walls dated to about 1550 BC, well out of range of the biblical timeline. Kenyon further concluded that Jericho was unoccupied during the Late Bronze Age, though subsequent excavations have shown evidence of meager occupation.[10]

That Jericho in the Late Bronze Period was a small, unwalled settlement is not seriously contested by archaeologists as a whole. Exceptions are found only in the writings of defenders of inerrancy, most notably Bryant Wood, a trained archaeologist and research director of the Associates for Biblical Research, a Christian apologetics organization. Beginning in 1990, Wood argued that Garstang was correct in dating the fall of Jericho to about 1400 BC, which supported not only the historicity of the Jericho story but also the early date of the exodus. But Wood's interpretation has gained no traction among archaeologists for *evidentiary* (not ideological) reasons. Further, placing Jericho's destruction in the Late Bronze period creates a whole other problem. The archaeological evidence for Israel's military conquest of Canaan is meager at best, and what little we have is from no earlier than the thirteenth century BC; placing Jericho's destruction in the end of the fifteenth century creates more of a problem than it solves. Wood's proposal is also extremely difficult to square with the ample archaeological evidence for an increase in hill country settlements in the twelfth century (consistent with the portrayal in Joshua and a thirteenth-century exodus), not the late fifteenth century, as Wood's position requires. Wood's theory has not convinced his peers, and subsequent work supports Kenyon's date (though not necessarily all the details of her arguments).[11]

Inerrantist scholars more in tune with the archaeological data have wisely settled for defending only the "essential" historicity of the biblical story, though such a posture is hardly problem free. Capitalizing

---

10. Kathleen M. Kenyon, *Digging Up Jericho: The Results of the Jericho Excavations 1952–1956* (New York: Praeger/Ersnt Benn, 1957).

11. Bryant G. Wood, "Did the Israelites Conquer Jericho? A New Look at the Archaeological Evidence," *BARev* 16, no. 2 (1990): 44–58. The matter is picked up one more time in articles by Wood and his critic Piotr Bienkowski in *BARev* 16, no. 5 (1990): 45–68. Elsewhere, Bienkowski confirms meager Late Bronze Age occupation of Jericho but that it "fell" because of economic rather than military factors (*Jericho in the Late Bronze Age* [Warminster: Aris and Phillips, 1986], 124–25, 155–56).

on the kernel of historicity granted by the presence of a small settlement in Jericho during the Late Bronze Age, evangelical scholars such as Kenneth Kitchen, Richard Hess, and more recently John Monson have argued in various ways that the archaeological data, though not directly supporting the historicity of the fall of Jericho, do not necessarily make impossible the presence of a walled city at the end of the Late Bronze Age. The scholars cite erosion as a possible reason for why the walls are undetected.[12] This line of argument is a common rhetorical strategy among inerrantists: if the archaeological evidence does not make the biblical view absolutely impossible, the biblical account remains historically possible and therefore should be given the benefit of the doubt, and external evidence should be interpreted generously to support that conclusion.

One can certainly argue this way, though I wonder if inerrantists would be willing to accept this type of argument from others. Would the "it's not impossible" argument be deemed compelling confirmation of other historical phenomena, for which there is meager or no clear evidence, if they were at odds with inerrancy, or is the need to defend inerrancy driving the argument? Moreover, I am doubtful that this line of argument is sufficient to support the notions of biblical reliability and sufficiency that are intended to be guaranteed by the CSBI specifically and the inerrantist model of Scripture in general. To say "it's possible / not impossible" seems far from the view of God that inerrancy intends to regard: a straightforward, historically accurate revealer of truth, who is not held hostage by things like archaeology or biblical scholarship. A defense of inerrancy that rests on the impossibility of disproving the possibility of historicity, in my view, is entirely circular and therefore demonstrates the implausibility of the premise and is its own refutation.

---

12. Kenneth Kitchen, *On the Reliability of the Old Testament* (Grand Rapids, Mich.: Eerdmans, 2003), 187–88; Richard S. Hess, *Joshua: An Introduction and Commentary*, Tyndale Old Testament Commentaries 6 (Downers Grove, Ill.: InterVarsity, 1996), 150–52; John M. Monson, "Enter Joshua: The 'Mother of Current Debates' in Biblical Archaeology," in Hoffmeier and Magary, *Do Historical Matters Matter*, 436–37. On the other hand, Bienkowski has shown that most Late Bronze settlements in Canaan (68 of 76) were unwalled (*Jericho in the Late Bronze Age*, 124). See also T. A. Holland, "Jericho," *Anchor Bible Dictionary*, 3.736. David Ussishkin argues directly against the notion of Late Bronze walls in Jericho being built on earlier Middle Bronze foundation ("Notes on the Fortification of the Middle Bronze II Period at Jericho and Shechem," *BASOR* 276 [November 1989]: 29–53).

Inerrantist responses notwithstanding, the dominant position held by archaeologists today is that the material evidence from Late Bronze Age Jericho supports only the presence of a small, unwalled settlement, not the walled city described in the Bible. Israeli archaeologist Amihai Mazar, hardly a skeptic of biblical historicity, puts it this way: "Undoubtedly, the biblical story of the battle of Jericho is *legendary*, but in this case archaeological evidence *does not run directly counter to the biblical tale*, as is asserted by some scholars."[13] Inerrantist scholars are understandably drawn more to the second half of Mazar's conclusion than to the first half. But granting a minimal historical core, as Mazar does here, is a far cry from asserting the *historical reliability of the biblical account* in the manner required by the prescriptive function of inerrancy in evangelicalism.[14] The biblical story of the fall of Jericho is perhaps a significant elaboration on a historical kernel, not a reliable record of a historical event.

Ironically, a train of thought lies open to inerrantist scholars for accepting this conclusion, which they themselves have articulated for another pressing issue of biblical historicity: the exodus from Egypt. Kenneth Kitchen, for example, speaks of the ancient Near Eastern "trend to 'mythologize' history [rather than historicize myth], to celebrate actual historical events and people in mythological terms."[15] Kitchen's point is to defend the basic historical reliability of the bibli-

13. Amihai Mazar, "The Iron Age I," in *The Archaeology of Ancient Israel*, ed. Ammon Ben-Tor (New Haven: Yale Univ. Press; Tel Aviv: Open Univ. of Israel, 1992), 283 (my emphasis), cited in J. Gordon McConville and Stephen N. Williams, *Joshua*, The Two Horizons Old Testament Commentary (Grand Rapids, Mich.: Eerdmans, 2010), 29. See also Amihai Mazar, *Archaeology of the Land of the Bible* (New York: Doubleday, 1990), 331, cited in Monson, "Enter Joshua," 436–37. Curiously, Monson considers Mazar's view to defend his inerrantist argument.

14. Note, too, Mazar's slightly veiled criticism of conservative Christian "biblical archaeology": "In America, the term biblical archaeology continues to be used by conservative Christian researchers, as evidenced in a new book entitled *The Future of Biblical Archaeology* (edited by J. K. Hoffmeier and A. Millard), which appeared in 2004. Similarly, the Biblical Archaeological Society and its magazine *Biblical Archaeology Review*, though private and nondenominational, reflect in their names a well-defined targeted public, much of it composed of conservative Christians who are interested in the Bible and its world. *There is a broad gap between this approach and the professional approach to archaeology as part of the larger fields of anthropology and history*, and this has resulted in the refutation of the term biblical archaeology by many scholars in the United States" (Israel Finkelstein and Amihai Mazar, *The Quest for the Historical Israel: Debating Archaeology and the History of Early Israel*, ed. Brian B. Schmidt [Atlanta: Society of Biblical Literature, 2007], 32–33, my emphasis).

15. Kitchen, *Reliability of the Old Testament*, 262.

cal account of the splitting of the sea: it has a historical core (how-ever defined) that the biblical writers present in mythic terms, rather than being, as some say, a myth dressed in fictional historical garb. Likewise, speaking of the crossing of the Sea of Reeds, James Hoff-meier argues, "Hebrew writers could use mythic language and images to depict specific historical situations," adding that this "in no way detracted from the historicity of the events being discussed."[16]

"Mythologized history" is potentially a fruitful line of discussion for understanding a number of biblical episodes, including the exodus and fall of Jericho,[17] though I am not sure Hoffmeier should get a free pass in his doctrinal conclusion. If biblical writers describe events mythically, it most certainly detracts from the historicity of the event. It may not eliminate the possibility of historicity, but one must admit that the heat is turned up a bit, since defending inerrancy must now be satisfied by merely asserting the possibility that "something happened" though we don't really know — and can't possibly know — what, other than it is not how the Bible presents it. One could reasonably question what value inerrancy holds in such a scheme. Also, claiming a histori-cal core for a biblical narrative, even if correct, does not determine how much history we actually have in the biblical account, a problem that besets inerrantist arguments of the Bible's "essential" historicity. The historical core for the exodus story could just as easily be, as many bib-lical scholars think, a small band of slaves who left or escaped Egypt and migrated over land (or across a shallow lake), and later generations retold this historical core in mythic language.[18]

Regardless, my only point here is that the principle Kitchen and Hoffmeier apply to the mythic telling of the Reed Sea crossing could be applied to the fall of Jericho: the biblical story reflects a small his-torical core (perhaps suggested by some archaeological evidence) that at some point was mythicized. This could prompt fruitful discussion,

---

16. James K. Hoffmeier, *Israel in Egypt: The Evidence for the Authenticity of the Exodus Tradition* (New York: Oxford Univ. Press, 1996), 213.

17. This is the general argument made by Douglas Earl, *The Joshua Delusion: Rethinking Genocide in the Bible* (Eugene, Ore.: Cascade, 2010).

18. Among other elements in the exodus story, the splitting of the sea clearly evokes the ancient Near Eastern imagery of the cosmic battle and taming of chaos, as seen, for example, in the Babylonian story Enuma Elish and reflected in the separating of the waters in Genesis 1:6–8 and more clearly in Psalms 74:12–17 and 136:10–15.

though we must also admit that once we follow this path, we have left the world of inerrancy as it functions in evangelicalism as a prescriptive doctrine. Rather than trying to find ever more problematic ways of preserving inerrancy, it seems more reasonable to affirm the deeply problematic nature of the evidence concerning Jericho and discuss its implications for inerrancy and the need for a new paradigm.

The gravity of this discussion becomes clearer when we consider the evidence concerning the conquest of Canaan in general. Here too the archaeological record does not support the biblical story. Of the thirty-one towns listed in Joshua 12:9–24, twenty have been identified, but only Hazor and Bethel (and perhaps Lachish) fit the biblical description. The other towns either were unoccupied during the Late Bronze Period, show no evidence of sudden change, or were destroyed before or after the time of the biblical conquest. Add to this the troubling fact that most of Transjordan, notably Heshbon of Ammon and Dibon of Moab (for example, Num. 21:30), was unoccupied during the Late Bronze Period, when the Israelites were said to pass through. Archaeological investigations do confirm overwhelmingly a significant increase in settlements in the hill country between 1200 and 1000 BC, which is generally consistent with the biblical accounts, but these were not founded by outside invaders.

The general scholarly conclusion, expressed here gently by Douglas A. Knight and Amy-Jill Levine, is not seriously contested: "Archaeologists have long tested the evidence for the sweeping military campaign portrayed in the book of Joshua, and their results are not encouraging for a Late Bronze Age setting [thirteenth century BC]."[19] The Jericho story is just one illustration of this larger issue. As discussed earlier, the core Christian principle of the incarnation opens up a more fruitful dialogue concerning the intersection of these sorts of historical data and a doctrine of Scripture. The evangelical discussion needs to begin there, not stall because of a faulty premise about what kind of Bible God would need to produce.

---

19. Douglas A. Knight and Amy-Jill Levine, *The Meaning of the Bible: What the Jewish Scriptures and Christian Old Testament Can Teach Us* (San Francisco: HarperOne, 2011), 20. An excellent and readable summary of the issues is Lawrence E. Stager, "Forging an Identity: The Emergence of Ancient Israel," in *The Oxford History of the Biblical World*, ed. Michael D. Coogan (Oxford: Oxford Univ. Press, 1998), 122–75.

The historicity of the conquest comes into play again below, where we consider the ethical and theological implications raised by God's command to exterminate the Canaanites.

Did Paul's Companions Hear Jesus' Voice or Did They Not? Luke, Historiography, and Inerrancy

Acts 9:7 and 22:9 give different accounts of Paul's vision of Christ on the way to Damascus.[20] In the former, we read that Paul's traveling companions heard Jesus' voice but saw no one. In the latter, they did not hear Jesus' voice but saw a light. What was or was not seen is not much of a problem for inerrancy. The companions could have seen no one (9:7) but still seen a light (22:9), and neither account needs to present both details. But whether Paul's companions heard (9:7) or did not hear (22:9) "the sound" (Greek *phōnē*) of Jesus' voice is difficult to skirt. (Both passages unambiguously equate the sound with Jesus' voice; see 9:4 and sound of the speaker in 22:9.) Unlike the synoptic problem in the Gospels and the historical books of the Old Testament (Kings and Chronicles), which is explained on the basis of the different historical settings, audiences, and perspectives of the authors, this discrepancy in Acts is within the same book and by the same author, and so poses a different sort of challenge to inerrancy.

One way of defending inerrancy is to reconcile the two accounts by translating Acts 22:9 as "did not understand the voice" (NIV).[21] This allows the companions in 22:9 to still hear the voice of Jesus, as in 9:7, but there is no reason to translate 22:9 any differently than 9:7, other than the perceived need to reconcile the two accounts. Elsewhere in the New Testament, the verb *akouō* followed by *phōnē* never means simply to understand what was said but to have heard it (and in places to obey, as in John 10:3, 16, 27; 18:37). Of course, hearing implies comprehension, but the expression in the Bible never means "to understand" as distinct from "to hear," and Acts 22:9 is no exception.

---

20. A third account, not discussed here and which further complicates the matter, is Acts 26:12–14.

21. Ajith Fernando's duplication of the translation problem is unfortunate but also understandable, given that the NIV is the base translation for his commentary (*Acts*, The NIV Application Commentary [Grand Rapids, Mich.: Zondervan, 1998]). See also Darrell L. Bock, *Acts*, Baker Exegetical Commentary on the New Testament (Grand Rapids, Mich.: Baker: 2007), 358–59.

Some commentators seem to think that the issue is hardly worthy of extended comment, and leave it at that. Ernst Haenchen, for example, asserts that the two verses differ in expression but not sense, though he doesn't give an explanation.[22] Hans Conzelmann briefly mentions that the differences are real but can be accounted for as "literary variations" for "stylistic reasons," though he does not say how.[23] Similarly, Simon Kistemaker, without breaking his stride, asserts that there is no contradiction and that the differing meanings are to be gleaned from the context, though he does not get into the important question of how the context relieves the contradiction.[24] More commonly, however, commentators recognize the clear discrepancy between the two accounts, though without always fully explaining why it exists. For example, Luke Timothy Johnson states matter-of-factly that the two accounts say "the exact opposite" and that Acts 22:9 "exactly contradicts the first version."[25] Ben Witherington III notes the discrepancy and attributes it to the freedom ancient writers have to bypass "minute details."[26] This is certainly correct in principle (of modern writers too), though some might quibble as to whether "they heard" and "they did not hear" is a minor detail.

In any case, strict inerrantists have difficulty accommodating transparent differences like this, since it challenges the underlying premise that God would be logically consistent and historically accurate. Any such contradictions are therefore only "apparent contradictions" that require the interpreter to be patient until a proper explanation arises. This "be patient" argument is another inerrantist strategy, similar to the "it's not impossible" argument mentioned in the previous section: problematic data are either interpreted favorably or held at bay in order to preserve the viability of a theological premise. But these two accounts, if read in any other piece of ancient literature, would be labeled "contradictory" without hesitation. To insist here, on

---

22. Ernst Haenchen, *The Acts of the Apostles: A Commentary* (Philadelphia: Westminster, 1971), 322.

23. Hans Conzelmann, *Acts of the Apostles*, Hermeneia (Philadelphia: Fortress, 1987), 72.

24. Simon J. Kistemaker, *Exposition of the Acts of the Apostles* (Grand Rapids, Mich.: Baker, 1990), 336.

25. Luke Timothy Johnson, *The Acts of the Apostles*, Sacra Pagina 5 (Collegeville, Minn.: Liturgical Press, 1992), 163, 389.

26. Ben Witherington III, *Acts of the Apostles: A Socio-Rhetorical Commentary* (Grand Rapids, Mich.: Eerdmans, 1998), 311. Witherington also suggests that the accounts may have been originally intended for different audiences (308–9).

(questionable) theological grounds, that one *must* see these accounts as noncontradictory in order to preserve the nonnegotiable doctrine of inerrancy, despite the words in front of us, is to tell lay readers that they cannot trust their own reading skills, and could thereby raise genuine concerns about the intellectual bias of inerrantists.

The issue before us is not whether these accounts differ or how they can be made to fit a treasured theological grid. We owe it to ourselves, the church, and Scripture's integrity to allow these differences to have their way in helping us shape a view of Scripture that closes the distance between how Scripture behaves and how we presume it to behave — thus honoring God in the process. In my opinion, that process puts us squarely in the arena of historical investigation, which is to ask why Luke in *his* time and place, not ours, would write as he did. I do not think the answer to this question is necessarily obvious, but there are some well-traveled paths worth noting that I think provide a better backdrop than imposing inerrantist requirements on an ancient author.

For one thing, biblical writers shaped history creatively for their theological purposes.[27] Few biblical scholars, including evangelicals, hesitate to acknowledge this, and we have already seen an example in the Jericho story. Such creative historiography is not the sole property of Old and New Testament writers but simply part and parcel of any historian, ancient or modern, who wants to write a compelling account of the past to persuade or inspire his or her readers. For example, in his account of the Peloponnesian War, the scrupulous historian Thucydides writes,

> In this history I have made use of set speeches some of which were delivered just before and others during the war. I have found it difficult to remember the precise words used in the speeches which I listened to myself and my various informants have experienced the same difficulty; *so my method has been, while keeping as closely as possible to the general sense of the words that were actually used, to make the speakers say what, in my opinion, was called for by each situation.*[28]

27. A brief evangelical articulation of this basic principle is V. Philips Long, *The Art of Biblical History* (Grand Rapids, Mich.: Zondervan, 1994).

28. Thucydides, *History of the Peloponnesian War*, trans. R. Warner, rev. ed. (London: Penguin, 1972), 47 (my emphasis).

Though an eyewitness to events, as Luke claims to be (at least for part of Acts), Thucydides nevertheless had to make up dialogue to communicate what in his opinion was "called for." Constructing a coherent picture from raw material by addition and elaboration is the task of any historian, and the only reason to protect Luke the historian from this very same process is to preserve, ironically, an ahistorical doctrine of how biblical writers wrote, which, once again, is implicitly rooted in a particularly modern view of what God's "truthfulness" requires.

Part of Luke's palette for his portrait of Paul is his own Scripture, Israel's story. New Testament writers were energetically engaged in talking about Jesus and the new people of God by drawing upon and transforming the symbols and images of the Old Testament. Commentators on Acts routinely, and correctly, appeal to the literary motifs of divine announcement, theophanies, and Old Testament prophetic call narratives as a backdrop against which to understand Luke's presentations of Paul's vision — particularly in Acts 22:9, where Paul, like his Old Testament counterparts, *alone* hears the divine voice. This does not solve, or even directly address, the question of the factual discrepancies between the two accounts. It should, however, pave the way for the more fundamental move of reorienting inerrantist expectations of the nature of Luke's historiography.

In other words, long before pondering why Luke would describe the same thing in two different ways (which already suggests that there is a problem here that needs to be solved), we need to ask why Luke describes *anything* the way he does. What is Luke's historiographical method, so to speak? The fact that Luke describes Paul's Damascus road experience in different ways already alerts us to the likelihood that recording "what happened" is not his primary focus, whereas interpreting Paul for his audience is.

In the Old Testament, servants of God chosen to bear a special message of an impending act of God are drafted into service by a divine encounter of some sort. These "call narratives" are hardly carbon copies of each other, but some are similar to Paul's call to take the gospel to the Gentiles. When Ezekiel is called by God to deliver good news to the exilic community, he sees a humanlike heavenly creature on a heavenly throne, glowing as if by fire, and surrounded by brilliant light. Ezekiel falls facedown to the ground and hears "the voice of one speaking," which comes to him privately (Ezek. 1:28). Similarly, an angel appears to Daniel, with arms and legs gleaming like burnished bronze and a voice like thunder — a vision that Daniel's companions do not experience but that leaves Daniel weak with his face to the ground; he is then commissioned to take the prophetic word to the people (Dan. 10:5 – 14).

I am not suggesting that Luke deliberately presents Paul in Acts 22:9 as a new Ezekiel or Daniel (although we should not discount the possibility), but the similarities suggest that Luke is appealing to precedent, perhaps a well-known literary device. This explanation is all the more compelling in view of the broader context of Acts 22:9, which is Jewish opposition to Paul's preaching (see 21:27 – 36). By presenting Paul as a present-day prophet challenging the status quo, Luke may be trying to defend Paul's status: as were the prophets of God before him, Paul is a chosen instrument of God for a great purpose.

The wider context of Jewish and Greco-Roman literature may also shed some light. Luke Timothy Johnson (among others) suggests an echo of the story Joseph and Asenath (possibly late first century BC to second century AD) in Luke's description of Paul.[29] In this legendary story of the patriarch and his Egyptian wife (see Gen. 41:45 – 50; 46:20), Asenath undergoes her own call of sorts (Joseph 14): the heavens open, a great light appears, she falls on her face, and an angel tells her to dress in new clothes, thus symbolizing her acceptance by God and marriage to Joseph. Richard Pervo lists numerous examples from Greco-Roman literature, and elsewhere, of divine blinding as a form of punishment (as it was for Paul).[30] These accounts are certainly not parallel to Acts 22:9, nor is Acts 22:9 dependent on these stories on a literary level. But the presence of a diversely articulated motif of divine encounter, with details similar to those we find in Acts 22:9, may help us understand the details of Luke's presentation of Paul. In fact, the persuasive force of Luke's presentation of Paul as a chosen prophet of God would be strengthened with the use of this motif. Luke's situation, like that of Thucydides, called for such a portrait of events.

The question remains, however, why Luke didn't shape his account of Paul's call the same way in Acts 9:7. I am not sure, though I would

---

29. Johnson, *Acts*, 167 – 78.

30. Richard I. Pervo, *Acts*, Hermeneia (Minneapolis: Fortress, 2009), 241 – 42, nn. 71, 73.

suggest again that the need to defend Paul as a Jewish prophet in Acts 22, and not in chapter 9, may help explain the difference between the two accounts. Regardless, I wish to make a less complex though no less important point here: a better grasp of the creative nature of ancient portrayals of the past can and should inform our understanding of how biblical portrayals work. Biblical historiography does not operate according to inerrantist expectations. But burdened by modern precisionist notions of truth as a requirement of a text-inspiring God, inerrancy—contrary to its intention—obscures what Scripture, read incarnationally as a historical phenomenon, has to say.

Shaping significantly the portrayal of the past is hardly an isolated incident here and there in the Bible; it's the very substance of how biblical writers told the story of their past.[31] In few places is this principle seen more clearly, and is its need to be understood more pressing, than in the Canaan conquest narratives.

The Extermination of the Canaanites: A Historical, Ethical, and Theological Problem for Inerrancy

God's order to kill every Canaanite man, woman, and child, as laid out in Deuteronomy 20:16–17, poses well-known, long-standing, and pressing theological challenges, not least for evangelical inerrancy. In recent years, the issue has surfaced on a popular level, in part because of the highly visible challenges to Christian morality by New Atheists.[32] It does not help Christian apologists that Christian history contains many examples of harsh treatment of "outsiders" by perpetrators who claimed to be following

---

31. This same principle is evident in the Old Testament. One familiar example is the account of Moses' birth, abandonment, and eventual exaltation in Exodus 2:1–10, which echoes the much older legend of Sargon (ancient king of Akkad, 2300 BC). Of humble birth, Sargon was (1) placed by his mother in a reed basket lined with pitch, (2) set afloat on a river, (3) found by the king's water drawer, who raised him as his son, and (4) eventually became king. These similarities to the Moses story, which are hardly coincidental, suggest that *how* the story of Moses' birth is told is not simply a report of "what happened." The Moses of Exodus emerges through the lens of an ancient Near Eastern literary convention of drawing on "precedent to certify a new event or a new leader" (Victor H. Matthews, *Old Testament Turning Points: The Narratives That Shaped a Nation* [Grand Rapids, Mich.: Baker, 2005], 62). Moses is not a country bumpkin but is destined for greatness. See further Tremper Longman III, who compares this ancient "abandoned child" motif to the modern version of a child wrapped in a blanket and left on the doorstep in a basket (*Fictional Akkadian Autobiography: A Generic and Comparative Study* [Winona Lake, Ind.: Eisenbrauns, 1990], 70–72).

32. For example, see Richard Dawkins, *The God Delusion* (Boston: Houghton Mifflin, 2008), 268–316.

biblical precedent (for example, the Spanish conquest of the West Indies, and the plight of Native Americans at the hands of British settlers).[33]

Addressing responsibly the matter of God's command to exterminate the Canaanites requires us to come to terms with at least three factors: (1) the genuine seriousness of the moral and theological issues this raises for Christian theology, compounded by (2) Jesus' teachings about how to treat sinners and enemies, which do not rest comfortably with God's order to slaughter men, women, and children, and (3) the discrepancies between the archaeological record and the biblical account of the conquest of Canaan, as we glimpsed above. Some may find this third point good news, relieved that Canaanite extermination may not have happened, which would get God off the hook. But for inerrantists, the archaeological data compounds the problem. An inerrantist model of Scripture "needs" the Canaanite genocide to be in some meaningful sense literally true, despite the resulting theological and moral problems. For inerrantists, an "errant" Bible is a greater theological threat than a God who orders the extermination of an entire people, since an entire theological system rests on the former.

In my opinion, inerrantist attempts to account for and defend Canaanite extermination on a moral and historical level have not addressed adequately these three factors. To preserve inerrancy, the inerrantist apologetic is required to counter the three points made above with three highly questionable (historically and theologically) counterassertions: the extermination of Canaanites (1) displays God's just moral judgment, (2) is not in any true conflict with Jesus' teachings, and (3) describes historical events with essential accuracy. Below, I will focus on the first two, since we touched on the third earlier.

Extermination of Canaanites as a Pressing Moral and Theological Problem

Deuteronomy 20:10–20 gives God's marching orders for Israel's imminent invasion of Canaan (see also Deut. 7:1–6). God encourages

---

33. Also relevant here is the much larger issue of God's violence outside of the conquest stories. Even though we see calls for international peace in the Old Testament, as illustrated by the forging of swords and spears into farming tools (Isa. 2:4; Mic. 4:3; though see Joel 3:10), God's dominant means of addressing sin and disobedience is through physical punishment and death, a pattern beginning in the flood story (Gen. 6–9) and continuing throughout Israel's historical narratives and prophetic literature. Killing or punishing by sword (enemy attack), famine, or pestilence is God's preferred method of dealing with stubborn, sinful people—whether Israel's enemies or Israel itself.

the Israelites not to be fainthearted, afraid, terrified, or panicked, as they were forty years earlier (Num. 13:1–35): "The LORD your God is the one who goes with you to fight for you against your enemies to give you victory" (Deut. 20:4). Israel need not be afraid like last time. Yahweh is with his people and will secure victory for them. The slaughter of the Canaanites is guaranteed.[34]

Two types of enemies are discussed in Deuteronomy 20:10–20, non-Canaanites and Canaanites, and the former is just as important for us as we consider Canaanite extermination. Non-Canaanites (vv. 10–15) are to be offered terms of peace, but this is no humane gesture. If the terms are accepted, all the people will be subjected to forced labor — which hardly leaves the residents with much of a choice but to fight and raises an additional moral issue of God commanding forced enslavement. If the inhabitants refuse to become slaves for life, Israel is to attack and God will give them the victory: all the men are to be "put to the sword" (v. 13), while the women, children, and livestock are "plunder" (v. 14) or "booty" (NRSV). God commanding the Israelites to treat women and children as booty should make us all stop in our tracks, even apart from the issue of Canaanite extermination.

Numbers 31, which is earlier in the narrative, gives us a glimpse of the treatment that awaits non-Canaanites when God is provoked. In that passage, God orders the Israelites to "take vengeance" on the Midianites (v. 2) by waging war against them. The Israelites comply and kill every man (v. 7), take captive the women and children, along with the livestock and property, as plunder (v. 9), and burn all the towns to the ground (v. 10). Upon the soldiers' return, however, Moses is incensed at how many Midianites are still alive. He commands that all the boys be killed, thus wiping out the line and removing the threat of war (see Pharaoh's similar move in Exod. 1:22). Midianite women who slept with Israelite men, thus tempting them to false worship, are also to be executed. Just imagine this scene in your mind's eye.

The virgin women and girls, however, are to be "spared," but not out of mercy or for the sake of justice. Virgin women were considered

---

34. Military conflict is foreshadowed at the very beginning of Israel's march to Canaan. Whenever the Israelites broke camp, Moses would say, "Rise up, LORD! May your enemies be scattered; may your foes flee before you" (Num. 10:35). From the outset, it seems, people met along the journey to Canaan are *God's* enemies. God is their enemy for no apparent reason other than they are in Israel's way.

property, and so were divided among the soldiers, civilians, and priests along with the rest of the plunder (vv. 25–47).[35] Without giving ourselves up to wild speculation, one may be justified in wondering exactly what the Israelite soldiers and other Israelites did with the captive virgin women. If we were dealing with a text from other ancient tribal cultures, we would likely not hesitate to point out how morally corrupt these people were.

This overview of the treatment of non-Canaanites is not a side issue. It helps us see that the extermination of the Canaanites ordered in Deuteronomy 20:10–20 cannot be viewed as a one-time outburst of God's wrath against a particularly deserving people; it can be viewed only as *part of a larger picture of Yahweh as a tribal warrior god* who commands not just the killing of enemy soldiers but also the killing and/or enslaving of civilians, including women and children. The extermination of Canaanites, however rightly troubling, is simply one element of that portrayal. The implication for inerrantists is this: *In order to defend or justify the extermination of the Canaanites as an expression of God's inscrutable standard of justice and goodness,[36] that same line of thought needs to be applied to the forced enslavement of women and children, and to prizing virgin women as plunder.* The same God does both.

Moving to the Canaanites, they are not offered terms of peace (Deut. 20:16–20). Rather the Israelites are to kill everything that draws breath—animal or human, whether men, boys, women, or girls, from infant to elderly. Why such a drastic measure? One reason is that Yahweh is a jealous God (Deut. 5:9), and verse 18 makes it clear that allowing any Canaanite to live runs the risk of leading the Israelites astray to worship other gods. Killing all the Canaanites obviates this problem (see also Deut. 7:2–4). God's command, in other words, is

---

35. God's command to treat virgins as property is disturbingly documented in Israel's legal tradition (Ex. 22:16–17; Deut. 22:28–29). Some virgins were given to Eleazar the priest and the Levites as an "offering to the LORD" (Num. 31:29 NRSV). This probably means they became cultic slaves to help with the priestly duties.

36. The various inerrantist strategies for addressing Canaanite genocide are succinctly summarized in Thom Stark, *The Human Faces of God: What Scripture Reveals When It Gets God Wrong* (Eugene, Ore.: Wipf & Stock, 2010), 85–114. Stark is particularly critical of Gleason Archer (*Encyclopedia of Bible Difficulties* [Grand Rapids, Mich.: Zondervan, 1982], William Lane Craig ("Slaughter of the Canaanites," *www.reasonablefaith.org.site/News2?page=NewsArticle&id=7911* (August 4, 2010), and Christopher J. H. Wright (*The God I Don't Understand: Reflections on Tough Questions of Faith* [Grand Rapids, Mich.: Zondervan, 2008]).

not rooted in a *moral* judgment against the Canaanites' unprecedented degree of sinfulness (which would allow God's command to be interpreted as a simple expression of his righteous indignation against sin). True, other passages cite Canaanite sinfulness as the reason for God's command (for example, Gen. 15:16; Deut. 9:4). But the Canaanites were not higher up on the ladder of moral offense to God than any other nation. Some defenders of God's actions here claim that Canaanite child sacrifice (Deut. 12:31) was the tipping point, but Canaanites hardly cornered the market on this act (see King Mesha of Moab's act, 2 Kings 3:27). By God's standard, all nations in the Old Testament were sinful, yet they were not treated as the Canaanites were. There is clearly another factor at work that explains the unique treatment of the Canaanites: they occupied the land to be given to Israel, and they had to be exterminated to prevent their impure, sinful behaviors from leading the Israelites astray to worship other gods.

How do we move forward on this issue?[37] If one is willing to step outside of the inerrantist paradigm, a solution arises almost naturally. Though possibly (I would say likely) rooted in the memory of ancient conflict, the biblical conquest narratives do not "report events" with inerrantist expectations of historical accuracy. These narratives are the rhetoric of a tribal people, who understood their own existence and their God's role among them in terms of the categories of tribal culture: gods are warriors who fight for their people against enemies, giving victory for faithfulness but withdrawing their hand for unfaithfulness. The Israelites were an ancient people and portrayed God and their relationship to him in that way.

Perhaps others will see a different solution, but an inerrantist model is inadequate to handle the issue of Canaanite extermination

---

37. Although we cannot address the matter here in any detail, it may be of some comfort to know that the Old Testament preserves an alternate view of the conquest that seems to exonerate the Israelites. According to Leviticus 18:24–28, the previous inhabitants of the land became defiled, and so "the land vomited out its inhabitants" (v. 25). "Vomited" leaves unstated what the metaphor refers to (whether violent conflict or some others means of ousting), but the past tense suggests that God had already dealt with the Canaanite problem before the Israelites left Mount Sinai. The Israelites therefore were not responsible for slaughtering men, women, and children. As we saw concerning the book of Acts above, the presence of alternate accounts so at odds with one another suggests that literary and theological fashioning is at work. As troublesome as such an approach may be for inerrantists, it at least potentially relieves Christian readers of Scripture of the burden of defending God's actions. If anything, we are reminded that the Bible is a book containing diverse voices.

in the Old Testament, and other models must emerge that accept the implications of a Bible that reflects how God is willing to meet his people where they are and allow them to tell the story in ways that reflect deeply their own cultural context. And such a model would need to account for not only the Old Testament depiction of God's violence toward outsiders but also Jesus' rejection of it.

What Would Jesus Do?

In the Sermon on the Mount (Matt. 5:43–48), Jesus tells his Jewish audience to love and pray for their enemies rather than hate their enemies and love only their neighbors. In doing so, Jesus says, they will become true children of God, for God sends the rain on the just and unjust alike. Loving only those who love you does not reflect the heart of God, for even tax collectors do that. True followers of God will take the much harder road of loving people who mean them no good. To do so is to be perfect (in love) as God himself is. As we seek to discern how Jesus' teaching here relates to God's violence in the Old Testament toward Israel's (and therefore God's) enemies, there are several points we must bear in mind.

Matthew's gospel as a whole presents Jesus as a new and improved Moses — which suggests that we might see Jesus go beyond what Moses said.[38] Specifically, Matthew presents the story of Jesus in five discreet sections, each ending with, "When Jesus had finished saying these things …" (see 7:28–29; 11:1; 13:53; 19:1–2; 26:1–2). The fivefold story of Jesus gives a "new Torah" for the people of God. Also, both Moses and Jesus escape a royal decree of mass infanticide (Moses was placed in a basket in the Nile, and Jesus was carried off to Egypt). Both return to be among their people to deliver them, and both endure a forty-day fast before ascending a mountain to bring to the people the law of God. And, rather unambiguously, Jesus' Sermon on the Mount (a plain in Luke 6) mimics Moses' declaration of the law from Mount Sinai and presents Jesus as the new mountaintop mediator of God's Word to the waiting people below.

Although much of the Sermon on the Mount pits Jesus against the hypocrisy of the religious leaders of his day (chaps. 6–7), the sixfold

---

38. This is a wholly noncontroversial point. See Jack Dean Kingsbury, *Matthew as Story*, 2nd ed. (Philadelphia: Fortress, 1998), and Dale C. Allison Jr., *The New Moses: A Matthean Typology* (Philadelphia: Fortress, 1994).

refrain in chapter 5 "You have heard that it was said ... but I tell you ..."
(or the equivalent; 5:21–22, 27–28, 31–32, 33–34, 38–39, 43–44)
contrasts Jesus' teaching to that of Moses. It is debatable whether Jesus
is simply expanding upon the implications of the Mosaic law or the
disjunction is more severe. At the very least, some sort of contrast is
made: Jesus claims an authority that bids his hearers to follow him,
not simply rely on Mosaic tradition. Murder and adultery are not only
about these physical acts but also about words and thoughts—matters
of the heart (5:21–30); Moses may have allowed divorce, but Jesus
allows it only for unfaithfulness (vv. 31–32; neither Mark nor Luke
mention this exception); under Moses, swearing oaths to Yahweh was
a way of certifying fidelity, but in Jesus' kingdom, no oaths are to
be made of any sort (vv. 33–37); an eye for an eye and a tooth for a
tooth insured just retribution under Moses, but Jesus commands that
personal injury should be answered with an extra measure of kindness
(vv. 38–42).

This contrast to—or at least going one better than—the Mosaic
law continues in Matthew 5:43–48. According to Leviticus 19:18,
Israelites are not to seek revenge or bear a grudge against a fellow
Israelite, that is, their neighbor. Their enemies, however—as we have
seen with bracing clarity in the previous section—are not afforded
this treatment. But Jesus says that now, true followers of God—those
who want to be like him, to be perfect as he is—must love their neighbors and their enemies with the same love. Who are these enemies?
Not simply people they happen to not like or not get along with but
those who persecute them (v. 44). Keeping in mind the distinction in
the Old Testament between "neighbor" (fellow Israelite) and "enemy"
(outsiders), the enemies Jesus refers to would seem to be primarily the
Romans, the current Gentile occupants of the Holy Land. These are
the ones with the power to persecute his Jewish audience, but Jesus
commands that the proper response to persecution is love and prayer.

Further, Kenton Sparks has made the compelling case that Matthew's gospel as a whole asks its readers "to interpret the Mosaic 'genocide' through the lens of Jesus' radical message of love."[39] He notes that
of the five women listed in Matthew's genealogy of Jesus (1:1–17), two

---

39. Kenton L. Sparks, "Gospel as Conquest: Mosaic Typology in Matthew 28:16–20,"
CBQ 68.4 (2006): 652.

have clear Gentile connections (Bathsheba and Tamar) and two are non-Israelites (the Moabitess Ruth and the Canaanitess Rahab). This favorable view of Gentiles continues in Jesus' birth narrative: the (Gentile) magi receive him, but King Herod and "all Jerusalem with him" (2:3) hold him in suspicion and fear, which parallels the account of the Roman centurion's faith in Jesus vis-à-vis Jewish rejection (8:5 – 13).[40]

Most telling is the Syrophoenician widow of Mark 7:24 – 30, labeled a Canaanite in Matthew 15:21 – 28, the only mention of Canaanites in the New Testament. Although on the surface the episode looks like a picture of Jewish exclusivism (the Canaanite woman is a dog eating the crumbs that fall from her master's table), Jesus declares at the end that this Canaanite woman has great faith (v. 28). Sparks reads this as a "tongue-in-cheek parody of Jewish exclusivism," intended to make a pointed statement of Canaanite inclusion.[41] Finally, Jesus calls his followers to go to "all nations" and make disciples, not conquer and kill them (Matt. 28:16 – 20). This farewell instruction in Matthew echoes *and reverses* that given by Moses at the end of his life (Deut. 31:1 – 8), when he says in essence, "Go to the nations [to wage war] and do all I have commanded you, and the Lord will be with you." In the Old Testament, as we have seen, God's presence with Israel among the nations was a promise of success in battle. In Matthew, God will bring about the conversion of the nations, even at great personal risk.

Jesus' admonition to love enemies, which appears only in Matthew, is a clear statement of Gentile (even Canaanite) inclusion directly contrasted to the dominant Old Testament / Mosaic estimation of the nations. This must have sent a shock wave through the audience (as did pretty much everything Jesus says in the Sermon on the Mount), in part because the Jews had been subject to Gentile rule in their own land ever since the destruction of the temple in 586 BC and the deportation of a significant number of the population to Babylon. After the return from exile, the Israelites were still subject to Gentile rule — first by the Persians, then the Seleucids, the Ptolemies, and finally the Romans. In Jesus' day, the various Jewish groups had different opinions of how they should relate to their Roman hosts. The upper-crust Sadducees seemed content to work with the Romans for their own

---

40. Ibid., 652 – 54.
41. Ibid., 654. The parallel between this woman and Rahab in Joshua 2 and 6 is striking.

social benefit. The Pharisees had a more anti-Roman undercurrent. But Roman rule was largely considered a problem or irregularity to be overcome, not a sign of God's blessing, especially in view of the Old Testament prophetic witness that promised Jerusalem's exaltation after some period of disciplining of the Israelites and eventual submission of the nations to Yahweh's rule (for example, Isa. 2:2). Both Jesus' call to love and pray for his people's enemies and his utter disinterest in establishing Jewish political independence were out of sync with the messianic hope so prevalent in the Old Testament.

Matthew's Jesus supersedes Moses, which leads to the following point: *Jesus' call to love and pray for one's enemies cannot be lined up neatly with the Old Testament and judged to be a simple extension or revealing of what the Old Testament really says.* Jesus' teaching is a *reversal* of the Old Testament's dominant tone of exclusivism. You do not hate your enemies; you love them. You do not kill them; you evangelize them. Killing the enemy among you to gain political independence and national security are no longer the goal; leaving your land to go out into the world and make disciples of the nations is. One might ask why God didn't enact this evangelistic policy the first time around, in the Old Testament. One answer, as I mentioned above, is that Israel's depiction of God vis-à-vis the nations unmistakably, and understandably, reflects the ubiquitous tribal culture at the time. Jesus said, in effect, "That was then, this is now; you have heard it said, but I say to you."

It seems clear to me that inerrancy, as it is usually promulgated within evangelicalism, cannot capture this dynamic that Scripture itself exhibits. Inerrancy is prone to seek "timeless truths" given by a God who ultimately transcends the particulars of history so that he can speak clearly to us today. But by failing to do justice to the time-conditioned nature of Scripture, inerrantists have great difficulty accepting what seems self-evident on the pages of Scripture: the portrayals of God reflect cultural and historical moments of the biblical writers, which therefore yield variant expressions of God. Scripture is a collection of historically situated narratives that develop, move, and transform; it is not a treatise from a distant land that requires legal consistency.

I suppose one could find a way to call this dynamic "inerrancy" if need be, but that is hardly what is intended by the term, and there is no compelling reason to confuse matters by pressing the term into awkward service. Inerrancy, particularly as it is expressed in the CSBI and functions within evangelicalism, does not clarify the nature of this dynamic; it obscures it under the false pretense of defending the Bible and the character of God behind it.

Concluding Thoughts

Simply put, inerrancy, however defined and nuanced, has great difficulty in addressing adequately and convincingly Scripture as a historical phenomenon. A common objection to my position is that we should not place the study of history over the Bible by allowing extrabiblical historical investigation to determine how we read the Bible. I reject fully this counterargument, if anything because inerrantists are more than willing to accept historical study if it supports their theory. The real problem isn't the simple *use* of outside information to address our understanding of the nature of the Bible but whether what we find there is amenable to a particular theory.

Inerrancy, in other words, is an a priori and prescriptive doctrine. However imprecisely the text itself exhibits this doctrine, we must nevertheless *assume* it of the text in order to engage the text appropriately and be faithful Christians. Leaving aside for the moment how this turns inerrancy into a kind of criterion for genuine Christian faith, and thus how it has functioned historically in evangelicalism as an identity marker and means of determining who is in and who is out, it must be admitted that this is a very awkward position to hold. We are told that the factual truthfulness of the Bible is essential to Christian faith, yet because inerrancy is a priori, we can allow historical investigation to bear upon our knowledge of the accuracy of the Bible only when that investigation supports inerrancy. When our doctrine demands that we believe what is contrary to disciplined observation, cognitive dissonance and faith crises take root. Must Christians truly believe that God left for the church a private epistemology, by which we know truth differently and better than others?

And if we are to be consistent in this position, shouldn't we also cease benefitting from other scholarly and scientific pursuits altogether? Shouldn't we stop using technology and stop seeking modern medical treatment? If the Bible alone gives us accurate knowledge, and if the methods that have produced the advancements we currently enjoy are rooted in spiritual rebellion, then why should Christians ever support any of them? It is just here where we see the schizophrenia that inerrancy forces upon evangelicals: we are free to benefit from the advances of modern science and critical study and can even participate in these fields, yet when it comes to that which is most central to our faith and understanding of the world — the Bible — we are told that scientific study constitutes a threat and is contrary to faith in God, that we must simply believe that the Bible is accurate, even if a preponderance of evidence suggests otherwise. From my perspective, while this leap of faith may seem a daring statement of nobility or piety, it is disingenuous and even duplicitous. Indeed, I wonder at times whether inerrancy asks of its adherents to be dishonest, or at least willingly numb, in order to hold to the truth. When protecting doctrine requires that we dismiss, mishandle, or vilify compelling information unfriendly to our doctrine, we are demonstrating not faithfulness to God's Word but a failure to trust God more than our theology.

If there is any sense in which the language of inerrancy can be retained, it is this: as a *descriptive* observation rather than a *prescriptive* declaration. Rather than bringing to the interpretive process a grid of allowable conclusions that are a priori deemed consistent with a particular notion of God, a descriptive model of inerrancy would try to take its cues from biblical behavior and so draw inferences about what qualities to expect of Scripture. Rather than being a nonnegotiable philosophical starting point for biblical interpretation, with prescriptive power, and adjusting biblical phenomena to fit the theory, a descriptive approach would be more a statement of faith on the part of the reader that *no matter what is encountered, the reader is in the presence of the wisdom and mystery of our God.* Such an approach, because it would be less threatened by genuine advances in our knowledge of antiquity, not only would help ease the hearts and minds of disquieted evangelicals but also would be better suited to engage people who have no inclination to respond to standard evangelical apologetics.

To anticipate an objection, I would agree that such a definition of inerrancy is really a complete redefinition and so hardly describes what inerrancy was devised in the CSBI to do, namely, provide parameters for interpretation that ensure that a particular view of the Bible and the God responsible for it remain intact. This is why I feel that the term *inerrancy* has run its course and that evangelicals need to adopt other language with which to talk about the Bible. As referenced repeatedly in this essay, one suggestion I have articulated is an incarnational metaphor: Scripture is a collection of a variety of writings that *necessarily and unashamedly* reflects the worlds in which those writings were produced. The implication of this metaphor is that an understanding of those historical settings can and should affect interpretive conclusions. This process, I believe, is what is presumed when we are dealing with a God who, in Christ, seems to be quite ready and willing to walk among us rather than keep his distance.

In evangelical culture, what I am advocating here should hardly seem out of place. C. S. Lewis, though not himself a trained theologian or biblical scholar, nevertheless had astute instincts that he was not shy about articulating.

> The human qualities of the raw materials show through. Naïvety, error, contradiction, even (as in the cursing Psalms) wickedness are not removed. The total result is not "the Word of God" in the sense that every passage, in itself, gives impeccable science or history. It [the Bible] carries the Word of God; and we (under grace, with attention to tradition and to interpreters wiser than ourselves, and with the use of such intelligence and learning as we may have) receive that word from it not by using it as an encyclopedia or an encyclical but by steeping ourselves in its tone or temper and so learning its overall message....
>
> [There] is one argument which we should beware of using ...: God must have done what is best, this is best, therefore God has done this. For we are mortals and do not know what is best for us, and it is dangerous to prescribe what God must have done—especially when we cannot, for the life of us, see that He has after all done it.[42]

Lewis's thoughts here are compelling and informed—I would even say commonsensical—and articulate well the Christian wisdom

---

42. C. S. Lewis, *Reflections on the Psalms* (San Diego: Harcourt, 1986), 111–12.

and necessity of leaving behind the inerrantist model. The pressing issue before evangelicalism is not to formulate longer, more complex, more subtle, and more sophisticated defenses of what we feel God should have done but to teach future generations, in the academy, the church, and the world, better ways of meeting God in the Scripture we have.

R. ALBERT MOHLER JR.

I am pleased to have the opportunity to engage the contribution of Peter Enns to this debate, and to respond to it. There can be no doubt that Enns considers the question of inerrancy with great seriousness, and that his chapter presents what can only be described as a very consistent and clear rejection of any claim that the Bible is inerrant. For his candor, we should be grateful.

As a matter of fact, his candor is a refreshing contrast to the efforts of many others to confuse the issue or to redefine inerrancy so that it loses its coherence and cogency. Enns does not do that. Indeed, he states that "redefining or nuancing inerrancy" is not his purpose at all. By the end of his chapter, he argues that "the inerrantist model" should be left behind. But the reader knows from the onset of Enns's presentation that this is where his argument must arrive.

To his credit, Enns acknowledges that inerrancy "has been a central component of evangelicalism for its entire history" (p. 84). In his telling of the tale, inerrancy has functioned within evangelicalism primarily as a response to the rise of higher criticism — as an essentially defensive doctrine.

There is truth in this assertion, of course. The very word insists on a negative claim: the Bible includes nothing rightly defined as an error. But, like many negative claims, it reflects a prior assumption and settled belief. Christians did not believe in the Trinity only after the ecumenical councils identified and refuted errors. Rather, the councils dealt with false doctrinal claims in order to assert with definitional precision what was previously believed by the faithful.

And yet, therein lies a fundamental difference. The sequential ecumenical councils, for the most part, settled the issues of their concern for centuries. This is true, at least, for Western Christendom. In that case, the prevailing intellectual climate adjusted itself to the creeds and theological formulations of the councils. This has not been the case with evangelicals today and their defense of biblical inerrancy. Indeed, the prevailing intellectual context of late-modernity makes the defense of inerrancy ever more difficult, even as it looms ever more necessary.

At the most fundamental level, Enns looks at the current intellectual situation and then sees inerrancy as a theological embarrassment that must be removed in order to minimize the evangelical scandal. I look at the same intellectual context and see inerrancy, in contrast, as ever more necessary to both evangelical faith and practice. Indeed, I am quite certain that without inerrancy evangelicalism will cease to be evangelical in any real sense. For, at the end of the day, inerrancy is the single issue that truly distinguishes evangelicalism from liberal Protestantism.

In his own way, Peter Enns seems to see this. Inerrancy, he says, "is encoded into the evangelical DNA" (p. 84). In this statement, Enns may have conceded more than he even recognized. For if you change the DNA of an organism, it is no longer the organism it once was. Evangelicalism without inerrancy would cease to be evangelicalism; it would be something else. In short order, that something else would be a new variant of *Kulturprotestantismus*.

Of course, this is not the most important question for the church or for intelligent Christians. The more important question is straightforward: is inerrancy true?

Enns believes that it is not true in that it makes a claim about the Bible that is neither true nor helpful. I believe that it is most assuredly true, as I argued in my own chapter. His litany of intellectual crimes charged against inerrancy is long and varied. Inerrancy, as defined by the Chicago Statement on Biblical Inerrancy, "obstructs the kind of critical dialogue clearly surfacing within evangelicalism, and therefore threatens to neutralize self-criticism, a necessary quality of any healthy intellectual pursuit" (p. 85).

This same claim has been made against every major evangelical doctrine. For that matter, the same claim has been leveled against every major doctrine of the Christian faith and, beyond these, against every creed and confession and theological statement. As soon as a doctrine is formulated and a theological boundary is drawn, someone rises to claim that intellectual integrity has been murdered and that self-criticism is now impossible.

The only way to avoid such a claim is to avoid the drawing of any meaningful theological boundaries. From its very inception, however, evangelicalism has understood the need to define those boundaries. In one sense, what has defined English-speaking evangelicalism is the determination to draw necessary boundaries while remaining open to engagement with the larger world. Enns seems to concede this very point when he refers to inerrancy's "definitive—and nonnegotiable— role in forming evangelical identity in the face of modern challenges" (p. 84).

Enns's rejection of inerrancy is rooted in a three-part argument. *First, he argues that inerrancy is an intellectual disaster for evangelicalism.* Much of his argument has already been noted in this regard; but his argument is more personal than many readers might recognize. He accuses inerrancy of serving as a "conversation stopper, and a means by which people are judged safe or dangerous" (p. 90). This, he declares, "prevents evangelicalism from honestly considering developments in biblical studies and other fields" (p. 90). In a passionate paragraph, he writes of witnessing firsthand "the spiritual and emotional fallout of holding scholarship at bay in order to protect, by force if necessary, evangelical views of inerrancy" (p. 90).

Of course, the issue here is the right and responsibility of evangelical institutions to maintain evangelical faith and witness. Once again, any theological statement or doctrinal formula functions as some form of a "conversation stopper"—at least within the group or church that established the boundary. The group is defined, in essence, by what it states must be truth commonly believed, commonly taught, and commonly preached. Those who differ are, by definition, either outside the group or working their way there.

Indeed, intellectual honesty requires us to acknowledge that every group in every realm of intellectual endeavor has some boundary beliefs that are, and are intended to be, conversation stoppers of some kind. Try finding a tenured professor in a medical school who denies the germ theory of disease. Enns writes movingly of "trained, experienced, and practicing biblical scholars, young, middle-aged, and near retirement, working in evangelical institutions, under inhuman personal and professional stress," who are trying to "negotiate the line" between their institution's affirmation of inerrancy and their own "academic integrity" (p. 90). That is indeed a perilous and difficult position. But Enns's answer is to abandon the belief that those institutions have every right to hold, and to expect their faculty members to hold. In other words, Enns straightforwardly calls for evangelicalism to abandon its own DNA—his term—in order to relieve professors of the difficulty of choosing to remain in a group while trying to redefine its boundaries.

That is sad enough. But what Enns never seems to recognize is that those evangelicals who encoded inerrancy into the movement's DNA did so not only because they believed that inerrancy is necessary, but because they believed that inerrancy is *true*—a true statement about what God has given us in his written Word. That explains the origin and substance of the Chicago statement, and it explains the continued determination of evangelicals to maintain inerrancy as a core belief.

Enns goes further in the second part of his argument, openly claiming that inerrancy is an erroneous concept. Referring back to his argument in *Inspiration and Incarnation*, Enns continues to insist that the incarnational model allows the Bible's "historically conditioned behavior" to correct claims of inerrancy (p. 87). The problem in his chapter here is only an extension of the problem in his book. The incarnational model of Scripture is, of course, genuinely helpful; it rightly recognizes the Bible to be both a divine and a human book. But the truth of this model does not lead to the conclusion that Enns would have us draw. The incarnate Christ was fully God and fully human, but his humanity was without sin. Just as theologians have for centuries argued over whether Jesus *could not* sin or merely *did not* sin, theologians may argue whether the Bible *cannot err* or merely *does not* err. But the end result is the same in any event—Jesus did not sin and the Bible is without error.

Enns believes that it is wrong—even untrue—to claim that the Bible is without error. Furthermore, he claims that God did not intend to give us a Bible that is without error. *That takes us to the third part of his argument: Enns believes that the Bible should be understood as ancient literature that reflects all the characteristics of other literature from the same eras.* He makes sweeping statements in this regard, but his argument becomes most clear with reference to the specific texts we were all asked to address.

He does not believe that Joshua 6 truthfully recounts the events considered. In his view, the archaeological data simply do not allow for Joshua 6 to be taken seriously as history. At the most, it "is perhaps a significant elaboration on a historical kernel, not a reliable record of a historical event" (p. 96). The chapter might be "mythologized history," but for Enns, it is far more myth than history. Lest we miss his point, he extends his argument to the Bible's account of the exodus: "The historical core for the exodus story could just as easily be, as many biblical scholars think, a small band of slaves who left or escaped Egypt and migrated over land (or across a shallow lake), and later generations retold this historic core in mythic language" (p. 97).

That comes astonishingly near to a candid rejection of the truthfulness of one of the Bible's central narratives — a narrative upon which hangs virtually all of the rest of the Bible. In an equally candid acknowledgement, Enns allows that following this kind of approach means that "we have left the world of inerrancy as it functions in evangelicalism as a prescriptive doctrine" (p. 98). That is an understatement. Inerrancy is hardly all that is left behind. With inerrancy taken off the table, what kind of truth does the Bible convey in Enns's view?

Along the same lines, Enns understands Acts 9:7 and 22:9 to be in conflict, even at the level of truth claim. He suggests that Luke is operating with a literary agenda, not a concern for historical accuracy. Luke was concerned to bolster Paul's prophetic status, and Enns argues that this (in one way or another) explains the contradiction between the two passages. We only have a problem, Enns insists, if we force the Bible into "modern precisionist notions of truth" (p. 104).

But "precisionist notions of truth" are not merely modern. There can be no doubt that Luke employs a literary agenda in both his gospel and in Acts, but it is Luke himself who told Theophilus that his purpose was "to write an orderly account" of the events he records and explains (Luke 1:3 ESV). We undermine the authority of the Bible when we oppose literary intention against historical accuracy if, as in Acts, the text clearly makes an historical claim.

The third biblical passage, Deuteronomy 20:16–17, brings us to an even more strident statement of Enns's position. He reviews the theological and moral questions about the text and finds the problems insurmountable unless "one is willing to step outside of the inerrantist paradigm" (p. 108). Having done that, Enns then explains that the Bible's conquest narratives (like the exodus narrative) "do not 'report events' with inerrantist expectations of historical accuracy" (p. 108).

Well, if not "inerrantist expectations of historical accuracy," then what? Enns sees almost no historical validity at all—certainly not in terms of God having actually ordered the killings involved in the conquest. Instead, the narratives are "the rhetoric of a tribal people" (p. 108). The Israelites were (among others) an ancient people who "portrayed God and their relationship to him in that way" (p. 108). The Bible does not reveal, in these passages at least, the real character of God. Enns argues: "Israel's depiction of God vis-à-vis the nations unmistakably, and understandably, reflects the ubiquitous tribal culture at the time" (p. 112).

So, taking Peter Enns at his word, the Bible contains numerous passages that not only fail the test of historical accuracy (even to the point of questioning whether the exodus took place), but also present a false and dangerous misrepresentation of God's very character and will.

To no surprise, the vehemence of Enns's rejection of inerrancy comes to full heat in his conclusion. He wonders aloud if the proponents of inerrancy are asking adherents "to be dishonest, or at least willingly numb, in order to hold to the truth" (p. 114). Inerrancy, he insists, "has run its course" and evangelicals had better find some better way of describing the Bible and its truthfulness.

What kind of language does Enns suggest? He urges a *descriptive* rather than a *prescriptive* approach. Better, he insists, to describe the Bible as it is (according to his rendering) rather than what the Bible must be. What does he then state about the Bible, *descriptively*? In the end, Enns suggests an approach that "would be more a statement of faith on the part of the reader that *no matter what is encountered, the reader is in the presence of the wisdom and mystery of our God*" (p. 114, emphasis original).

This tragically minimal statement about the Bible, offered in the full crescendo of his concluding section, entails not only a rejection of inerrancy, but a rejection of anything remotely connected to the church's faithful consensus on Scripture through the ages. Whether he realizes it or not, Peter Enns has moved far outside of any recognizable evangelical model of biblical inspiration or authority. At times, it seems clear in his chapter that he knows this. And yet, he demands that evangelicals surrender inerrancy in order to save themselves.

I appreciate the candid nature of the chapter Peter Enns has provided us. I appreciate the fact that he destroys any pretensions within the evangelical movement to moderate or redefine inerrancy. He demands, quite straightforwardly, that evangelicals surrender inerrancy in any meaningful form. And yet, he also makes clear that inerrancy is but the first truth claim to be surrendered.

What Peter Enns proposes is the death of evangelicalism by changing its DNA in order to excise inerrancy. Tragically, he leaves us with the full evidence of how little is left after that excision. But evangelicalism does not need to be rescued from itself.

Of far greater importance is this: the Bible does not need to be rescued from itself and its own very clear claims to truthfulness. "The grass withers, the flower fades, but the word of our God will stand forever" (Isa. 40:8).

MICHAEL F. BIRD

Peter Enns' views on Scripture and inerrancy have courted more controversy than Kim Kardashian's attending a Jihadists-for-Jesus fundraiser. Enns is either the bad boy or the maverick of evangelicalism depending on who is telling the story. So I am glad for the opportunity in this volume to dialogue with him rather than make denouncements against him, as has too often been the norm.

I wholeheartedly agree with Enns on two principal areas. First, one cannot rely on a priori ideas of God as the sole basis for developing a doctrine of Scripture because one must also inform such a doctrine by examining the phenomenon of Scripture. That means, in practice, carefully investigating the physical materials that preserve Scripture, ancient languages, an array of genres, narrative structures, literary devices, socioreligious contexts, and the history of interpretation as factors that form our discourse about Scripture. Study of these factors will leave us better informed as to how Scripture is God's *Word* in human *words*. Second, I also concur that the doctrine of inerrancy has impacted contemporary evangelical theological discourse and shaped societies, churches, confessions, and boundaries. Formulations of inerrancy have been deployed more often than not for political purposes than for theological utility. Taken together, Enns is right on the money when he points out that evangelicals can end up suffering "cognitive dissonance" when they cannot reconcile the phenomenon of Scripture with the magisterial authority often attributed to formulations of inerrancy.

That said, I do depart from several elements of Enns' proposal by way of either nuance or negation as to what he claims.

First, I would contest his claim that inerrancy has been "a central component of evangelicalism for its entire history" and that inerrancy is "encoded into the evangelical DNA" (p. 84). If that were true, a revision of inerrancy would require a revision of evangelicalism in its entirety. While evangelicalism — historic and global — has always upheld biblical authority and biblical infallibility, it has not always been crafted in the specific forms of the American inerrancy tradition (AIT) and the Chicago Statement on Biblical Inerrancy (CSBI) that Enns is pushing back against. In fact, Enns implies as much when he states that inerrancy emerged as a "response to the challenges of biblical higher criticism of the eighteenth and nineteenth centuries" (p. 84). As I've argued, the AIT is both a retrieval of what Christians have always believed about Scripture and also a recent reaction against biblical criticism resourced in the philosophical framework of modernity and worked out in the fundamentalist versus liberal debates that took place in mainline denominations.

Second, I categorically reject Enns' proposal of an "incarnational model" for explaining Scripture as a divine-human book. I am aware that such a model is merely a starting point for explaining how the Bible is both a divine and human work. However, this incarnational model is, as John Webster calls it, "Christologically disastrous." It's disastrous because it threatens the uniqueness of the Christ event, since it assumes that hypostatic union is a general characteristic of divine self-disclosure in, through, or by a creaturely agent. Furthermore, it results in a divinizing of the Bible by claiming that divine ontological equality exists between God's being and his communicative action.[43]

Third, concerning the test cases, Enns states that "The biblical story of the fall of Jericho is perhaps a significant elaboration on a historical kernel, not a reliable record of a historical event" and "The historical core for the exodus story could just as easily be, as many biblical scholars think, a small band of slaves who left or escaped from Egypt and migrated over land (or across a shallow lake), and later generations retold the historical core in mythic language" (p. 96). My response is, well, if so, prove it. I can understand that some scholars will find reasons to say that the biblical stories of the exodus and conquest did not happen or did not happen precisely the way that the Bible says they did. I'm open to suggestions that narratives about the births of heroes and campaign stories were embellished as part of ancient Near Eastern

---

43. John Webster, *Holy Scripture: A Dogmatic Sketch* (Cambridge: Cambridge Univ. Press, 2003), 22.

chronicling. However, in order to say that we know what really happened, and it was not A but B, someone needs to lay their evidential cards on the table. Just because you have a theory about what was behind a certain biblical story does not therefore make that theory immediately more probable than the extant biblical account. That holds true all the more if you believe in a God who can and does act in history and uses Scripture as a mode of his self-communication. A point of principle is that biblical criticism should be digested critically and its presuppositions, procedures, and findings made susceptible to the same scrutiny to which the biblical narratives are themselves made subject.

I think I could cope with Enns' reading with the Old Testament narratives only because deep down inside me, as with most evangelicals, is a repressed Marcionite. Yet the problem is that if you allow the Old Testament to be fictionalized or allegorized away, the result would be a spiritually impoverished and theologically heterodox faith. I also wonder if Enns would apply the same explanatory paradigm he uses on the Old Testament narratives to Jesus' miracles or resurrection. In all seriousness, if I became convinced that the conquest never happened, I think I could reload and reboot my faith to suit the data. However, if the resurrection is based on a "historical kernel" of something like the disciples' believing that despite the fact that Jesus was truly and permanently dead, his cause still lives on, and if they employed the mythic language of resurrection simply to describe how Jesus' message has brought them to a new spiritual awareness, then, to be honest, I'd probably resign from my job as a seminary professor, and go on an existential bender that oscillates between depression and debauchery. Because, as St. Paul says, "If the dead are not raised, 'Let us eat and drink, for tomorrow we die'" (1 Cor. 15:32, citing Isa. 22:13; 56:12 [NIV]). I believe in reading Scripture with all of the erudition and expertise that I can muster from both historical theology and historical criticism. Yet at the end of the day, I have to choose whether I will believe the testimony of biblical authors to the acts of God in history, and I choose to believe. In a faith seeking understanding, that will mean a discerning appropriation of biblical scholarship and a hermeneutically informed listening to biblical testimony.

Fourth, I cannot go along with Enns' facile pitting of the Matthean Jesus versus the Old Testament. While my inner Marcionite is cheering, the biblical theologian inside me is rather irate (which is a reminder that I should probably get tested for a possible multiple-personality disorder). I would point out that the tension between exclusivism and inclusivism and between God's anger and God's love runs across the entire breadth of the biblical canon. The God who smote the Canaanites is the same God who sent Jonah to Nineveh. The Jesus who told us to love our enemies is the same Jesus who will tread the winepress of the fury of God's wrath in the future. What we find in the Gospels is not the replacement of Old Testament tribalism with New Testament cosmopolitanism. Jesus does not negate the Old Testament as much as he interprets it around a constellation of values that the Old Testament in fact contains: messiah, mercy, Spirit, sacrifice, justice, judgment, Israel, nations, wisdom, warnings, sin, and salvation. Jesus' teaching from and about the Law and Prophets provides a definitive account of how to prioritize certain commandments when they conflict, and of how to discern the overarching will of God when biblical values like purity and compassion clash. It is not the case that Jesus said in effect, "That was then; this is now." More likely, Jesus was saying something in the order of, "Now that the kingdom of God has come, now that God's salvation is here, this is how we live out the love we heard about in the Law."

Finally, I would have liked to see Enns be more constructive than deconstructive in his approach to the doctrine of inerrancy. He does this very briefly towards the end of his essay when he proposes a "descriptive model of inerrancy" that takes its cues from the shape of the biblical materials (p. 114). He proposes an affirmation of biblical authority where it is asserted that Scripture draws us into the presence of God's wisdom and mystery, and such an affirmation would then leave us better equipped to deal with the various complexities we might encounter in the study of Scripture. Such a project is interesting to consider, and I would like to see it properly fleshed out. Of course, it is one thing to criticize the CSBI; it is another thing to come up with something better.

Drawing inspiration from Enns, a revision of the CSBI probably would be a very good idea. Enns is right that the CSBI leaves a lot to be desired since it fails to grapple appropriately with the "hermeneutical and theological complexities" of Scripture. The CSBI demands a consistently literalistic hermeneutic and requires adopting a conflict model of science and religion, neither of which I support. Even so, not every affirmation or denial in the CSBI is fool's gold. The vast bulk of statements are straightforward and sober. So if one were to revise the CSBI, then I would suggest (1) a better appropriation of the phenomenon of Scripture, (2) a more sophisticated theory of linguistics and hermeneutics undergirding it, (3) deliberate incorporation of insights from church history, and (4) aiming for consensus among global evangelical churches. Then we might come up with a statement on biblical authority that has consent and catholicity even to the Enns of the earth.[44]

---

44. If one were to convene another "International Council on Biblical Inerrancy" to revise the CSBI, then I would suggest making it actually international. Assemble believers from Nigeria to Norway, from Vietnam to Venezuela, then hold sessions in Beijing, Bogota, and Brisbane to shape a document about the doctrine of Scripture. To prevent any national group from dominating the council, representation should be proportional. Since North American evangelicals make up only about 5 percent of global evangelicals, they should only have 5 percent of the delegates to such a council. Though it sounds like a great idea, I sincerely doubt that key evangelical leaders in the USA would agree to such proportional representation and would not submit themselves to the wisdom and will of the global evangelical church. Perhaps I'm being hypercritical, but (1) many conservative American evangelical leaders seem to have a keen sense of their own cultural and tribal superiority over the rest of the world's Christians, and (2) the inerrancy debates are not just about "what should thoughtful Christians believe about Scripture" but are to some degree about power games in certain tribes and territories. That said, I do not doubt that a great many American evangelicals, even committed inerrantists, genuinely cherish their brothers and sisters in Christ beyond the borders of their own lands and see them as partners in discerning the truth of God's Word.

RESPONSE TO PETER ENNS

KEVIN J. VANHOOZER

I am glad that Peter Enns is participating in this volume as a representative of biblical (OT) studies. He does in his essay what every good biblical scholar has to do with theologians: he holds their systematic feet to the textual fire, ensuring that theologians' doctrinal formulations attend to biblical particularities—the textual phenomena. He signals his zeal for the text in the opening lines, with a fine phrase about the Bible being "open to all but impossible [for any] to master" (p. 83). It is for the sake of this impossible-to-master, historically conditioned collection of texts that Enns launches his full-scale frontal assault on the doctrine of inerrancy. Why the hostility? Because, in his view, inerrancy functions as a quasi-Nietzschean will-to-truth/power, generating an interpretive violence that evangelicals wreak on biblical things.

Charity leads me to view Enns as a champion of the text rather than the bogeyman of conservative evangelicalism. He is trying to educate evangelicals about the "assured results" of modern biblical scholarship. Of course, inerrantists see themselves as champions of the text in view of their own insistence on Scripture's entire truthfulness. No doubt each contributor to the present volume sincerely believes his own view to be right. Unfortunately, sincerity is no guarantee of truth. Sincerity needs tempering by other intellectual virtues, such as humility, patience, and charity. I leave it to the reader to decide which contributor displays these qualities in greatest measure. Of course, we also need to examine the arguments themselves, and it is to this task that I now turn.

I endorse Enns' call to conform our doctrine of Scripture to the Bible that we actually have rather than the one we think God ought to have written. My own essay contrasts an "inerrancy of glory" (aka "perfect book inerrancy," a cultural construct) with an "inerrancy of the cross." I draw this distinction in order to urge an inerrancy of the cross that recognizes the wisdom of God in the surprising textual form he has given it rather than the form we may think it ought to have had. Enns simply identifies inerrancy with perfect book theology, however, and then devotes most of his essay to exposing its nakedness. I agree that perfect book inerrancy, "by placing on it expectations it is not designed to bear" (p. 84), fails to do justice to Scripture. However, in my own chapter, I explore a constructive alternative. I wish Enns had tried to do this too.

Instead, Enns spends most of his chapter reacting to what I judge to be a caricature of inerrancy—what David Dockery, whom I discuss in my own chapter, calls "naive" rather than "critical" inerrancy. Enns would have been better off discussing the original drawing—namely, the definitions offered by John Frame or Paul Feinberg—rather than demeaning the assumptions and interpretive practice of anonymous inerrantists. Who are these faceless villains ("is it I, Peter")? Enns nevertheless makes a valid point: the doctrine of inerrancy has been hijacked by various bands of exegetical pirates who insist that the gold of true Bible knowledge is secure only in their own interpretive treasure chests.

Enns thinks the core issue is "how inerrancy *functions* in contemporary evangelical theological discourse" (p. 83, my emphasis). Why should the function rather than the *nature* of inerrancy be the crux of the matter? We don't throw away other doctrines, like divine sovereignty or the atonement, just because some people misunderstand or misuse them. No, we try to set them right. Curiously, Enns is not interested in definitions. Even his title focuses on function: "Inerrancy, However Defined, Does Not Describe What the Bible Does." This is strange. Why should inerrancy—the claim that the Bible is without error—describe what the Bible does? Enns' essay suffers from two confusions: (1) a failure to distinguish the nature of inerrancy from its use and (2) a failure to distinguish inerrancy's right use from various abuses.

Enns' discussion of the Chicago Statement on Biblical Inerrancy (CSBI) is uniformly negative in tone. He thinks it functions as a political weapon ("a boundary marker against ... misguided hermeneutical approaches"; p. 84) and catalyst for intellectual dishonesty. And that's only the preface!

Enns criticizes the statement for loading the theological deck by linking Jesus' view of Scripture to inerrancy before defining the latter. Ironically enough, he follows much the same strategy, though in reverse: he links inerrancy to abuses of Scripture before defining it. Note well: Enns is not rejecting a particular definition of inerrancy as much as a set of interpretive practices that have come to be associated with inerrancy. Inerrancy is, in Enns' court, guilty by association, and apparently there is no appeal ("however defined").

Yes, inerrancy has something to do with Scripture's truthfulness, though Enns thinks that it gets "truth" *wrong*. Why? Because inerrancy (allegedly) fails to deal with "the manner in which God speaks truth, namely, *through the idioms, attitudes, assumptions, and general worldviews of the ancient authors*" (p. 87). By way of contrast, Enns' "incarnational" model takes historical conditionedness seriously. If you're keeping score: inerrancy, with its assumption of the Bible's absolute truthfulness, generates bad interpretive practices that cannot do justice to the text; "incarnationcy," with its assumption of the Bible's historical conditionedness, does not generate bad interpretive practices (though what it does encourage remains to be seen).

Enns' underlying concern here begins to come into focus. He believes the CSBI defines truth abstractly, without regard for the Bible's literary forms and historical context. It's a legitimate concern: if I thought that inerrancy could not account for what the Bible actually is, I would reject it too. But it can, so I don't.

Enns says he has evidence that supports his point. He cites article 12, which says that no scientific hypothesis about earth history can be used to overturn the Bible's teaching on creation and the flood. He infers from this that inerrancy commits us to six-day creationism — that is, to reading the Bible literalistically, against its literary grain. The salient question, however, is, what *does* the Bible teach about creation? Article 13 says, "We deny that it is proper to evaluate Scripture according to standards of truth and error that are alien to its usage or purpose." This gives us interpretive breathing room with regard to Genesis 1 – 2 inasmuch as it allows us to ask what standards of truth, and ways of communicating truth, were in force in the ancient Near East.[45]

---

45. One can also point to other articles (8, 18) in the CSBI that clearly signal the importance of reading the Bible according to its diverse literary genres.

Enns confuses the definition of inerrancy with what interpreters do in its name, collapsing the nature of inerrancy into the tradition of its use.[46] This is most regrettable. For the only way to speak of *abuses* of inerrancy is to maintain the nature/use distinction. Indeed, the thrust of my own chapter is to distinguish between *literalistic* applications of inerrancy (boo!) and affirmations of the Bible's *literal* truth (hurrah!), where *literal* means "according to the communicative intent of the author and his literary genre." Sadly, however, there is no room for literate, hermeneutically informed inerrantists in Enns' inn.

A misleading picture of inerrancy holds Enns captive. He thinks that inerrancy requires a strict, literalistic correspondence between the text and the external world, and that it implies that God is "a straightforward, historically accurate revealer of truth" (p. 95). I share his concern that we not foist our ideas of perfect truth onto the Bible instead of acknowledging the book God has actually given us. But I dispute his claim that inerrancy requires us to read the Bible as if it were always making the kind of claim that would satisfy a modern historian — or fundamentalist. On the contrary, in maintaining that Scripture is "without error," inerrancy insists only that the Bible makes good on its claims, *whatever these claims may be*. Neither inerrantists nor their critics should judge this matter before undertaking the hard work of literate interpretation.

But Enns does. He mistakenly thinks that inerrancy is joined at the hip with an unsound hermeneutic. On the contrary: inerrancy tells us only that "what is said" is true; it cannot tell us "what is said" nor defend the truth of "what is said." I agree with Frame: "Inerrancy is a belief about the truth of a document, not about the interpretation of it."[47] Yes, there are dangers in the way inerrancy can be applied to biblical interpretation. However, when inerrancy is properly understood, many of these interpretive dangers can be avoided.

My essay contrasts the original concept of inerrancy (which I associate with Augustine, J. I. Packer, and John Frame) with the pale

---

46. Failing to perceive the difference between the doctrine of inerrancy and subsequent interpretations is like failing to see the difference between Scripture and the tradition of its interpretation.

47. John Frame, *The Doctrine of the Word of God* (Phillipsburg, N.J.: P&R Publishing, 2010), 168.

caricatures of inerrancy against which Enns is (often rightly) reacting. In the Packer/Frame/Vanhoozer model, there is no a priori requirement to read biblical narrative with the expectation that God's speech will conform to the norms of modern historiography. Rather, we have humbly to ask what kind of claim a particular text is making. The best inerrantists — those who combine a robust affirmation of the Bible's truth with a sensibility to grammar, historical context, and literary form — have always known this. My chapter can be viewed as a blast against the monstrous regiment of illiterate inerrantists (where *illiteracy* pertains to the inability to appreciate what kinds of books one is reading in the Bible). Evangelicals today may need remedial education about inerrancy; they don't need to abandon it.

Evangelicals should be open, in principle, to Enns' (and Kitchen's) suggestion that Joshua may include "mythologized" history. Yet this need not detract from its essential historicity, or truth, *unless* one insists on a modern understanding of historiography. C. S. Lewis (to whom Enns makes frequent appeal) was uncompromising in his dismissal of the suggestion that the New Testament narratives of Jesus were mythical, despite certain similarities to the Exodus narrative depicting Jesus' power over the water and the sea (symbolic in much ancient literature of the forces of chaos): Jesus turns water into wine (John 2:7–9), stills the sea simply by speaking (Mark 4:39), and demonstrates his utter sovereignty over water by walking on it (Matt. 14:26). How might Enns interpret these passages given his "incarnation" model?

Enns thinks the two passages from Acts about the circumstances surrounding Paul's conversion would quickly be labeled contradictory if they were read like any other piece of ancient literature. He summarily dismisses the "be patient" argument that asks interpreters to wait until apparent contradictions can be resolved. Yes, there are textual difficulties, which is why my Augustinian approach counsels faithful patience, and a love of God's Word that endures all things, including criticism.

Why is Enns in such a hurry to capitulate to the prevailing scholarly consensus? Theories, consensus opinions, and schools of thought all come and go. Christians are not to be blown about by every wind of academic fashion. I wonder: does he think, in light of the problem of evil, that we should concede that God does not exist? After all, there is considerably more evidence of gratuitous evil in the world than there is that ancient Jericho had no walls. It's not clear to me how, on Enns' scorecard, the theist fares any better than the inerrantist. Should we therefore reframe our doctrine of God to fit the prevailing extratextual "evidence"?

Enns says the inerrantist "needs" God to have commanded the Canaanite genocide in order to "save" inerrancy, despite the resulting theological and moral problems. What is Enns' alternative suggestion? His solution to the problem of genocide is to read the texts as "the rhetoric of a tribal people" (p. 108) that understands gods to be warriors who fight on their behalf. Is Deuteronomy 20 therefore true or false (or something else)? He doesn't say, but instead runs to Jesus (always a good move!). The Gospels present us with a "new and improved Moses," a contrast made all the more poignant to the extent that Jesus' Great Commission ("Go into all the world") countermands Moses' "great commission" ("Spare nothing alive"). Enns faults inerrancy for failing to "capture this dynamic that Scripture itself exhibits" (p. 112).

I don't get it. Why, on Enns' view, should the Old Testament be the church's Scripture, unless it is to see how far the people of God have advanced in their understanding of God? Can Enns, an Old Testament scholar, really be advocating a Marcionite view, according to which Yahweh (or at least Israel's understanding of Yahweh) is time-worn, primitive, and obsolete, while the early church's understanding of God is theologically developed and morally advanced? I was flabbergasted to see Enns chalk up the alleged lack of appreciation for the universal scope of God's love in the Old Testament to "the ubiquitous tribal culture at the time" (p. 112). I am all for seeing development in the history of redemption, but I dispute any suggestion that the Old Testament reflects an inferior doctrine of God because its authors were part of a tribal culture. Talk about chronological snobbery.

Enns' contrast between the tribal warrior God of the Old Testament and the loving Father of Jesus Christ in the New Testament is seriously overdrawn. There is ample counterevidence: the Abrahamic covenant itself mentions the blessing Israel was to be to *all* nations, not simply its own twelve tribes (Gen. 12:3); Moses depicts the ways of God not in terms of tribal vindictiveness but rather in terms of mercy and steadfast love and faithfulness (Exod. 34:6–7). Moreover, Jesus himself never distances himself from the actions of Yahweh in the Old Testament. Furthermore, Jesus' Olivet Discourse (Matt. 24) is every bit as violent as the Old Testament command about genocide, and there is nothing in this context (or the book of Revelation) about God loving his enemies at the last battle.

Despite the helpful warnings about bad interpretive practice, then, I found Enns' essay to be generally disappointing, for two reasons. First, as I have repeatedly mentioned, it founders on a category mistake: he insists on seeing inerrancy as "an a priori and prescriptive doctrine" (p. 113) that assumes what kind of truth the Bible has (i.e., literalistic) and insists that people read it that way: "We are told that the factual truthfulness of the Bible is essential to Christian faith" (p. 113). Really? Where are we told that, and by whom? Not by the CSBI, which never uses the term *fact* or *factuality* in the preface, short statement, or any of the articles. My own essay sets forth a view of inerrancy that is a posteriori and descriptive. In other words, I make no prior assumptions as to what kind of claims I will find in Scripture, other than my first theological assumption that, because God is true in the sense of utterly reliable, God is as good as his word. Interestingly, Enns deals with what I take to be the Packer/Frame/Vanhoozer view only in the last paragraphs of his essay, when he (finally) admits that we might retain the term *inerrancy* as a descriptive observation rather than prescriptive requirement. But this is precisely how I, and many others, regularly use the term! It would have helped had Enns acknowledged this.

My second disappointment is that Enns never gives us the recipe for a positive, constructive doctrine of Scripture. He never tells us what makes the Bible God's Word or, if it is God's Word, what positive qualities it may have (e.g., inspiration) and how these ought to affect our interpretation and use. If there *are* contradictions in the Bible, what are the implications for biblical authority? Do we listen to all texts as God's Word or only some? The closest he comes to giving an answer is his gloss on descriptive inerrancy, which he suggests is the reader's expression of faith that "no matter what is encountered, the reader is in the presence of the wisdom and mystery of our God" (p. 114). This is a good start, though I note that he still can't bring himself to use the dreaded t-word ("truth"). In sum, what I missed from Enns' chapter is any sense that we can, after all, affirm with the psalmist, "The law of the Lord is perfect … the testimony of the Lord is sure" (Ps. 19:7 ESV), or that we can say, with Jesus, "Your word is truth" (John 17:17 ESV) or, if we could, what that would mean.

JOHN R. FRANKE

The essay by Pete Enns is at the other end of the spectrum from that of Mohler and is different in character from the other contributions in this volume. His title makes it clear that he has dispensed with the notion of inerrancy after supporting it for many years as a faculty member at Westminster Theological Seminary. It is important to note that while Enns has moved away from inerrancy, he has not given up on the importance of the Bible for Christian faith. It is still for him "the book of God for the people of God" (p. 83). He has simply come to the conclusion that the term and the ideas behind the term are not helpful to describe what the Bible is all about and how it functions. As I noted in my own essay, I have some sympathy with this view and do not think that inerrancy is a particularly helpful term since it so easily conjures up false notions about the Bible. Even many of the most vigorous proponents of the concept go to great lengths to nuance exactly what the term does and does not mean. It is prone to be taken in simplistic ways and misunderstood. Having said that, I still appreciate what I regard to be the chief insight it signifies, namely that the Bible is an inspired, faithful, and trustworthy witness to the God revealed in Jesus Christ and the divine mission.

In reading his essay, I can't shake the impression that Enns is still in reaction to his departure from Westminster and the controversy his work has created among evangelicals. He takes the posture of one who is simply trying to come to terms with the evidence before him and offer a rendering of that evidence for the work of biblical scholarship. I think he should be commended for this basic posture since Christianity has little future as a significant voice in the discourse of our culture if it does not grapple seriously with the results of scientific investigation. We might also posit that if we take these results with the seriousness they deserve, our understanding of the faith will be challenged at places and may be in need of reformulation and restatement. There is nothing new in this. The history of the church is replete with new thinking and ideas in the face of shifting cultural circumstances that have brought changes to the accepted norms of Christian faith.

In these contexts there are always reformers who want to reimagine matters in ways that they feel are more faithful to new circumstances and discoveries as well as those who defend the status quo. Enns sees himself as a reformer who is calling the Christian community to a more rigorous examination of the biblical text. Many of his evangelical critics see him as one who has betrayed the tradition and must therefore be refuted and cast aside. From my perspective, such an approach to those who offer dissenting views, especially in the world of intellectual discourse and scholarship, is unhelpful. Healthy traditions need reformers, and treating such persons harshly only serves to diminish the life of the community and its standing in the wider world. I believe that evangelicals ought to embrace the valuable work Enns is doing and learn from it, even if they do not agree with him. I still remember listening to him on a local radio program with a call-in component and hearing a listener, who described himself as an ex-Christian, say that if the Bible had been presented to him in the way that Enns was describing, his departure from the faith might have been delayed or possibly stopped altogether.

Having said this, it seems to me that Enns has overstated the implications of views he wishes to critique. For instance, he says of the CSBI that its assumption of "God as a truth-teller requires a text that is only superficially, if at all, circumscribed by the idiom of the day." He goes on to say that the implications of this view mean that if Christians are to trust what God says about salvation, God *"must* at all costs avoid any hint of the Bible's mingling with ancient ways of thinking about where the cosmos comes from and with ancient conventions of history writing. God *must* keep his distance from the human drama, and Scripture must bear witness to how well he transcends the fragile landscape of antiquity" (p. 89). While acknowledging that few would deny the Bible's historical rootedness, this gets muted in the interest of affirming inerrancy. This critique simply does not do justice to the state of evangelical biblical scholarship as practiced by those committed to inerrancy. I find extensive engagement with the ancient setting and considerable effort to understand Scripture in its ancient context. Further, the CSBI specifically acknowledges that inspiration does not override the personalities and literary contexts of the writers (Article VIII). This is an embrace of the significance of Scripture's ancient setting, not a rejection of it.

I have no doubt that some inerrantists hold the sort of dehistoricized views of the Bible that Enns describes, perhaps particularly in some systematics departments, but I do not think this is indicative of many inerrantist biblical scholars. Now it is certainly fair to ask if the ancient context is being taken seriously enough, but Enns goes well beyond this sort of stance in his criticism. This is unhelpful to his argument and is perhaps related to the fact that, for over a decade, he was an advocate of inerrancy at Westminster seminary and as a member of the Evangelical Theological Society. Since I am fairly certain that as a professor of Old Testament he himself never held the sort of dehistoricized view of the Bible he describes, even while he was committed to inerrancy, it would be more helpful (and interesting) to hear him explain the problems he now perceives with it based on his own previous commitments, rather than on views he (most likely) never held in the first place.

With respect to this particular essay, it seems to me that its primary thrust is more deconstructive than constructive. It is clear that he does not think inerrancy is an appropriate way to describe the nature of biblical authority, but he does not offer much in the way of an alternative formulation, apart from a brief mention of the incarnational model he has offered. But even this proposal is more descriptive in nature rather than prescriptive. How does he think Scripture ought to function in the church? What is the purpose behind the inspiration of the texts? What does God want us to know from the texts of Scripture? How do these texts shape the life and witness of the Christian community? He does mention that he spends less time developing the philosophical and theological issues in order to concentrate more on the texts at hand, but also that he does so primarily for a deconstructive purpose—to lay out clearly why they are "problematic for inerrancy" (p. 92). This is fair enough given the scope of this volume, but it still leaves me wondering about his constructive framings. Perhaps these are the sorts of questions that theologians tend to ask and that biblical scholars can sometimes find annoying. It seems clear throughout his essay that Enns wants to preserve the status of the Bible as the Word of God; however, it would be interesting and helpful to hear more about his prescriptive constructions. If the Bible really is, as Enns asserts, the book of God for the people of God, it would seem appropriate to inquire about the contemporary function of Scripture.

While Enns is focused on being faithful to the ancient elements of the Bible—and rightly so—it is also important to remember that the meaning of the ancient texts is not exhausted by the supposed intent of the authors. As I mentioned in my essay, texts take on a life of their own. Speaking of the biblical text, Walter Brueggemann suggests that it "has generative power to summon and evoke new life" and holds out an eschatological vision that "anticipates and summons realities that live beyond the conventions of our day-to-day, take-for-granted world."[48] However, we must remember that while world construction is closely related to the text, it is ultimately the work of the Spirit speaking through the texts of inspired Scripture for the purpose of creating an alternative and counter-cultural community that exists for the common good. In this way the Bible functions as the instrumentality of the Spirit for the purpose of guiding the church into participation in the mission of God.

Such a model would offer a compelling supplement to the incarnational model offered by Enns and bridge the gap between the ancient text and its contemporary appropriation. It also has the advantage of expanding the incarnational metaphor into the present as indicative of the work of the Spirit throughout history. Enns asserts that based on the texts of Scripture, we see that God speaks truth "through the idioms, attitudes, assumptions, and general worldviews of the ancient authors" (p. 87). This is true, but it can be expanded beyond the ancient world to include all societies. The incarnational metaphor suggests that God speaks truth to people where they are, entering into their contexts for the purpose of establishing relationship. Through the work of the Spirit, the pattern we see in Scripture is extended throughout history through the witness of the church as the instrument of God's mission to the world.

---

48. Walter Brueggemann, *Finally Comes the Poet* (Minneapolis: Fortress, 1989), 4–5.

In missiological terms, Andrew Walls has referred to this as the indigenization principle.[49] It is rooted in the core gospel affirmation that God comes to us where we are and accepts us as such through the work of Christ, and not on the basis of what we have been, are, or are trying to become. God does not relate to us as isolated, self-sufficient individuals, but rather as people who are conditioned by the particular times and places in which we live and are shaped by the families, societies, groups, and cultures in which we participate. In Christ we are accepted by God in the midst of all the relations, experiences, and cultural conditioning that make us who we are. The impossibility of separating ourselves from our social relationships and the societies in which we belong should lead to an unwavering commitment to the indigenization principle.

The account of the Jerusalem Council in Acts 15 provides an affirmation of this notion with the decision that the Gentiles should be permitted to enter into the faith without being bound to the rituals and practices of the Jewish Christians. The most significant of these decisions was the determination that male Gentile converts would not need to undergo circumcision. The affirmation that God accepts people as they are means that those who have not participated in such customs as circumcision, dietary restrictions, and ritual cleansings need not do so in order to be part of the community of Christ's disciples. In light of this, Walls asserts that no particular group of Christians "has therefore any right to impose in the name of Christ upon another group of Christians a set of assumptions about life determined by another time and place."[50] The inerrancy of Scripture affirms the truthfulness of this missional pattern and its faithfulness to the incarnational character of God's love for the world. It affirms that plurality and mutuality are at the very heart of the gospel as the blessing and intention of God, who invites all people to participate in the liberating and reconciling mission of Jesus Christ.

---

49. Andrew F. Walls, *The Missionary Movement in Christian History: Studies in the Transmission of Faith* (Maryknoll, N.Y.: Orbis, 1996), 3–9.

50. Ibid., 8

INERRANCY IN
INTERNATIONAL
PERSPECTIVE

INERRANCY IS NOT NECESSARY FOR EVANGELICALISM OUTSIDE THE USA

MICHAEL F. BIRD

Introduction[1]

It falls to me now to write a *minority* report on inerrancy, from a position that approximates the view of Scripture held by the *majority* of evangelicals who make up the global evangelical church.[2] I will endeavor to show that while the American inerrancy tradition possessed a certain utility in the "Battle for the Bible" in the twentieth century, it is not and should not be a universally prescriptive article of faith for the global evangelical church. That is because the American inerrancy tradition, though largely a positive concept, is essentially modernist in construct, parochially American in context, and occasionally creates more exegetical problems than it solves.

Obviously, there is no way I can represent every view on Scripture as held by the multiplicity of evangelical churches around the world. What is more, I have my own specific conclusions to argue for as biblical scholar–cum–theologian, and not everyone from Azerbaijan to

---

1. My thanks goes to Dr. Jason Sexton (Ridley Hall, Cambridge) for reading an earlier draft of this paper, though naturally, any remaining deficiencies are my own.

2. Let me acknowledge that there are American-influenced congregations around the world, mostly with very good and godly fruits, as America has a wonderful history as a missionary-sending nation. But I have also met some peculiar Christians from Africa and Europe with oddly American beliefs about taxation, end-times theology, the King James Bible, and prescribed styles of worship. I'm excluding these Americanized colonies from what I mean by "global evangelical church."

Zimbabwe will agree with everything I say.[3] So my objective is to modestly articulate a view of the veracity of Scripture that is genetically independent of the American inerrancy tradition and then to evaluate inerrancy from such a position.

But do not think I have come therefore to preach an errant or erroneous Bible, *mē genoito* (may it never be!). Let the record show that in other writings, I have defended the historicity of the virgin conception and Jesus' bodily resurrection from the dead.[4] My point is that the American inerrancy tradition is not an essential facet of the faith, because most of us outside of North America get on with our mission without it, and we are none the worse for not having it! Our churches uphold Scripture as the inspired Word of God. We therefore study it, teach from it, and preach it, but without the penchant to engage in bitter divisions over which nomenclature best suits our theological disposition. While the contexts for the international evangelical church are varied, in no place has it been necessary to construct a doctrine of inerrancy as a kind of fence around evangelical orthodoxy. In what I have observed, such doctrinal fences, far from preserving orthodoxy, tend to divide believers, inhibit Christian witness by assuming a default defensive stance, and risk making the Bible rather than Christ the central tenet of Christian faith. What best represents the international view, in my opinion, is a commitment to the *infallibility* and *authority* of Scripture, but not necessarily a doctrine of Scripture conceived in the specific terms of the American inerrancy tradition as represented in the Chicago Statement on Biblical Inerrancy (CSBI). This is the centre of gravity for my thesis.

Reflections on the CSBI

Preliminary Thoughts

The CSBI is a robust and forthright statement of biblical authority for which I am genuinely appreciative. For the most part, I find myself in agreement with the CSBI. I am quite fond of its preface, with its reso-

---

3. See my earlier essay, "Introduction: From Manuscript to MP3," in Michael F. Bird and Michael Pahl, eds., *The Sacred Text: Artefact, Interpretation, and Doctrinal Formulation* (Piscataway, N.J.: Gorgias Press, 2010), 1–18, and relevant portions of my book *Evangelical Theology: A Biblical and Systematic Introduction* (Grand Rapids, Mich.: Zondervan, forthcoming 2013).

4. See Michael F. Bird and James Crossley, *How Did Christianity Begin? A Believer and Non-believer Examine the Evidence* (London: SPCK; Grand Rapids, Mich.: Baker, 2008).

lute affirmation of the "total truth and trustworthiness of Holy Scripture," its recognition that one can be a genuine disciple of Jesus and not be an inerrantist, as well as its call for reformation in the church. But thereafter I do have concerns and qualifications about what is said in the section titled "A Short Statement" and in the articles.

1. A Defective View of the Genre of the Biblical Creation Account and Its Relationship to Scientific Models

The CSBI is freighted with huge and unacknowledged hermeneutical assumptions. The statement masks several implied claims about what the Bible is and how it should be interpreted. This is evident in what the CSBI says about God and creation. The short statement declares that the Bible is true, not only in the sphere of salvation but also "in what it states about God's acts in creation, about the events of world history, and about its own literary origins under God." And in article 12, the point is reinforced with a denial that "scientific hypotheses about earth history may properly be used to overturn the teaching of Scripture on creation and the flood."

In this, the CSBI seems to commit one to a strict literal hermeneutic that demands a literal seven-day creation and a young earth. This is no mere affirmation that the biblical creation story is true, for the principle of inerrancy insists equally on *how* it is true. Such notions of truth rely on modern presumptions of precision and exactitude. The framing here also assumes a conflict model between science and religion, and where the two clash, deference must be given to the biblical text — or more precisely, to one particular interpretation of the biblical text. Now, I am not an advocate of a secular scientism, but the problem here is that the CSBI covertly embeds a particular interpretation of Genesis 1–3 into its assertions about inerrancy, and all scientific alternatives to the literalist interpretation in geology, biology, and cosmology are rebuffed. Thus inerrancy becomes a clandestine method that smuggles one particular interpretation of the biblical creation story into its doctrine, with the concomitant result that to deny this literalist interpretation is tantamount to denying the inerrancy and authority of the text.

For many biblical interpreters, Genesis 1–3 is not a blow-by-blow literal account of creation as much as it is about establishing a monotheistic worldview of God as Creator in the context of competing creation accounts in the polytheistic environment of the ancient Near East. No conflict with science exists about origins, because Genesis 1–3 is not intended as a scientific account of creation.[5] In addition, I should point out that in an infallibilist view, which I will expound below, there is no preempting of interpretations and no presumptions about science and religion. An infallibilist can maintain the veracity of the biblical creation story on the terms of its historical and canonical location, all with due respect to the text's diverse reception in the Christian church.

2. An Assumption That Biblical Veracity Rests on the Harmonization of Discrepancies

In chorus with the CSBI, I affirm the unity and consistency of Scripture. Yet just when I think we are on the same page, the CSBI makes a peculiar and problematic remark in article 14: "We deny that alleged errors and discrepancies that have *not yet been resolved* vitiate the truth claims of the Bible" (my emphasis). I suspect that the CSBI's focus on reconciling the minutia of detail is a dead end. Infallibilists do not take the unity of Scripture to rest on our abilities to resolve all apparent discrepancies; instead the unity of both Testaments rests in their singular testimony to Jesus Christ.

The story of Jesus healing a blind man near Jericho illustrates the futility of some efforts at harmonization (Matt. 20:29–34; Mark 10:46–52; Luke 18:35–43). In Luke, Jesus heals a blind man on the way to Jericho, while in Matthew and Mark he does this on the way out of Jericho. Luke and Mark have one blind man, while Matthew has two blind men. The setting, the plea of the blind man, the rebuff of the crowd, and Jesus' response in all three versions make it clear that it is the same story. Matthew just likes doublets and often turns ones into twos, and Luke has altered the account on an incidental detail.

You cannot resolve these differences, so it is futile to wait for a day when some bright spark might find a way to resolve the differences, but my point is that we do not need to. The point of the story is surely that Jesus is the Son of David, who heals the blind and shows compas-

---

5. I heartily recommend John H. Walton, *The Lost World of Genesis One: Ancient Cosmology and the Origins Debate* (Downers Grove, Ill.: InterVarsity, 2009).

sion to the outcasts, all as a sign of messianic salvation. Beyond that, the details are incidental and are open to rearrangement by the storyteller. This is a good example of what John Calvin said: "We know that the Evangelists were not very exact as to the order of dates, or even in detailing minutely everything that Christ did or said."[6] Now, the CSBI recognizes that the Bible does not contain "modern technical precision," but whether the framers of the document would extend a lack of precision to details in the Synoptic tradition, given their affirmation of inerrancy in the details of history, is moot (articles 12–13). Alternatively, we could say that Christology, not chronology, is the unity and coherence of Scripture![7] Taking this line, our focus will be on the person and work of Christ, and we will not get distracted in wrangling over incidental details and trying to develop unconvincing explanations to account for minor variations of detail.

3. A Revisionist View of the History of Biblical Interpretation and a Lack of Reflection on the Contingent Conditions behind Inerrancy

The CSBI goes on the defensive in article 16 when it affirms that inerrancy "has been integral to the Church's faith throughout its history" and denies that it "is a doctrine invented by Scholastic Protestantism, or is a reactionary position postulated in response to negative higher criticism." There is a grain of truth here, but some palpable problems as well.

First, Christian believers over the course of history have repeatedly affirmed that the Holy Scriptures come from God, they are to be read and studied in the churches, they are the inscripturated form of the rule of faith, they emit divine authority, they are without falsehood, and they are true and trustworthy.[8] However, to insist that the CSBI understanding of inerrancy is and always has been normative in church

6. John Calvin, *Commentary on a Harmony of the Evangelists*, trans. William Pringle, vol. 1, Calvin's Commentaries, vol. 16 (Grand Rapids, Mich.: Eerdmans, 1989), 216.

7. See also R. T. France, "Inerrancy and New Testament Exegesis," *Themelios* 1 (1975): 12–18.

8. Cf. John D. Woodbridge, *Biblical Authority: A Critique of the Rogers/McKim Proposal* (Grand Rapids, Mich.: Zondervan, 1982); Woodbridge, "Evangelical Self-Identity and the Doctrine of Biblical Inerrancy," in Andreas J. Köstenberger and Robert W. Yarbrough, eds., *Understanding the Times: New Testament Studies in the 21st Century* (Wheaton, Ill.: Crossway, 2011), 104–38.

history is a bit of a stretch.[9] Someone like an Augustine seems close to what the CSBI affirms in his explicit statements on Scripture. The bishop of Hippo wrote, "Only to those books which are called canonical have I learned to give honor so that I believe most firmly that no author in these books made any error in writing."[10] Yet John Chrysostom was somewhat more restrained in his proposal: "But if there be anything touching time or places, which they have related differently, this nothing injures the truth of what they have said ... [but those things] which constitute our life and furnish out our doctrine nowhere is any of them found to have disagreed, no not ever so little."[11] Chrysostom sounds more like infallibility than inerrancy (more on the distinction later). And then again, Origen could write, "But let these four [Gospels] agree with each other concerning certain things revealed to them by the Spirit and let them disagree a little concerning other things."[12] For Origen, something like inerrancy applied only to the level of spiritual interpretation, not to the historical details of Scripture.[13] While it is undoubtedly true that Christians have historically affirmed the truthfulness of Scripture and denied allegations of falsehood, I want to suggest that there might have been a bit more diversity in the history of the church as to precisely how Scripture is true and without grievous error.

Second, the focus on the autographs of Scripture is somewhat of a red herring. B. B. Warfield believed, somewhat naively, that if we possessed the original texts, then all *real* discrepancies would vanish and we'd be left with only *apparent* discrepancies.[14] Of course, this assumes that we can discern the difference between the two species of discrepancy, and it

---

9. Cf. David F. Wright, "Soundings in the Doctrine of Scripture in British Evangelicalism in the First Half of the Twentieth Century," *TynBul* 31 (1980): 88–89.

10. Augustine, *Epistles*, 82.1.

11. John Chrysostom, *Hom. Matt.* 1.6. The essential doctrinal unity of Scripture, according to Chrysostom, is "that God became man, that He wrought miracles, that He was crucified, that He was buried, that He rose again, that He ascended, that He will judge, that He hath given commandments tending to salvation, that He hath brought in a law not contrary to the Old Testament, that He is a Son, that He is only-begotten, that He is a true Son, that He is of the same substance with the Father, and as many as are like these; for touching these we shall find that there is in them a full agreement."

12. Origen, *Comm. Joh.* 10.4.

13. I think Origen and Chrysostom would fall afoul of the CSBI's article 12, which denies that infallibility and inerrancy are "limited to spiritual, religious, or redemptive themes, exclusive of assertions in the fields of history and science."

14. B. B. Warfield, "Inerrancy of the Original Autographs," in *Selected Shorter Writings of Benjamin B. Warfield*, vol. 2, ed. J. E. Meeter (Nutley, N.J.: P&R, 1973), 580–87.

asserts that our current editions of the Bible are somehow full of real discrepancies even though God has preserved the Scriptures in the church. Augustine and John Owen are routinely cited as vouching for the biblical autographs. Augustine wrote, "I confess to your Charity that I have learned to yield this respect and honour only to the canonical books of Scripture: of these alone do I most firmly believe that the authors were completely free from error. And if in these writings I am perplexed by anything which appears to me opposed to truth, I do not hesitate to suppose that either the manuscript is faulty, or the translator has not caught the meaning of what was said, or I myself have failed to understand it."[15] John Owen referred to "the purity of the present original copies of the Scripture, or rather copies (*apographa*) in the original languages, which the Church of God doth now and hath for many ages enjoyed as her treasure."[16] However, Augustine was writing at a time when every Tomiani, Dickianaeus, and Harrios was producing poor Latin texts of the New Testament, creating much confusion, and John Owen was responding to Catholic apologists who were producing Greek texts that had variants which supported Roman Catholic doctrines. Thus their appeal to the autographs was based on text-critical concerns, not on the theological quality of the autographs per se. I would add that some church fathers, such as Eusebius,[17] could attempt to solve textual discrepancies by assuming a scribal error and making a conjectural emendation, but this is for the most part a desperate move.[18] The authoritative Bible is not just that which replicates the autographs; it is also the Bible as it is received and believed in the church.

To maintain that divine inspiration is confined to the initial autographs is a position that is textually problematic, as it is theologically indefensible. For a start, what do we do if there were additions made to the biblical books, such as the account of Moses' death added in

15. Augustine, *Letter to Jerome*, 82.3.

16. Cited in Theodore P. Letis, *The Ecclesiastical Text* (Philadelphia: Institute for Renaissance and Reformation Biblical Studies, 1997), 43.

17. Eusebius, *Gospel Problems and Solutions to Marinus* 2.8.

18. On the challenges that textual criticism presents to the inerrancy of the *autographa*, see Michael A. Grisanti, "Inspiration, Inerrancy, and the OT Canon: The Place of Textual Updating in an Inerrant View of Scripture," *JETS* 44.4 (2001): 577–98, and John J. Brogan, "Can I Have Your Autograph? Uses and Abuses of Textual Criticism in Formulating an Evangelical Doctrine of Scripture," in Vincent Bacote, Laura C. Miguelez, and Dennis L. Okholm, eds., *Evangelicals and Scripture: Tradition, Authority, and Hermeneutics* (Downers Grove, Ill.: InterVarsity, 2004), 93–111.

Deuteronomy 34, or if an editorial colophon was added in John 21:24 to confirm the testimony of the Beloved Disciple? Were these secondary elements inspired too? Or what if there were two editions of some biblical books, such as Jeremiah's prophecy that had to be rewritten after it was destroyed; which one was inspired (Jer. 36:26–28)? Indeed, the text of Jeremiah is quite a conundrum, since our English Bibles are based largely on the twelfth-century Masoretic Text, which is some 30 percent longer than the Septuagintal version (that is, Greek translation of the Old Testament), which itself was based on an underlying Hebrew source from before the time of Jesus. The earliest attestation of the text of Jeremiah is considerably shorter than our "canonical" edition.[19] Limiting inspiration to an initial autograph creates a host of problems when we realize that our biblical texts sometimes had secondary additions and subsequent editions, since it would imply that our inspired autographs have noninspired sections overlaid upon them. On top of that, if the New Testament authors were so slavishly concerned with preserving the original text of the Old Testament, then why were they relatively free in their citation of the Old Testament in the New Testament, such as Peter's citation of Joel 2 in Acts 2, which is an inexact replication of the Hebrew text? Perhaps, as J. I. Packer points out, the New Testament authors were more concerned with the text's original meaning than with its original wording.[20] Finally, what does it say about a God who inspires the original text and yet allows the subsequent history of the church to struggle with a corrupted version of his inscripturated revelation? Doesn't this make God disinterested in preserving or unable to preserve his revelation effectively? Surely, it is the faithfulness of God to his revelation in Scripture which is precisely what the inerrantists are trying to demonstrate. Yet their focus on the original autographs seems not only to detract from that but also to constitute capitulation to skeptics who are quick to point out the corruptions in the Bibles that we currently have and use. The solution, I believe, is not to think that God reinspires every copy of Scripture (such as every

19. Cf. J. Daniel Hays, "Jeremiah, the Septuagint, the Dead Sea Scrolls and Inerrancy: Just Exactly What Do We Mean by the 'Original Autographs'?" in Bacote, Miguelez, and Okholm, *Evangelicals and Scripture*, 133–49. Be warned, reading Hays's article might blow your theory of inspiration apart!

20. Cf. J. I. Packer, "Inspiration," in I. H. Marshall et al., eds., *New Bible Dictionary*, 3rd ed. (Downers Grove, Ill.: InterVarsity, 1996), 508.

papyrus, scroll, or codex), nor to say that one particular modern version is inspired (such as the King James Bible), but to see inspiration as extending to the human literary processes which preserved the meaning and power of God's Word to achieve the ends for which it was given.

Third, the CSBI denies that there were any contingent circumstances that shaped the development of the American inerrancy tradition in the modern period. But Charles Hodge and B. B. Warfield did not write in philosophical isolation or in a historical vacuum. Both men were shaped largely by Common Sense Realism and were thus susceptible to the failings of that epistemological system, with its view that epistemic foundations and proper method would lead to some kind of God's-eye view of reality. Facing the challenge of religious skepticism, Hodge and Warfield were essentially apologists for Scripture, a project that was only marginally undertaken in patristic, medieval, and Reformation eras.[21] The duo was responding largely to the critique of revealed religion in modernity, so it is inevitable that their theologies of Scripture were shaped by the philosophical currents of their time. The Princetonians developed the doctrine of infallibility, taking it further, extending the Bible's truthfulness to matters both salvific and scientific, and more explicitly denying that revelation and error can coexist.[22] Of course, that does not mean that what they wrote was merely reactionary or that development is always a bad thing, but it is hard to imagine either man writing what he did without René Descartes, Immanuel Kant, or F. C. Baur lurking in the background.

Fourth, inerrantists sometimes engage in some anachronistic history in order to defend their view. If it can be proven that revered figures from church history held to inerrancy, then there is said to be another reason for believing in inerrancy. This occasionally results in some desperate and overcooked attempts to prove that the said person believed in inerrancy. The logic often proceeds like this:

1. Good and godly people believe what the CSBI says.
2. John Calvin was a good and godly person.
3. Therefore John Calvin believed what the CSBI says.

---

21. Wright, "Soundings in the Doctrine of Scripture," 91.

22. Cf. Kevin J. Vanhoozer, "Scripture and Hermeneutics," in *The Oxford Handbook of Evangelical Theology*, ed. G. R. McDermott (Oxford: OUP, 2010), 37–38.

My point is not whether John Calvin held to inerrancy as the CSBI defines it; I think he would have been very much in the same ballpark.[23] My point is that the context for studying John Calvin is not late 1970s Chicago as a response to the Jack Rogers and Donald McKim view[24] but medieval Catholicism, which had a high view of Scripture but deployed Scripture in subjection to the Roman Catholic magisterium. We must resist the temptation to turn our heroes of the faith into advocates of our own positions in light of our own contemporary debates.

The other thing to pursue is how ancient views of inerrancy were married to philosophical frameworks and hermeneutical applications. It is one thing to hold to inerrancy because Augustine apparently did so. But it is quite another thing to pull inerrancy out of Augustine's Neoplatonic framework, his view that the Greek and Hebrew versions of the Old Testament (including the Apocrypha) were equally inspired, and his allegorical interpretation of the days of creation. Note this: *why* Augustine believed in inerrancy and *what* he did with it might strike modern inerrantists as quite disturbing. My point is that modern defenders of inerrancy have not given sufficient attention to the philosophical, theological, and hermeneutical paradigms that have often accompanied inerrancy-like affirmations in church history. Proponents of inerrancy have not adequately broached the matter as to whether these accompanying paradigms are extrinsic or intrinsic to a doctrine of inerrancy.

4. An Unfortunate Trend toward Theological Colonialism

Perhaps most concerning of all is that the framers of the CSBI arrogate to the point that they demand that if we do not accept this statement of "total divine inerrancy" and if we fail to incorporate inerrancy into our confessions of faith, then we are guilty of disregarding Scripture and bringing grave consequences to the church. The framers are equally insistent that infallibility is not enough by itself and must be cojoined with inerrancy in order to be theologically healthy (see article 11).

---

23. On Calvin and inerrancy, see J. I. Packer, "John Calvin and the Inerrancy of Holy Scripture," in *Inerrancy and the Church*, ed. J. D. Hannah (Chicago: Moody, 1984), 143–88.

24. See Jack B. Rogers and Donald K. McKim, *The Authority and Interpretation of the Bible* (San Francisco: Harper & Row, 1979) and Woodbridge, *Biblical Authority*.

Here is the problem: there are thousands of churches around the world that are both evangelical and orthodox and get on with their ministry without ever having heard of the CSBI and without ever using the word *inerrancy* in their statement of faith. The reason is that global evangelical churches have been informed by a broad creedal and confessional tradition that already had the theological heritage and hermeneutical tools to deal with challenges to the Bible without having to marry its apologetics to the philosophical terms of modernity. To insist that churches and parachurch organizations around the world must suddenly add the word *inerrancy* to their doctrinal standards in order to be faithful usurps for oneself an authority that is reminiscent of the ancient councils.

The International Council on Biblical Inerrancy was not an ecumenical council with representatives from near and far, representing all traditions, bringing collective wisdom to bear on the doctrine of Scripture. It looks to me to be mainly a conservative in-house American thing. The international council was international to the same extent that winners of the World Series or the Super Bowl are "world" champions. There were a few ring-ins such as J. I. Packer, John Wenham, and Roger Nicole (all Western European males), but I detect no voices from Africa, Asia, or South America having any real input into the formulation of the CSBI. I would suggest that the Lausanne Covenant and Vatican decree *Dei Verbum* might have wider appeal to many churches than the CSBI in terms of commanding the assent of the global church.

G. K. Beale's remarks on globalism and postmodernism embody the type of theological paternalism that I'm concerned about.[25] The mere fact that he puts global perspectives in theology as a tag-on to an appendix arguing against postmodern hermeneutical errors suggests that Beale portrays global views on Christian faith as something to be negotiated in the quest for a sound doctrine of Scripture. He feels the need to assuage his implied reader that there is a perspective on globalism "that is good and healthy, indeed, biblical" in that the church in one part of the world may focus on methods, interpretation, biblical

---

25. Greg K. Beale, *The Erosion of Inerrancy in Evangelicalism: Responding to New Challenges to Biblical Authority* (Wheaton, Ill.: Crossway, 2008), 261–65.

ideas, doctrines, or applications that are not known or emphasized in other parts of the worldwide church.[26] That sounds all right, but Beale then proceeds to talk about the global church as if we are all enthralled by Western liberalism, or else we are just in the infancy of theological formation. He believes that these global churches may benefit from considering the conservative Western sector of scholarship because of the conservative Western "emphasis on the authority of the Bible, text-based interpretation, and affirmation of the supernatural in the Bible," the unstated premise being that global churches are somehow deficient in these areas.[27] I have to say that Beale's remarks are well-intended, and he desires genuine fellowship with global churches; it is a pity then that he does so with such a paternalistic attitude.

First, in many cases, conservative American evangelical biblical interpretation is not only parochial but also weird and whacky. Only American evangelicals use Scripture to argue against gun control, against environmental care, and against universal healthcare.[28] Second, while there is a great blessing in American evangelical scholarship, one I've benefited from immensely (not least of all from Beale's brilliant *Revelation* commentary), we do not need Americans to teach us that the Bible is authoritative and how to do text-based interpretation. Here's the thing: we already knew that; in some cases we knew it a millennium before the Americans, and why do Americans presume to teach us a proper doctrine of biblical authority and biblical interpretation when they live in the same country as Joel Osteen, Joyce Meyer, and the Left Behind series! Third, to read between the lines, I think Beale is, consciously or not, reassuring his own conservative constituency of the theological superiority of their doctrine of Scripture vis-à-vis the world, and he tacitly suggests that the American conservative response to global Christianity it is to colonize the world with a proper doctrine of Scripture that reflects the American inerrancy tradition. Beale acknowledges that the global and American churches can learn from each other, but I want to suggest that when

26. Ibid., 262.
27. Ibid., 263.
28. Outside of America (and even inside it), Wayne Grudem's book *Politics According to the Bible: A Comprehensive Resource for Understanding Modern Political Issues in Light of Scripture* (Grand Rapids, Mich.: Zondervan, 2010) is mystifying and mortifying to global evangelicals.

it comes to the doctrine of Scripture, *the dialogue and teaching should flow both ways*.

Final Thoughts on the CSBI

First, the CSBI derives primarily from inferences about God's character as truthful and righteous rather than from the literary phenomena of Scripture. The doctrine of Scripture obviously remains umbilically connected to our doctrine of God. Yet somewhere along the way, you have to engage the phenomena of Scripture, its diversity and nature, its content and the challenges that it raises, and then revise your doctrine of revelation accordingly.[29] Yet such wrestling with the phenomena of Scripture is mostly lacking here. The CSBI looks like a statement compiled primarily by theologians rather than by biblical scholars.

Second, for the most part, the affirmations and denials in the articles of the CSBI are relatively straightforward and mostly unproblematic (commendable in places!). However, when it assumes a certain epistemology (such as foundationalism)[30] or promotes a certain view of hermeneutics (such as consistent literalism), then one can see the CSBI as the attempt to smuggle in certain presuppositions and to covertly legitimize them by linking them to belief in inerrancy.

Third, the CSBI is not really intended as a way of gauging the mind of the global church on Scripture. Its primary function is to define American evangelicalism as a bounded set, to use inerrancy as a way of forcing conformity to certain biblical interpretations, and to weed out dissenters in denominational politics. If, in any debate on doctrine, one plays the inerrancy card against one's opponents, then one can effectively remove these opponents on the grounds that they are denying the prestigious moniker of inerrancy.[31] Thus inerrancy is primarily a weapon of religious politics to define who is in and who is out. That is why some inerrantists preach the inerrancy of the text but practice the inerrancy of their interpretation.

---

29. Cf. Everett F. Harrison, "The Phenomena of Scripture," in *Revelation and the Bible*, ed. Carl F. Henry (London: Tyndale, 1959), 237–59.

30. I would consider myself a "chastened foundationalist," given that there is an external reality, it is knowable, but it is never known independently of the knower and his or her subjectivities.

31. Exactly what Carl Henry (*God, Revelation and Authority*, 4:365) warned us about!

What Does the Bible Say about Itself?

When it comes to the Bible's claims about itself, an initial problem is that even inerrantists cannot agree as to whether the Bible explicitly teaches its own inerrancy. The idea of inerrancy as an implicate of inspiration was influentially argued by Carl F. H. Henry, who put forward a mix of a priori assumptions and deductive reasoning from Scripture on this point. Henry contended that if God is the ultimate author of Scripture, even through human authors, then its content must be trustworthy, even inerrant.[32] Similarly, Millard J. Erickson reasoned, "It is obvious that belief in the inerrancy of the Scriptures is not an inductive conclusion arrived at as a result of examining all the passages of the Bible. By its very nature, such a conclusion would be only probable at best. Nor is the doctrine of biblical inerrancy explicitly affirmed or taught in the Bible. Rather, it is a corollary of the doctrine of the full inspiration of the Bible."[33] In contrast, others such as Jim Hamilton and Greg Beale have maintained that the biblical testimony explicitly supports a claim to biblical inerrancy.[34] It does not bode well for claiming that the Bible teaches its own inerrancy when inerrantists themselves dispute the claim.[35]

Rather than "inerrancy," a better categorization of Scripture's claims for itself would be "veracity," or "divine truthfulness." Instead of stating how or in what way the Bible is not untrue—which is an odd thing to say, when you think about it—we are better off simply asserting that God's Word is true as it correlates with God's intent for what Scripture is to achieve, because he is faithful to his world and to his Word.[36] In the Psalter, we read things like "The words of the LORD

---

32. Carl F. H. Henry, *God, Revelation and Authority*, 6 vols. (Carlisle, UK: Paternoster, 1999).

33. Millard Erickson, *Christian Theology* (Grand Rapids, Mich.: Baker, 1985), 229.

34. Jim M. Hamilton, "Scripture: The Evangelical View," in Bird and Pahl, *The Sacred Text*, 215–40; G. K. Beale, "Can the Bible Be Completely Inspired by God and Yet Still Contain Errors? A Response to Some Recent 'Evangelical' Proposals," *WTJ* 73 (2011): 1–22.

35. Note that the CSBI preface declares that inerrancy is part of the "claims of God's own Word," but later article 15 proffers, "We affirm that the doctrine of inerrancy is grounded in the teaching of the Bible about inspiration."

36. I like how Ben Witherington puts it: "The terms inerrant and infallible are modern ways of attempting to make clear that the Bible tells the truth about whatever it intends to teach us about. I much prefer the positive terms truthful and trustworthy. When you start defining something negatively (saying what it is not) then you often die the death of a thou-

are flawless, like silver purified in a crucible, like gold refined seven times" (Ps. 12:6), "The law of the LORD is perfect, refreshing the soul. The statutes of the LORD are trustworthy" (Ps. 19:7), "The word of the LORD is right and true; he is faithful in all he does" (Ps. 33:4), "Never take your word of truth from my mouth, for I have put my hope in your laws" (Ps. 119:43), "Your word, LORD, is eternal; it stands firm in the heavens" (Ps. 119:89). In the testimony of the Beloved Disciple, Jesus himself said, "Scripture cannot be set aside" (John 10:35), meaning that Scripture cannot prove to be inconsistent with itself. John the Seer constantly emphasizes that the words of his prophecy are "trustworthy and true" (Rev. 21:5; 22:6) because they come from Messiah Jesus, who is himself faithful, holy, just, and true (Rev. 3:7, 14; 15:3). From all this, Donald Bloesch's position on the "truthfulness or veracity of Scripture" is the preferred point of affirmation.[37] I would add that such an affirmation corresponds nicely with one of the key assertions in the CSBI, that Scripture is "true and trustworthy" (article 9).

The testimony of God's Word about itself is that God's Word is an authentic and authoritative account of God's actions in creation, redemption, and consummation. God speaks in revelation, and it is true because God identifies with and even invests his own character in his Word. The language of revelation is accommodated to the worldview and expectations of its audience in matters of cosmology and historiography, but the accommodation is never a capitulation to error. God does not speak erroneously, nor does he feed us nuts of truth lodged inside shells of falsehood. G. W. Bromiley put it aptly: "While it is in no doubt a paradox that eternal truth is revealed in temporal events and witnesses through a human book, it is sheer unreason to say that truth is revealed in and through that which is erroneous."[38]

An important upshot is that we are now well placed to ascertain the reason why God's Word is always true in what it affirms. Against

---

sand qualifications, not to mention you have to define what constitutes an error. I am happy to say that the Bible has three main subjects—history, theology, and ethics, and that it tells us the truth about all three" ("Ben Witherington on Scripture," *http://euangelizomai.blogspot. com/2007/09/ben-witherington-on-scripture.html* (September 9, 2012).

37. Donald G. Bloesch, *Holy Scripture: Revelation, Inspiration, and Interpretation* (Downers Grove, Ill.: InterVarsity, 1994), 116.

38. G. W. Bromiley, "The Authority of Scripture," in F. Davidson, A. M. Stibbs, E. F. Kevan, eds., *The New Bible Commentary* (London: IVF, 1954), 22.

the inerrantist position as articulated in the CSBI, I do not agree that inerrancy is established by our ability to demonstrate that the Bible is without error. I say that simply because there are, honestly speaking, bits of Scripture, inconsequential for the most part, that do not agree in their precise details. (I know this is controversial, but do read on, to where I deal with them!) This was one of the chief drawbacks with B. B. Warfield's doctrine of inerrancy, in the mind of the Scottish theologian James Orr. Now, Orr was no liberal; he was a contributor to the important twelve-volume collection *The Fundamentals*, published in the early twentieth century. Orr responded to Warfield's project as follows: "It is urged ... that unless we can demonstrate what is called the inerrancy of the biblical record down even to its minutest details, the whole edifice of belief in revealed religion falls to the ground. This, on the face of it, is the most suicidal position for any defender of revelation to take up."[39] We might say that Warfield and the inerrantists who followed him went a bridge too far, since they seized more intellectual terrain than they could effectively defend. They allowed modernity to fight on the philosophical ground of their choosing and with the epistemological weapons of their choosing. The Battle for the Bible was always rigged in favor of modernity, and a better strategy would have been to deconstruct modernity as its philosophical DNA. So we shouldn't anchor the truth of Scripture in our apologetic capabilities to beat the skeptics at their own game; I think there are better ways.

An International View of Scripture

There are a number of ways in which the truthfulness of Scripture has been expressed in the global evangelical churches. Many of these churches are denominationally aligned and proudly hold to their confessional heritage. So the 60 million Anglicans in the global south hold to the Thirty-Nine Articles, with its reference to the "authority" and "sufficiency" of Scripture for salvation, leaving open how Scripture relates to history and science. The 75 million Presbyterians

39. James Orr, *Revelation and Inspiration* (London: Duckworth, 1909), 197–98, cited in Andrew T. B. McGowan, *The Divine Spiration of Scripture: Challenging Evangelical Perspectives* (Leicester: Apollos, 2007), 127.

around the world, with major concentrations in Brazil and Korea, hold to the Westminster Confession of Faith, which affirms the "infallible truth and divine authority" of Scripture. The 2 million members of the Church of Southern India believe that "the Scriptures are the ultimate standard of faith and practice." The Baptist World Alliance, representing some 41 million Baptists, in their Centenary Congress of 2005 declared that "the divinely inspired Old and New Testament Scriptures have supreme authority as the written Word of God and are fully trustworthy for faith and conduct." The Fellowship of European Evangelical Theologians, in its statement of faith, acknowledges "the divine inspiration of Holy Scripture and its consequent entire trustworthiness and supreme authority in all matters of faith and conduct." The Evangelical Affirmations conference held at Trinity Evangelical Divinity School in 1989 nowhere used the word *inerrancy*, instead affirming "the complete truthfulness and the full and final authority of the Old and New Testament Scriptures as the Word of God written."[40] The British Universities and Colleges Christian Fellowship (UCCF) has a statement of faith held by university chapters all around the world and even used by many churches and parachurch organizations globally; on Scripture, this statement reads, "The Bible, as originally given, is the inspired and infallible Word of God. It is the supreme authority in all matters of belief and behaviour." The Word in Action convention, held in Bath, England, and affiliated with the Keswick Convention, recognizes "the divine inspiration of Holy Scripture and its consequent entire trustworthiness and supreme authority in all matters of faith and conduct." The Jerusalem Declaration of the Fellowship of Confessing Anglicans contains the article "We believe the Holy Scriptures of the Old and New Testaments to be the Word of God written and to contain all things necessary for salvation. The Bible is to be translated, read, preached, taught and obeyed in its plain and canonical sense, respectful of the church's historic and consensual reading." Finally, let us consider the Lausanne Covenant, representing evangelical believers from all corners of the globe, which in article 2 says,

---

40. Kenneth S. Kantzer and Carl F. H. Henry, eds., *Evangelical Affirmations* (Grand Rapids, Mich.: Zondervan, 1990), 32.

> We affirm the divine inspiration, truthfulness and authority of both Old and New Testament Scriptures in their entirety as the only written word of God, without error in all that it affirms, and the only infallible rule of faith and practice. We also affirm the power of God's Word to accomplish his purpose of salvation. The message of the Bible is addressed to all men and women. For God's revelation in Christ and in Scripture is unchangeable. Through it the Holy Spirit still speaks today. He illumines the minds of God's people in every culture to perceive its truth freshly through their own eyes and thus discloses to the whole Church ever more of the many-colored wisdom of God.

You may notice that the words *inerrant* and *inerrancy* are absent from all of these statements, though the Lausanne Covenant's "without error in all that it affirms" perhaps comes closest. There are reasons for this. First, it is important to remember that the Battle for the Bible that took place in American denominations in the twentieth century was very much an intra-American affair.[41] As Daniel J. Treier comments, "Conflict over scriptural inerrancy has not defined evangelicalism elsewhere as it did in the United States."[42] The global church had other problems to deal with, ranging from polygamy to persecution, from syncretism to secularism, from nominalism to nationalism, from colonialism to communism, and various humanitarian crises. Rather than a Battle for the Bible, many global churches had a Battle for Survival, which is not conducive to theological hairsplitting.

Second, the nomenclature of "inerrancy" is a relative latecomer on the theological scene. As J. I. Packer writes, "Evangelicals are accustomed to speak of the Word of God as *infallible* and *inerrant*. The former has a long pedigree; among the Reformers, Cranmer and Jewel spoke of God's Word as infallible, and the Westminster Confession of the 'infallible truth' of Holy Scripture. The latter, however,

---

41. Ronald F. Satta, *The Sacred Text: Biblical Authority in Nineteenth-Century America*, Princeton Theological Monograph (Eugene, Ore.: Pickwick, 2007).

42. Daniel J. Treier, "Scripture and Hermeneutics," in Timothy Larsen and Daniel J. Treier, eds., *The Cambridge Companion to Evangelical Theology* (Cambridge: Cambridge Univ. Press, 2007), 40. See further David F. Wright, "Soundings in the Doctrine of Scripture in British Evangelicalism in the First Half of the Twentieth Century," *TynBul* 31 (1980): 87–106, and Stephen R. Holmes, "Evangelical Doctrines of Scripture in Transatlantic Perspective," *EQ* 81 (2009): 38–63.

seems not to have been regularly used in this connection before the nineteenth century."[43] *Inerrancy* is a recent entry in the theological lexicon, and thus it is odd to turn it into a kind of theological shibboleth.

For the most part, global churches have focused on Scripture as "infallible" and "authoritative." By "biblical infallibility," we mean that the biblical teachings are true and without falsehood in all that they affirm, with specific reference to God's revelation of himself as Savior. It is often unclear exactly how infallibility and inerrancy materially differ from each other, since both deny that God's revelation is encased in falsehood. Sometimes it is said that inerrancy entails freedom from error in all that is mentioned in Scripture — regardless of whether it pertains to historical, scientific, or theological claims — while infallibility is more modest in scope and pertains only to matters of faith and doctrine.[44] That is of course the root of the inerrantist objection, that infallibility is too soft and not assertive enough. I want to say that infallibility is not a retreatist position; rather it focuses on the perfection of God's revelation, with a view to the purpose for which God has revealed himself.[45] The Bible was not intended as a handbook on astronomy, so it is pointless to treat it like one. Instead the Bible was intended to impart knowledge of God as Creator and Redeemer, and under that premise, the Bible is completely true in all that it says. The primary feature of infallibility is that God's Word will never mislead us and it is a safe and reliable guide in all matters to which it speaks.

Before we proceed, I need to unpack the doctrines of revelation, inspiration, and veracity embedded in biblical infallibility. First, on revelation, the Bible, as God's inscripturated revelation of himself,

43. J. I. Packer, *"Fundamentalism" and the Word of God* (Grand Rapids, Mich.: Eerdmans, 1958), 94–95.

44. See Peter Jensen, *The Revelation of God* (Downers Grove, Ill.: InterVarsity, 2012), 197–203. McGowan (*The Divine Spiration of Scripture*, 123–64) argues that infallibility is superior to, and therefore preferable over, inerrancy.

45. See Roger Olson, "Why Inerrancy Doesn't Matter," *The Baptist Standard* (February 2, 2006), *www.patheos.com/blogs/rogereolson/2010/08/why-inerrancy-doesnt-matter/*: " 'Infallible,' to me, means the Bible never fails in its main purpose which is to identify God for us, to communicate his love and his will to us, and to lead us into salvation and a right relationship with our Creator, Savior and Lord." See also McGowan, *The Divine Spiration of Scripture*, 162: "It [infallibility] has the sense of purpose, meaning that God will infallibly achieve what he has determined to achieve in and through his Word."

was given to reveal God in the language of human authors so that God would communicate and commune with others. Revelation is not mere propositions about God waiting to be decoded from the morass of biblical genres. Revelation is God's work in imparting cognition of his person, plan, purposes, and the entire reality which he represents. Viewed this way, revelation consists of worldview, beliefs, ethics, tasks, and behaviors that are created by the act of revealing. Now, obviously the Bible says things about God and God's action which are true. However, the goal of revelation is not only knowing facts about God but also enjoying fellowship with God.

Second, inspiration describes how God publicizes and preserves the special revelation of himself through the medium of human authors in what is now the biblical canon. God directly inspires persons, not pages (see 2 Peter 1:20–21; Acts 1:16; 4:25), so inspiration happens principally at the conceptual level, though of course concepts and words overlap, creating a degree of verbal inspiration. While *inspiration* may be the term we use to describe the relationship of a divine self-communicative act to a textual entity, we may heed John Webster's suggestion and talk about a "sanctification" of the textual processes that led to the formation of the biblical canon. This sanctification is understood as "the overall process of God's ordering of creaturely realities as servants of his self-presentation."[46] In this sanctifying work of God, in both the autographs and in any subsequent textual formation, the veracity of Scripture is retained for the purpose for which God has given Scripture: "teaching, rebuking, correcting and training in righteousness" (2 Tim. 3:16).

Third, the veracity and verification of Scripture sits between the Holy Spirit and the church. I would not place the doctrine of Scripture at the head of a system of theology (an innovation introduced with the Second Helvetic Confession); I would place it in between the doctrine of the Holy Spirit and the doctrine of the church. On such a scheme, Scripture is veracious because it is ratified by the inner witness of the Holy Spirit and then validated by the testimony of the church as our canon. Yet I would press that point even further, beyond the testimony of Spirit and church, and argue that ultimately if the Word of God is

---

46. John Webster, *Holy Scripture: A Dogmatic Sketch* (Cambridge: Cambridge Univ. Press, 2003), 10.

God's own Word, then its veracity is rooted not in personal experience, not in church councils, much less in our apologetic efforts, but in divine fidelity.[47] That is to say, the truthfulness of Scripture is secured by the faithfulness of God to his own Word. God's Word is always conformed to his character as just, holy, righteous, and true. Unsurprisingly, Psalm 119 and Revelation 21–22 fasten the trustworthiness of God's Word to the very faithfulness of God. God is the theological grounds for the veracity of Scripture—God and nothing else. I trust God the Father, I trust his Son, the Spirit leads me to that truth, so I trust God's Holy Book.

On biblical authority, to say that the Bible is authoritative is to affirm that the Bible is divinely authorized because the Holy Spirit speaks to us through it—exactly what the Westminster Confession and London Baptist Confession both affirm.[48] Therefore Scripture must be obeyed in its entirety and not treated as an item for negotiation. There is the story about Adolf Schlatter, who, when interviewed for a professorial appointment in Berlin, was asked by a churchman on the interview panel if he as an academic "stood on the Bible." Schlatter replied, "No, I stand under the Bible."[49] As followers of Jesus, we do not sit in judgment of God's Word; we allow it to stand in judgment of us. We strive to obey its precepts and live out its story. Indeed, a focus on the Bible's authority moves us from the abstract toward the practical. For how we live under the Bible is the ultimate test of what we believe about God and the Bible. John Stott wrote, "The hallmark of authentic evangelicalism is not subscription but submission. That is, it is not whether we subscribe to an impeccable formula about the Bible, but whether we live in practical submission to what the Bible teaches, including an advance resolve to submit to whatever it may later be shown to teach."[50]

---

47. See Paul Helm and Carl R. Trueman, eds., *The Trustworthiness of God: Perspectives on the Nature of Scripture* (Grand Rapids, Mich.: Eerdmans, 2002) and Timothy Ward, *Words of Life: Scripture as the Living and Active Word of God* (Downers Grove, Ill.: InterVarsity, 2009), 132.

48. WCF I.10; LBC I.10.

49. Andreas J. Köstenberger, L. Scott Kellum, and Charles Quarles, *The Lion and the Lamb: New Testament Essentials from the Cradle and the Cross* (Nashville: Broadman, 2007), 16–17.

50. John Stott, *Evangelical Truth: A Personal Plea for Unity, Integrity, and Faithfulness* (Downers Grove, Ill.: InterVarsity, 1999), 73–74.

Three Test Cases

In accordance with the goals of this volume, what follows is a brief examination of several texts that demonstrate how conceptions of the nature of God, hermeneutics, and the practice of exegesis all impact how the texts are interpreted.

1. Historical Accuracy: The Fall of Jericho (Josh. 6)

Archaeology has always been a battleground in debates about the historicity of the Old Testament. Indeed, experts debate whether we should even use the name "biblical archaeology," and many prefer instead the much less freighted designation "Syro-Palestinian archaeology."[51] On the matter of archaeological excavations of the city of Jericho and their bearing upon the story in Joshua 6 about the supernatural sacking of the city by the Israelites, we can begin by noting a few things.

First, dating the destruction of Jericho's City IV has been notoriously difficult. Dates proposed have included 1400 BCE (John Garstang, Bryant Wood), 1550 BCE (Kathleen Kenyon), and 1230 BCE (William Albright, G. E. Wright). Limited excavations by Italian archaeologists in 1997–98 failed to contribute new data to the dating of the destruction of Jericho's Late Bronze Age city.[52]

Second, whereas the biblical picture presents the Israelite tribes bursting into Canaan with the ferocity of an armored cavalry division, there are ancient Near Eastern historians who doubt there ever was a conquest of Canaan by a nomadic tribe of Israelites from Egypt. Issues raised include: (1) No evidence exists to unequivocally link the destruction of the Canaanite cities to the Israelites; (2) Some historians have questioned Israel's ability to successfully assault well-defended city-states in such a short time span; (3) Some historians question why, since Egypt controlled and garrisoned troops in Canaan during

---

51. William G. Dever, "Retrospects and Prospects in Biblical and Syro-Palestinian Archaeology," *Biblical Archaeologist* 45 (1982): 103–4.

52. J. Garstang and J. B. E. Garstang, *The Story of Jericho*, 2nd ed. (London: Marshall, Morgan, & Scott, 1948); K. M. Kenyon, "Jericho," in *New Encyclopedia of Archaeological Excavations in the Holy Land*, ed. E. Stern (New York: Simon & Schuster, 1993), 2:679–80; Bryan Wood, "Did the Israelites Conquer Jericho?" *BAR* 16 (March-April 1990): 45–48; G. Ernest Wright, *An Introduction to Biblical Archaeology* (London: Duckworth & Co., 1960), 44–52.

the Late Bronze Age (1500–1200 BCE), no Israelite activity is mentioned in extant Egyptian records; (4) There is an expectation that more material evidence would be available if a new people group were to decimate and then inhabit a land; and (5) There are alternatives to a large-scale and violent conquest, including the notion of the Israelites as an entirely indigenous development in Canaan, a gradual and peaceful migration into Canaan, a small-scale conquest, or a combination of these options.[53]

What are we to make of this? In regard to the conquest, a close reading of the biblical text indicates that the scale of this event was probably much smaller than usually imagined. Only the cities of Jericho, Ai, and Hazor were demolished and burned (Josh. 6:24; 8:19–21, 28; 11:11). Many cities were besieged and their populations hit hard, but annihilation and destruction was not the norm. The normal practice was more toward driving out the inhabitants and preserving their cities, minus pagan shrines, for usage (Exod. 23:23–30; Num. 33:50–56; Deut. 6:10–11; 19:1–2). Most probably, the Israelites seized key locations and attacked the inhabitants but did not conquer the region completely (Josh. 13:1; 15:63; 16:10; 17:11, 16).[54] In regard to the destruction of Jericho, we have to accept that we just do not know when City IV was destroyed nor by whom, based on archaeological evidence. Nothing here falsifies the biblical account that it was conquered by the Israelites during the Late Bronze Age, but neither can much evidence for such a conquest be found. As G. E. Wright wrote, "Jericho provides no evidence either for the manner or for the precise date of its fall to the Israelites."[55] The problem is that the location was subject to a long process of erosion, which explains the lack of evidence.[56] The jury will always be out because of our lack of material evidence and because the evidence we have will always be subject to redating and revision. We should heed the words of Dillard and Longman: "Today's archaeology too often becomes tomorrow's footnote about earlier mistaken efforts. One can only hope that further excavation will eventually put

53. James K. Hoffmeier, *The Archaeology of the Bible* (Oxford: Lion, 2008), 66–67.
54. Ibid., 67–68.
55. Wright, *Introduction to Biblical Archaeology*, 48.
56. Gordon Wenham, "History and Old Testament," in *History, Criticism and Faith*, ed. C. Brown (England: IVP, 1976), 60.

the question of date beyond reasonable doubt."[57] As such, it is impossible to tie faith or even nonfaith to archaeological records, since such records are continually subject to scholarly revision.

In any case, the key function of the Jericho story is to mark Israel's transition from wandering in the wilderness to reaching their promised inheritance in the land (Josh. 4:13). The emphasis is on the victory given to the Israelites by God alone (Josh. 5:13–6:5), and Jericho is the only city named in Joshua's recollection of the conquest of the land, highlighting its importance as a memorial of the acts of God in Israel's salvation history (Josh. 24:11). An infallibilist reading of this story will always be interested in its historical reliability, since it narrates an act of God in history; however, the main thrust of the story is God's promise to take his people into the Promised Land, and it's on this point that our faith is said to rest.

2. Intracanonical Accuracy: Discrepant Points in Accounts of Paul's Conversion (Acts 9:7; 22:9)

Without going into the debate about the compatibility of the Paul of the Epistles with the Lucan Paul of Acts,[58] there are details in Luke's own portrayal of Paul that do not always line up. Our example here pertains to what Paul's companions did or did not see and hear during Paul's christophany. In Luke's narrations of Paul's vision of the risen Jesus, Paul's companions heard a sound but did not observe anybody; they saw a light, but not the person whom Paul saw. The details seem a bit hazy as to what Paul's companions did or did not see, probably because the details were hazy in Paul's own mind. In any case, it looks innocuous to me.

I doubt that either Luke or his readers were quite so befuddled with such details, as ancient historians were more concerned with reporting the gist of events than with describing the minutiae with pinpoint precision. Ancient historians were storytellers, not modern journalists, so naturally they were given to creativity in their narratives and filled in the gaps on details where necessary. The function of Scripture

---

57. Raymond B. Dillard and Tremper Longman, *An Introduction to the Old Testament* (Grand Rapids, Mich.: Zondervan, 1984), 111.

58. See Michael B. Thompson, "Paul in the Book of Acts: Differences and Distance," *ExpT* 122.9 (2011): 425–36.

here is to communicate the unexpected and arresting nature of Paul's conversion and calling. What is more, readers should accept that God called Paul to do this new work among the Gentiles. Luke's narration is flexible on the details simply because the genre in which he was writing allowed him to be so without any discredit to his reputation for reliability. The use of such genres in biblical revelation indicates that the truthfulness of revelation is not tied to incidental details.

3. Theological Plurality: The Canaanite Genocide and the Sermon on the Mount (Deut. 20:16 – 17; Matt. 5:43 – 48)

How are we to reconcile the divine command for the Israelites to commit genocide against several Canaanite tribes (Deut. 20:16–17) with Jesus' rigorous demands to love our enemies and to show a scandalous mercy to others (Matt. 5:43–48)?

I have visited the Holocaust Museum in Sydney, Australia, and seen the visual testimony to the genocidal violence perpetrated by a supposedly Christian nation against God's historical covenant people. Years ago, when serving in the Australian Defence Force, I assisted in the debriefing of Australian peacekeepers who served in Rwanda during the intertribal massacres that took place in that country, and the firsthand accounts were terrifying; grown men held back tears as they described the process of counting thousands of corpses spread throughout a valley. How could the God of Jesus allow, let alone command, violence like this against men, women, and children? Part of me thinks that maybe the ancient heretic Marcion was right! Maybe the God of the Old Testament was a mean, wrathful God, and Jesus came to give us a new religion, antithetical to the old one. But then again, I know that Marcion was a fruitcake, and I would be wise not to take him too seriously. Yet I am still in desperate need of some way to resolve the dissonance I feel about an apparent dissociative identity disorder in the divine mind when we juxtapose these two passages.

One strategy would be to point out that God's revelation addresses people in their context and that God's commands often present practical resolutions which, though far from ideal, are nonetheless necessary in the situation. Then, as redemptive history progresses, God reveals more of what he expects of his covenant people, with a view to how things will be at the end of history. For example, it is true to say that Jesus forbids what the Law allows (that is, divorce [Mark 10:2–12]) and allows what the Law forbids (that is, eating unclean foods [Mark 7:1–23]). That is not because God changed his mind on divorce and the food laws but because Jesus reveals God's original intention for humanity—lifelong marriage between man and woman, and Gentiles and Jews united in the family of Abraham. The role of the Mosaic law in redemptive history is a book on its own, but I would be prepared to argue that the Mosaic law was in many ways an interim legal code which, among other things, addressed the hardness of the human heart in marital relationships and enabled Israel to remain separate from the pagan nations of Canaan. This explains why the Law permitted divorce and prohibited certain foods common to Canaanite tribes, and why Jesus could seemingly contravene these commands.

If we apply this model of progressive revelation that supersedes much of the interim legislation, then we can say that the command to commit genocide was a less-than-ideal option but a necessary pathway for the survival of Israel, given the way that tribal and ethnic warfare was conducted in the ancient Near East, and a way to prevent Israel from worshiping pagan deities. However, God's intention was for his *shalom*—his peace—to reign over the earth, and thus in the fuller revelation that we receive in the teachings of Jesus, love for enemies, rather than the destruction of foes, is to be the norm.[59] A commitment to biblical veracity does not entail trying to reconcile irreconcilable propositions about killing your neighbors and simultaneously loving them; instead it requires a recognition of the contingency of divine commands in less-than-ideal situations, and an acknowledgment that some commands are more indicative of God's original and eschatological intentions than others. In other words, while all biblical commands are "true," some commandments are "truer" than others in terms of revealing God's character and eschatological purpose for humanity.

Let us be honest: Old Testament texts on genocide are difficult passages to study, and my fail-safe is to engage in a hermeneutic of trust

---

59. Note too that Jesus' commands have continuity with the Old Testament. Jesus' command for us to love our neighbor is rooted in the Old Testament (Lev. 19:18), and the Mosaic legislation does have laws about the merciful treatment of women taken into captivity after war (Deut. 21:10–14). So we have to take into account both the discontinuity and the continuity between Jesus and the Mosaic law.

because God is faithful to his world and to his Word. I am reminded of Abraham's petition that the Lord would spare Sodom from destruction: "Far be it from you to do such a thing — to kill the righteous with the wicked, treating the righteous and the wicked alike. Far be it from you! Will not the Judge of all the earth do right?" (Gen. 18:25). I trust God, in his infinite sense of right, to do what is just and proper, even when I do not understand it myself. I can speculate on God's reasons for commanding the genocide of the Canaanite tribes and pontificate on why these tribes were somehow deserving of such a punishment. But in the end, judgment is a divine prerogative, and God judges justly. When it comes to ethically difficult texts, we should let our doctrine of God formed out of the wider canonical witness shape our reading.

I am also reminded that God's mercy and grace abound in the Old Testament in his acts of sparing Adam and Eve, saving Noah and his family from the judgment of the flood, calling an undeserving pagan to be father of a new people, redeeming the Israelites from Egypt, and giving his people chance after chance to repent of their evil deeds and return to his covenant love. One of the most repeated refrains in the Old Testament is that God is compassionate and gracious, abounding in love and faithfulness (Exod. 34:6; Num. 14:18; Neh. 9:17; Ps. 86:5, 15; 103:8; Joel 2:13; Jonah 4:2). This is the same God who sent forth his sinless Son to save sinners in the world (John 3:16; Rom. 5:8), and the same God who appoints Jesus as judge for the final day (John 5:22; Acts 17:31; Rom. 2:16; 2 Tim. 4:1). God's plan to repossess the world for himself and to put the world to rights involves a series of redemptive events that reveal both the graciousness and justice of his character. When I feel a dissonance between God's character and his actions, when I doubt his love, then, like the psalmist, "to this I will appeal: ... I will remember the deeds of the LORD" (Ps. 77:10–11). A resolution to our theological dissonance is reached by our hermeneutic of trust and by our remembrance of God's covenantal acts undertaken within the believing community.

Conclusion

The global evangelical churches affirm that the Bible is infallible and authoritative, but we have not normally used the language of "inerrancy." The Bible does not strictly teach its own inerrancy but declares that God's revelation is always true and trustworthy, and this is anchored in the faithfulness of God. What I'm arguing for is not the same as the American inerrancy tradition, but it is hardly a completely different species. I think that the American inerrancy tradition, as expressed in the CSBI, provides a robust affirmation that God's Word is true, but this tradition can be problematic when it meets the specific phenomena of Scripture, and I'd rather not create more problems for myself than I need, either exegetically or apologetically. Furthermore, the CSBI is a mixed blessing. It is a clear statement of Scripture's veracity, but it covertly smuggles in several questionable hermeneutical projects, and its sociological function is to fortify the hegemony of certain leaders and the particular brand of theological conservatism that they represent. In the end, I am partial to the thoughts of the late Donald Bloesch, who thought that *inerrancy* was "not the preferable word," given its baggage and limitations, but maintained that perhaps "it should not be abandoned, for it preserves the nuance of truthfulness and is necessary for a high view of Holy Scripture."[60]

To insist on inerrancy as the singular doctrinal device for global evangelicalism's affirmation of scriptural authority makes about as much sense as insisting that African, Asian, or Australian sports fans abandon their enthusiasm for local sports and start following American football instead. We internationals have our own form of tackle football; it is called rugby. We like it better than American football because American football looks wimpy in comparison. Rugby is an international sport with a world cup, while American football is played by the USA — oh, and Canada. Rugby is continuous, whereas American football has more breaks than a Harley-Davidson motorcycle on Route 66. Rugby was the game played by the great Scottish missionary Eric Liddell, while American football was the game played by O. J. Simpson. I rest my case!

Finally, irrespective of what term we prefer to use — *inerrancy* or *infallibility* — the tirade against God's Word never ceases. Yet despite the barrage of assaults from many quarters, ranging from ancient pagans such as Celsus to modern atheists such as Richard Dawkins, God's Word remains sure and secure. The critics come and go, like chaff in the wind, but the Word of the Lord endures forever. I love how John Clifford put it in his famous poem "The Anvil."

---

60. Bloesch, *Holy Scripture*, 116.

Last eve I passed beside a blacksmith's door
And heard the anvil ring the vesper chime;
When looking in, I saw upon the floor,
Old hammers worn with beating years of time.

"How many anvils have you had," said I,
"To wear and batter these hammers so?"
"Just one," said he; then with a twinkling eye,
"The anvil wears the hammers out, you know."

And so, I thought, the anvil of God's Word,
For ages, skeptic blows have beat upon;
Yet, though the noise of falling blows was heard,
The anvil is unharmed — the hammers gone.

Thanks be to God for his Holy Word, and may it dwell richly in our hearts until the day when God is all in all.

R. ALBERT MOHLER JR.

It falls to me now to write a response to Michael F. Bird, whose chapter I found interesting, clever, and a bit frustrating at times. His essay is interesting in that it raises a host of important and worthy issues. It is clever in that it appeals to an international context but remains solidly situated within English-speaking evangelicalism. It is frustrating because, in the end, I believe that Michael Bird affirms inerrancy but throws some obstacles in the path along the way.

Then again, maybe that is why I enjoyed reading his essay so much. I will classify Bird as a friendly critic, and I think we can benefit from his approach.

At the onset, it is revealing to juxtapose statements from the beginning and the end of Bird's essay. He starts with a clear purpose: "I will endeavor to show that while the American inerrancy tradition possessed a certain utility in the 'Battle for the Bible' in the twentieth century, it is not and should not be a universally prescriptive article of faith for the global evangelical church" (p. 145). But at the end of his essay, Bird agrees with Donald Bloesch and cites him to the effect that, though inerrancy is "not the preferable word," perhaps "it should not be abandoned, for it preserves the nuance of truthfulness and is necessary for a high view of Holy Scripture" (p. 172).

So, Bird begins with concerns that inerrancy is basically an American concept that should not be prescriptive for global evangelicalism, and then ends by agreeing that inerrancy is, nonetheless, necessary for a high view of Scripture. This is a man I can work with. I think his approach corresponds to the experience and thinking of many evangelicals today, and that is made even more evident in the full context of his essay.

Bird does level three charges against inerrancy: it is "essentially modernist in construct, parochially American in context, and occasionally creates more exegetical problems than it solves" (p. 145). Even though he affirms that inerrancy "is largely a positive concept," Bird wants to take American evangelicals to task for their particular use of inerrancy and the Chicago statement's definition of it (p. 145).

In the most passionate section of his essay, Bird claims that global evangelicalism is "none the worse for not having [inerrancy]" and asserts that even American evangelicalism is often not well served by it. He argues that American evangelicalism has attempted to use inerrancy as a doctrinal parameter to protect orthodoxy, that it has failed to do so, and that it has tempted evangelicals to risk the impression that the Bible rather than Christ stands at the heart of the Christian faith.

Those are important concerns to which we will return. But it is better to first address Bird's issues with the Chicago Statement on Biblical Inerrancy because his essay there reveals how much we actually have in common. Bird believes that a commitment to the infallibility and authority of Scripture is more important than a commitment to inerrancy. I agree, as would most, if not all, of the framers of the Chicago statement. The affirmation of inerrancy was never meant to assert or to imply that inerrancy is the most important hallmark of the Bible — not even for American evangelicalism. The inspiration and authority of Scripture are more important issues — *prior* issues. The framers of the Chicago statement did not take up inerrancy because it is the loadstar of all doctrinal disagreements, but because it was being increasingly denied as a description of the Bible's self-witness. It is unfair to accuse the Chicago statement, or its framers, of arguing otherwise.

Once again, though, Bird seems mostly to agree with the substance of inerrancy as a truth claim. He clearly resonates with much of the Chicago statement's actual language, and he especially likes the prefatory emphasis on the "total truth and trustworthiness of Holy Scripture." And so do I. As a matter of fact, I argue in my chapter that truthfulness and trustworthiness are probably the best words in the English language to serve us in this regard. I affirm the effort by Paul Helm and others to assert the total truthfulness and trustworthiness of the Bible as the Word of God. Truthfulness and trustworthiness frame the perfection of the Bible in positive terms — always more easily understood — and they better communicate the personal nature of

God's assurance that the revelation he has given us in the Bible is both true and trustworthy because *he* is true and trustworthy.

But inerrancy becomes necessary when the truthfulness and trustworthiness of the Bible are undermined by the claim that the Bible contains error.

Bird's essay reveals that many of his concerns about inerrancy and the Chicago statement are misplaced, based on an erroneous reading. He asserts that the statement is "freighted with huge and unacknowledged hermeneutical assumptions" (p. 147). (What statement of any merit is not?). But his first example falls flat. Citing the Chicago statement's denial that "scientific hypotheses about earth history may properly be used to overturn the teaching of Scripture on creation and the flood," Bird complains that the statement "seems to commit one to a strict literal hermeneutic that demands a literal seven-day creation and a young earth" (p. 147). The Chicago statement, however, does not demand this commitment. I personally believe in both a seven-day creation and a young earth, as do many evangelicals, but several of the most prominent framers of the Chicago statement did not. And they were known not to have these commitments. So Bird's lengthy and passionate section that frames this concern in detail is actually not germane to the discussion about the Chicago statement. His charge may hit some inerrantists for sure, but not the Chicago statement itself.

Bird also complains that the Chicago statement is too concerned with resolving "alleged errors and discrepancies" in the Bible. He is especially irritated by the statement's reference to those matters that have "not yet been resolved." Bird "suspects" that the Chicago statement's "focus on reconciling the minutia of detail is a dead end" (p. 148).

And yet, once again, I look to Bird's actual argument and find, oddly enough, mostly what you would expect a signer of the Chicago statement to say. Not entirely; he does go too far in suggesting that Matthew and Luke altered the account of the blind man's healing near Jericho. Bird would be wiser, I think, to leave the matter where he started with his principle that it is not necessary to resolve such "incidental details." Bird also argues that the Chicago statement is wrong to imply that we should seek to resolve all differences in detail or to "wait for a day when some bright spark might find a way to resolve the differences" (p. 148). But here as well, I think the framers would agree—I know this American evangelical does.

Reading Michael Bird's essay reminded me of the quip (attributed to both Oscar Wilde and George Bernard Shaw) that the Unites States and Britain are "two nations divided by a common language." I am now tempted to extend that point to Australia. Many of Bird's concerns are just not germane to the Chicago statement itself.

On the three passages we were asked to consider, Bird offers only a very short assessment. Interestingly, this is clearly not where he wants to focus. He states, quite rightly, that the account of Jericho should not be left to the archaeologists. In his words, "it is impossible to tie faith or even non-faith to archaeological records, since such records are subject to scholarly revision" (p. 168). And he is untroubled by the accounts of Paul's conversion in Acts because "the use of such genres in biblical revelation indicates that the truthfulness of revelation is not tied to incidental details" (p. 169).

With reference to the conquest of Canaan, Bird appeals to a model of progressive revelation to walk a careful line that does not invalidate the truthfulness of God's command to kill the Canaanites. He points to the Sermon on the Mount as more revealing of God's ultimate purpose for humanity and urges a "hermeneutic of trust because God is faithful to his world and to his Word" (p. 170). Bird affirms that all biblical commands are true, but he oddly states that some are "truer" than others (p. 170). While I do not think this particular expression is at all helpful, it is a proposal of progressive revelation that could (and should) be made more carefully. In the main, Bird's argument is perfectly consistent with inerrancy—right down to calling Marcion a "fruitcake" (p. 169).

I claim no ability to read another's mind, but it does seem that Bird's essay generally makes the case *for* inerrancy rather than against it. So what is his real concern?

Bird accuses inerrantists of confining divine inspiration to the original autographs of Scripture. But this is not what any inerrantist I know has ever done. The autographs do serve a necessary and logical function, but divine inspiration is certainly not "confined" to the autographs.

Bird accuses the Chicago statement of denying "that there were any contingent circumstances that shaped the development of the

American inerrancy tradition in the modern period" (p. 153) But where, I ask, is that denial? This is an accusation from silence. In that case, the creeds of Nicaea and Chalcedon would also be guilty of denying their historical contingencies. Every creed, confession, and theological statement is written and affirmed within a specific set of historical and cultural circumstances. That is hardly a radical observation. But the usefulness and, more importantly, the truthfulness of any statement is revealed in terms of its content over time and through changing circumstances.

This gets back to Bird's concern that inerrancy is basically a modernist concept. To a certain extent, he is undeniably right. The varieties of error and the conceptions of truth to which B. B. Warfield and Charles Hodge were responding were categorically different from the concerns faced by the patristic and medieval theologians. But, to put it bluntly, modernity happened. And the church had to respond to modernity as it happened, answering the unique questions that modern knowledge and worldviews posed. Of course inerrancy developed out of the modern age with concerns raised by modernist thinkers. And it happened here first, so to speak. It happened in Europe and North America, and Christians in these lands had to respond. I believe that inerrancy is crucial to any faithful response, and I believe that this will remain so wherever modernity arrives.

That takes me to Bird's concern about inerrancy as a form of "theological colonialism" (p. 154). I read his sections on this concern with the greatest interest. My basic response is this: modernity will find you, wherever you are.

I want to learn from Michael Bird and his international context. At the same time, it is hard to read another Christian as representing a truly global context when he speaks English as a native language. Furthermore, the vast majority of sources Bird cites in his chapter (and in his larger written corpus) are from English-speaking evangelicalism, and even from the United States. But he does land some good blows here. In retrospect, the International Council on Biblical Inerrancy was, embarrassingly enough, not very international. Point made. Furthermore, Bird accuses American evangelicalism of sending decidedly mixed signals when the Chicago statement is put alongside "Joel Osteen, Joyce Meyer, and the Left Behind series" (p. 156).

Ouch. (It would be unseemly of me here to point to the same pattern in Australia.)

In the end, Bird states that it is wrong to demand of churches and parachurch organizations all over the world that they add inerrancy to their doctrinal statements or be found unfaithful. But, again, the Chicago statement itself makes no such demand.

Ultimately, I see Michael Bird as a friendly critic of the American inerrancy tradition who ends up where most inerrantists have always been — that is, seeking to state the positive truth about the total truthfulness and trustworthiness of the Bible, but at the same time needing to say that the Bible is, indeed, inerrant. Bird's chapter helped me to see this even more clearly.

RESPONSE TO MICHAEL F. BIRD

PETER ENNS

It's always good to hear Bird's lighthearted but insightful thoughts. Reading his essay was stimulating and refreshing, particularly his assessment of the problematic nature of inerrancy. I share Bird's concern over the American fundamentalist and evangelical preoccupation with inerrancy, and look on with some jealousy that his own experiences have not been burdened with a "penchant to engage in bitter divisions over which nomenclature best suits our theological disposition," as such defensive fence-building tends to "divide believers" and "inhibit Christian witness" (p. 146). At this juncture, though, I might suggest that, although non-American's may be more relaxed about nomenclature, I am not sure they would be as relaxed about the concept behind it when pushed a bit. I see this tension in Bird's own responses to at least two of the passages, that, though as remote from Mohler's treatment as the Fall Classic is to a cricket test match, inerrantist concerns remain for Bird, even if couched in more nuanced phrasings.

Bird's critique of the Chicago statement as "freighted with huge and unacknowledged hermeneutical assumptions," not to mention "notions of truth [that] rely on modern presumptions of precision and exactitude" (p. 147), is spot on, and his extended engagement of that document is lucid. One small—at least at this point—correction on a specific matter: Bird comments on the CSBI's handling of the creation story by remarking, "for *many* biblical scholars, Genesis 1–3 is not a blow-by-blow literal account of creation" (p. 147, my emphasis). Perhaps Bird is hedging so as not to cause unnecessary offense, but his understatement borders on false advertising. To say "many" could leave the impression that there are a good number (just not the majority) who read Genesis 1–3 as a blow-by-blow historical account, thus giving some credibility, if only minimal, to the CSBI's assertion. The truth is *no one*, outside of literalist fundamentalism, reads Genesis 1–3 this way, including nearly every inerrantist evangelical scholar I know. As minor as this may seem, I draw it out to put into even clearer relief than Bird does — namely, that a mistaken genre identification of the biblical creation accounts is the assumed default position of literalist inerrancy and that of the CSBI.

I also appreciate Bird's comments on the problems inherent in harmonization (though hardline inerrantists would make short work of Bird's critique by asserting a priori that the details of the stories *must* harmonize or the Word of God is rendered null and void). It strikes me, though, that focusing on "incidental" and "minor variations of detail" (p. 149) is a relatively easy problem to address within an inerrantist scheme. Bird feels that we should not focus on these harmless incidentals but on "the point of the story" (p. 148) that isn't affected by them. Although we do run into variations that are minor and incidental in the Synoptic Gospels, the synoptic problem on the whole is more pressing and cuts more to the core of the CSBI's shortcomings. The conquest accounts in Joshua and Judges, or the accounts of Judah by the Deuteronomistic Historian and the Chronicler, are not minor variations but significantly different retellings of the past. So rather than posing a solution (minimize details in favor of the overall "point" of the story) that works some of the time, I would rather critique the CSBI for failing to address a problem that is in fact far more serious for its assumptions about the nature of Scripture.

Still, in these matters I am largely supportive of Bird's analysis, as I am in many other issues he raises in his critique of inerrancy, such as the following: "inerrancy," as it is understood in the evangelical and fundamentalists mainstream, has not been the church's doctrine of Scripture through its entire history; Augustine was not an "inerrantist"; we do not (and never will have) the autographs, and even if we did, the discrepancies (the very stuff of the author's works) would remain; biblical books were added to well beyond the time of the purported original author; free citations of the Old Testament by the New Testament writers indicate no pressing concern to preserve original wording; inerrancy as it is used today arose out of a particular philosophical context of the nineteenth century; Bird's chastising of the "theological colonialism" inherent in CSBI and the "theological paternalism" of its promoters (p. 155); inerrancy's function as a political weapon, as a means of enforcing conformity and squelching dialogue. In sum, Bird concludes that the CSBI does not deal seriously (or even knowledgeably) with the diverse historically contextualized phenomena of Scripture or allow those phenomena to affect one's notion of the nature of Scripture. In Bird's view, these shortcomings reflect the relative absence of biblical scholars among the CSBI framers.

I began to have some questions, though, when Bird moved from critique to a positive statement of Scripture, which he then applies to our three passages. Bird prefers the terms "veracity" or "divine truthfulness" (p. 158) to *inerrancy* and cites in support several psalms that speak of God's truthfulness, one from John and another from Revelation. Bird's point, of course, is that "truthfulness" is a biblical concept, whereas inerrancy is not. But as he continued his discussion, I began to wonder how much different in substance is his view from a down-the-middle signer of the CSBI.

I was particularly struck by statements like the following: "God speaks in revelation, and it is true because God identifies with and even invests his own character in his Word. The language of revelation is accommodated to the worldview and expectations of its audience in matters of cosmology and historiography, but the accommodation is never a capitulation to error. God does not speak erroneously, nor does he feed us nuts of truth lodged inside shells of falsehood" (p. 159). This is inerrantist language, even if Bird does not adopt the nomenclature. Furthermore, "true," "error," "erroneously," and 'falsehood" are left floating. I am not sure what Bird means by them—at least at this point. And most important, to say that God accommodates without capitulating to error is a nice idea, but does not discriminate his view from Mohler's or any other literalist/inerrantist. The devil is in the details.

Bird then revisits an earlier point, that a truthful Bible is not hampered by the presence of "bits of Scripture, inconsequential for the most part, that do not agree in their precise details" (p. 160). In my experience, this is part of common American inerrantist rhetoric—claiming a higher level of inerrancy that does not require mathematical precision, as the fundamentalist version does. But an inerrantist's (or "veracitist's") job is hardly done until he or she has left the minor details and moved to the major ones. Inerrancy is not defended by accounting for the presence of relatively harmless discrepancies.

In the quote above, Bird avers that God accommodates to the ancient audience with respect to history and cosmology, though without capitulating to error. Yes, but the manner of accommodation to an ancient audience is not simply a matter of God's being fine with a lack of precision in details. The real challenges to inerrancy—including Bird's "veracitism" (my word)—are considerable matters of substance: myth, alternate and incompatible retellings of the monarchy, etc. Focusing on the details rather than the larger perennial issues—the very ones that deeply challenge notions of truth and error—is playing it safe. In this respect, I don't think Bird's decision to opt for *infallible* as the better term moves us far enough along the path. I agree it is better than *inerrant*, but, since it focuses on "faith and doctrine" (as Bird claims), it simply sidesteps the substantive challenge of history to an inerrantist/infallibilist/veracitist model of Scripture. What would need to be addressed are questions like, "How does Genesis 1–3 accommodate to ancient Near Eastern myth yet still not capitulate to error?" Or, "How are the two widely divergent accounts of David's reign infallible for faith and doctrine?"

When we arrive, then, to Bird's treatment of our three passages, I was beginning to sense that Bird might pull back a bit from where I thought he was going. I was hoping for Bird to drive home the implications of his earlier theoretical critique, but instead I saw more of an apologetic for a view that, if one had not read the first two-thirds of the essay, would be labeled inerrantist, quite at home on American soil, though of a more progressive type than Mohler's. For the most part, whereas I could see Mohler quite unhappy with Bird's critique of inerrancy by which he began his essay, I am not so sure he would be as alarmed by Bird's articulation of his own view of Scripture (see especially his final paragraphs before the three test cases) or by his handling of the passages.

Concerning the fall of Jericho, Bird understates—as does Mohler—when he says that "some" (p. 166) historians doubt that the conquest of Canaan ever happened in a manner resembling the biblical story, thus leaving the impression that there are a good many who think it did. As I mentioned in my response to Mohler on this issue, and above regarding Genesis 1–3, the archaeological data concerning Jericho is no longer seriously debated among noninerrantist archaeologists and historians (for reasons Bird himself outlines). Bird, however, creates the inaccurate impression that the matter of Jericho really is up in the air in the scholarly community. Bird then cites W. F. Albright from 1939 along a few inerrantists who have written on the subject, thus further creating the impression that the question of Jericho is so unclear and the data are so open to scholarly revision that to question its historical value is jumping to unwarranted conclusions. This does not reflect the current state of affairs.

Bird tips his hat to inerrantism, saying historical reliability (not defined) is important, but then turns to focus on the "key function" (p. 168) of the Jericho story, to articulate the faithfulness of God in bringing his people into the land. That moves the issue without handling the problem. In fact, it exacerbates the issue, since even this "key function" presumes Israelites as a people entered the land, which is one of the very issues the archaeological investigation has seriously called into question. Though Bird acknowledges historical problems, he quickly funnels them through trusted sources so he can move to what he sees as the real point. It's like tossing up a baseball in order to hit it, as opposed to facing a real pitcher. Or, to use another American sports analogy (knowing how much Bird likes them), it's fourth and long, and Bird is punting from his end zone.

Concerning Acts 9 and 22, I agree with Bird that these sorts of discrepancies in details are hardly worth fretting about—though for hardline inerrantists they are. But here, too, Bird's dismissal of the discrepancy *because* it is merely one of detail is not satisfying. Bird claims that "ancient historians were more concerned with reporting the gist of events than with describing the minutiae with pinpoint precision" (p. 168). Perhaps, but this way of putting it suggests that Luke was hurriedly knocking out his account of Paul, got some of the details mixed up between chapters 9 and 22, but … whatever. It is still incumbent upon us to try to explain the discrepancy, and in doing so might come to learn that neither an inerrantist nor an infalliblist "the gist of it all is just fine" approach explains the text. (I would add, too, that Bird, like Mohler, seems to think the discrepancy was over what was seen/not seen, when in fact it concerns who heard/did not hear.)

My strongest disagreement with Bird is in his handling of the problem of Canaanite extermination. He carves a path forward by defending the biblical account along the following lines: (1) exterminating the Canaanites was a necessary, practical solution, at an early and provisional stage in redemptive history; (2) the Mosaic law was only an interim legal code designed for the harsh realities of tribal life; (3) though the command to exterminate the Canaanites was "true," God's "truer" ultimate intention was *shalom* for the nations, and Canaanite extermination was an unfortunate but necessary way of getting there; (4) Jesus in Matthew 5:46–48 follows the deeper intention of God in number 3, and hence is not truly in conflict with what God said in Deuteronomy 20:16–18. Bird further contends that we should not ponder the imponderable of why God said what he said, trust that his judgments are always just, keep in mind the larger canonical context, and remember that in the Old Testament, God is plentifully merciful.

I won't respond to each point, as I have addressed these in my essay, but in general I would contend that Bird's path forward falsely minimizes the challenge by either being unnecessarily speculative or too distant from what the texts in question actually say. The provisional nature of the Old Testament does not address why God needs to be provisional in *this* way. The deeper intention of *shalom*, though a popular contention, is not at all obvious in the Old Testament — and hardly a major theme when reading through the Deuteronomistic History. And positing command to exterminate the Canaanites as imponderable does not do justice to the fact that the texts persistently give very clear reasons as to why God says what he says. Reasons for the Canaanite extermination are not a mystery in the Old Testament, which is why the episode creates such a dilemma.

RESPONSE TO MICHAEL F. BIRD

KEVIN J. VANHOOZER

As one who has studied and taught in England and Scotland, respectively, for a dozen years, I am sympathetic to Michael Bird's plaintive minority report. It's true that the doctrine of Scripture feels different in British evangelicalism, and this despite our common language. It is also true that, until recently, UK statements of faith express their views of Scripture in terms other than inerrancy. Does it therefore follow, to cite Bird's title and principal thesis, that inerrancy is "not necessary outside the USA"? Is Bird's thesis about the non-necessity of inerrancy necessarily true?

Necessity is a fascinating category and, as anyone who has read Alvin Plantinga's *The Nature of Necessity* knows, fairly complex.[61] Plantinga develops the notion of "transworld identity" to suggest that a property is necessary only if an entity has that property in *every* possible world. Bird, for his part, simply needs to argue that inerrancy is not intrinsic to evangelical identity in *this*, our actual world. I belabor the point because, in my own essay, I asked whether inerrancy is a uniter or divider of evangelicals (though, truth be told, I wasn't thinking of global evangelicalism: sufficient for the day are the problems closer to home). I presented four possibilities: inerrancy is (a) essential/necessary, (b) inimical/dangerous, (c) incidental, or (d) expedient. Bird ends up choosing (c), though he flirts with (b); my essay makes a case for (d).

I do not wish to exaggerate the differences. There's quite a lot in Bird's essay with which I agree, especially when he sets out his own doctrine of Scripture. For example, we both appeal to God's faithfulness to his word to account for the Bible's truthfulness. This leads me to wonder whether what differences that remain are less substantive than strategic, perhaps even pastoral. At the end of the day, I'm very

---

61. Alvin Plantinga, *The Nature of Necessity* (Oxford: Oxford Univ. Press, 1974).

glad we have his minority/majority world report. As is often the case in discussions of global theology, it is salutary to be reminded that we see through a context dimly (1 Cor. 13:12). North American evangelicals need to get out of their big fat Western ghettoes more often. Bird forces us to confront an important perennial issue: are we genuinely contextualizing the gospel, and biblical truth, or are we forcing our cultural-contextual concerns onto the text?

Bird comes out swinging from his corner Down Under: he acknowledges that while inerrancy possessed "a certain utility" in the twentieth-century "Battle for the Bible," it is not something to which the global evangelical church should be required to subscribe: "the American inerrancy tradition, though largely a positive concept, is essentially modernist in construct, parochially American in context, and occasionally creates more exegetical problems than it solves" (p. 145). "Essentially modernist" hurts as much as "parochially American." The basic problem seems to be that the doctrine of inerrancy was begat at a particular time and place.

I am here inclined to ask, with regard to the genesis of this or any doctrine, "Is there an alternative?" Bird claims to espouse not a view from nowhere but rather one that is "genetically independent of the American inerrancy tradition" (p. 146). His "international" view employs words like *authority* and *infallibility*, and he thinks they work quite well in enabling the church to get on with her mission. It is not necessary, he opines, to use the doctrine of inerrancy "as a kind of fence around evangelical orthodoxy" (p. 146). Doctrinal fences apparently don't make good neighbors, and they "risk making the Bible rather than Christ the central tenet of Christian faith" (p. 146). This is a legitimate concern, to be sure, but the contrast is perhaps overdrawn: many inerrantists take the position they do precisely to preserve the integrity of the prophetic and apostolic witness to Jesus Christ.

Still, Bird makes an important point. In what is perhaps my favorite line in the essay, he says: "The Battle for the Bible was always rigged in favor of modernity, and a better strategy would have been to deconstruct modernity as its philosophical DNA. So we shouldn't anchor the truth of Scripture in our apologetic capabilities to beat the skeptics at their own game" (p. 160). I agree: inerrancy works best not as an apologetic strategy but as part of a dogmatic description of the

Bible's ontology (i.e., its properties as the Word of God). The point in confessing the Bible's entire truthfulness is not to encourage us to lord it over scientists but rather to trust God's Word to the limit, even when what is said is difficult.

Bird prefers the term *infallibility* to inerrancy and cites article 2 of the Lausanne Covenant, according to which Scripture is "without error in all that it affirms." Yes, the term *inerrant* is missing, but the basic *concept* is front and center. Bird says that *infallibility* has a soteric focus (as opposed to *inerrancy*'s scientific preoccupation): God did not give us a handbook on astronomy but a map that leads us (infallibly!) to Jesus Christ. Bird rightly reminds us of the essentially redemptive purpose of Scripture, and of revelation more generally.

How significant is the difference between inerrantists and infallibilists?[62] I personally prefer the term *infallibility* (when I get to define it) because it suggests that the Bible does not fail to achieve the purpose for which God has given it, whether that purpose is asserting, promising, commanding, exhorting, praising, etc. On this view, inerrancy is a subset of infallibility: the Bible is inerrant because its assertions are infallible.[63] I recognize that my use of the term *infallible* is different from Bird's, possibly even idiosyncratic. The problem, however, is that many people in my context (North American evangelicalism) use the term *infallibility* as a contrast term to *inerrancy*, meaning something like "true in matters of faith and practice." In other words, in my context, *infallibility* often means "limited inerrancy" (i.e., limited to matters concerning God and salvation).

It is not necessary to insist that everyone use words in exactly the same way I do; however, it is necessary to keep track of the various ways in which people use terms if meaning is use, and if we are to avoid serious misunderstandings. It is one thing to clarify terms, quite another to get caught up in "disputes about words" (1 Tim. 6:4). Paul

---

62. Cf. J. I. Packer: "Inerrancy and infallibility thus become synonyms, differing only in nuance and tone.... Neither word need be used; both may be used to advantage" (from lectures in systematic theology at Regent College, cited in Alister McGrath, *J. I. Packer: A Biography* [Grand Rapids, Mich.: Baker, 1997], 202).

63. Cf. John Frame, who says that *infallible* is the stronger term because it means not simply that there are no errors in the text but that there *can* be no errors. See the helpful discussion in his *The Doctrine of the Word of God* (Phillipsburg, N.J.: P&R Publishing, 2010), 168–69.

is of the opinion that disputing about words "does no good" (2 Tim. 2:14). We are all familiar with discussions which "have gone beyond the stage of a useful exchange of ideas" and are thus unedifying.[64] It may seem at times that the "battle for inerrancy" is such a dispute, especially when it gives way to suspicion and dissension in the church. In this regard, it is ironic that the term *logomachia* (lit. "word battles") is found only in the New Testament, not in secular literature.

Debates about inerrancy are ultimately not about words but about concepts, however, in particular the concept of truth. Bird fears that the North American concept of inerrancy is infected with modernist assumptions (e.g., a literalistic concept of truth). In relation to the Chicago statement's stance toward the Genesis creation narrative, he says "the principle of inerrancy insists equally on *how* it is true" (p. 147). That is not how I read the Chicago statement, nor does J. I. Packer: "The conservative evangelical differs from his liberal brother, not by committing himself to interpret the Bible in a different way, but by committing himself in advance to believe whatever the Bible turns out to be saying."[65] It's worth noting that many of the members of ETS affirm the CSBI but *not* a literal seven-day creation. There are other ways for words to correspond to reality than literalistically (a point my essay tries to hammer home).

I want to devote the rest of my response to Bird's charge that the Chicago statement is an example of American parochialism. I do so with some diffidence, because I agree that, as Bird archly observes, the ICBI "was not an ecumenical council" (p. 155). There was no significant input from Africa or Asia, so the likelihood increases, he avers, that the prevailing philosophical and hermeneutical paradigms of the time and place may have exercised a disproportionate influence on the council. By way of contrast, Bird's international view is informed "by a broad creedal and confessional tradition" (p. 155). Intriguingly, he does not call his view "catholic," but this is really the substance of his critique: Chicago is not sufficiently catholic to be "required believing."

To be sure, Chicago is no Nicaea. However, I argue in my own chapter that the conviction Chicago tries to preserve — that the Bible

---

64. Philip H. Towner, *The Letters to Timothy and Titus* (Grand Rapids, Mich.: Eerdmans, 2006), 395.

65. J. I. Packer, "Questions about IVF," *Breakthrough* 11 (May 1962): 15.

is wholly truthful and trustworthy—is essentially the same as that of the catholic tradition. The "sameness" in question, however, is not that of numerical (*idem*) identity but rather of narrative (*ipse*) identity. In other words, it's the same doctrine the church has always professed about Scripture, only a bit more grown up, as it were: developed. What I want to say about inerrancy to the global evangelical church parallels what I want to say about *homoousios*, the operative concept at the Council of Nicaea: in each case, what is normative for the global church is not the particular term, or even the specific concept, but rather the underlying judgment that the terms and concepts express.

Why should the rest of the world care about North American evangelicalism's doctrinal obsession with inerrancy? First, it may be only a matter of time, given globalization and patterns of higher education, until the rest of the world is faced with similar challenges to biblical authority posed by biblical criticism, naturalistic scientism, and skeptical historicism. If you can find McDonald's or Starbucks in Taiwan and Timbuktu, can Richard Dawkins or Bart Ehrman be far behind? Second, it may be that one way to universal (i.e., catholic) truth is by way of an intensification of particular (i.e., contextual) conversations. We should no more despise or relativize the notion of inerrancy simply because it is culturally situated than we should relativize Newton's Second Law of Motion—F = ma (force = mass × acceleration)—just because he was a seventeenth-century Englishman.

Does the doctrine of inerrancy continue or develop a catholic trajectory in emphasizing the truthfulness of Scripture? Does the CSBI exhibit "sameness in difference"—sameness (in underlying judgment about Scripture's truthfulness) with the catholic tradition despite a certain contextual difference (in the particular concepts used to express the judgment)? I'm sure that Bird does not want to commit the genetic fallacy and claim that the doctrine of inerrancy can't be right *because* it was made in the USA ("can anything good come out of North America?"; cf. John 1:46). Like it or not, the North American church is part of the catholic church, and hence an ingredient in global theology.

Is it possible that the framers of the Chicago statement, despite the culturally conditioned and contingent nature of the North American discussion, have discovered a necessary implication of what Christians elsewhere might one day have to say about Scripture's truth? Is it possible that inerrancy represents a legitimate development of the doctrine of Scripture that arose in response to the needs and challenges of our twentieth-century context? I don't see why not.

At the end of the day, then, it's not as important that Bird uses the term in his particular context as that he not *deny* it. Yet this is not quite right either because, as we see elsewhere in this book, some versions of inerrancy (which I would prefer to call distortions) ought to be repudiated. What I hope Bird would not deny, then, is what I have attempted to spell out in my essay as "well-versed" inerrancy: a well-wrought contextual expression of a catholic truth.

JOHN R. FRANKE

Michael Bird's essay underscores the contextual nature of the American inerrancy tradition. He states that it is "essentially modernist in construct, parochially American in context, and occasionally creates more exegetical problems than it solves" (p. 145). Doubtless, there will be those who dispute the particulars of this statement, but it serves to underscore an important element of all doctrinal assertions and constructions. They are not universal. They are always second-order affirmations that are shaped by the particular social and historical settings in which they are formulated and articulated. Bird offers a compelling account of some of the ways in which the notion of inerrancy formulated in the Chicago Statement on Biblical Inerrancy is reflective of a particularly American set of issues and concerns.

I find Bird particularly compelling when he points out the trend toward theological colonization. He notes that the framers of the CSBI assert that if its statement and particular articulation of total divine inerrancy is not affirmed, then "we are guilty of disregarding Scripture and bring grave consequences to the church" (p. 154). As he points out, there are thousands of churches around the world that are "both evangelical and orthodox and get on with their ministry without ever having heard of the CSBI and without ever using the word *inerrancy* in their statement of faith" (p. 155). To suggest that these churches are somehow unfaithful to the Bible because of differences on biblical authority or inerrancy is disastrous for the unity of the church.

From my perspective, Scripture itself gives rise to a plurality of approaches to Christian doctrine in general and the doctrine of biblical authority in particular. In addition to the diversity of the biblical witness, differences and plurality in doctrine and teaching are also related to the situation of the interpreters of the Bible. Bird's analysis of the colonialism implied by the language of the CSBI comes into even sharper relief when considered from the perspective of the linguistic and cultural settings that shape all human discourse, including theological. We do not view the world from an objective or neutral vantage point, but instead structure our world through the concepts we bring to it, particularly language. Human languages function as social conventions and symbol systems that attempt to engage and describe the world in a variety of ways that are shaped by the social and historical contexts and perceptions of various communities of discourse. No simple, one-to-one relationship exists between language and the world and, thus, no single linguistic description can serve to provide an objective conception of the world since language structures our perceptions of reality.

In addition, language has multiple functions, and this leads to the important concept of "language games." Rather than functioning in a general and universal fashion, each particular use of language occurs within a separate and apparently self-contained system, complete with its own rules. Similar to playing a game, we require an awareness of the operative rules and significance of the terms within the context of the purpose for which we are using language. Each use of language, therefore, comprises a separate language game. And any particular setting or game may have little or nothing to do with the other language games. From this perspective, meaning is not directly related to an external world of facts, though it may appear this way from the inside of a particular linguistic system. Instead, meaning is an internal function of language because the meaning of any statement is dependent on the context or language game in which it appears. In this sense, any sentence may have as many meanings as contexts in which it is used. Further, the development of these language games is a social phenomenon; linguistic systems are the product of social convention. This perspective is in contrast with older conceptions that viewed language as a natural phenomenon that developed according to fixed and discoverable laws.

Viewing language in this fashion presumes that it does not have its genesis in the individual mind grasping a truth or fact about the world and then expressing it in statements. Rather, language is a social phenomenon, and any statement acquires its meaning within the process of social interaction. In this social process of world construction and identity formation, language provides the structure of our particular and collective experience, perspective, and understanding. We learn to use language and make sense of it in the context of our participation in a community of users that are bound together through common social conventions and rules of practice. Since language is a socially constructed human product forged in the context of ongoing interactions, conversations, and engagements, our words and linguistic conventions do not have timeless and fixed meanings that are independent from their particular usages in human communities and traditions.

From this perspective, the CSBI is reflective of a particular language game and, therefore, cannot be imposed on other communities that do not participate in that game. Indeed, no such statement can truly serve in a universal fashion. This is what it means to say that all such statements are local and contextual. This is true even of ecumenical statements that are drafted by a representative group of members from the broader church. However, as Bird points out, the International Council on Biblical Inerrancy "was not an ecumenical council with representatives from near and far, representing all traditions, bringing collective wisdom to bear on the doctrine of Scripture." He also makes the humorous but pointed observation that the international council "was international to the same extent that the winners of the World Series or the Super Bowl are 'world' champions." There are no voices from Africa, Asia, or South America that had "any real input into the formulation of the CSBI" (p. 155).

To assert that such a statement must be affirmed by the whole church if it is not to be guilty of disregarding Scripture is the height of cultural imperialism. Bird is quite right to assert that the CSBI is problematic for evangelicals outside of the American context who make up the majority of the global evangelical church. But it is also a problem for evangelicalism in the USA. The ICBI was not representative of North American evangelicalism as a whole, but rather a particular segment of that constituency, and the CSBI never spoke for the North American evangelical community even at its inception. There have always been large numbers of self-identified evangelicals who did not share its convictions. With large and growing numbers of immigrant and ethnic communities that identify as evangelical, the current distance between the CSBI and the broader evangelical community is greater still. For some, the tendency of a particular group of evangelicals, dominated by a particular ethnic and cultural perspective, to make definitive claims and then assert that they should be embraced as authoritative for all evangelicals is an example of the cultural captivity of the hegemonic expressions of evangelicalism.

Indeed, it is difficult to attend a meeting of the Evangelical Theological Society and not be struck by what an overwhelmingly white and male group it is. Can it really be said to be reflective of the ethnic, racial, and gender diversity that make up the population of American evangelicalism? Even this current volume, with its worthy goal of highlighting the diversity of opinion on inerrancy and sparking conversation about differences, is still locked into a particular set of traditions and assumptions about inerrancy because of the cultural location of its contributors. As one of my Facebook friends suggested, they should call the book, "Five White Guys Talk about Inerrancy." Clearly this is a conversation that is reflective of only one particular language game and set of cultural assumptions and meanings. This does not mean it is not an important and worthwhile conversation, particularly for people who are a part of the language game we share. But it does mean that we should not overestimate its significance and authority for global Christianity.

Bird's warning about the trend to colonialism is coupled with an invitation to consider alternative expressions of biblical authority that have emerged from global evangelicalism but do not employ the term inerrancy. As he says, while these reflect positions that are different from the American tradition, they do not represent "a completely different species" and that to insist on the adoption of inerrancy "as the singular doctrinal device for global evangelicalism's affirmation of scriptural authority makes about as much sense as insisting that African, Asian, or Australian sports fans abandon their enthusiasm for local sports and start following American football instead" (p. 172).

The plurality of Scripture leads to the conclusion that there will not be a single statement of biblical authority that will be able to do justice to the full scope of the biblical witness. We need a variety of formulations that allow the diverse witness of the different communities, cultures, and language games that make up the body of Christ to flourish. Such flourishing is hindered by the demand that only one approach be viewed as normative. I remember listening to a theological commentator say that it seemed like many evangelicals practiced theology in the following way: They come upon the great forest of the Christian tradition, with its complex and richly developed ecosystem. They start moving from tree to tree with the Bible in hand and ask if each tree represents faithful biblical teaching. If not, they tear it down and rip up its roots to ensure that nothing grows on that spot ever again, and then move on to the next tree. At the conclusion of their work, they had razed the entire forest, except for one solitary tree. They stood back, admired their work, and said, "Behold the beauty of biblical Christianity!"

In order for the vision of healthy and diverse evangelical witness to grow and flourish, a particular challenge must be embraced by those who represent the hegemonic forms of theology that have served to marginalize alternative evangelical voices in the church as well as in the schools and seminaries where so many traditional Christian leaders are trained. We must be willing to subject the dominant theological traditions and intellectual assumptions of the North American evangelical church to critical scrutiny and intentionally decenter them in relation to other voices and traditions. We must be willing to give up the assumption of self-supposed theological and intellectual supremacy and be prepared to listen rather than to speak. In so doing we will be in a position to receive the larger witness of the church and be liberated from the cultural imperialism that has served to deafen us to the voices of so many and blind us to the work of God.

While this task will be difficult and often painful to those of us who have been formed and privileged by the dominant traditions of evangelicalism, such a process is necessary for the witness of the church to the character of God and the gospel of Jesus Christ. Thus, for the sake of the gospel and the community that is called to bear living witness to it, we must in humility consider the interests and concerns of others before our own in keeping with the example of the Lord of the church, "Who, being in very nature God, did not consider equality with God something to be grasped, but made himself nothing, taking the very nature of a servant" (Phil. 2:6–7).

PERSPECTIVES ON RENEWING AND RECASTING INERRANCY FOR TODAY

AUGUSTINIAN INERRANCY: LITERARY MEANING, LITERAL TRUTH, AND LITERATE INTERPRETATION IN THE ECONOMY OF BIBLICAL DISCOURSE

KEVIN J. VANHOOZER

Introduction: "It Is a Truth ..."

"It is a truth universally acknowledged, that a single man in possession of a good fortune, must be in want of a wife." Jane Austen could not in 1813 have foreseen the dramatic social changes that have led, in our day, to cohabitation, prenuptial agreements, and female CEOs. Despite its grand claim, therefore, the contemporary reader is hard-pressed to say that the opening line of *Pride and Prejudice*, though justly famous, is also an inerrant statement, which we can provisionally define as a proposition that is unfailingly true.[1] Austen writes prose divinely, but we must not confuse her words with God's. What is the literary meaning, literal truth, and literate interpretation of this first line? What is Austen doing with her words? Is she affirming the truth "that a single man ...," or is she speaking ironically? When we take context (that is, the rest of the novel) into consideration, what she really means is that a single *woman* must be in want of a rich husband—a quite different proposition.

---

1. A proposition is the content of a communicative act. Coming to appreciate both the distinction and the relation between sentences and propositions will prove crucial to my account.

Scripture nowhere says of anything, "It is a truth universally acknowledged," though its wisdom literature comes close. The book of Proverbs contains parental advice to a son, and many commentators suppose that the son in question—a man born to be king—is indeed in possession of a fortune, in want and in search of a wife. Is there an overarching "message" in Proverbs—"The fear of the LORD is the beginning of knowledge" (Prov. 1:7), or perhaps a moral variation on Newton's third law of motion: "For every action there is a happy or unhappy consequence"—or is each single proverb an individual pearl on a proverbial necklace? Is it a truth universally acknowledged that "those who work their land will have abundant food" (Prov. 12:11)—even during droughts?

Jesus spoke in proverbs too, though his favorite mode of teaching was the parable. What happens in Jesus' stories, unlike in Austen's novels, is anything but truth universally acknowledged. Jesus' stories contain shocking subversive developments that go *against* the status quo. Is it a truth, universally acknowledged or not, that a father will always welcome home a son who has squandered his inheritance (Luke 15:11–32)? What *kind* of truth is Jesus teaching (that is, *about what* and *in what way* is he communicating truth)? How is Jesus able to teach truth about the kingdom of God by means of metaphors and stories? Is Jesus teaching a single proposition in each parable or several? Similar questions pertain to the Gospels—which Martin Kähler famously calls "passion narratives with long introductions." Is Jesus' passion narrative true in the same way that proverbs, parables, and *Pride and Prejudice* are true, or is biblical truth always and everywhere a matter of historical fact?

The doctrine of inerrancy must be *well-versed* because the textual truth of Scripture is comprised of language and literature. Well-versed inerrancy is alert to the importance of rhetoric as well as logic. Poorly versed accounts of inerrancy—accounts that fail to address the nature of language, literature, and literacy—do not ultimately help the cause of biblical authority, and may in fact constrict it.[2]

---

2. John Stott says that one reason why inerrancy makes him uncomfortable is because God's revelation in Scripture is so rich "that it cannot be reduced to a string of propositions which invites the label *truth* or *error*" (*Evangelical Truth: A Personal Plea for Unity, Integrity, and Faithfulness*, rev. ed. [Downers Grove, Ill.: InterVarsity, 2003], 61). He also worries that inerrancy seems "to make us excessively defensive in relation to apparent discrepancies" instead of encouraging us to search the Scriptures to grow in grace and knowledge of God (Ibid.).

Inerrancy and Evangelical Christianity: The State of the Question

Evangelicalism, as a renewal movement at the heart of Protestant Christianity, affirms Scripture's supreme authority over belief and life. Such "biblicism" has long been thought to be a distinguishing feature of evangelicalism.[3] However, evangelicals have come to understand biblical authority in two contrasting ways, with some emphasizing Scripture's authority for faith and practice alone ("infallibilists"), others its authority over all domains it addresses, including history and science ("inerrantists"). Does the Bible tell us how the heavens go as well as how to go to heaven? Calvin says that if you want to learn about astronomy, you should ask the astronomers, not Moses, since his purpose was not to deliver supernatural information about the movement of planets.[4] Evangelicals disagree about the *extent* of the Bible's authoritative *domain*, with infallibilists limiting it to "religious" matters, and inerrantists expanding it indefinitely.[5] The critical question at present is whether inerrancy is a divisive distraction or an essential feature, perhaps even the rallying cry, of evangelical biblicism.[6]

What Is Inerrancy For (and How Important Is It)?

Inerrancy is not the issue that separates the sheep from the goats; inerrantists are not necessarily "truthier than thou." The doctrine of inerrancy is not a blunt instrument with which to bludgeon people who are unable in good conscience to subscribe to the notion. Nor is inerrancy a means of eliminating all biblical difficulties or of ensuring particular biblical interpretations or of proving the Bible to be true. Nor should we use inerrancy to determine in advance what kind of truths we will find in Scripture or to stipulate that what matters most in the Bible is the information it conveys. Inerrancy is neither a hermeneutical shortcut nor a substitute for good exegesis. What, then, is inerrancy good for?

3. See David W. Bebbington, *Evangelicalism in Modern Britain: A History from the 1730s to the 1980s* (London: Unwin Hyman, 1989), 3–19.

4. John Calvin, *Commentary on Genesis* (Grand Rapids, Mich.: Baker, 1981), 1:86.

5. Michael Rea suggests that Scripture has authority over "the domain defined by the text itself" ("Authority and Truth," in D. A. Carson, ed., *The Scripture Project*, 2 vols. [Grand Rapids, Mich.: Eerdmans, forthcoming]).

6. See John D. Woodbridge, "Evangelical Self-Identity and the Doctrine of Biblical Inerrancy," in Andreas J. Köstenberger and Robert W. Yarbrough, eds., *Understanding the Times: New Testament Studies in the 21st Century* (Wheaton, Ill.: Crossway, 2011), 104–38.

God's Word will accomplish the purpose for which it has been sent (Isa. 55:11). It follows that the Bible is authoritative over any domain God addresses. Inerrancy points out how the efficacy of God's Word works out with regard to assertions in light of divine omiscience. To anticipate: inerrancy means that *God's authoritative Word is wholly true and trustworthy in everything it claims about what was, what is, and what will be.* While inerrancy is not a full-orbed hermeneutic, it does give believers confidence that Scripture's teaching is ultimately unified and coherent. God does not contradict himself, despite surface textual appearances to the contrary (Isa. 45:19). If exegesis without presuppositions is not possible, then inerrancy is one of the right presuppositions, enabling us to name what some see as errors for what they are: not errors but difficulties.

The Bible contains difficulties — *this* is a truth universally acknowledged. Honesty compels us to acknowledge it; integrity compels us not to skim over it. Some of these difficulties may be quickly dispatched; others require prayer and fasting. In any case, difficulty is the operative concept, and George Steiner helpfully distinguishes three kinds.[7] Looking things up can resolve *contingent* difficulties. *Modal* difficulties have to do not with surface infelicities (that is, there is nothing to look up) but with the reader's inability to relate to the text's overall style and subject matter. *Tactical* difficulties arise from the author's willful intention to be ambiguous or obscure, perhaps to spur the reader to think further and read again.

Many contingent difficulties in Scripture have now been resolved thanks to discoveries in archaeology. Nevertheless, there are still some difficulties that we do not yet know how to resolve. Steiner's modal difficulties are often *moral* or *spiritual* difficulties, offenses not merely to reason but to the hardened human heart. And, of course, a poet's tactics are child's play in comparison with those of the divine rhetor. Inerrancy does not make the difficulties go away. Rather it expresses faith's conviction that, to use Shakespeare's phrase, "the truth will out,"[8] and this gives us a reason to endure critical questioning, to continue trusting each and every part of God's Word, and humbly yet

---

7. George Steiner, "On Difficulty," in *On Difficulty and Other Essays* (Oxford: Oxford Univ. Press, 1978), 18–47.

8. *Merchant of Venice*, act 2, scene 2.

boldly to read again. The purpose of inerrancy is to cultivate readers who confront biblical difficulties as did Augustine: "And if in these writings I am perplexed by anything which appears to me opposed to truth, I do not hesitate to suppose that either the manuscript is faulty, or the translator has not caught the meaning of what was said, or I myself have failed to understand."[9] Difficulties are not necessarily indications of the dark side of Scripture's moon, only spots in its sun.[10]

Is inerrancy a uniter or a divider with respect to the evangelical movement? There seem to be three possibilities: (1) inerrancy is *essential* for the unity and integrity of evangelicalism; (2) inerrancy is *inimical* to the unity and integrity of evangelicalism; (3) inerrancy is *incidental* to the unity and integrity of evangelicalism, a matter of indifference.

Stephen Holmes concedes that it is technically correct to say that church tradition affirmed the truth of Scripture's propositions, but "this is not an especially interesting or important claim."[11] Even Warfield would not say that inerrancy is the essence of Christianity. In other words, inerrancy is not a doctrine of first dogmatic rank — a doctrine on which the gospel stands or falls — as is the doctrine of the Trinity. On the other hand, a high view of biblical authority that affirms its entire trustworthiness is necessary to preserve the integrity of the gospel, and other candidate terms (for example, *infallibility*) that have sought to capture this notion have become diluted over time. So while inerrancy is clearly not part of the *substance* of the gospel (union and communion with Christ), it is connected to the *proclamation* of the gospel: "Specifically, it is an outworking of the *trustworthiness* of Scripture."[12] Still, inerrancy pertains directly to assertions only, not to the biblical commands, promises, warnings, and so on. We would therefore be unwise to collapse everything we want to say about biblical authority into the nutshell of inerrancy. The term *infallible* — in the sense of "not liable to fail" — remains useful as the broader term

---

9. Augustine, *Letter to Jerome*, 82.3.

10. Contra Kenton L. Sparks, *Sacred Word, Broken Word: Biblical Authority and the Dark Side of Scripture* (Grand Rapids, Mich.: Eerdmans, 2012).

11. Stephen R. Holmes, "Evangelical Doctrines of Scripture in Transatlantic Perspective," *Evangelical Quarterly* 81.1 (2009), 62.

12. Timothy Ward, *Words of Life: Scripture as the Living and Active Word of God* (Downers Grove, Ill.: InterVarsity, 2009), 130.

204 • FIVE VIEWS ON BIBLICAL INERRANCY

for biblical authority, with *inerrancy* a vital subset (that is, not liable to fail *in its assertions*).[13]

Inerrancy is neither inimical nor incidental to the present and future of evangelicalism. To say it is essential is to go too far, though it is a natural outworking of what is essential (authority), and thus a mark of a person who is *consistently* evangelical. I agree with Packer: inerrancy "ought always to be held as an article of faith not capable of demonstrative proof but entailed by dominical and apostolic teaching about the nature of Scripture."[14] Perhaps, in order to be at peace with as many evangelicals as possible, we could agree that inerrancy, if not *essential*, is nevertheless *expedient* (there was a fourth possibility after all!). Even the faculty of Fuller Theological Seminary, which dropped the phrase "free from error in the whole and in the part" from their doctrinal statement in 1971 in favor of "infallible rule of faith and practice," appears ready to use the term again if *properly* defined: "Where inerrancy refers to what the Holy Spirit is saying to the churches through the biblical writers, we support its use."[15] The problem, however, is that there are various definitions, and caricatures, in circulation. What the evangelical world needs now is an account of "well-versed" inerrancy.

Why "Well-Versed"?

Accounts of inerrancy are well-versed, first, when they understand "the way the words go."[16] Well-versed inerrancy acknowledges that biblical truth involves form as well as content. Well-versed inerrancy thus takes account of the importance of rhetoric as well as logic for "rightly handling *[orthotomeo]* the word of truth" (2 Tim. 2:15 ESV). To be well-versed is to have a *literate* understanding of the *literal* sense. The early Christians had "an addiction to literacy."[17] My primary concern

---

13. Ward views inerrancy as a true description of the Bible, but not in the top rank of attributes inasmuch as it derives from inspiration (Ibid.).

14. J. I. Packer, "Upholding the Unity of Scripture Today," in *Honouring the Written Word of God*, Collected Shorter Writings of J. I. Packer, vol. 3 (Vancouver: Regent College Publishing, 2008), 141.

15. Fuller Theological Seminary, "What We Believe and Teach," *http://documents.fuller.edu/provost/aboutfuller/believe_teach.asp* (April 12, 2013).

16. Eugene Rogers's paraphrase of Thomas Aquinas's description of the literal sense ("How the Virtues of the Interpreter Presuppose and Perfect Hermeneutics," *Journal of Religion* 76 1996. , 64–81).

17. William A. Graham, *Beyond the Written Word: Oral Aspects in the History of Religion* (Cambridge: Cambridge Univ. Press, 1987), 123.

about inerrancy today is that too many contemporary readers lack the literacy needed for understanding the way the words go, or for rightly handling the word of truth. Biblical inerrancy in the context of biblical illiteracy makes for a *dangerous* proposition.

Second, and more important, a well-versed doctrine of inerrancy gives priority to the Bible's own teaching about God, language, and truth. "Well-versed" thus stands in for "the whole counsel of God" (Acts 20:27 ESV)—the overarching story line of the Bible that features the economic Trinity (that is, the words and acts of God in history). My primary intent is not to react to immediate challenges (many others are doing this, often quite effectively) but rather to probe further into the deep theological roots of the idea of inerrancy, which involves the truthfulness of God and God's relationship to Scripture—the economy of truth and triune rhetoric.

Inerrancy is not a speculative postulate but an inference from God's self-communication in word and deed. It is always a temptation to assume that we know what God is like simply by unpacking the concept of "infinitely perfect being." Elsewhere I have cautioned against "perfect being" theology, not least because God's revelation in Christ has confounded the wisdom of this world.[18] We must make every effort to avoid identifying God with *our* ideas of Perfect Being, and inerrancy with *our* ideas of what a Perfect Book must be. I want to distinguish, following Luther, an "inerrancy of glory" (that is, a natural theology of inerrancy derived from our culturally conditioned concept of perfection) from an "inerrancy of the cross" (that is, a revealed theology of inerrancy derived from the canonically conditioned concept of perfection). A well-versed doctrine of inerrancy that takes its bearings from Scripture understands truth not merely in terms of the philosopher's idea of correspondence but, biblically first and theologically foremost, in terms of covenantal faithfulness and testimonial endurance. God's truth endures and hence proves itself over time, but not without opposition from critics or suffering on the part of its witnesses.

Scripture's truth does not depend on interpreters acknowledging it as such. The reality of God, the world, and ourselves is what it is independently of our thoughts and words about it. Nevertheless, only

18. See my *Remythologizing Theology: Divine Action, Passion, and Authorship* (Cambridge: Cambridge Univ. Press, 2010), 94–98.

readers born from above, by the Holy Spirit, can be "well-versed" in the dual sense in which I am using the term: grammatical-rhetorical and biblical-theological. A well-versed approach to inerrancy is *Augustinian* ("faith seeking understanding") and *sapiential* in orientation, for it sees truth not simply as information to be processed but as life-giving wisdom: "the truth will set you free" (John 8:32).

Is the Chicago Statement Well-Versed?

The Chicago Statement on Biblical Inerrancy was agreed upon in 1978 by a coalition of some three hundred evangelical scholars and leaders representing a variety of constituencies. Can anything good come out of the 1970s?

It is unfair to hold the statement itself responsible for the less than edifying use that others have made of it. The preface alone belies the objection that inerrancy is a distraction from more important Christian concerns, by emphasizing, in a spirit of humble conviction, the importance of biblical authority for Christian faith and discipleship and by acknowledging that those who deny inerrancy may still be evangelical (albeit less consistently so). As to the short statement, it does a fine job in locating the doctrine of Scripture in the doctrine of the triune God, thereby keeping it theological.[19]

In asking whether the Chicago statement is well-versed, I have four major concerns: (1) whether its definition of inerrancy is clear; (2) whether it gives primacy to a biblical-theological rather than a philosophical understanding of truth; (3) whether it is sufficiently attentive to the nature and function of language and literature; (4) whether it produced a theological novelty.

The Definition of Inerrancy

"People surely accept or reject the word [*inerrancy*] without agreeing or even knowing what someone else means by it."[20] This is a shrewd insight. I regularly refuse to say whether I hold to inerrancy until my interlocutor defines the term (or allows me to do so).

---

19. For a further elaboration of this point, see Robert W. Yarbrough, "Inerrancy's Complexities: Grounds for Grace in the Debate," *Presbyterion* 37, no. 2 (2011), 85–100.

20. Paul Feinberg, "The Meaning of Inerrancy," in Norman L. Geisler, ed., *Inerrancy* (Grand Rapids, Mich.: Zondervan, 1980), 293.

Everything hinges on a clear and careful definition, and once this is in hand, many objections will be seen to be attacking either a caricature or a false implication of the doctrine.

The statement's first eleven articles treat biblical inspiration. It is clear that inerrancy is an entailment of divine authorship and that the peculiarities and particularities of human authorship do not call Scripture's truth into question. However, we do not get an explicit definition of inerrancy in any one article, though we are told that Scripture is "true and reliable in all the matters it addresses" (article 11) and "free from falsehood, fraud, or deceit" (article 12). Is the Bible inerrant because it happens not to have erred or because, as God's Word, *it could not have erred*?

Paul Feinberg's celebrated definition gathers up the various threads of the Chicago statement into a conceptual coat of many colors (that is, qualifications): "When all facts are known, the Scripture in their original autographs and properly interpreted will be shown to be wholly true in everything they affirm, whether that has to do with doctrine or morality or with the social, physical, or life sciences."[21] The Chicago statement is also compatible with David Dockery's briefer formula: "The Bible in its original autographs, properly interpreted, will be found to be truthful and faithful in all that it affirms concerning all areas of life, faith, and practice."[22] This definition is attractive because (1) it is a positive statement, (2) it says that the Bible has to be properly interpreted, and (3) it argues that the Bible is true not in everything it mentions but in what it affirms (Dockery calls this critical rather than naive inerrancy).[23]

I propose the following definition: to say that Scripture is inerrant is to confess faith that *the authors speak the truth in all things they affirm (when they make affirmations), and will eventually be seen to have spoken truly (when right readers read rightly).*[24] I shall unpack this definition further below.

---

21. Ibid., 294.

22. David Dockery, "Can Baptists Affirm the Reliability and Authority of the Bible?" *SBC Today* (March 1985), 16.

23. David Dockery, "Variations on Inerrancy," *SBC Today* (May 1986), 10–11.

24. By "right readers," I mean right-hearted and right-minded readers: those who read in faith and humility, not to mention the general prerequisites for literary competence. Strictly speaking, I should also say "as originally given" to specify that I am not claiming that any particular copy or translation is inerrant (and thus I am acknowledging the importance of textual criticism). However, because this qualification does not distinguish my position from others, and because I have nothing else to add to standard evangelical explanations of why it is important, I have seen fit to consign it, not to the margins of my discourse, but to this footnote.

Truth, Language, Literature, and Interpretation

One of the most common objections to the idea of inerrancy is that it is essentially modern, unequally yoking biblical authority to a particular theory of meaning (that is, referential), knowledge (that is, foundational), and truth (that is, correspondence). It is therefore incumbent on the inerrantist to set forth a theological account of meaning and truth. Does the Chicago statement deliver?

The short statement opens powerfully with declarations that God "is Himself Truth and speaks truth only" and that biblical authority is "inescapably impaired" if inerrancy is "made relative to a view of truth contrary to the Bible's own." The terms *true*, *truth*, and *truthfulness* appear again in articles 9, 11, 13, 14, and 17. The CSBI never explicitly defines them but would seem to presuppose a correspondence view of truth. This alone is hardly modernist, for some kind of correspondence is implied in Aristotle's celebrated definition: "To say of what is that it is, and of what is not that it is not, is true."[25] It is perhaps better to think of correspondence as an intuition about the way in which language accords with reality rather than as a full-blown theory, since theories, even about truth, come and go. Whether the correspondence view makes sense of the CSBI's claim that "God ... is himself Truth" or of Jesus' own claim to be "the truth" (John 14:6) is a point to which we shall return in the next section.

Curiously, the CSBI does not explicitly identify what in Scripture are the *bearers* of truth (for example, words, sentences, statements, propositions, or texts). The lack of any mention of "propositions" is, however, a surprising and conspicuous absence, especially given its prominence in subsequent material on inerrancy.

The statement is at its best when it situates its discussion in terms of the Bible and theology, as it does in article 4, which reminds us that God uses language, and neither human finitude nor fallenness render language "inadequate as a vehicle for divine revelation."[26] Article 8

---

25. *Metaphysics*, 1011b25.

26. Some evangelicals radicalize Calvin's notion of accommodation, arguing that God adopts not only the raw communicative materials at hand but also the fallen and therefore errant human perspectives as well. It is not clear, however, why everything humans say should be somehow mistaken or faulty. If the incarnation is the paradigmatic divine accommodation, and if the man Jesus is *impeccable* (incapable of sinning), then we may say that God

similarly affirms the appropriateness of the "distinctive personalities and literary styles" of the human authors as vehicles of revelation, and article 13 stipulates that truthful language need not be technically precise (that way lies modernity) but can include figurative language. And article 18 helpfully reminds us that Scripture employs various literary forms to speak the truth.

We can identify two areas of concern: (1) whether inerrancy pertains to those portions in Scripture (and there are large swaths of them) that are *not* affirmations, and (2) how language and literature "correspond" to reality. As to the first point, J. L. Austin criticized the philosophers of his day (the mid-twentieth century) for their tendency to think that the purpose of language is to "state facts" or to describe "states of affairs." The notion of a speech act is now well established in the literature; we know now that authors do many things with words besides asserting.[27] Language can be used to describe the world and report history, and that it is able to do so is vital to Christian faith, where the main message is indeed historical: "He is risen!" But not all sentences in the Bible state facts. To be sure, we have to assume certain things to be true in order to make sense of other speech acts. Jesus commanded his disciples to fetch a donkey from a nearby village (Matt. 21:2) and in doing so tacitly assumed certain truth conditions (that is, that there was a village with a donkey in it). Yet what Jesus did with words was *command*, not assert.[28]

As to assertions themselves, my opening example of *Pride and Prejudice* reminds us that the relationship of language to reality is not always simple or linear, as if we could draw a straight line between words and things in the world. While the Chicago statement does not officially subscribe to the idea that meaning is reference, it may inadvertently encourage it. Some of its most enthusiastic and vociferous supporters have appealed to the statement as warrant for reading all biblical narrative as if it were a species of the genus *Modern Historiography*. The

---

assumes the createdness but not the fallenness of humanity, in which case inerrancy is the textual counterpart of impeccability.

27. J. L. Austin, *How to Do Things with Words*, 2nd ed. (Cambridge, Mass.: Harvard Univ. Press, 1975).

28. Jesus also predicted that the disciples would find a donkey, and they did (Matt. 21:6), so strictly speaking, we should say that he commanded and asserted. Speakers and authors can do more than one thing at once with their words.

main problem, with the statement and with much twentieth-century philosophy of language, is that it appears to take individual sentences (for example, "The cat is on the mat," "Jesus wept") as paradigmatic illustrations of how words refer to or picture the world. To insist that true statements are always exact representations of extralinguistic reality leads to overly literalistic interpretations.[29] A picture of "literality" holds us (moderns) captive.[30] To say, "I believe in the literal truth of the Bible" may mean something quite different when uttered in the modern world than it did in the time of Augustine.

Truth is indeed about reality, but there is more than one way to render reality in language.[31] We have truth "when what is said is that this is how things are." The map of the Paris métro is about the Paris métro — it says, "This is how the Paris métro is" — but "the way the words go" (if maps could speak!) is not like the way a picture corresponds. The tracks that take tourists to the Eiffel Tower are not really orange, as they are on the map, nor are they only a centimeter wide. Most users understand the convention. Truth is the "fit" between text and reality, between what is written and what is written about, but one can speak about (map) the same terrain in many ways. Some maps highlight topography, others points of scenic interest, and still others buried treasure. A road map need not contradict one that points out historical landmarks or topography. Each type of map reflects a certain interest and highlights what it wants its readers to know. There is no such thing as a universal, all-purpose map. The metaphor of the map reminds us that *there is more than one kind of fit.*[32] I worry that some theories of inerrancy imply that there is only one way to map the world correctly.[33]

---

29. See the helpful critique of the "mental-picture theory" of truth and reference in Vern S. Poythress, *Inerrancy and the Gospels: A God-Centered Approach to the Challenges of Harmonization* (Wheaton, Ill.: Crossway, 2012), chap. 7.

30. See James Barr, "Literality," *Faith and Philosophy* 6 (1989), 412–28.

31. Cf. C. S. Lewis: "Truth is always about something, but reality is that about which truth is." (Lewis, "Myth Became Fact," in *God in the Dock: Essays on Theology and Ethics* [Grand Rapids, Mich.: Eerdmans, 1960], 66.)

32. See my *Drama of Doctrine: A Canonical-Linguistic Approach to Christian Theology* (Louisville: Westminster, 2005), 295–97.

33. Something counts as an "error" only if it fails to make good on its own claim. It is wrong to say that a map (or a text) is an error for not doing something it does not set out to do. Readers should judge a text by its own standards of correctness and precision only. Error is a context-dependent notion. What might count as an error in the context of scientific historiography (or the natural sciences) might not count as an error in the context of less exacting, "ordinary" forms of discourse.

Biblical inerrancy requires biblical literacy. The literate interpreter understands the language and the literary form. The biblical books are like different kinds of maps. To read a biblical map correctly requires a certain familiarity with its conventions: one needs to know its scale, key, and legend. The biblical books speak of how things are, and thus correspond to the eternal reality of God, God's mighty acts, the world of nature and of human beings, but not always in the same way. The literate reader needs to follow the way the biblical words go, especially when they speak of the reality of the past. *Go* is the key term because biblical revelation is indeed progressing, moving with increasing speed to their ultimate referent: what God has done, is doing, and will do in Jesus Christ. The Chicago statement does well to highlight both the progressive nature of the Bible's teaching (article 5) as well as the importance of reading the parts in light of the whole, and the whole in light of the parts (article 6).

In recognizing the importance of reading Scripture according to its own standards of truth, figures of speech, and literary forms, the Chicago statement largely succeeds in following an "inerrancy of the cross" and avoiding an "inerrancy of glory." I resonate with the way the exposition of the statement puts it: "Scripture is inerrant, not in the sense of being absolutely precise by modern standards, but in the sense of making good its claims and achieving that measure of focused truth at which its authors aimed." If inerrancy has acquired a bad name, it is less the fault of the Chicago statement than of the way its proponents deploy the notion in defense of certain literalistic interpretations.[34] I agree with Mark Thompson: "[Inerrancy] should not be judged by the abuse of it or by inadequate explanations."[35] Nor ought we to expect too much of it. Inerrancy alone does not a hermeneutic make: "Inerrancy does not set down any principle that requires certain sections of Scripture to be treated as intended to be either largely historical or largely metaphorical."[36] Stated differently: inerrancy tells you that what is said is true,

---

34. Unfortunately, I am not as enthusiastic about the 1982 Chicago Statement on Biblical Hermeneutics, which to my mind is a retrograde effort because of an overemphasis on historical reference (that is, factuality) and a subsequent lack of emphasis on the literary sense (that is, form).

35. Mark D. Thompson, "Toward a Theological Account of Biblical Inerrancy," in James K. Hoffmeier and Dennis R. Magary, eds., *Do Historical Matters Matter to Faith? A Critical Appraisal of Modern and Postmodern Approaches to Scripture* (Wheaton, Ill.: Crossway, 2012), 72.

36. Ward, *Words of Life*, 134.

but it cannot tell you what is said. Nor, alas, is professing inerrancy sufficient to keep a person orthodox. No such necessary correlation exists between having the right doctrine of Scripture and getting the right doctrine out of Scripture.[37] We must be careful neither to inflate nor deflate inerrancy's role in interpretation.

A Theological Novelty? What Does Chicago Have to Do with Nicaea?

Article 16 states "that the doctrine of inerrancy has been integral to the Church's faith throughout its history." It also denies that inerrancy is "a reactionary position postulated in response to negative higher criticism." To refute the claim that the doctrine of inerrancy was "invented" by nineteenth-century Princeton is also to rebut the objection that inerrancy, along with the Chicago statement, is a provincial and parochial concern. Can it be done?

A full-orbed demonstration of inerrancy's historical pedigree is beyond the scope of the present essay. Others have been there, done that.[38] I propose instead to compare and contrast the Chicago statement to the creedal statement on the Trinity of the Council of Nicaea. To be sure, the framers of the Chicago statement explicitly say in the preface that they do not propose to give the statement "creedal weight," but this is not the salient feature of my comparison. I propose to focus instead on a certain parallel between inerrancy and *homoousios*.

Chicago is not Nicaea: the gospel itself is not directly at stake in inerrancy, nor is it clear whether there was in Chicago a counterpart to Athanasius. I am nevertheless struck by four similarities: (1) the notions of *homoousios* and inerrancy both arose at a time when the truths they express—in the one case, the full deity of the Son, in the other, the divine truth of the Scriptures—were being challenged; (2) both *homoousios* and *inerrancy* are technical terms that have proven to be stumbling blocks to many; (3) neither term is biblical, in the sense of occurring in Scripture; yet (4) both terms reflect underlying biblical convictions or judgments.

---

37. Arthur Carl Piepkorn, "What Does 'Inerrancy' Mean?" *Concordia Theological Monthly* 36, no. 8 (1965), 591.

38. See John D. Woodbridge, *Biblical Authority: A Critique of the Rogers/McKim Proposal* (Grand Rapids, Mich.: Zondervan, 1982).

My thesis, in brief, is this: while the term *inerrant* or the concept of inerrancy may be new, the underlying judgment is not.[39] I owe the concept/judgment distinction to David Yeago, who in a seminal article developed it in connection to Nicaea. Yeago thinks that Paul's language in Philippians 2:6, about the Son's *isos theos* ("equality with God"), is saying the same thing as Nicaea's very different concept *homoousios* ("of the same substance"). It is essential "to distinguish between judgments and the conceptual terms in which those judgments are rendered" so that "the same judgment can be rendered in a variety of conceptual terms."[40] Similarly, I submit that *inerrancy* is saying (nearly) the same thing as John's language in Revelation 21:5 about the Word of God being *pistoi kai alethinoi* ("trustworthy and true").

The doctrine of inerrancy expresses a nonidentical equivalence to what Scripture teaches about itself. The problem with concepts, however, is that they gradually acquire a medley of associations, each of which affects the core meaning. Although it expresses a biblical judgment, the concept of inerrancy also shows signs of its cultural and historical locatedness. The challenge, then, is to affirm the underlying judgment together with the concept of inerrancy, provided that we can free the latter *from* unhelpful cultural accretions in order to free it *for* ministering the whole counsel of God.[41]

Well-Versed Inerrancy: An Augustinian Theology of Veracity

Augustine is the patron saint of well-versed inerrancy because (1) his thinking was thoroughly theological and he judged Scripture to be entirely true and trustworthy, and (2) he was not only familiar with but also proficient in the liberal arts, writing on the nature and interpretation of language, concerned for what he called the literal meaning of Genesis, but also alert and attentive to biblical figures of speech. Augustine would surely agree with the judgment expressed by my definition of inerrancy: *the authors speak the truth in all things they affirm*

39. Augustine believed that the Bible is "without error" *[sine errore]*, but he also interpreted the Bible in ways that go beyond grammatical-historical exegesis.

40. David Yeago, "The New Testament and the Nicene Dogma: A Contribution to the Recovery of Theological Exegesis," in Stephen Fowl, ed., *The Theological Interpretation of Scripture: Classic and Contemporary Readings* (Oxford: Blackwell, 1997), 93.

41. See the helpful survey by Jason S. Sexton, "How Far beyond Chicago? Assessing Recent Attempts to Reframe the Inerrancy Debate," *Themelios* 34, no. 1 (2009), 26–49.

(when they make affirmations), and will eventually be seen to have spoken truly (when right readers read rightly). In this section, I want to frame my definition in biblical and theological terms, attending in particular to divine authorship, the nature of truth, the meaning of the literal sense, and the role of the reader in the economy of interpreting Scripture's divine communication.[42]

God and Truth: Covenantal Correspondence ("Speak the Truth")

Augustine defines truth as "what is"[43] or "that which shows what is."[44] Scripture clearly affirms that God speaks the truth: "Your words are true [*emeth*]" (2 Sam. 7:28 ESV); "Thy word is truth [*aletheia*]" (John 17:17 KJV); "Let God be proved true [*alethes*] [and every man a liar] [*pseustes*]" (Rom. 3:4 NRSV). What kind of truth is in view here? Does the Bible subscribe to a correspondence theory of truth?

Before we answer that (and we will), we must pause to consider, and marvel at, inerrancy's most important presupposition: *God speaks.* Better: God is a communicative agent who employs human language and literature as means of communicative action. Moreover, because the works of the Trinity are undivided [*opera trinitatis ad extra indivisa sunt*], we must ultimately identify God's speaking as *triune discourse*, in which discourse is "something someone says to someone about something in some way for some purpose."[45]

What is language for? Carl Henry was right to protest against the neoorthodox attempt to avoid the cognitive nature of divine revelation. Yet he goes too far in saying of language that "its basic function is cognitive,"[46] that "the minimal unit of meaningful expression is a proposition,"[47] that only propositions can be true or false,[48] and that most of the

---

42. In terms of David Dockery's categories, my well-versed approach is a combination of his third and sixth types, hence a "critically nuanced" inerrancy (see Dockery, "Variations on Inerrancy," 10–11).

43. *Soliloquies*, 2.5.8.

44. *On True Religion*, 36.66.

45. On the various elements of discourse, see my "Apostolic Discourse and Its Developments," in Markus Bockmuehl and Alan J. Torrance, eds., *Scripture's Doctrine and Theology's Bible* (Grand Rapids, Mich.: Baker, 2008), 191–207.

46. Carl F. H. Henry, *God Who Speaks and Shows*, God, Revelation, and Authority, vol. 3 (Waco, Tex.: Word, 1979), 401.

47. Ibid., 453.

48. Ibid., 456.

sentences in Scripture "are historical assertions or explanations of such assertions."[49] Given his view of the nature of language and truth, it is not surprising that he concludes that the Bible is propositional revelation, that is, that the Scriptures "contain a body of divinely given information actually expressed or capable of being expressed in propositions."[50]

In linking biblical authority with propositional revelation, Henry carries on a venerable theological tradition. I do not wish to be heard as affirming anything less, though I do want to say something *more*. While Henry is right to emphasize the cognitive nature of biblical revelation (that is, that it conveys content that can be thought about and assented to), he tends to treat declarative sentences as "the privileged class" of biblical discourse.[51] By way of contrast, the words of Truth incarnate privilege "the poor" (that is, forms of discourse that traditional philosophers and theologians typically neglect): the bulk of Jesus' earthly teaching consists of figures of speech, enigmatic sayings, and parables. To be sure, these forms too are cognitive, though it is harder to draw a straight line between individual sentences and the propositions they convey.

Whereas Henry thinks that the basic function of language is to transfer information, I believe that God gives us language to communicate, which is a broader category: "Language never exists simply to state propositions: its primary role is a means by which one person acts in relation to others."[52] If we attend to all that the Bible depicts God as doing to engage human persons by means of language—if we give a well-versed account—we will see that both God and Scripture do more with propositions than teach or impart information.

Among the various divine speech acts we could consider, the *oath* is particularly important. God makes solemn promises out of words (that is, God commits himself to doing things for others) and seals his commitments with an oath.[53] *God covenants*. A covenant is

49. Ibid.
50. Ibid., 457.
51. For views on propositions in medieval and modern logic and rhetoric, see Gabriel Nuchelmans, *Late-Scholastic and Humanist Theories of the Proposition* (Amsterdam: North-Holland, 1980).
52. Ward, *Words of Life*, 136. See also William Alston, *Illocutionary Acts and Sentence Meaning* (Ithaca: Cornell Univ. Press, 2000), 277–80.
53. See Paul R. Williamson, *Sealed with an Oath: Covenant in God's Unfolding Purpose* (Downers Grove, Ill.: InterVarsity, 2007).

a communicative act that establishes or ratifies a personal relationship and aims at communion: "A *berit* is a relationship involving an oath-bound commitment."[54] All discourse, to the extent that it is a medium of social interaction, has a quasi-covenantal dimension.[55] Language is a divinely ordained institution, a rich and supple medium of communicative action oriented to communion. Of course, as with everything else God created, language too can be corrupted, and the peculiar corruption of language is the lie, leading not to communion but to alienation.

"Let God be proved true" (Rom. 3:4 NRSV). Throughout the Scriptures, God proves himself true by keeping his word. He fulfills his promises; he does what he says. There is thus a *covenantal correspondence*, a faithful fit, between God's words and God's deeds. The Hebrew term that signifies this covenantal correspondence is *emeth*: "to be reliable, trustworthy, *true*." *Emeth* is paired with *hesed* ("steadfast love") in five of its eleven occurrences in the Pentateuch (for example, Ex. 34:6). "Truth" here is a quality not simply of statements but of a person: *faithfulness*.[56] We hear an echo of this in medieval marriage ceremonies, in which a person pledges or swears by his or her *troth* (cf. "betrothed"). The idea is that true words are words that can be relied on, words that provide firm ground on which to stand. Five other instances of *emeth* in the Pentateuch are in the context of a "trial" of truth, that is, determining whether something is the case (for example, Deut. 13:14). Indeed, the criterion for recognizing false prophecy is that the false prophet's words do not come to pass (Deut. 18:22). There is in this case "a fissure between thought and utterance,"[57] a lack of correspondence between what is said and what is, a breaking of the

---

54. Peter J. Gentry and Stephen J. Wellum, *Kingdom through Covenant: A Biblical-Theological Understanding of the Covenants* (Wheaton, Ill.: Crossway, 2012), 132.

55. See further my "From Speech Acts to Scripture Acts: The Covenant of Discourse and the Discourse of the Covenant," in *First Theology: God, Scripture, and Hermeneutics* (Downers Grove, Ill.: InterVarsity, 2002), 127–58.

56. 56. See Dennis T. Olson, "Truth and the Torah: Reflections on Rationality and the Pentateuch," in Alan G. Padgett and Patrick R. Keifert, eds., *But Is It True? The Bible and the Question of Truth* (Grand Rapids, Mich.: Eerdmans, 2006), 16–33, and Roger Nicole, "The Biblical Concept of Truth," in D. A. Carson and John D. Woodbridge, eds., *Scripture and Truth* (Grand Rapids, Mich.: Zondervan, 1983), 287–98.

57. Paul Griffiths, *Lying: An Augustinian Theology of Duplicity* (Grand Rapids, Mich.: Brazos, 2004), 25.

bond that binds true words to the world, and a damnable disruption in the covenant of discourse.[58]

Both the prophets and apostles are divinely commissioned spokesmen charged with putting the word of God into words. God speaks through human authors who nevertheless remain fully human. They speak on Christ's behalf, about Christ, through Christ's Spirit, who guides them in the truth (John 16:13–14). In addition to the other things they do with words, the prophets and apostles are *testifying to Christ* (Luke 24:27). Testifying is a speech act that reports, and thus relates to others, the truth about something. Inerrancy is ultimately a matter of claiming that the biblical testimony is entirely trustworthy and true, and of trusting that it will eventually be seen to be true through enduring the process of critical testing and cross-examination.[59]

Jesus is the truth (John 14:6), God's own Word expressed in time and space in the form of a human being. Jesus is God's own truth claim — but what is it about? Augustine compares the incarnation with the way in which we humans "beget" our thoughts in words. I submit that Jesus is the truth because he is God's true and trustworthy Word and because as God's Word, he corresponds to God himself. The Son is the visible "image of the invisible God" (Col. 1:15), the "exact imprint of God's very being" (Heb. 1:3 NRSV). The Son corresponds to deity in every way except that he is the Son rather than the Father. Jesus is God's promise made good. Jesus is the truth because he is the Word that covenantally corresponds to, faithfully fits, and measures up to the reality of God. *Jesus is the truth because he communicates what*

---

58. See George Steiner, *Real Presences* (Chicago: Univ. of Chicago, 1989). My own view corresponds (!) most closely to minimalist accounts of truth as correspondence as found in William P. Alston, *A Realist Conception of Truth* (Ithaca, N.Y.: Cornell Univ. Press, 1996), 22–26, and David Clark, *To Know and Love God: Method in Theology* (Wheaton, Ill.: Crossway, 2003), 380–82.

59. Testimony features in the Ten Commandments: "You shall not bear false witness" (Ex. 20:16 ESV). Moses's law also requires the testimony of at least two witnesses in trials involving capital punishment (Deut. 17:6; 19:15). John the Baptist "came for testimony *[martyrion]*, to bear witness to the light" (John 1:7 RSV). Jesus' works, the Scriptures, and the voice from heaven all bear witness to who he is (John 5:30–39). The author of the fourth Gospel, who claims to be an eyewitness, explicitly says he is giving testimony about the things that took place in fulfillment of Scripture (John 19:35–36) so that his readers may believe the best of all propositions: *that Jesus is the Christ* (John 20:31). See my "Trials of Truth: Mission, Martyrdom and the Epistemology of the Cross," in *First Theology*, 337–73.

God is.[60] From this particular truth, I derive the following about truth in general: *true words communicate what is.* Words that purport to communicate what is yet fail to do so are false—unreliable, untrustworthy, perhaps even lies. Correspondence is covenantal because "our word is our bond."[61] The lie is a breach of the bond that ties word and world together. It is a sundering of what God originally put together. God cannot lie, and hence neither does Scripture.[62] It remains to be seen, however, just what kind of testimony Scripture gives.

God and Language: Literal Sense and Literary Sensibility ("In All Things They Affirm")

Truth presupposes meaning. To understand what truth a given discourse communicates, we must first understand the type of discourse with which we have to do. A poem harbors truth in a different way than does a physics manual, a narrative history, or a theology textbook. In William Alston's words: "*It is only after the proposition has been assigned that the question of truth value can be raised.*"[63] Truth is always about *what is*, but there are many kinds of reality and many ways of talking about it (for example, to what do metaphors refer?). We must first discern what a passage or a text is *about*, and then ask *how* it is about it. As Aristotle commented, "being may be said in many ways." The same goes for history. The issues are complex, but the following distinctions may help clarify matters.

Critics and commentators only confuse matters when they suggest that inerrantists believe in the literal truth of every word of the Bible. Individual words are neither true nor false, for they do not *assert* anything. To assert something—to say what is the case—is a thing people do by using words. There is a difference between "sentence meaning" and "speaker meaning." It is therefore not enough to speak about the *semantics* of biblical literature (its propositional content, sentence meaning); we must also account for the *pragmatics* (kinds of communicative

60. If time and space permitted, I would reflect on 1 John 5:6–10 to expand on the Spirit's role in the triune economy of testimony.

61. Austin, *How to Do Things with Words*, 10.

62. Mark Thompson rightly identifies God's personal veracity as a pillar of the doctrine of inerrancy ("Toward a Theological Account of Biblical Inerrancy," 83–86).

63. Alston, *A Realist Conception of Truth*, 260 (italics his).

action, speech act meaning). This distinction is particularly important when we try to determine what precisely the authors are affirming (when they are affirming).[64] Well-versed inerrancy here comes into its own by calling attention to Scripture as composed of various kinds of discourse and to the necessity of asking, *what is the author doing in his discourse, and what is the discourse about?* For the proposition on the page (sentence content) may not be the proposition the author is affirming (speech act content).

Proponents of inerrancy must take great care to distinguish the notion of literal truth from a literalism that runs roughshod over the intent of the author and the literary form of the text. Was Jesus *affirming botanic truth* when he called the mustard seed "the smallest of all the seeds" (Mark 4:31 ESV), or was he *drawing an analogy* that his hearers would have understood, in order to communicate a nonbotanical truth? Here we may recall the Chicago statement's call to take account of Scripture's literary forms and to avoid evaluating Scripture with standards of truth "that are alien to its usage or purpose" (articles 18 and 13, respectively).

For the sake of clarification, let us define *literalism* as the view that equates *what is said* (that is, meaning) with *semantic content* (that is, the proposition semantically expressed by the sentence regardless of context).[65] At the limit, literalism runs roughshod over figures of speech and forms of discourse such as irony, in which what one says is often the opposite of what one means.[66] Irony is an especially interesting case study for inerrancy: is the proposition it puts forward as truth the text or the subtext, the sentence meaning or the speaker's meaning? To appreciate the irony in the book of Job or John's gospel, we must do more than read for the semantic content or literalistic sense.[67] We must

---

64. "Every statement accurately corresponds to truth *just as far forth as affirmed*" (A. A. Hodge and Benjamin B. Warfield, *Inspiration* [Grand Rapids, Mich.: Baker, 1979], 29, my emphasis).

65. For a spirited defense of what I am calling literalism, see Herman Cappelen and Ernie Lapore, "A Tall Tale in Defense of Semantic Minimalism and Speech Act Pluralism," in Gerhard Preyer and Georg Peter, eds., *Contextualism in Philosophy: Knowledge, Meaning, and Truth* (Oxford: Clarendon, 2005), 197–219.

66. See further François Recanti, "Literal and Contextualism: Some Varieties," in Preyer and Peter, *Contextualism in Philosophy*, 171–96.

67. E. M. Good, *Irony in the Old Testament*, 2nd ed. (Sheffield: Sheffield Academic Press, 1981); Paul Duke, *Irony in the Fourth Gospel* (Richmond, Va.: John Knox Press, 1985).

specify the author's communicative intent in order rightly to say what he is *doing* with his words. Inerrantists read for the *literal* sense, that is, for the *speech act content* of an author's discourse (in other words, the proposition pragmatically expressed by the sentence in its particular context). We need to know something about both the sentence (semantics) and the speaker's intention (pragmatics) in order rightly to discern the literal sense (that is, what the author is saying in tending to his words in just this way).[68] Only in the context of its particular use can we determine *what is said*.

A well-versed approach to biblical discourse acknowledges that what is said is not always an affirmation. Authors can do many things with words and can affirm things in many ways. Well-versed inerrancy thus takes special care with the qualification "in all things they affirm." Is every passing mention of something an affirmation? According to Alston, an author asserts *p* when he takes responsibility for explicitly presenting *p* in his discourse (that is, by saying in so many words, "*that p*"). Alston too wants to combine semantics and pragmatics, sentence and speaker meaning, and does so by defining sentence meaning as "illocutionary act potential."[69] An illocution refers to what a speaker *does* in speaking (for example, promise, command, assert, and so on). The sentence provides the propositional content that the author then uses to mean something, that is, "to perform *acts* of a certain sort."[70] I propose that we *identify the literal sense with the illocutionary act an author is performing.*[71] In sum: the literal sense of what we say is not the sentence content (the words considered apart from the context of their use) but the speech act content.

"In all things *they* affirm." These words represent an important qualification — or rather *specification* — of my definition of inerrancy. The "they" refers not to sentences but to authors. Consider again Jesus' claim about the mustard seed. The proposition semantically

---

68. Strictly speaking, semantics (the dictionary meaning of words) depends on pragmatics (how speakers *use* words in various contexts). The meaning of a word or a sentence is its capacity to be used to do certain things in communication (Alston, *Illocutionary Acts*, 154).

69. Alston, *Illocutionary Acts*, 160.

70. Ibid., 162.

71. Cf. Thomas Aquinas, who defines the literal sense as "that which the author intends, and the author of Holy Scripture is God" (*Summa theologiae* I.1.10). See Adina Miriam Yoffie, "Biblical Literalism and Scholarship in Protestant Northern Europe, 1630–1700" (unpublished PhD dissertation in history at Harvard University, 2009), chap. 1.

expressed—the claim taken out of the context of Jesus' (and Matthew's) use—is false, prompting this response from the Christian Apologetics and Research Ministry: "No, the mustard seed is not the smallest of all seeds. Jesus was speaking proverbially. That is, he wasn't making a statement of absolute fact but using a proverbial style of communication."[72] In the terms of the present essay, Jesus was not *affirming* as scientific fact the proposition semantically expressed by his sentence. The subject matter of Jesus' authoritative teaching was not mustard seeds but the kingdom of God, and he was communicating truth about the kingdom in terms his audience could understand. Jesus was not making a *literalistic* truth claim (about mustard seeds), but he was speaking the *literal* truth (about the kingdom).[73] This is no game of semantic smoke and mirrors; it is the way linguistic communication works.

What is true of Jesus' teaching applies to all the other forms of biblical discourse as well. In order to know what the biblical authors are affirming, we need to determine the nature of their discourse: what are they talking about and in what way are they talking about it? Warfield puts it well: "No objection is valid which overlooks the prime question: what was the professed or implied purpose of the writer in making this statement?"[74] What complicates matters is that, with a few exceptions, the biblical authors typically write in longer forms of poetry and prose, and to determine what is said in, say, a narrative, we have to do more than consider isolated sentences. For the proposition(s) an author expresses may be a function not of one sentence only but of a whole paragraph, many paragraphs, or perhaps the whole story. That to which we ascribe truth may not be the propositions semantically expressed in serial sentential form but the proposition(s) expressed by the discourse taken as a whole.[75]

---

72. http://carm.org/is-mustard-seed-smallest-of-all-seeds.

73. Hodge and Warfield helpfully distinguish "exactness of statement," which they equate with absolute literalness (my "literalistic"), from accuracy (my "literal"), which is a measure of authorial intent (*Inspiration*, 28–29). Similarly, Reformation commentators trained in the humanist tradition distinguished between *scriptum* and *voluntas*: what was *written* and what was *intended* (Kathy Eden, *Hermeneutics and the Rhetorical Tradition: Chapters in the Ancient Legacy and Its Humanist Reception* [New Haven: Yale Univ. Press, 1997], 6–8).

74. Hodge and Warfield, *Inspiration*, 42.

75. I say *proposition(s)* to leave open the possibility that narratives may convey neither a single macroproposition nor a series of one-per-sentence micropropositions but rather several propositions "nested" at different levels of the discourse (a clarification I owe to Daniel Treier).

The moral of this story is that we have first to discern the literal sense before saying "true or false." And it helps to discern what is being affirmed ("what someone says about something") when we attend to the form of the discourse and literary genre ("in some way"). Moisés Silva identifies a problem with unversed approaches to inerrancy when he notes that traditionally, "grammar books have stopped at the sentence level when describing syntax."[76] The best way to discover what sentences are being used for is to determine the literary form of which they are a part. Stated differently: the literary form is part of the context of use and thus stands at what we could view as the intersection of the semantics and pragmatics of meaning and truth. Interpreters need literary sensibility in order to determine which proposition(s) a discourse explicitly expresses or affirms.

The best biblical examples of sentences that correspond to propositions in a one-to-one relationship are probably the aphorisms in Proverbs and certain doctrinal one-liners from the Epistles and elsewhere (for example, "God is light" [1 John 1:5]). Yet even the book of Proverbs has a distinctive literary form that affects the way we take its propositions: "The biblical books were meant to be read as wholes and that is the way we should read them."[77] "Strong propositionalists" are tone-deaf to everything in Scripture but the truth content conveyed and seem not to feel the difficulty of extracting propositions from complex forms of discourse. Gordon Clark's comment is representative: "Aside from imperative sentences and a few exclamations in the Psalms, the Bible is composed of propositions."[78] Such a view is simply unable to appreciate the significance of, say, the narrative form as anything other than packaging for a series of propositions ("and then, and then, and then"). *Tone-deaf* may be too harsh: strong propositionalists hear the music, but only the melody. They therefore think they have assimilated Beethoven's truth when they can whistle the tune of the Fifth Symphony. Strong propositionalists resemble C. S. Lewis's "unliterary reader," who looks only for the Event: "[Such a

76. Moisés Silva, *God, Language and Scripture: Reading the Bible in the Light of General Linguistics* (Grand Rapids, Mich.: Zondervan, 1990), 118.

77. Ibid., 125.

78. Gordon H. Clark, *Karl Barth's Theological Method* (Nutley, N.J.: Presbyterian & Reformed, 1963), 150.

reader] ignores nearly all that the words before him are *doing*; he wants to know what happened next."[79]

A Rhetoric (and Hermeneutic) of Truth: Inerrancy and Literate Interpretation ("When Right Readers Read Rightly")

Well-versed inerrancy puts a premium on the responsibility of the interpreter to understand the text correctly. The reader is part of the economy of biblical discourse. Is the Bible's truth somehow dependent on the activity of interpreters? Hardly. The Bible teaches truth whether or not its students learn their lesson. Nevertheless, a certain degree of biblical literacy is required for Scripture's truth to be appreciated for what it *is* rather than something else. Scripture ultimately tests us, revealing how "true" (that is, sound) our eyes, ears, and hearts are. Are we the kind of right-minded and right-hearted people who can recognize and receive the truth, not simply bits of information but truth's "robust presence" — the collective testimony of the Scriptures to Jesus Christ?[80]

God's Word can be relied upon to accomplish the purpose for which it has been sent, and when this purpose is *making affirmations*, it does so inerrantly. As we have seen, however, texts can be "about" reality in different ways (there is more than one kind of map), and they can focus on different aspects of reality — from the smallest details to the big picture. To interpret Scripture rightly means recognizing what *kinds* of things the biblical authors are doing with their words. Are we reading history, story, apocalyptic, wisdom, science, or something else? We must not underestimate the importance of rightly determining the literary genre, or the challenge of rightly discerning the proposition(s) a narrative or parable or psalm explicitly presents.

In sum: God's words are wholly reliable; their human interpreters, not so much. God's words do many things, and while their affirmations are critical to Christian faith ("He is risen!"), we must also remember that God uses language to communicate for other purposes

---

79. C. S. Lewis, *An Experiment in Criticism* (Cambridge: Cambridge Univ. Press, 1961), 30, my emphasis.

80. I take the phrase "robust presence" from Kurt Pritzl's "Aristotle's Door," in Pritzl, ed., *Truth: Studies of a Robust Presence* (Washington, D.C.: Catholic Univ. of America Press, 2010), 15–39.

than to transmit information. Finally, we must be realistic about how far inerrancy takes us as interpreters. While inerrantists believe that biblical discourse ultimately coheres, inerrancy itself "does not set down any principle that requires certain sections of Scripture to be treated as intended to be either largely historical or largely metaphorical."[81] Inerrancy is compatible "with widely varying views about what (if any) propositional messages are asserted or conveyed by biblical texts."[82] Truth may be said in many ways, by story and history, direct and indirect teaching, maxims and metaphors. What the authors are doing with their words must be discerned through right biblical interpretation. Inerrancy alone does not a hermeneutic make, as the following case studies will no doubt show.

Well-Versed Inerrancy in the Dock: Three Counts of Aggravated Textual Assault

We turn now to an examination of three challenging case studies, each of which represents, in its own way, a "hard saying" of Scripture, and hence a test for well-versed inerrancy.

The Poetics of Biblical Narrative: Jericho, Joshua 6, and the Question of a Historical "Fall"

How can we hold to the inerrancy of the Bible if the archaeological data contradicts what the text says actually happened? Joshua 6 depicts a key moment in the outworking of God's plan of salvation and is thus an excellent proving ground for would-be biblical interpreters, presenting a number of challenges on the literary, historical, and theological levels. Our primary focus is on the historical level, but as we shall see, this cannot be neatly separated from the other two.

Was there, in fact, a historical fall of Jericho? Many, though not all, scholars believe that the archaeological record is at odds with Joshua's account. One colleague refers to the problem of Israel's entry into Canaan as the "mother of all current debates" in biblical archaeology.[83]

---

81. Ward, *Words of Life*, 134.
82. Rea, "Authority and Truth."
83. John M. Monson, "Enter Joshua: The 'Mother of Current Debates' in Biblical Archaeology," in Hoffmeier and Magary, *Do Historical Matters Matter*, 427–57.

That the issues are complex is no reason not to engage them. Stephen Williams rightly observes, "The historical facticity of the grant of land to an exodus people is a foundational piece of history and grounds the claim of both Testaments to be speaking truly of the God who acts."[84] One proposition that Joshua 6 explicitly affirms, then, is that it is *God* who gives Jericho into Israel's hand (Josh. 6:2). The truth not only of Joshua but also of the divine promise therefore hinges on this being historically the case.

The underlying question concerns the nature of Israel's emergence in Canaan. Archaeologists have gone back and forth on this issue. W. F. Albright proposes a "conquest model" that correlates the Joshua narrative with archaeological evidence for the thirteenth-century destruction of various Canaanite cities.[85] Score one for the inerrantists. The problem, however, is that most contemporary scholars reject Albright's model, not only because new archaeological evidence has come to light but also "because of its literal, simplistic reading of Joshua."[86] Albright's reading was poorly versed; like other literalists, he was too concerned with establishing what happened (the "Event"). There is good textual reason to question his conquest model. In order to do justice to Joshua 6, we need to attend not only to the *story* (what happened, the chronology of events) but also to the *discourse* (how the story is told, what it is about).[87]

Archaeology, like science, can neither confirm nor deny whether God acts, though it can lend credence to whether space-time events happened the way they were reported to have happened. The past leaves material "traces" that, like texts, call for interpretation. Archaeology deals with solid objects, yet it is not a hard but a hermeneutical science, and there is a conflict of interpretation over how to read the evidence. There is evidence at Jericho of collapsed city walls, but the dates do not seem right. There is evidence of grain amidst the burned-out city,

84. J. Gordon McConville and Stephen N. Williams, *Joshua*, The Two Horizons Old Testament Commentary (Grand Rapids, Mich.: Eerdmans, 2010), 209.

85. W. F. Albright, "The Israelite Conquest of Canaan in the Light of Archaeology," *BASOR* 74 (1939), 11–23.

86. K. Lawson Younger, "Early Israel in Recent Biblical Scholarship," in D. Baker and B. T. Arnold, eds., *The Face of Old Testament Studies: A Survey of Contemporary Approaches* (Grand Rapids, Mich.: Baker, 1999), 179.

87. Seymour Chatman, *Story and Discourse: Narrative Structure in Fiction and Film* (Ithaca, N.Y.: Cornell Univ. Press, 1978).

which suggests to some that the city fell because of something other than a lengthy siege. Some of the fiercest debate concerns the dating of pottery. The long and short of it is that the evidence, taken on its own material terms, is inconclusive.[88] Given the complexity of the evidence, scholars should use extreme caution before pronouncing the text to be in error.[89] It is also debatable how wise it is to engage in archaeological apologetics given the underdetermined nature of the data. There is no need to ask, as one scholar does tongue-in-cheek, "If Jericho was not razed, is our faith in vain?"[90]

The prior question for a well-versed approach to inerrancy must rather be, *what is the author of Joshua saying/doing with his words?* Specifically, is the main thrust of Joshua to give the kind of factual reporting that Americans have come to expect of newspapers such as the *New York Times?* We might expect this, but if we do, it says more about us than about the biblical authors, who could hardly be considered journalists. Rather what we have in Joshua is historical testimony, presented in an artful narrative way (that is, as a story-shaped history) and intended to highlight certain theological themes, all for the purpose of shaping the identity of the believing community and of encouraging them (us!) to walk faithfully before God.

A well-versed approach to inerrancy thinks, *"Literary understanding is a necessary condition of historical understanding."*[91] We should not oppose literature to history; in many cases, narrative is "true history artfully presented."[92] Narrative histories do more than convey pictures that correspond exactly to what actually happened; there is a *poetics* and *rhetoric* proper to historical narrative which help us appreciate what they do and how they work.[93] Just as we must first determine the meaning of a text before we assess its truth, so we must first appreciate Joshua 6 as narrative before we judge its historical truth or falsity.

---

88. See Iain Provan, V. Philips Long, and Tremper Longman III, *A Biblical History of Israel* (Louisville: Westminster, 2003), 174–76.

89. See Bernard Ramm, "The Relation of Science, Factual Statements and the Doctrine of Biblical Inerrancy," *Journal of the American Scientific Affiliation* 21 (1969), 98–104.

90. George W. Ramsey, *The Quest for the Historical Israel* (Atlanta: John Knox Press, 1981), 107.

91. Provan, Long, and Longman, *A Biblical History of Israel*, 81.

92. Ibid., 88.

93. Ibid., 91–3. See further Meir Sternberg, *The Poetics of Biblical Narrative: Ideological Literature and the Drama of Reading* (Bloomington, Ind.: Indiana Univ. Press, 1985).

Some philosophers of history think that all sources are fallible because of "their inherent inability to provide anything but a partial, incomplete, and necessarily biased view of the events they ostensibly report."[94] But to judge a text to be in error simply because it does not give us a complete and unbiased account of events is to work with an inordinately high, somewhat arbitrary, and quintessentially modern standard. As with witnesses in court, textual testimony can tell the truth, and nothing but the truth, even if it is not the *whole* truth but rather a particular angle on the truth. Incompleteness is not necessarily a defect, especially when an author is narrating history with a particular purpose, as is John's gospel, which admits that Jesus did "many other things" (John 21:25) but contents itself with recording the events it does in order to inculcate belief in Jesus as the Christ (John 20:30–31).

Well-versed inerrancy insists on reading Joshua 6 in canonical context while taking into account the literary conventions its authors employ. This involves recognizing "an intermingling of the texts' figurative and ideological aspects" typical of other ancient Near Eastern histories.[95] For example, the claim in Joshua 10:40 that Joshua utterly destroyed southern Palestine and "left no one remaining, but utterly destroyed all that breathed" (NRSV) is likely hyperbolic and "should not be read in a flat, literalistic way, as if hard statistical information were intended."[96] Jericho's fall as depicted by the text owes less to a battle than to a liturgical act that ends with a shout of jubilee.[97] Moreover, the conquest of Canaan may not have been as complete as a literalistic reading of the text might initially suggest, not least because later in Joshua the inhabitants of the land are still present. A careful reading of the whole of Joshua will perceive an intended tension between the initial *subjugation* of the land (a gift from God) and the later *occupation* of the land (Israel's responsibility). The main proposition that Joshua 6 sets forth — what the text *affirms* — is that God has indeed made good on his promise to give Israel the land and that the people on their part must respond to God's faithfulness in like manner.

---

94. Martha Howell and Walter Prevenier, *From Reliable Sources: An Introduction to Historical Methods* (Ithaca: Cornell Univ. Press, 2001), 2.

95. K. L. Younger Jr., *Ancient Conquest Accounts: A Study in Ancient Near Eastern and Biblical History Writing*, JSOTS 98 (Sheffield: JSOT Press, 1990), 265.

96. Provan, Long, and Longman, *A Biblical History of Israel*, 153.

97. McConville and Williams, *Joshua*, 32–33.

Biblical narrative marches to the beat of a different drummer than does the company of historians to which modern readers are accustomed. Indeed, reading Joshua simply to discover "what actually happened" is to miss the main point of the discourse, which is to communicate a theological interpretation of what happened (that is, God gave Israel the land) and to call for right participation in the covenant. It does not follow, however, that the accounts in Joshua are myths, or even legends. On the contrary, Joshua 6 is artful narrative testimony to an event that happened in Israel's past, an event that reveals both who God is (faithful to his promise) and who Israel is to be in response (obedient to the covenant). Readers, especially those who believe that God raised Jesus from the dead, are within their epistemic rights to trust this testimony until shown otherwise.

Harmonizing on the Damascus Road (Acts 9:7; 22:9)

There are three accounts of Paul's encounter with the risen Christ on the road to Damascus in Acts (9:1–19; 22:6–11; 26:12–18), but we are concerned with the first two only and, in particular, with the apparent contradiction in the description of the experience of Paul's companions. In Acts 9:7, the narrator says they were speechless, "hearing the voice but seeing no one" (ESV), while in Acts 22:9 Paul himself reports that his companions "saw the light but did not hear the voice of the one who was speaking to me" (NRSV). According to the law of noncontradiction, it cannot be true both that *A* and *non-A* (that is, "they heard" and "they did *not* hear"). And this is not the only discrepancy (for example, in 9:7, Paul's companions saw no one, but in 22:9, they saw the light). As Fetherstone's sixteenth-century translation of Calvin's commentary on Acts 9:7 quaintly notes, "it seemeth that this narration doth not in all points agree with that of Paul [in Acts 22:9]."[98] A more recent commentator goes further, asserting that these two passages "contain a formal contradiction."[99]

Modern biblical critics are willing to live with this contradiction, chalking it up to the possibility that Luke used two conflicting

98. Calvin, *Commentary on the Acts of the Apostles*, vol. 1 (Edinburgh: Calvin Translation Society, 1844), 375.

99. Horst R. Moehring, "The Verb *akouein* in Acts IX 7 and XXII 9," *Novum Testamentum* 3 (1959), 80.

sources. The typical inerrantist reflex, when one is confronted with intratextual wrinkles like this one, is to iron them out—to harmonize. (Thankfully, we have been spared the suggestion that Paul met Christ *two times* on the Damascus road). Sure enough, the most popular "solution" to this contradiction is to point out that the Greek verb in question (*akouein*) means "to hear the sound" with a genitive and "to understand" with an accusative. Calvin anticipated this solution, suggesting that Paul's companions heard the sound of the voice but could not understand what was said (or who was speaking). J. H. Moulton says that this distinction "saved the author [Luke] from a patent self-contradiction."[100] A. T. Robertson agrees, and in his Greek grammar takes issue with the translators of the RSV, who accentuate the contradiction by repeating *hear* instead of substituting *understand* for the second instance: "That is lack of good will or even respect for the Word of God. And it falsifies Luke's witness."[101] If only grammar books today were as feisty!

There are two problems with this solution. First, many scholars question whether the evidence supports the distinction.[102] But second, resolving the difficulty this quickly, and grammatically, short-circuits our attempt to plumb the depth of Luke's communicative intent and literary artistry.

A biblically literate reader will note parallels between the story of Paul's conversion and other incidents in which the Lord appears to select individuals or groups in ways that stretch human auditory and visual sensibilities. Consider, for example, how Moses reminds Israel of God's appearing with thunder and lightning at Mount Horeb: "You heard the sound of words but saw no form" (Deut. 4:12). *Phos* (light) and *phone* (voice) are standard features of biblical theophanies. In Acts 9, Paul's companions do not see the light; in Acts 22, they do not hear the voice. If the intent is to show that only Paul truly experienced the appearance of Christ, then the two accounts express essentially the same proposition: "Paul's companions had no share

---

100. J. H. Moulton, *A Grammar of New Testament Greek* (Edinburgh: Clark, 1882), 249.

101. A. T. Robertson, *Grammar of the Greek New Testament in the Light of Historical Research* (New York: Hodder & Stoughton, 1914), 448–49.

102. See in particular Moehring, "The Verb *akouein* in Acts IX 7 and XXII 9" and Robert G. Bratcher, "*Akouo* in Acts 9:7 and 22:9," *Expository Times* 71, no. 8 (1960), 243–45.

in his christophanic encounter." In one commentator's words, "It is only the means of expression which are changed, not the sense of the statement."[103]

The way forward, once again, is to ask not only what words Luke used but also what Luke was *doing* with them in the context of his overall narrative. Acts is a narrative history that recounts the history of the early church ("story") in a theologically significant manner ("discourse"). Repetition with slight variations was one of the rhetorical tools ancient authors had in their arsenal to reinforce their message or to highlight certain themes. I have already noted the allusion to Israel's encounter with God at Mount Horeb. Moses came away from that theophany with a shining face; Paul comes away blind. That Paul's companions heard the voice (Acts 9:7) underscores the objectivity of the encounter.

Commentators agree that Luke hints at the structure and theme of his book—the expanding scope of Christ's witnesses from Jerusalem to the ends of the earth—in Acts 1:8. A case can be made that the three accounts of Paul's encounter on the road to Damascus serve the purpose of enhancing Paul's stature as a witness to the gospel "to the ends of the earth."[104] The change in wording ("they heard," "they did not hear") serves Luke's purpose by progressively reducing the role of the companions, eventually excluding them altogether from the revelatory event, which turns out to be not merely a theophany but a commissioning service.[105] Paul *alone* is a witness to this christophany; Paul *alone* will serve as Christ's witness. This literary repetition with a difference is Luke's way of ensuring that Paul's companions decrease so that Paul's stature as a witness to the Lord will increase.[106] In sum: the companions' hearing in Acts 9 confirms the reality of the christophany; their not hearing in Acts 22 shows that the divine commissioning is intended for Paul alone.

---

103. Ernst Haenchen, *Acts of the Apostles: A Commentary* (Philadelphia: Westminster, 1971), 322.

104. See Ronald D. Witherup, "Functional Redundancy in the Acts of the Apostles: A Case Study," *JSNT* 48 (1992), 67–86.

105. Charles W. Hedrick, "Paul's Conversion/Call: A Comparative Analysis of the Three Reports in Acts," *Journal of Biblical Literature* 100, no. 3 (1981), 424.

106. Witherup notes that Acts 26 does not say whether the companions saw or heard anything; they simply fell to the ground (Acts 26:14).

Racial Violence vs. Radical Love (Deut. 20:16 – 17; Matt. 5:43 – 48)

A college student once told me that her professor often mentions the Bible, but never without the qualification "that handbook of racism, genocide, and oppression." Deuteronomy 20:16 – 17 implicates God in what strikes many as evil, and is a good example of what Kenton Sparks calls the "dark side" of Scripture.[107] It also seems to fly in the face of the ethic that Jesus taught his disciples: "Love your enemies" (Matt. 5:44). There are two problems: first, that the Old Testament here depicts God as a "moral monster"; second, that Jesus teaches a different view of God.

This is not the place to undertake a doctrine of God; our topic is inerrancy, not theodicy. Nevertheless, the topics are related, as Wesley Morriston makes clear in an essay that argues that the "genocide passages" in the Old Testament provide us with a strong prima facie reason to reject biblical inerrancy. Why? In short, because "that is not what a perfectly good God would do."[108] The longer argument is that the explanation Deuteronomy gives for God's commanding Israel to exterminate the various nations in Canaan does not constitute a morally sufficient reason for obeying.[109]

The challenge for the inerrantist is to resolve the apparent contradiction between what God commands Israel and what Jesus commands his disciples. This is a real difficulty, and there is a distinct temptation to want to make it go away. For example, Randall Rauser "solves" the problem by insisting that a morally perfect God would never order a human being to kill a human baby, and thus concludes that God did *not* command genocide. The cost of giving in to temptation here, however, is the loss of biblical inerrancy.[110]

It was the Gnostics who first pitted the loving God of the New Testament against the "wrathful" God of the Old. This will not do:

---

107. Kenton L. Sparks, *Sacred Word, Broken Word: Biblical Authority and the Dark Side of Scripture* (Grand Rapids, Mich.: Eerdmans, 2012).

108. Wesley Morriston, "Did God Command Genocide? A Challenge to the Biblical Inerrantist," *Philosophia Christi* 11, no. 1 (2009), 8.

109. See Paul Copan, "Is Yahweh a Moral Monster? The New Atheists and OT Ethics," *Philosophia Christi* 10 (2008), 7 – 37.

110. "'Let Nothing That Breathes Remain Alive': On the Problem of Divinely Commanded Genocide," *Philosophia Christi* 11 (2009), 27 – 41.

first, because the Old Testament affirms the love and mercy of God (Ex. 34:6–7); second, because the New Testament affirms the wrath and judgment of God; and third, because Jesus never distances himself from the way in which the Old Testament depicts God.[111] This latter point is the most important, and the clue to the way forward. Why did Jesus himself not find Deuteronomy's depiction of God abhorrent? Probably because he was not working with the concept of "morally perfect being." I find it interesting that Rauser and Morriston treat their own moral intuitions about what a perfect being *must* do as more reliable (dare I say inerrant?) than the biblical text. As Christians, they should know that the wisdom of the world is the foolishness of God.[112]

Our task, again, is not (in this context) to justify the ways of God but rather to explain how Jesus could have promulgated his law of love and not felt a tension with the Old Testament depictions of God as Divine Warrior. I submit that it was because Jesus saw himself as fully a part of the same story of what happens when holy love meets unholy rejection, or when the Creator-Redeemer engages the forces of chaos. Stated differently: Jesus read the Old Testament not literalistically (as do some of its critics) but in a literal-typological manner that keeps the overarching plot (that is, salvation history) in view at all times. I can here only provide a brief sketch of the redemptive-historical hermeneutical framework that Christians need to bring to such difficult passages.

If we view Scripture with the widest of wide-angle lenses, we see that God finally succeeds in forming a fit habitation in which to dwell: a cosmic temple. A number of commentators have pointed out that ancient Near Eastern kings typically built temples to commemorate victory in battle, and Yahweh does something similar, creating a garden temple in Eden after subduing chaos.[113] That garden temple becomes corrupt, however, and so begins a long restoration project that

---

111. Christopher J. H. Wright, *The God I Don't Understand: Reflections on Tough Questions of Faith* (Grand Rapids, Mich.: Zondervan, 2008), 77.

112. The concept of "perfect being" carries a heavy theological load. Whence its authority? Moral intuitions are fickle, as we are learning from the national debate about same-sex marriage. My worry is that "perfect being" foists culturally conditioned notions of perfection onto God.

113. See, for example, G. K. Beale, *The Temple and the Church's Mission: A Biblical Theology of the Dwelling Place of God* (Downers Grove, Ill.: InterVarsity, 2004).

concludes only with the establishment of new heavens and a new earth: the cosmic temple. This may seem miles away from our immediate textual issue, but it is not.

Israel's entry into the Promised Land hearkens back to the exodus from Egypt: in both cases, God enables Israel to pass through the waters (symbolic of chaos) and to anticipate the consummation of his drama of redemption at the final judgment, when the last battle will be fought by the Divine Warrior, and Satan and his minions will be defeated forever. This is the overarching framework that puts God's command in Deuteronomy 20 into right perspective: it's all about cleansing a temple space for God to dwell with his people (that is, not ethnic but *ethic* cleansing). The *herem*—the requirement to "dedicate" the Canaanites to destruction—ultimately pertains to holiness, not hostility: "It was not driven by genocidal or military considerations, but the need to eradicate evil and prevent evil from spreading to the new population."[114] It is noteworthy that the divine command strictly circumscribed the *herem* in space and time, that God threatened Israel with the same fate in case of disobedience (and made good his threat—see Jer. 25:9), and that it is a type of the ultimate destiny of people who oppose God.[115] The reason why Jesus can say "Love your enemies" without condemning the Old Testament is because the conquest of Canaan was a unique and limited event—a single scene, now past—in the drama of redemption. Wright is correct when he says that the conquest of Canaan "was never meant to become a model for how all future generations were to behave towards their contemporary enemies."[116]

The violence we see in the Old Testament, though real, is also typological, an anticipation of the bloody violence (the *herem*?) directed to Jesus on the cross, and thence of peace for all the nations. A biblically literate interpreter ought to hear overtones of the conquest narrative in the passion narrative as well; here too God spares nothing that breathes. The definitive battle over evil is indeed accomplished on the cross, where Jesus *"breathed his last"* (Matt. 27:50 NRSV, my emphasis).

---

114. Daniel I. Block, *Deuteronomy*, The NIV Application Commentary (Grand Rapids, Mich.: Zondervan, 2012), 483.

115. Ibid., 476–86.

116. Wright, *The God I Don't Understand*, 90.

Jesus worked some violence himself when he "cleansed" the temple, driving out people who profaned it with their money (Mark 11:15–16). In other words, *Jesus himself displayed the same jealous zeal* for the house of God that Yahweh had earlier for his land and people. What is God's must be consecrated to God, and to him alone. I believe that the difficulty we moderns have with the *herem* stems from an anemic sense of holiness and an underestimation of the scandal of idolatry, but that is a matter for another time.

The divine command (to a specific generation of Israelites) to kill the Canaanites, when properly interpreted in its redemptive historical context and viewed in the shadow of the cross, no more contradicts Jesus' teaching (to his disciples, playing a different scene in the drama of redemption) than God's holiness contradicts God's love. The "answer" is simplicity itself: *divine simplicity*, namely, the idea that the divine attributes do not name "parts" of God but offer a perspective on the *whole* of God's being. The two passages under consideration threaten inerrancy only if they contradict one another theologically, but they no more cancel each other out than does the holy love God displayed on the cross.

Conclusion: The Cost of Inerrancy

"Prefer the more difficult reading" is tried-and-true advice in the realm of text criticism, where the aim is to discern the most reliable manuscripts. The reasoning is straightforward: scribes and copyists are more likely to smooth out textual wrinkles than to introduce them.

The three case studies above are indeed difficult and, in each case, what generates the difficulty is the doctrine of inerrancy. If it were not for inerrancy, we could simply remove the difficulty by pronouncing the text to be in error: there was no historical fall of Jericho; Luke corrected himself and got his account of Paul's conversion right the second time; God did *not* command Israel to exterminate the Canaanites. To be sure, inerrantists too sometimes seek to alleviate the difficulty by adducing historical "proofs" or resolving theological tensions. By contrast, a well-versed inerrancy, while it does not take pleasure in textual difficulties, is nevertheless willing to engage and, if need be, *endure* them.

We must beware of "cheap inerrancy" that merely professes belief in biblical truth but stops short of *doing* or *enduring* it. To insist that the doctrine of inerrancy is all that matters is but a half-truth. Implicit in my definition of inerrancy is that we be not only literate readers who rightly see what proposition an author is proposing (the literal sense) and what kind of attention to this proposition is required (literary sensibility) but also right-minded and right-hearted readers who respond rightly to each and every communicative act in Scripture (Spirit-given literacy). Ultimately, a well-versed approach to inerrancy constitutes nothing less than a standing requirement that the community of Scripture's interpreters become persons capable of understanding, loving, and participating in the truth (Eph. 4). To know the truth, in the deep biblical and covenantal sense, is not merely to comprehend intellectually that to which the language corresponds but to respond in such a way that our lives correspond or conform to the truth. We must be passionate truth-seekers, truth-tellers, truth-doers, *and* truth-sufferers: interpreters who bear truthful witness to the truth of Scripture, not least by enduring its difficulties.

The last word in a well-versed, Augustinian approach to inerrancy belongs to Augustine: "And if in these writings I am perplexed by anything which appears to me opposed to truth, I do not hesitate to suppose that either the manuscript is faulty, or the translator has not caught the meaning of what was said, or I myself have failed to understand."[117] Indeed.[118]

---

117. Augustine, *Letter to Jerome*, 82.3.

118. My thanks to Dan Treier, Ike Miller, James Gordon, David Moser, the members of the Deerfield Dinner Discussion Group, and the editors for their comments on a previous draft.

R. ALBERT MOHLER JR.

I can only imagine that the experience of reading Kevin Vanhoozer's essay must be something like the experience of sitting in his classroom. He is a keen thinker and a careful teacher, precise and measured in his arguments and expansive in the range of his intellectual engagements. I appreciate his scholarship and consider him a gift to evangelicalism.

His affirmation of inerrancy is strong—perhaps even stronger than he realizes. He tells us that when asked if he affirms the inerrancy of the Bible, he regularly refuses until "my interlocutor defines the term (or allows me to do so)" (p. 206). After reading his essay, I think evangelicalism might be better served if Vanhoozer would first affirm inerrancy and then use his gift of teaching to present what he calls a "well-versed" understanding of inerrancy.

Vanhoozer is concerned to avoid association with less than "well-versed" understandings of inerrancy. That is understandable and commendable. What he calls "poorly versed accounts of inerrancy" can do great harm, he argues, and "do not ultimately help the cause of biblical authority" (p. 200). That is true, of course, but it must also be stated, with even greater forthrightness, that denials of biblical inerrancy have often caused far greater damage—in some cases leading to a repudiation of essential doctrines of the Christian faith.

Vanhoozer's essay contains a specific, clear, and sophisticated defense of biblical inerrancy as a truth claim and as a theological principle. He proposes that inerrancy, properly defined, means that the biblical authors "speak truth in all things they affirm (when they make affirmations), and will eventually be seen to have spoken truly (when right readers read rightly)" (p. 213).

Before getting to his definition, Vanhoozer considers the utility and importance of inerrancy as an evangelical conviction. He suggests that there are three possibilities: inerrancy is either *essential* to evangelicalism, *inimical* to evangelical unity, or *incidental* "to the unity and integrity of evangelicalism" (p. 203). But before working through them, he rightly asserts that inerrancy is not "the essence of Christianity" — it is not a doctrine of "first dogmatic rank" (p. 203). I agree and would add that inerrancy, in itself, is not a doctrine that Martin Luther, for example, would have classified as *articulus stantis vel cadentis ecclesiae* (an article by which the church stands or falls).

On the other hand, Luther did insist that the material principles of the faith (including justification by faith alone) rest upon the foundation of the formal principle, which is the authority of Holy Scripture. Vanhoozer is certainly right to argue that inerrancy is not a universal mark of the church in the same way that the doctrine of the Trinity is "a doctrine on which the gospel stands or falls" (p. 203). And yet, inerrancy is important, he asserts, because "a high view of biblical authority that affirms its entire trustworthiness is necessary to preserve the integrity of the gospel, and other candidate terms (for example, infallibility) that have sought to capture this notion have been diluted over time" (p. 203). So inerrancy is very important because it preserves something that must be said of Scripture and it says it better than any other term. Still, I agree with Vanhoozer that it would be unwise "to collapse everything we want to say about biblical authority into the nutshell of inerrancy" (p. 203).

In Vanhoozer's final analysis, inerrancy is "neither inimical nor incidental to the present and future of evangelicalism" (p. 204). But nor is it essential. Vanhoozer settles for *expedient* as perhaps the best understanding of inerrancy's utility and importance to evangelicalism. So, perhaps Vanhoozer's approach should be considered an argument for the *expediency* of a well-versed understanding of biblical inerrancy for the present and future of evangelicalism.

But this raises an interesting point about Vanhoozer's essay. He strongly affirms inerrancy. But his essay reveals more of a concern with misconstruals of inerrancy than with the very real concessions made by so many who claim to be evangelicals while not just misconstruing inerrancy but outright rejecting it. After reading his essay, it appears to me that Vanhoozer is far more concerned to prevent evangelicals from claiming too much than claiming too little about the truthfulness and trustworthiness of the Bible.

Vanhoozer does affirm the need to define inerrancy carefully. (That was, of course, the very challenge undertaken by the framers of the Chicago Statement on Biblical Inerrancy.) Curiously, however, Vanhoozer explains that after Fuller Theological Seminary's 1971 removal of language from its doctrinal statement affirming that the Bible is "free from all error in the whole and in the part," the faculty is now apparently ready to use inerrancy again *if they can define it in their own terms*. Vanhoozer cites a recent statement from Fuller that offers a definition of inerrancy in these terms: "'Where inerrancy refers to what the Holy Spirit is saying to the churches through the biblical writers, we support its use'" (p. 204). But that is precisely the sort of minimalistic definition of inerrancy that the Chicago statement framers sought to oppose and to expose as sub-evangelical. Tellingly, it is hard to imagine that Rudolf Bultmann would oppose such a definition of inerrancy.

So, to follow Vanhoozer's presentation to this point, inerrancy is not exactly essential, though it is expedient — so expedient, in fact, that no other word accomplishes what inerrancy accomplishes. But what is needed is a "well-versed" understanding of inerrancy that avoids making the wrong kind of claims about the truthfulness of the Bible, while preserving every sense in which the Bible is true.

For Vanhoozer, a well-versed understanding of inerrancy is informed by an understanding of language and literary forms. What he then offers is a far more detailed and (arguably) sophisticated understanding of language than what is found in the Chicago statement. A well-versed concept of inerrancy "acknowledges that biblical truth involves form as well as content" and "takes account of the importance of rhetoric as well as logic" for understanding the Bible (p. 204). A well-versed understanding of inerrancy "gives priority to the Bible's own teaching about God, language, and truth" and is not based on a philosophical pre-understanding of perfection. Vanhoozer argues for a "canonically conditioned concept of perfection" for a proper understanding of both God and his Word (p. 205).

In this regard, Vanhoozer's argument for an "inerrancy of the cross" rather than an "inerrancy of glory" (*pace tua* Luther) is helpful — as is his excellent argument for an Augustinian approach based on faith seeking understanding.

So, what about the Chicago statement? Vanhoozer says many more good things about it than bad. Although he suggests that the statement would be strengthened by more attention to several points of definition (such as a definition of propositions), Vanhoozer seems to register basic agreement with the statement as a whole, understanding the intellectual conditions of the late 1970s and the historical context of the times. He even defends the statement against charges that the concern for inerrancy is basically modern, arguing that even Aristotle affirmed a form of the correspondence view of truth.

And yet, Vanhoozer makes two very interesting moves as his argument unfolds. First, he argues that inerrancy, properly speaking, refers only to affirmations found within the Bible. He asserts that "large swaths" of the Bible are passages that are not affirmations (p. 209). He explains that affirmations are assertions of fact and that "not all sentences in the Bible state facts" (p. 209).

Second, he seems very clearly to assert that inerrancy pertains to propositions, and to propositions only. He is certainly correct to point out that many sentences in the Bible are not, properly speaking, propositional statements at all. But the framers of the Chicago statement acknowledged the fact that much of the Bible contains non-propositional sentences. The statement itself acknowledges many different forms of biblical literature and argues for no comprehensive hermeneutical system, other than an affirmation of historical-grammatical interpretation.

I am concerned that Vanhoozer's constriction of inerrancy is based on his own limitation of its domain to propositional sentences, or what he calls affirmations. This is inconsistent with his own sophisticated affirmation of the pluriform richness of the literary forms in the Bible. Surely he would agree, at least to some degree, that every text of Scripture, understood in its proper literary form, is making some form of affirmation. He criticizes some evangelicals (fairly I think) for claiming too much in terms of the propositional character of all biblical texts. I fear Vanhoozer *claims too little* in terms of the affirmations found within every text of Scripture—whatever its literary form.

After all, one of the problems directly addressed by the Chicago statement is the subversion of the biblical text by those who simply dehistoricize a text that clearly and irreducibly makes an historical claim.

Vanhoozer's use of speech-act theory is always informative (as in his discussion of divine speech acts such as oaths and covenants), though it leaves me wondering exactly where we are to locate the inspiration of the biblical text. After reading Vanhoozer's substantial corpus of writings, the question remains—and it is a question that hangs over his essay.

He says so many good and important things about the Bible, its truthfulness, and its proper interpretation. His emphasis on "right-hearted and right-minded readers" is brilliant and altogether healthy (p. 235). His argument for inerrancy with reference to the Council of Nicaea and *homoousios* is exceedingly helpful, affirming that "while the term inerrant or the concept of inerrancy may be new, the underlying judgment is not" (p. 213). His warning about excessive literalism is cogent, as is his reference to the importance of irony in the Bible. The careful reader of the Bible will pay close attention to the literary form of every text and a well-versed understanding of inerrancy "puts a premium on the responsibility of the reader to understand the text correctly (p. 223).

When approaching the three specific texts we were all asked to consider, Vanhoozer does not linger. He argues that archaeological findings are not sufficient to overcome the truthfulness of Joshua 6 and concludes that the chapter is "artful narrative testimony to an event that happened in Israel's past" (p. 228). But he does not claim historical accuracy for the passage as a whole. Vanhoozer is right to argue that reading Joshua "simply to discover 'what actually happened'" is to miss the larger point and purpose of the passage (p. 228). And yet, the text certainly does claim to record, in rather specific (though "artful") detail, "what actually happened."

Vanhoozer's oddest statement comes at the end of his consideration of this passage: "Readers, especially those who believe that God raised Jesus from the dead, are within their epistemic rights to trust this testimony until shown otherwise" (p. 228). *What*, I must ask, *could* show us otherwise? Vanhoozer's words here seem incongruous with the entire thrust of his argument.

The accounts of Paul's conversion are explained as serving a theological purpose through literary art. But, when Vanhoozer writes of the "revelatory event," is he limiting that to the theophany? What about

Luke's writing of Acts? I'm left wondering how Vanhoozer would propose that we determine when Luke intends to make a clearly historical claim and when he is using literary devices to serve a theological purpose.

Vanhoozer's consideration of the conquest of Canaan and the Sermon on the Mount is based on his own argument for a redemptive-historical hermeneutical framework. His argument is very brief, and leaves many questions unresolved. But he rightly calls readers to read Deuteronomy 20 "in the shadow of the cross" (p. 234).

Vanhoozer concludes that the three problematic biblical texts "are indeed difficult and, in each case, what generates the difficulty is the doctrine of inerrancy" (p. 234). If not for inerrancy, he says, "we could simply remove the difficulty by pronouncing the text to be in error" (p. 234). While he makes a cogent point, he also points to what a rejection of inerrancy would then allow: a wholesale reconceptualization of the Christian faith. Vanhoozer's much needed and welcomed advice: a well-versed inerrancy will take no pleasure in textual difficulties, but will both engage and *endure* them (p. 234).

Kevin Vanhoozer is certainly correct to warn against "cheap inerrancy" that affirms the truthfulness of the Bible without *doing* or *enduring* the Word of God (p. 234). And he is equally correct, and even more urgent, when he calls evangelicals to a well-versed inerrancy that "constitutes nothing less than a standing requirement that the community of Scripture's interpreters become persons capable of understanding, loving, and participating in the truth (Eph. 4)" (p. 235).

I join Kevin Vanhoozer in praying that evangelicals will show themselves to be that community of interpreters who rightly read the Scriptures. I believe that inerrancy is more than *expedient* to that end; it is *essential* to our full and well-versed affirmation of the total truthfulness and trustworthiness of Holy Scripture.

PETER ENNS

Here, as always, I appreciate Vanhoozer's efforts in laying out a constructive theological landscape. I also value the perspective Vanhoozer brings to the discussion, that of a theologian engaging philosophical hermeneutics and the history of Christian thought, and bringing this to bear on the nature of contemporary biblical interpretation. There is always a wider spectrum of Christian thought and church tradition to be considered as we engage Scripture in our unique moment, and I resonate with much of Vanhoozer's thinking.

Vanhoozer poses the question of whether inerrancy is a distraction (with *infallible* being a better term) or evangelicalism's rallying cry. His essay is in essence a defense of retaining *inerrancy*, when properly defined; there are good (well versed) and bad (poorly versed) articulations of inerrancy. While the latter fixes on what I might call "brute propositions," the former understands the truth of Scripture as a theological articulation that accounts for *how* Scripture works, i.e., as literature and as speech-act communication. In my opinion, this leitmotif in Vanhoozer's body of work is a genuine contribution to evangelical theology.

With that generally supportive posture in mind, and seeing myself very much in conversation with Vanhoozer, I want to restrict my comments here to those aspects of his essay that either raise some questions for me or that I feel do not adequately address the problem before us. For example, Vanhoozer states early on that "inerrancy" entails only that "the Bible is authoritative over any domain God addresses" (p. 202) This type of assertion is common among inerrantists, intended (wisely) to keep one from pressing inerrancy too far (as, I imagine, Vanhoozer would contend Mohler has done). Of course, Vanhoozer's essay expands this definition, but at the end I was still not sure what a "domain" is, what it means for God to address one, or what factors help determine when that is happening. I sensed already here that this language could be used to deflect the matter of Canaanite extermination or the fall of Jericho artificially away from the troubling historical issues by relegating these narratives to some other "proper" theological domain. This suspicion seemed to be confirmed later in Vanhoozer's handling of these issues.

Elsewhere Vanhoozer notes that, though historical problems of Scripture still remain, archaeology has resolved "many" of them. My initial reaction to this seemingly incidental comment was confirmed when I got to Vanhoozer's handling of the fall of Jericho and Canaanite extermination. I do not wish to be unnecessarily repetitive of my similar comments in responding to Mohler and Bird, but, as innocent as this comment may seem, "many" unwittingly underrepresents the problem before us. Archaeology is not an enemy to Christian faith as sometimes caricatured, but to say "many" issues have been resolved is misleading. In fact, one of the very troubling aspects of archaeological study is the serious challenges it has posed to the overall plot of Israel's historical narrative — a discreet people group that was enslaved in Egypt, delivered en masse, and then invaded and conquered Canaan as an outside force. The issue is not entirely dismal, of course, as some elements of the biblical story have generally been confirmed or at least found to be consistent with the archaeological record, but Vanhoozer's casual comment suggests a more positive picture than is warranted, which inhibits the kind of conversations needed concerning inerrancy.

Vanhoozer's apparently unqualified endorsement of Augustine's handling of interpretive challenges raised some questions for me too: "The purpose of inerrancy is to cultivate readers who confront biblical difficulties as did Augustine: 'And if in these writings I am perplexed by anything which appears to me opposed to truth, I do not hesitate to suppose that either the manuscript is faulty, or the translator has not caught the meaning of what was said, or I myself have failed to understand.' Difficulties are not necessarily indications of the dark side of Scripture's moon, only spots in its sun" (p. 203). Taken without qualification, this suggests there are in fact no genuine challenges to inerrancy, only our interpretation of an inerrant text. I am not exactly sure how, practically speaking, this claim differs substantively from some of Mohler's. But more important, as Bird points out in his essay,

Augustine's comment pertains to the careless production of Latin texts and should not be applied to an evangelical defense of inerrancy, and will certainly not serve to guide us in handling our three passages. It is counterproductive to "cultivate readers" who would approach archaeological problems, for example, by applying Augustine's mindset here.

Several other assertions concerning what inerrancy necessarily entails were more distracting to me than helpful, and could potentially obstruct careful consideration of our three passages, if taken at face value. For example, inerrancy is not essential to the Gospel per se but is essential to its proclamation; inerrancy pertains only to what Scripture asserts, not to "biblical commands, promises, warnings, and so on" (p. 203; I don't know what "asserts" means or on what basis that distinction is made); inerrancy is a mark of those who are "*consistently* evangelical" (p. 204); inerrancy cannot be proven but is "entailed by dominical and apostolic teaching about the nature of Scripture" (p. 204; citing J. I. Packer). These are some of the very issues that need to be brought to the table and evaluated by observing how the Bible "behaves," rather than introducing them as a priori commitments. For example, on the last point, the midrashic handling of the Old Testament by Jesus and the apostles—an observation that results from historical study—should temper any appeal to their "teaching about the nature of Scripture" that does not bring front and center the manner in which the New Testament writers actually handle Scripture.

Similarly, when defining "well-versed inerrancy," Vanhoozer counsels to give "priority to the Bible's own teaching about God, language, and truth" (p. 205), by which he means keeping in view the "overarching story line of the Bible that features the economic Trinity (that is, the words and acts of God in history)" (p. 205). Vanhoozer is saying, in essence, that well-versed inerrancy keeps in mind everything the Bible says about "God, language, and truth" by means of a canonical and Trinitarian reading. I think Vanhoozer's thinking is vastly more nuanced than others, but is not the entire issue before us what it *means* to adhere to the Bible's teaching on "God, language, and truth?" I don't think any of the contributors of this volume would disagree, yet the final products diverge significantly.

What I like most in Vanhoozer's model of well-versed inerrancy is his "inerrancy of the cross," which "understands truth not merely in terms of the philosopher's idea of correspondence but, biblically first and theologically foremost, in terms of covenantal faithfulness and testimonial endurance" (p. 205). This seems a theologically wise orientation in general, though I would be more overt in including the notion of the humiliation of the cross as a way of informing our expectations of the nature of Scripture. He picks up this train of thought later by tying the matter of inerrancy to the person of Christ, in that both Christ and Scripture communicate truth about "what God is" (p. 205). I find the summation promising, though, again, I wonder how this will be applied to the thorny challenges we face. What alerts me to a potential problem is Vanhoozer's following sentence: "Words that purport to communicate what is yet fail to do so are false—unreliable, untrustworthy, perhaps even lies" (p. 000). But again, the entire question before us is the manner in which the words of Scripture "purport to communicate what is." As stated, and trying to integrate Vanhoozer's discussion thus far, I am still unclear how a statement like this can handle conflicting historical assessments in Scripture. How does Vanhoozer's theory work itself out when handling the particulars of the biblical texts? I am not yet certain where this is going.

Vanhoozer's assessment of the Chicago statement is more positive than I feel is warranted. Vanhoozer seems convinced that, when all the facts are in, the inerrancy of the autographs, when properly interpreted, are faithful and true guides to faith and practice (citing David Dockery). I align myself more with Bird's criticisms on this matter specifically and the CSBI in general, that autographs neither exist nor would they help if they did. I also find unhelpful Vanhoozer's summative definition of inerrancy: "the authors speak the truth *in all things they affirm* (when they make affirmations), and will *eventually* be seen to have spoken truly (when right readers read rightly)" (p. 207, my emphasis). This is common evangelical language, echoing the CSBI, and I am never quite sure what to do with it when I see it. For one thing, we have the perennial problem of what "affirm" actually means, and Vanhoozer's subsequent thoughts did not clear this up for me. Further, "eventually" raises flags. Though on one level a wise call to patience in interpretation, it can be (and is regularly) used as a means of forestalling serious objections to inerrancy (what I outline in my essay as the "be patient" and "not impossible" apologetic).

I am sympathetic to Vanhoozer's caution that "to insist that true statements are always exact representations of extralinguistic reality leads to overly literalistic interpretations" (p. 210). Still, as I commented in my response to Bird, allowing for inexact representations of extralinguistic reality in Scripture is not the main challenge confronting inerrancy. Far more pressing is the perennial inerrantist problem, pervasive in Scripture, of the relationship between text and event, which our three passages touch on. I am left wondering how Vanhoozer will deal with the difficulties of the three passages, i.e., to what extent he would see them as truly challenging to inerrancy, or simply challenging to a poorly versed version of inerrancy. I contend they are challenges to Vanhoozer's well-versed definition as well.

Related is Vanhoozer's view that "we must first discern what a passage or a text is *about*, and then ask *how* it is about it" (p. 218). Yet discerning what a text is about — by which I take it Vanhoozer means the author's intention for writing it — is the very thing that so quickly eludes us. He illustrates his principle by referring to the often-cited comment by Jesus that the mustard seed is the smallest of all. Vanhoozer resolves this difficulty by telling us that Jesus did not intend to "affirm a botanical truth" but merely intended to draw an analogy that his hearers would understand. I am sympathetic to Vanhoozer's speech-act theory of inerrancy that lies behind this comment, but at the end of the day, I am not sure how Vanhoozer knows what Jesus' illocutionary intention is for referring to the mustard seed. A simpler and more convincing solution for me is that Jesus' claim about the kingdom was illustrated by an assumed "truth claim" *for that time* about mustard seeds. I do not see what is lost by affirming that Jesus was a first-century man and thought like one. That is one of the implications of the "irreverent doctrine" of the incarnation, as C. S. Lewis put it.

Concerning the fall of Jericho, I am not entirely sure where Vanhoozer lands. On the one hand, it is clear that "what happened" matters to Vanhoozer, in that he contends that the accounts in Joshua are not "myths, or even legends" (p. 228). On the other hand, asking "what happened" is a misreading of the text, for it fails to do justice to the "main point of the discourse, which is to communicate a theological interpretation of what happened" (p. 228). Despite Vanhoozer's arguments, I am still left feeling he is sidestepping the historical problems.

Along the way, Vanhoozer contends that the archaeological data are ambiguous and "inconclusive," and he repeats his opinion that modern precision or "factual reporting" was never the author's intention anyway. But as I mentioned in my previous responses, (1) outside of inerrantists, archaeologists don't see the ambiguity, and (2) modern precision is not the issue but whether the basic plot of the biblical story reflects historical events. Vanhoozer seems to remain noncommittal on the specific matter of whether the walls of Jericho actually fell. The text says they did. So did they? Must they? Does Vanhoozer's focus on discourse have space for an interpretation of the story where its main historical element—the sacking of Jericho—did not happen but was, perhaps, only recalled to have happened by the writers for theological reasons? But if, on the other hand, it is necessary for Vanhoozer that Jericho's fall is genuinely historical, on what basis does he make that claim, other than the doctrinal requirement of inerrancy?

I appreciate Vanhoozer's handling of Acts 9 and 22. He accurately depicts the problem as one of hearing (not seeing), and explores exegetical issues concerning the Greek texts. He and I are in substantive agreement that Luke's depiction of Paul is analogous to Old Testament call narratives (he mentions Moses' call), and that the details of Acts 22 suggest that Luke was portraying Paul *alone* as God's messenger to the "ends of the world."

Vanhoozer's handling of Canaanite extermination is less agreeable to me. He cautions against judging God on the basis of our own moral code, and I agree in principle, though his reason for this caution is the preservation of inerrancy, which is the cart pulling the horse. Also, I feel Vanhoozer is shortchanging his opponents, since the moral code that raises such trouble for Christian readers is not entirely their own but from Jesus' own words. Further, a key factor in handling this issue, routinely marginalized or missed entirely in evangelical discussions, is how Yahweh's behavior toward the Canaanites is utterly at home in ancient tribal ways of thinking. The truly pressing questions are not abstract philosophical ones, like, "How can a good and loving God order the extermination of the Canaanites?" but questions informed by Israel's historical context, like, "How is it that Yahweh is acting so much like the gods of other nations and not like what Jesus says about him?"

248 • FIVE VIEWS ON BIBLICAL INERRANCY

It will also not do to ameliorate Canaanite extermination by appealing to passages where God shows mercy, since that mercy is shown to the Israelites, his own people, not to the nations. One day, as the biblical story goes, the nations will come around and submit to Yahweh, but for now they pose a threat to the chosen people of God (and the story of Jonah is the exception that does not cancel out this dominant theme). Neither is it useful to understand *herem* as an issue of holiness and not hostility. In brief, concerning Canaanite extermination, I see Vanhoozer repeating common but erroneous arguments. If one can look past his indelicate style of engagement, Thom Stark's responses, in my judgment, put these common defenses to rest.[119]

119. Thom Stark, "Is God a Moral Compromiser? A Critical Review of Paul Copan's 'Is God a Moral Monster?'" *thomstark.net/copan/stark_copan-review.pdf*, and *The Human Faces of God* (Eugene, Ore.: Wipf and Stock, 2010), esp. 83–124.

RESPONSE TO KEVIN J. VANHOOZER

MICHAEL F. BIRD

Kevin Vanhoozer begins his essay with a quote from Jane Austen's *Pride and Prejudice*. In turn, I reply with a quote from Shakespeare's *Othello*—specifically, the words of the arch villain, Iago, who said, "I'd rather have this tongue cut from my mouth than it should do offence to Michael Cassio." Although Iago very much intends both to speak and do great offense to Michael Cassio, I'd rather be forced to listen to several hours of Al Gore speeches than to give offence to Kevin Vanhoozer. Vanhoozer is my favorite American theologian, who has provided me with much succor. During my doctoral studies, I was routinely chastised by postmodern professors at postgraduate seminars for my presumption of authorial intent and belief in textual realism. As such, Vanhoozer's book *Is There a Meaning in This Text?* was my sword and shield, enabling me to intelligently articulate the view that authors are not dead, texts are not just mirrors, and communities are not corporate papacies who can make stuff up ex nihilo.[120] Furthermore, Vanhoozer's work on theological prolegomena has significantly shaped my own formulation as to how to make the triune God's self-communication fundamental to evangelical theology.[121]

There are several commendable features of Vanhoozer's "Augustinian Inerrancy," including (1) his placement of inerrancy in the domain of divine affirmations given in Scripture; (2) his definition of inerrancy: "God's authoritative Word is wholly true and trustworthy in everything it claims about what was, what is, and what will be" (p. 202), which is satisfactory for both a biblical scholar and a global evangelical; (3) his claim that inerrancy is not "essential" but

---

120. Kevin J. Vanhoozer, *Is There a Meaning in This Text? The Bible, the Reader, and the Morality of Literary Knowledge* (Grand Rapids, Mich.: Zondervan, 1998).

121. Kevin J. Vanhoozer, *First Theology: God, Scripture, and Hermeneutics* (Downers Grove, Ill.: InterVarsity, 2002); Vanhoozer, *The Drama of Doctrine: A Cognitive-Linguistic Approach to Christian Theology* (Louisville, Ky.: Westminster John Knox, 2005).

"expedient," which is worthy of consideration; (4) his rejection of inerrancy based on abstract notions of a Perfect Being with a Perfect Book, and his replacing it with a version of inerrancy based on the triune God's self-disclosure in his canonical-linguistic speech-acts, which is indeed preferable for its nuanced linguistics, of which the Chicago Statement on Biblical Inerrancy is lacking; (5) his equally admirable recognition that while the precise concept of inerrancy is actually new and culturally located, nonetheless the underlying value and concern of inerrancy is universal and valid in the church's historic faith; (6) his giving a reasonable amount of weight to Scripture's textual phenomena and how it constrains the claims we can make about what the text affirms and its overall veracity; and (7) finally, his Yoda-like aphorism that "Inerrancy alone does not a hermeneutic make" (p. 224). Indeed, Vanhoozer brings the hermeneutical sophistication, literary sensitivity, and theological depth that the American inerrancy tradition so desperately needs if it is to be more than a shibboleth in North American evangelical tribalism.

Those are the positive aspects, but now, alas, it is time to get my Iago on and get all Shakespearean villain on Vanhoozer.

First, Vanhoozer relies initially on a rather superficial approach to hard textual questions. Vanhoozer's preliminary comments on inerrancy set out the doctrine within the context of the efficacy of God's Word within the domain of God's knowledge and the purpose for which the Word is given. This guarantees from the outset that God's Word is unified, coherent, and noncontradictory. He then recognizes the Bible's many textual "difficulties," but he resorts to addressing them in standard yet simplistic ways: wait for an explanation to emerge, rethink your interpretation, or else the manuscript you are using must be faulty (p. 202). The problem here is twofold: (1) Several of the "difficulties" are not simply interpretive problems, like a Gordian's knot sitting there idly waiting for some wise exegetical knight on an archaeological steed to break it with the sword of a new interpretation, a new artifact, or a new manuscript find. Many of these "difficulties" are contradictions particularly when one presupposes the type of precision that the CSBI attributes to Scripture.[122] Vanhoozer's Augus-

---

122. How many demoniacs did Jesus heal in the Decapolis? One or two? Was it in Gedara, Gerasa, or Gergesa? See Matt. 8:28–34; Mark 5:1–20; and Luke 8:26–39.

tinian inerrancy needs to wrestle with some up-close and personal Origenesque exegesis to see how hard it is to solve these problems with stock-standard explanations. (2) The opening précis on inerrancy was all the more odd since Vanhoozer goes on to develop a more compelling approach to inerrancy that is consistent with how literary intentions, artistic license, and ancient writing conventions explain that these "difficulties" are completely congruent with the truth claims made in Scripture. Thus, I wonder if Vanhoozer's Augustinian Inerrancy really needs Augustine's explanation that all "difficulties" are just a matter of figuring out what went wrong with my interpretation, translation, or manuscript.

Second, I am not sure that Vanhoozer has completely demonstrated a necessary link between the Bible's historical referentiality and its theological coherence. Vanhoozer claims that inerrancy functions to give believers confidence that Scripture's teaching is "ultimately unified and coherent" (p. 202), and he marries that to an Aristotlean and Augustinian correspondence theory of truth (pp. 218, 214). This provides the grounds for his notion of "covenantal correspondence," with a faithful fit between God's words and God's deeds (p. 216). In terms of how that plays out, with reference to the destruction of Jericho, Vanhoozer states that what is at stake is not simply the veracity of Joshua's account but that the entire divine promise hinges on the conquest being a historical reality (p. 225). I believe that Vanhoozer is right that the biblical account of the conquest is true history artfully presented, not literalistic, somewhat hyperbolic even, and the main point of the story is that God has made good on his promise to give Israel the land. However, I'm left with several questions, such as, Does the fulfillment of the divine promise require a historical event behind it approximate to what is recorded in Joshua's account of Jericho? Could the promise still be made good if in fact several thousand Hebrew slaves from Egypt spasmodically drifted into Canaan over a generation? How much hyperbole or artistry would disqualify the account from being historical? At the end of the day, I believe with Vanhoozer that the God who raised Jesus from the dead can and does work in history. Even so, I want to know what prevents Vanhoozer from being an ahistorical coherentist (i.e., what actually happened does not matter as long as the biblical claims are coherent at a theological level). I still want from Vanhoozer a thicker account of God's revelation in history and its relationship to his notion of "covenantal correspondence."

Third, Vanhoozer's engagement with the CSBI was critical and yet constructive. In terms of his opening question ("Can anything good come out of the 1970s?"), I would have to reply, "Yes, the movie *Star Wars* and the musical *Evita*." But before I sing, "Don't cry for me Chewbacca," I have to protest that Vanhoozer has not addressed one of my concerns about the CSBI, namely its lack of catholicity and its deficient interest in global perspectives. That said, I think Vanhoozer's Augustinian model is one of the better ways to infuse some creedal theology and to retrieve some patristic voices to shape future discussions of inerrancy.

Let me finish by saying that Kevin James Vanhoozer's approach is praiseworthy; it assuages many concerns about inerrancy; it retains a strong affirmation of biblical veracity; and my hope is that any revision to popular and official statements of inerrancy should give the KJV perspective, despite some contested points, strong consideration.

RESPONSE TO KEVIN J. VANHOOZER

JOHN R. FRANKE

The work of Kevin Vanhoozer is on the cutting edge of evangelical theology. In numerous works he has sought to enlarge the evangelical theological project and bring it into conversation with intellectual currents beyond its standard profile. In doing this work, he employs the label postconservative to describe some elements of his work, while at the same time resists association with the postconservative movement. As one who is quite happy with the contours of the postconservative approach to evangelical theology, I confess that I often feel as though Vanhoozer is trying to have his theological cake and eat it too. On the one hand, he pushes the envelope of evangelical theology, while on the other hand he often seems, from my perspective, to shrink back from the logical conclusion of his positions. I appreciate this first tendency, but I find the second puzzling. Of course, I have little doubt that he would respond that I have misunderstood him or failed to grasp the nuances of his views and that, if I did, I would see why the conclusion I draw from his work pushes matters too far.

I mention this because his essay in this volume is one with which I resonate at many levels, perhaps more than any of the others. Vanhoozer has articulated my concerns about the Chicago Statement on Biblical Inerrancy better than I have and, at many points in his essay, I found myself thinking, "Well said. I wish I had thought to put it that way." Of course, no one is able to match Vanhoozer's rhetorical flourish, although I confess that I sometimes find it a bit wearisome and feel that, with a good editor, he could say the same things with more brevity and, hence, more clarity. Nevertheless, he has a marvelous way of challenging many aspects of the evangelical *status quo*, while remaining in good standing with most of the evangelical community. That is a gift.

I particularly appreciated his use of the metaphor of the biblical canon as a collection of different kinds of maps, coupled with the

253

assertion that maps reflect certain interests and points of view that are specific to their particular concerns. He concludes that there is in fact "no such thing as a universal all-purpose map. The metaphor of the map reminds us that there is more than one kind of fit" and worries that "some theories of inerrancy imply that there is only one way to map the world correctly" (p. 210). In his book, *The Drama of Doctrine*, he puts the matter quite well: "strictly speaking, the diverse canonical parts neither contradict nor cohere with one another, for both these notions presuppose either the presence or absence of conceptual consistency. But this is to assume that the various books of the canon are playing the same language game. They are not. Two notions that occupy different conceptual systems are nevertheless compatible if neither negates the other."[123] Here I am in general agreement with Vanhoozer, as is evident in my own approach to inerrancy. Where we differ concerns the implications of this approach for the discipline of theology. It is on this question that I will focus my response.

In my essay, I assert the following: "A single, normative systematic interpretation of the whole Bible is neither attainable nor desirable. Like the problematic notion of a cultural melting pot in which numerous distinct cultures come together and form one new universal culture made up of all the others, something of value is always left out or excluded. When we attempt to ease the difficulties of the multiple perspectives in Scripture to make matters more compact, clear, and manageable, we suffer the loss of plurality and diversity that is woven into the very fabric of Scripture, and by extension, the divine design of God" (p. 277). This seems to me to be the clear implication of the diverse plurality of Scripture. Based on my reading of his essay in this volume as well as his other works, my assumption is that Vanhoozer would generally agree with this statement, especially given his assertions that there is no such thing as a universal all-purpose map and that while the diverse parts of the biblical canon do not contradict or negate each other, neither do they cohere.

However, a recent exchange between us covering similar territory in the *Southeastern Theological Review* indicates that Vanhoozer does

---

123. Kevin J. Vanhoozer, *The Drama of Doctrine: A Canonical-Linguistic Approach to Christian Theology* (Louisville: Westminster John Knox, 2005), 275.

not share my conclusions about the implications of biblical plurality.[124] He does agree that Scripture is characterized by plurality: "What we have in Scripture, a plurality of human perspectives, is the divinely inspired refraction of this light—a canonical coat of many colors. Each of these canonical perspectives gives us access to a particular aspect of God's truth and reality. Franke will shout 'Huzzah!' when I say that it takes a plurality of canonical perspectives fully to render theological truth. This is my working assumption: that systematic theologians need to attend to the variety of authorial voices, forms of biblical discourse, and theological perspectives in Scripture."[125] While I am in substantial agreement with this statement, an important difference between us is worth noting. For Vanhoozer, it is a plurality of *canonical* perspectives that are required to fully render theological truth. I believe that while the canon norms theological discourse, it does not exhaust it. Put another way, theological truth cannot be fully rendered only with reference to the canon. As a paradigmatic as well as normative witness to truth, the Bible invites greater plurality, both practical and theological, than that contained in its pages in order that the mission of God might be continually expanded and incarnated among all people. I hold this conviction based on the shape and content of the canon. While I agree with my critics that this perspective will lead to a very different approach to theology, I see no reason whatsoever why this position is inconsistent with inerrancy. In fact, I believe that inerrancy pushes us in precisely this direction.

A second concern I have with Vanhoozer is a fear that what he grants with one hand, the plurality of Scripture and the necessity for multiple maps, he takes away with the other through an insistence on a universal ontology. Space does not permit full citation or full discussion here, and I urge readers to examine the full text of his remarks in the *Southeastern Theological Review*. While acknowledging Aristotle's assertion that being may be spoken of in many ways, Vanhoozer admits that he does not think that there can be numerous (a plurality?) of

124. See John R. Franke, "God, Plurality, and Theological Method: A Response to Kevin Vanhoozer's *Remythologizing Theology*," and Kevin J. Vanhoozer, "Vanhoozer Responds to the Four Horsemen of an Apocalyptic Panel Discussion on *Remythologizing Theology*," *Southeastern Theological Review* 4, no. 1 (2013): 41–51, 67–82.

125. Ibid., 72.

256 of FIVE VIEWS ON BIBLICAL INERRANCY

ontologies of God. He says that it seems to him that there can only be one right answer to certain ontological questions and worries that I have inadvertently "short-circuited the move from exegesis to theology, and hence faith's search for understanding, by exaggerating the inadequacy of second-order theological discourse to its subject matter."[126] I do not believe I have questioned the adequacy of theological language for the purpose of establishing right relations with God. Rather, I have asserted its limitations for the task constructing a universal theology. Perhaps in my zeal to deconstruct the pretensions of systematic theology, ontology, and metaphysics and the damage they have done to the witness of the gospel I have sometimes overstated matters, in which case I am open to some course correction.

Nevertheless, I continue to believe that the limitations of human language present serious challenges to the optimism of Vanhoozer concerning the ability of systematic theologians to ascertain the supposedly deeper and underlying unities of the text. He states, "I do not concede the point that the exegete is more biblical than the systematic theologian simply because the latter works with abstract constructions. On the contrary: theologians too clarify the grammar of the text, though on a deeper level . . . Implied in what we say about things is what we think these things are. I believe that our grammatical analysis of biblical discourse is theologically incomplete until we have spelled out its ontological implications."[127] The challenge of course is that ontology is just as contextual and situated as any other human intellectual undertaking. It is reflective of particular situations and circumstances. Yet to my ear it seems that Vanhoozer might be resistant to this notion. His assertion that ontology probes the deeper order of reality sounds like yet another enterprise in getting behind the text of Scripture to its deeper and more unifying substructure.

Interestingly, Vanhoozer acknowledges this concern while suggesting that his own approach will avoid these pitfalls: "I agree with Franke about the pretension of metaphysics if by 'metaphysics' we mean a ready-made set of categories that we impose on Scripture. There are numerous examples of theologians doing this. It is all too tempting

---

126. Ibid.
127. Ibid., 73.

to ride the categorical coattails of whatever metaphysic happens to be the most fashionable. The aim of remythologizing, however, is the countercultural way of deep exegesis and theo-ontology."[128] I fear that in spite of his awareness of the dangers of metaphysical pretension, the assumption of ontological universality will produce the very difficulties he is seeking to correct.

Alternatively, I suggest that the inerrant plurality of Scripture points us away from the traditional assumptions of systematic theology. In its place I propose a missional approach to theology that takes issues of location, culture, and context far more seriously. It is shaped by a commitment to missiology at its center. Missional theology takes into account the plurality that is contained in the biblical canon and does not proceed on the assumption that various genres and strands of the canon can be arranged into a uniform system of teaching. As such, it resists the danger of sectarianism inherent a systematic approach to theology. This occurs when different expressions of the church conclude that they have arrived at the one true system of doctrine. Inevitably such communities find themselves in conflict with other traditions that have come to different conclusions. The resulting fragmentation and divisiveness in the church is in clear contrast to the work of the Spirit in promoting the unity of the church. More important than this practical concern for the relationship between Christian communities is the failure of systematic theology to bear proper witness to the infinite qualitative distinction between God and ourselves. Much more needs to be said about this, but for the time being, I will leave the last word about systematization in theology to Karl Barth:

> In this work—it cannot be otherwise in view of its object—we have to do with the question of truth. It is, therefore, inevitable that as a whole and in detail the aim must be definiteness and coherence, and it is to be hoped that the definiteness and sequence of the truth will actually be disclosed. But this being the case, is it not also inevitable that "something like a system" will assert itself more or less spontaneously in dogmatic work? Why, then, should a "system" be so utterly abhorrent? If it asserts itself spontaneously

128. Ibid.

in this way, can it not be forgiven? And if so, why should we be frightened away by a law forbidding systems? May it be that a "system" which asserts itself spontaneously (not as a system, but as a striving for definiteness and coherence) signifies obedience and is therefore a shadow of the truth? It may well be so. But even in this case the danger is still there. The fact that unauthorised systematisation may be forgiven does not mean that the tendency to systematisation is authorised. Nor does the fact that even in the fatal form of an intrinsically unauthorised systematisation true obedience may finally be demonstrated and a shadow of the truth disclosed.[129]

---

129. Karl Barth, *Church Dogmatics* 1/1, 869.

RECASTING INERRANCY: THE BIBLE AS WITNESS TO MISSIONAL PLURALITY

JOHN R. FRANKE

I have always had mixed feelings about inerrancy. On the one hand, I deeply appreciate the core idea that it affirms: the character of the Bible as an inspired, faithful, and trustworthy witness to the being and actions of God. I believe that the Bible is the Word of God in human words, and that as such its stories and teachings, taken as a whole, are true and not a lie. This belief is one of the central convictions of my Christian faith. Insofar as inerrancy functions to assist in the affirmation of this conviction about the Bible, I have been willing to endorse it.

On the other hand, I have often been dismayed by many of the ways in which inerrancy has commonly been used in biblical interpretation, theology, and the life of the church, as though it served as some kind of panacea for resolving difficult and complex questions related to Christian faith and life in the world. Of even greater concern is the way in which inerrancy has been wielded by dominant groups as a means of asserting power and control. In addition, I've never thought the term *inerrancy* was a particularly helpful way of articulating the core idea of the authority of Scripture as a witness to the mission of God. For so many people inside and outside of Christian communities, it conjures up artificial notions of precision and exactitude that are decidedly unhelpful in the task of reading and understanding the Bible.

For eighteen years, I taught on the faculty of an evangelical seminary that was and is committed to inerrancy, and every year I signed the school's doctrinal statement and reaffirmed my support of this idea. As a faculty member, department chair, and dean of the faculty, I was involved in many spirited and fruitful conversations with my colleagues as we wrestled together over the meaning, usefulness, and limitations of the term. When I started writing sympathetic books and articles on postmodern theology, nonfoundationalism, and Karl Barth, I was regularly asked by friend and foe alike, "Do you really believe in inerrancy?" My answer was always the same: "Yes, as long as I get to define it." At the same time, I don't think I've ever used the word *inerrancy* in anything I've written for publication until this essay, including several book chapters and articles on the Bible and its role in theology.

What follows is an attempt to address my internal conflict about inerrancy by trying to remove it from the confines of the static biblicism that has plagued it, recasting the term in a dynamic direction more in keeping with the being and character of God and embracing its contextual plurality as an essential part of its witness. As such, it is an experiment in postconservative or progressive evangelical theology.[1]

Inerrancy, Evangelicalism, the Chicago Statement, and Foundationalism

Being conflicted about inerrancy presents a particular challenge for participation in the North American evangelical community, because of the ways in which inerrancy functions as both a theological and political symbol. While there are certainly many persons who self-identify as evangelical but do not affirm inerrancy, it nevertheless remains one of the central doctrinal commitments in evangelical churches, colleges, and seminaries, as well as one of the two doctrinal standards (the other being an affirmation of the Trinity) for the Evangelical Theological Society. In this context, the Chicago Statement on Biblical Inerrancy has become highly influential as providing a definition for the doctrine. For many, the Chicago statement interpretation of inerrancy is the hallmark of true evangelicalism, and to deny it is to be deemed outside the boundaries of evangelical faith.

This is perhaps rooted in the notion that the doctrine of inerrancy has always been a central component in the tradition of the church.

---

1. For a detailed discussion of such an approach to theology, see John R. Franke, *The Character of Theology: An Introduction to Its Nature, Task, and Purpose* (Grand Rapids, Mich.: Baker Academic, 2005).

Article 16 of the Chicago statement says "that the doctrine of inerrancy has been integral to the Church's faith throughout its history." Insofar as inerrancy simply means that all of Scripture is true, this assertion is fairly accurate. However, it must also be recognized that this commitment has been held in the midst of a variety of notions concerning God, truth, and the interpretation of the Bible. Hence, ancient Christian luminaries such as Origen, Gregory of Nazianzus, Ambrose, Augustine, and Gregory the Great all affirmed that Scripture was truthful and without error, but did so with philosophical, hermeneutical, and theological assumptions that allowed them to downplay and even sometimes discount the literal meaning of Scripture in favor of spiritual and allegorical interpretation.[2] It is doubtful that any of these early Christian leaders would affirm the details of inerrancy as they have come to be articulated in the Chicago statement.

Of course, the Chicago statement is not primarily concerned with ancient Christian thinkers. The framers were concerned about people who were maintaining that parts of the Bible were errant and could not be trusted. In response to the perceived erosion of biblical authority, the Chicago statement maintains in its short statement summary that since the Bible is inspired by God, who is the "Truth and speaks truth only," it is "God's own Word" and is of "infallible divine authority in all matters upon which it touches." Therefore, being "wholly and verbally God-given, Scripture is without error or fault in all its teaching, no less in what it states about God's acts in creation, about the events of world history, and about its own literary origins under God, than in its witness to God's saving grace in individual lives." Articles of affirmation and denial then add detail and nuance.

As a whole, the Chicago statement is reflective of a particular form of epistemology known as classic or strong foundationalism. This approach to knowledge seeks to overcome the uncertainty generated by the tendency of fallible human beings to error, by discovering a universal and indubitable basis for human knowledge. This conception

---

2. For a discussion of biblical interpretation in the early church, see Christopher A. Hall, *Reading Scripture with the Church Fathers* (Downers Grove, Ill.: InterVarsity, 1998). On spiritual interpretation in the writings of the figures mentioned here, see John R. Franke, ed., *Joshua, Judges, Ruth, 1–2 Samuel*, Ancient Christian Commentary on Scripture: Old Testament 4 (Downers Grove, Ill.: InterVarsity, 2005), xviii–xxvii.

of knowledge became one of the dominant assumptions of intellectual pursuit after the Enlightenment and decisively shaped the cultural discourse and practices of the Western world.[3]

The doctrine of inerrancy formulated in the Chicago statement and worked out in evangelical theology gives every indication that Scripture is to be viewed as just the sort of strong foundation envisioned by classical foundationalists. In this framing, Scripture is the true and sole basis for knowledge on all matters which it touches. It is equally authoritative on matters of science and history as on spiritual and religious concerns. Hence, for many people committed to inerrancy, if the Bible says that the earth was created in six literal, twenty-four-hour days, then that is what must be believed, no matter what other evidence is produced by scientific inquiry. If Scripture teaches that the first humans were created from the dust of the ground, then evolution must be declared false no matter what other evidence is produced. In matters of history, the biblical accounts must be affirmed no matter what evidence or lack thereof is produced by archaeology. The list could go on and on. In addition, this approach maintains that if there is a single error at any place in the Bible, none of it can be trusted. I have heard it said many times from this perspective that if there is one error in the Bible, there may as well be a thousand and none of it can be trusted. Of course, this is nonsense. As though an error in one of the books of the Old Testament means that the witness to the resurrection in the New Testament is somehow suspect or less trustworthy. This is classic foundationalism in action, even if the term is not acknowledged.

The problem with this approach is that it has been thoroughly discredited in philosophical and theological circles. There are other forms of foundationalism, often termed weak or modest foundationalism, and these are often in conversation with nonfoundationalism. Many, perhaps even most, of the philosophers in the Evangelical Theological Society subscribe to this chastened form of foundationalism. The details of these various positions need not detain us here; suffice it to say that all of these alternative epistemologies are characterized by fallibilism. Fallibilism is the philosophical principle that human beings

---

3. For a detailed discussion of foundationalism and its influence on theology, see Stanley J. Grenz and John R. Franke, *Beyond Foundationalism: Shaping Theology in a Postmodern Context* (Louisville: Westminster, 2001), 3–54.

can be wrong about their beliefs and that absolute certainty about knowledge is impossible.

I have little doubt that the Chicago statement was drafted with no intention of conforming to classic foundationalism, but I am concerned that it is nevertheless indicative of the assumptions of this approach. Inerrancy has certainly been used in a manner consistent with classical foundationalism. And yet most evangelicals these days appear to claim that they are not strong foundationalists but weak ones. In the framework of weak foundationalism, inerrancy could be mistaken and should be subject to critical scrutiny. The question should be asked: Is inerrancy really the best way to articulate the content of Scripture as the Word of God, based on what we read in the texts? What might the doctrine of inerrancy look like in a fallibilist perspective? On the other hand, if, as I suspect, a significant number of evangelicals are in fact classical foundationalists, they ought to say so and be prepared to defend their position. What I find frustrating is that many evangelicals claim that they are not classic foundationalists and then defend beliefs such as inerrancy as though they were.

From my postfoundationalist perspective, inerrancy is a second-order theological construction that is derived from the teaching of Scripture, rather than a direct assertion from the Bible. In other words, I don't believe that inerrancy is specifically taught as such in the pages of the Bible. It is rather the product of a series of inferences based on direct biblical statements that are construed as leading to the doctrine of inerrancy. The second-order status of inerrancy points to the interpretive character of the doctrine.

As a theological construction, inerrancy is the product of reflection on the primary stories, teachings, symbols, and practices contained in Scripture and therefore must be distinguished from these first-order commitments. Theological constructions and doctrines are always subservient to the content of Scripture and therefore must be held more lightly. Those who defend inerrancy do so based on an argument that it is a necessary consequence of divine inspiration, based on their understanding of God and the nature of truth. However, Christians in other traditions also affirm inspiration, but not inerrancy. They believe that such a notion does not do justice to the texts, themselves, or their understanding of God. The challenge is that conceptions of God and truth are interpretive and have varied throughout the centuries among those who have been committed to the authority of the Bible as the Word of God.

Even the Chicago statement acknowledges, in article 13, that it is improper "to evaluate Scripture according to standards of truth and error that are alien to its usage or purpose." This opens up a vast arena of interpretive possibilities with respect to the "usage or purpose" of Scripture in relation to standards of "truth or error." This seemingly allows for the possibility that the statements of Scripture are not timeless axioms but time-sensitive claims that must be understood according to their historical and canonical context. Yet the CSBI reveals its tendency toward foundationalism in article 12, which asserts, "We deny that Biblical infallibility and inerrancy are limited to spiritual, religious, or redemptive themes, exclusive of assertions in the fields of history and science."

But must we view Scripture as a foundation for human knowledge? Is it really necessary to burden Scripture with the commitments of classical foundationalism? I believe that doing so is "to evaluate Scripture according to standards of truth and error that are alien to its usage." Scripture provides us with knowledge of God that is reliable and truthful and yet not axiomatic. For this reason, I do not believe that the Chicago statement is able to serve as the standard-bearer for inerrancy. I will offer an alternative model.

The God of Scripture

Notions of inerrancy are connected to wider theological convictions. Any conception of inerrancy will carry with it a set of theological assumptions, stated or unstated, that shape the way in which it functions with respect to the interpretation of Scripture. One of the challenges in articulating a view of inerrancy—or any other doctrine, for that matter—is that the framing ideas are all contested in the Christian tradition. Hence, differences over inerrancy can quickly become related to differences over other questions. One of the strengths of this volume is that the contributors are asked to be clear about the broader assumptions that shape their view of inerrancy. At the same time, one of the challenges is that space does not permit the development of a detailed rationale for these assumptions.

In order to understand Scripture as the Word of God, it would seem to be important to first say something about the God of Scripture. While space permits only a cursory mention of several convictions about God, it is important to bring them into relief as the context in which my understanding of the Word of God is framed.

God Is God (and We Are Not)

One of the most basic assertions of the Bible is the creator-creature distinction. In Isaiah 55:8, we are told that God's thoughts are not our thoughts and that our ways are not God's. Second Peter 3:8 declares that for God, "a day is like a thousand years, and a thousand years are like a day." The Christian tradition has concluded from these and many other texts that the infinite God is radically different from finite creatures. This infinite qualitative distinction means that even revelation is not able to provide human beings with a knowledge that exactly corresponds to that of God. It also points to the accommodated character of all human knowledge of God.

God Is Living and Active

God is best understood as a being-in-act, meaning that God cannot be comprehended apart from God's actions and ongoing active relations. In the same way, the relationship of human beings to God is best conceived of in active rather than static terms. Relations with God are not something that can be possessed once and for all but rather are events that must be continually established by the ongoing work of God.

God Is Love

Since God is a being-in-act, his identity is known through his actions, and what God does is love. From all eternity, God has been in an active loving relationship characterized by the giving, receiving, and sharing of love between Father, Son, and Holy Spirit. We might also say that this active, relational participating in the divine fellowship of love is characteristic of the mission of God throughout eternity and in relation to the created order.

God Is Missional

God is a missionary, and therefore the Christian tradition speaks of the mission of God *(missio Dei)*. Love characterizes the mission of God from all eternity and is the basis for the sending of his Son into the world: "This is how God showed his love among us: He sent his one and only Son into the world that we might live through him" (1 John 4:9). The mission of God in Jesus is continued through the Spirit-guided witness to the gospel of churches in every culture that are sent into the world after the pattern by which the Father sent the Son: "As the Father has sent me, I am sending you" (John 20:21). This means that mission is not a product of the church; instead it is derived from the very nature of God. As missiologist David Bosch has observed, the logic of the classical doctrine of the *missio Dei*, expressed as God the Father sending the Son and then the Father and the Son sending the Spirit, must be expanded to include yet another movement: "Father, Son, and Spirit sending the church into the world."[4]

God Is Plurality-in-Unity and Unity-in-Plurality

The statement "God is love" refers primarily to the eternal, relational intra-Trinitarian fellowship among Father, Son, and Holy Spirit, who together are the one God in their interdependent relationality. The plurality-in-unity and unity-in-plurality that characterizes the life of the triune God means that difference and otherness is part of the divine life. It is important to note in this context that the love of God is not an assimilating love. It does not seek to make that which is different the same; rather it lives in harmonious fellowship with the other through the active relations of self-sacrificing, self-giving love. The Father, Son, and Spirit are indeed one God, but this unity does not make them the same. They are one in the very midst of their difference. With these convictions in view, I am now in a position to articulate an understanding of the Word of God that arises from them.

Divine Accommodation, Truth, and Scripture

In articulating an understanding of the Word of God, I believe we must keep the infinite qualitative distinction between God and ourselves at the forefront of our concerns, lest we fall into the idolatry of imagining that our thoughts and conceptions of God and truth corre-

---

4. David Bosch, *Transforming Mission: Paradigm Shifts in Theology of Mission* (Maryknoll, N.Y.: Orbis, 1991), 390.

spond to those of God. As finite creatures, we are not able to grasp the truth as God, who is truth, knows that truth to be. This situation gives rise to the theological adage *finitum non capax infiniti*—the finite cannot comprehend the infinite.

In order to respect this reality while still affirming that God has been made known in the act of revelation, John Calvin, one of the most influential theologians among evangelicals, appeals to the notion of divine accommodation.[5] This means that in the process of revelation, God "adjusts" and "descends" to the limited capacities of human beings and "lisps" to us, as adults do to infants, in order to be made known. Apart from such accommodating action, the knowledge of God would, by its very nature, be beyond the capabilities of human creatures to grasp because of the limitations that arise from our finite character. These limitations extend not only to the cognitive and imaginative faculties but also to the very mediums by which revelation is communicated to us.

For instance, language is contingent on the contexts and situations that give rise to particular vocabularies that shape and are shaped by the social circumstances in which they arise. As such, each language is a particular conceptual scheme that lacks the capacity and universality required to provide a description of God or ultimate truth that can be thought of as absolute. The plurality and flexibility of particular vocabularies provide a pointed reminder of the perspectival nature of language itself.

In making this assertion, we can appeal to the ecumenical Christian tradition and the conclusions of the Council of Chalcedon in 451. The Chalcedonian definition affirms that the divine nature of Jesus remains divine, even in the context of its relationship with the human nature, and the human nature remains human, even in the context of its relationship with the divine nature. One of the implications of this formulation is the denial of the "divinization" of the human nature of Jesus. Since the human nature employed as the medium of revelation is not divinized, it remains subject to its historically and culturally conditioned character.

5. John Calvin, *Institutes of the Christian Religion* 1.13.1. On Calvin's understanding of divine accommodation, see Edward A. Dowey Jr., *The Knowledge of God in Calvin's Theology*, 3rd ed. (Grand Rapids, Mich.: Eerdmans, 1994), 3–24.

By analogy, we can posit that what is true of the human nature of Jesus Christ with respect to divinization is also true of the words of the prophets and apostles in Scripture. The use that God makes of the creaturely medium of human speech and language in the inspiration and witness of Scripture does not entail its divinization. Language, like the human nature of Jesus, remains subject to the historical, social, and cultural limitations and contingencies inherent in its creaturely character, without compromising its suitability as a medium for the Word of God.

The notion of divine accommodation means that in fulfilling its purpose to form witnessing communities, Scripture functions like a map that effectively guides our journey into the mission of God. It pragmatically points us in the right direction without the necessity of being photographically precise or drawn exactly to scale. The application of divine accommodation to Scripture as the written Word of God points to the contextual character of the Bible and suggests an important element in the way in which Scripture is truth. Human language is incapable of providing descriptions of God that are fully faithful to the reality of God as God is in Godself. This is the very reason for positing the notion of divine accommodation. This means that while God's use of language in the act of self-revelation allows us to speak in authentically informative ways about God, we must still acknowledge the inherent mystery and otherness of God even in the act of bearing witness to God through our speech. The early church theologian Irenaeus captured this idea by asserting that while it is true and faithful to say that God is light, it is also true that God is unlike any light that we know.[6] Hence, our affirmation of God as light provides us with a measure of genuine understanding about God but does not eradicate the infinite qualitative distinction between us and God.

This conception of human language, as a vehicle of analogical reference for God, points to a distinction that must be made between the way in which the self-revelation of God in Jesus Christ is truth and the way in which the inspired words of Scripture are truth. As forms of the Word of God, both are true, but as inspired witnesses to revelation, or revelatory witnesses, the words of Scripture are not divin-

---

6. Irenaeus, *Against Heresies* 2.13.4.

ized and remain subject to the limitations of their creaturely character. We might make the distinction in the following way: the truth as God experiences it and knows it to be is capital-t (or ultimate) Truth; the inspired witnesses to truth contained in the human speech-acts of Scripture are situated and fragmentary and are therefore small-t truth. By inspiration, they bear a proper relationship to God, but inspiration does not enable them to transcend their limitations as a finite crea-turely medium. Hence, in this analogy, they are small-t truth rather than capital-t Truth, since only God has the knowledge of capital-t Truth. In this framing, all human knowledge, experience, and com-munication is understood as being situated in particular circumstances, and these circumstances have a significant effect on the character and content of human experience and knowledge. Only the living God transcends the limitations of time and place that are characteristic of finitude.

In keeping with the conviction that God has been revealed in the person of Jesus Christ, we can affirm the reality of ultimate or tran-scendent truth even as we acknowledge the interpretive character of human knowledge. At the same time, by virtue of the grace of divine revelation, we are able to know something about reality even if we cannot know it exhaustively or perfectly. Scripture is truth written (small t), in that it provides a series of faithful witnesses to the Truth of God's self-revelation without itself becoming a manifestation of capital-t Truth. This means that while Scripture is truthful and trust-worthy, we must be careful to respect the creator-creature distinction in our use of it.[7]

From this perspective, inerrancy is a theological category that applies to the Bible within the finite limitations of the particular con-textual vocabularies in which the texts were produced. It functions within the context of language as a finite, socially constructed medium and does not transcend those limits. Inerrancy affirms that narratives, propositions, and assertions—in fact, all the genres of Scripture— are true but are still relative to their context. Inerrancy should not be used to suggest, then, that the words of Scripture transcend their

---

7. For a more detailed discussion of the rationale for this way of delineating the distinc-tion between Truth and truth, see Merold Westphal, *Overcoming Onto-Theology: Toward a Postmodern Christian Faith* (New York: Fordham Univ. Press, 2001), 75–88.

situatedness as a form of decontextualized, absolutist theological language. I would say it this way: inerrancy functions only within the limits of language alone. It applies to Scripture only in the context of the original settings in which the texts that we have were constructed, and its affirmations and teachings cannot be abstracted from those contexts and offered as absolute truth, because only God knows and is Truth.

Word and Spirit

In keeping with the actualistic character of God's being, the Word of God is always an *act* which God performs or an *event* in which God has spoken, speaks, and will speak. In this conception, the Word of God may be viewed as having three forms: the act of revelation itself, the Spirit-inspired attestation and witness to revelation in the words of Scripture, and the Spirit-guided witness to revelation in the proclamation of the Christian community. In seeking to explain this event, we might imagine three concentric circles that represent three movements in the communication and reception of the Word of God. The innermost circle of the three is the Word of God as divine speech-act authored and spoken by God; however, this divine speech is represented to us and made expressible and approachable through the Spirit-inspired and Spirit-guided human and creaturely speech-acts contained in Scripture and the witness of the church. Hence, the Word of God may be described as the Word revealed, the Word written, and the Word lived and proclaimed.

Here I will focus on the function of Scripture as a form of the Word of God in relation to the work of the Spirit. The Protestant tradition has always been concerned to bind Word and Spirit together as a means of providing the conceptual framework for authority in the Christian faith. In the sixteenth century, John Calvin affirmed this Protestant principle in response to two tendencies with respect to the separation of Word and Spirit, that of "collapsing" the Spirit into the text, and that of ignoring the text in the name of following the Spirit. Calvin asserts the principle that the church is to be governed by the Spirit, but also maintains that the Spirit is bound to Scripture in order to ensure "that this government might not be vague and unstable."[8] I believe it would be more appropriate to affirm that Scripture is bound

---

8. John Calvin, "Reply to Sadolet," *Calvin: Theological Treatises*, ed. J. K. S. Reid (Philadelphia: Westminster, 1954), 229.

to the Spirit, who, in the divine economy, inspired it and continues to speak through it. To say that the Spirit is bound to Scripture runs the risk of collapsing the Spirit into the text and thus allowing human beings to move from a position of epistemic dependency with respect to the knowledge of God to one of mastery. From this perspective, I maintain that ultimate authority in the church is the Spirit speaking both in Scripture as well as through Scripture.

The assertion that our final authority is the Spirit speaking in and through Scripture means that Christian belief and practice cannot be determined merely by appeal either to the exegesis of Scripture carried out apart from the life of the believer and the believing community or to any supposed word from the Spirit that stands in contradiction to biblical exegesis. The reading and interpretation of the text are for the purpose of listening to the voice of the Spirit, who speaks in and through Scripture to the church in the present. This means that the Bible is authoritative in that it is the vehicle through which the Spirit speaks. In other words, the authority of the Bible, as the instrument through which the Spirit speaks, is ultimately bound up with the authority of the Spirit. Christians acknowledge the Bible as Scripture because the Spirit has spoken, now speaks, and will continue to speak with authority through the canonical texts of Scripture.

Through Scripture, the Spirit continually instructs the church as the historically extended community of Christ's followers in the midst of the opportunities and challenges of life in the contemporary world. The Bible is the instrumentality of the Spirit in that the Spirit appropriates the biblical text for the purpose of speaking to us today. This actualistic appropriation does not come independently of the so-called original meaning of the text. Indeed, careful historical exegesis is a crucial component in attempting to understand the meaning of Scripture. However, the speaking of the Spirit is not bound up solely with the supposed original intent of the authors and editors of the biblical texts. Contemporary proponents of textual intentionality, such as Paul Ricoeur, explain that although an author creates a literary text, once it has been written, it takes on a life of its own.[9] While the ways in

---

9. For a discussion of the significance of Ricoeur's work for the task of theology, see Dan R. Stiver, *Theology after Ricoeur: New Directions in Hermeneutical Theology* (Louisville: Westminster, 2001).

which the text is structured shape the meanings the reader discerns in the text, the author's intentions come to be distanced from the meanings of the work. In this sense, a text can be viewed metaphorically as having its own intention. This textual intention has its genesis in the author's intention but is not exhausted by it.

Therefore we must not conclude that exegesis alone can exhaust the Spirit's speaking to us through the text. While the Spirit appropriates the text in its internal meaning, the goal of this appropriation is to guide the church in the variegated circumstances of particular contemporary settings. Hence, we realize that the Spirit's speaking comes through the text not in isolation but rather in the context of specific historical-cultural situations and as part of an extended interpretive tradition.

The assertion that the Spirit appropriates the text of Scripture and speaks in and through it to people in a contemporary setting leads to the question of the goal or effect of the Spirit's speaking. What does the Spirit seek to accomplish in the act of speaking through the appropriated text of Scripture? An appropriate response to this inquiry suggests that through the process of addressing readers in various contemporary settings, the Spirit creates world. Sociologists point out that religion plays a significant role in world construction through a set of beliefs and practices that provide a particular way of looking at reality. For this reason, Paul Ricoeur asserts that the meaning of a text always points beyond itself in that the meaning is "not behind the text, but in front of it." Texts project a way of being in the world, a mode of existence, a pattern of life, and point toward a possible world.[10] The Bible stands in a central position in the practice of the faith in that the Christian community reads the biblical text as Scripture and looks to it as the focal point for shaping the narrative world it inhabits. In short, as John Goldingay declares, the text "calls a new world into being."[11] However, the point that needs to be stressed here is that this capacity for world construction, while bound closely to the text, does not lie in the text itself. Instead this result is ultimately the work of the Spirit speaking in and through the text as the instrumentality of world cre-

10. Paul Ricoeur, *Interpretation Theory: Discourse and the Surplus of Meaning* (Fort Worth: Texas Christian Univ. Press, 1976), 87.

11. John Goldingay, *Models for Scripture* (Grand Rapids, Mich.: Eerdmans, 1994), 256.

ation. The world the Spirit creates is neither the world surrounding the ancient text nor the contemporary world but rather the eschatological world God intends for creation as disclosed, displayed, and anticipated by Scripture.

Truth, Eschatological Realism, Christian Community, and Missional Plurality

The ongoing work of the Spirit is manifest in the appropriation of the biblical narrative in order to speak to the church for the purpose of creating a socially constructed world that finds its coherence in Jesus Christ in accordance with, and in anticipation of, the real world as it is willed to be by the Father. However, the world as God wills it to be is not a present reality; rather it lies in the eschatological future. Thus, while acknowledging that there is indeed a certain objective actuality to the world, it is important to recognize that this objectivity is not that of a static actuality existing outside of, and cotemporally with, our socially and linguistically constructed realities. It is not what some might call the world as it is. Instead the biblical narratives set forth the objectivity of the world as God wills it. Hence, Jesus taught his disciples to pray, "Your will be done, on earth as it is in heaven" (Matt. 6:10). The most real world is the future, eschatological world that God will establish in the new creation. Because this future reality is God's determined will for creation, as that which cannot be shaken (Heb. 12:26–28), it is far more real, objective, and actual than the present world, which is even now passing away (1 Cor. 7:31). In this way, the biblical narratives point to what might be called eschatological realism.

In relating this eschatological realism to the insights of social constructionists, we note that human beings, as bearers of the divine image, are called to participate in God's work of constructing a world in the present that reflects God's eschatological will for creation. This call has a strongly linguistic dimension because of the role of language in the task of world construction. Through the constructive power of language, the Christian community anticipates the divine eschatological world that stands at the climax of the biblical narrative, in which all creation finds its connectedness in Jesus Christ (Col. 1:17), who is the Word (John 1:1) and the ordering principle of the cosmos. Hence, Christian mission may be construed as Christocentric in its communitarian focus and Christotelic in its eschatological orientation. This eschatological future is anticipated in the present through the work of the Spirit, who leads the church into truth (1 John 2:27). From this perspective, the Christian community bears witness to the truth of the gospel of Jesus Christ through the construction of a social linguistic world that finds it coherence in Christ in accordance with the will of the Father. As such, the church is called to be a provisional demonstration of God's will for all creation.

The shape of this community of Christ followers is connected to the missional character of God's eternal life of love reflected in the biblical witness to God's love for the world. This is manifest in the sending of the Son and the Spirit for the purpose of reconciliation and redemption, in order that the world might participate in the fellowship of love shared by Father, Son, and Holy Spirit. This mission is at the heart of the biblical narratives concerning the work of God in human history. The Spirit bears witness to this mission in the inspiration of Scripture, for the purpose of forming witnessing communities that participate in the divine mission by living God's love in the way of Jesus Christ for the sake of the world.

The connection of the Word of God with truth invites a consideration of the nature of truth as relational and life-giving rather than simply a matter of right cognition or a proper conception and expression of facts and propositions. The content of this relational understanding of truth is love. Hence, we read the exhortation in Scripture to love: "Dear friends, let us love one another, for love comes from God. Everyone who loves has been born of God and knows God. Whoever does not love does not know God, because God is love" (1 John 4:7–8). Love is fundamental to truth. Hence, the prominent early church theologian Augustine of Hippo asserts that if we read Scripture in ways that lead us to love, we read it truthfully. Likewise, if we read it in ways that do not lead us to love, then we misread it, no matter what else we affirm that it teaches.[12]

A final element of the witnessing community that the Spirit forms through the agency of Scripture is plurality. One of the entailments of the contextual character of the Bible that is the result of divine accom-

---

12. Augustine, *On Christian Doctrine*, bk. 1, chap. 36.

modation and its witness to the being and character of God is its diversity. Indeed, the Bible is not so much a single book as it is a collection of texts from different settings and perspectives in the story of God's mission in the world. In other words, the Bible is polyphonic. Perhaps the presence of four gospel accounts offers the most straightforward and significant demonstration of plurality in the biblical canon. The inclusion of Matthew, Mark, Luke, and John, each with its distinct perspective on the life and ministry of Jesus, alerts us to the pluriform character of the gospel. This stands as a powerful reminder that the witness of the Christian community to the gospel of Jesus Christ can never be contained in a single universal account. Instead it is always situated in and characterized by a diversity of forms and perspectives, in keeping with the tradition of the biblical canon.

The multiplicity of the canonical witness to the gospel is not incidental to the shape of the community from which it emerged and which it envisions for the future. Attempts to suppress the plurality of the canonical witness by means of an overarching, universalistic account lead to serious distortions of the gospel and the community that is called to bear witness to it. Now, if Scripture as a form of the Word of God is truth written, and if Scripture is characterized by plurality, we must conclude that truth is characterized by plurality.[13]

It is worth mentioning at this point that this plurality should not be construed as leading to an "anything goes" sort of relativism. While the meaning of Scripture as the Word of God is pluriform and inexhaustible, this does not mean that all interpretations are therefore true. Some, even many, are false and untrue. The history of the church is filled with erroneous and destructive understandings of the Bible that have led to the oppression and marginalization of others.

In addition, as witness to the revelatory speech-act of the triune God, the plurality of Scripture should not be used as a denial of the unity of the canon. In keeping with the conviction that the Bible is inspired by the Spirit for the purpose of bearing witness to the self-revelation of God and guiding the church into truth, Christians affirm that the Bible constitutes a unity as well as a plurality. The unity of

---

13. For a fuller delineation of this idea, see John R. Franke, *Manifold Witness: The Plurality of Truth* (Nashville: Abingdon, 2009).

Scripture is found in its witness to the revelation of God in Jesus Christ. But this unity is a differentiated unity expressed in plurality. In this way, Scripture as the Word of God serves also as a witness to, and a reflection of, the plurality-in-unity and unity-in-plurality that characterizes the life of the triune God. Hence, the plurality of Scripture is the result of both the complexity and situatedness of language as a finite human medium as well as the identity and self-revelation of God, who enters into the setting of finitude as an accommodation to human limitation.

Scripture itself authorizes multiple perspectives within a set of possibilities that are also appropriately circumscribed by the shape and content of the canon. The plurality of the church is a faithful expression of the plurality of Scripture, which is in turn a faithful witness to the plurality of truth lived out in the eternal life of God and expressed in the act of revelation. As the Word of God and *normative* witness to revelation, Scripture consists of inspired human speech-acts that bear authentic witness to the divine speech-act of the event of revelation. As such, Scripture is truth written, and its pages bear witness to the plurality of truth. As the Word of God and *paradigmatic* human and creaturely witness to the event of revelation, Scripture also invites greater plurality than that contained in its pages, in order that the witness of the church to the missional love of God may be continually expanded and incarnated among all people.

The Nature, Status, and Function of Inerrancy

Viewed from this perspective, Scripture is inerrant in its witness to the plurality of perspectives that are indispensable to the practice of missional Christian community. *Inerrancy* is a technical theological term that serves to preserve the dynamic plurality contained in the texts of Scripture by ensuring that no portion of the biblical narrative can properly be disregarded or eclipsed because it is perceived as failing to conform to a larger pattern of systematic unity. This is a tendency among those who are not committed to any notion of inerrancy. Since some portions of the Bible do not fit into a particular individual or community's assumptions concerning God or Christian faith, those details are eliminated from the narrative as false or in error and then conveniently ignored. A well-known example of this approach is the so-called Jefferson Bible, in which the life and teachings of Jesus from the Bible are presented with the notable exclusion of the miracles of Jesus, references to his divinity, and the resurrection. These did not fit into Jefferson's views, and so they were eliminated.

This temptation can be strong, even among those with a commitment to the inspiration and authority of the whole Bible, particularly in the face of texts that seem to challenge deeply held theological convictions. One famous example is Martin Luther's suggestion that the epistle of James be metaphorically thrown into the fire since it appeared to challenge his formula that justification is by faith alone and not works with its statement that a person "is considered righteous by what they do and not by faith alone" (2:24). In the face of the temptation to declare certain portions of the Bible in error and to therefore eliminate them from consideration in the articulation and proclamation of the Christian faith, inerrancy functions to ensure that all of Scripture is taken seriously and viewed as authoritative.

This particular function of inerrancy is an important distinctive of those communities that are committed to the doctrine and its assertion that the whole of Scripture is truthful and trustworthy as the Word of God. It is inerrancy's second function, though, that presents a greater challenge to such communities. Inerrancy means that none of the texts of Scripture should be forced into conformity with others for the sake of systematic unity. To do this is to impose on the text an illegitimate interpretive assumption that truth must be characterized by a universal, systematic unity and that, this being the case, the texts of Scripture must be coherent with each other in ways that allow the underlying unity to be ascertained. I believe that inerrancy challenges this notion and serves to deconstruct the idea of a single normative system of theology.

Instead the notion of biblical inerrancy, wed to a pluralist notion of truth, functions to ensure that orthodox, biblical faith will be understood not as an entirely coherent, single, universal, and systematic entity but rather as an open and flexible tradition that allows for the witness and testimony of plural perspectives, practices, and experiences as the love of God revealed in Jesus Christ is incarnated in the witness of communities from every tribe, nation, and ethnicity. A single, normative, systematic interpretation of the whole Bible is neither attainable nor desirable. As with the problematic notion of a cultural melting pot in which numerous distinct cultures come together and form one new universal culture made up of all the others, something of value is always left out or excluded. When we attempt to ease the difficulties of the multiple perspectives in Scripture to make matters more compact, clear, and manageable, we suffer the loss of plurality and diversity that is woven into the very fabric of Scripture and, by extension, into the divine design of God.

The significance of this is connected to the purpose of Scripture to form witnessing communities that participate in the divine mission by living God's love in the way of Jesus Christ for the sake of the world. When notions of inerrancy are connected with the idea of absolute truth as a single system of doctrine revealed by God that can be grasped by human beings, the result is conflict and colonization. A particular understanding of theology and truth is developed and then taken to be universal, absolute, and inerrant by the people who framed it. They believe that in propagating and defending this system, they are doing God's will and that other people who do not share their convictions are not really faithful to God or the teaching of the Bible. This results in conflict between individuals and communities that have reached alternative conclusions. These conflicts have shaped the history of Christianity as competing communities have struggled to achieve hegemony. In the history of Christian mission, this approach has led to the colonization, oppression, and marginalization of people in the name of God, Jesus, the Bible, and truth because they did not conform to the standards that were claimed to be the only right way to be faithful to God. This is not in keeping with the self-giving love of God lived out in fellowship with the difference of the other.

The inerrant plurality of Scripture frustrates attempts to establish a single universal theology. It reminds us that our interpretations, theories, and theologies are always situated and perspectival; none simply rise above the social conditions and particular interests from which they emerge. Missionary theologian Lesslie Newbigin points out that this is true even with respect to our understanding of the gospel itself: "We must start with the basic fact that there is no such thing as a pure gospel if by that is meant something which is not embodied in a culture.... Every interpretation of the gospel is embodied in some cultural form."[14]

One of the dangers of cultural hegemony is that people in the dominant culture will be tempted to conclude that their outlook is universal. Such a conclusion will lead to the marginalization of other people who do not share in the outlooks and assumptions of the dominant group. Inerrancy calls on us to surrender the pretensions of a universal and timeless theology. Where we are unwilling to do this, we propagate forms of cultural, ethnic, and racial imperialism under the guise of Scripture and the Word of God. Positively, inerrancy wed to the plurality of truth holds great promise, for the witness of the church, as a practical research program in missional theology.

Reading the Bible

This view of the Bible and inerrancy invites us to read and assess texts on their own terms rather than demanding that they fit into overarching interpretive schemes. We will see their truth not in absolute terms but rather in terms of temporal witness in the midst of particular circumstances. It will produce an open and flexible theology in keeping with the mission of God as it is displayed in the Bible itself.

As an example of this, consider the question of circumcision as a covenantal identity marker of the people of God. In Genesis 17, God makes an everlasting covenant with Abraham that requires as its sign the circumcision of every male. This extends to all male members of the community, those born into it or those who enter it from the outside, such as those purchased from a foreigner. All are to be circumcised, and any who are not are cut off from the community because the covenant has been broken. Contrast this with the decision of the Jerusalem Council in Acts 15 on the question of circumcision for Gentiles as a requirement of being part of the community of God's people. While some believers from the party of the Pharisees argued that Gentile converts must be circumcised in keeping with the Torah, the council, following the testimonies of Peter, Paul, and Barnabas, decided not to make it difficult for the Gentile believers by requiring that they be circumcised. I

---

14. Lesslie Newbigin, *The Gospel in a Pluralist Society* (Grand Rapids, Mich.: Eerdmans, 1989), 144.

don't think it would be going too far to say that the council decided that the Gentile converts did not need to follow the scriptural mandate in Genesis 17, doubtless to the consternation of the Pharisees. The council members determined that the action of God in accepting the Gentiles by giving them the Holy Spirit required that they make a decision consonant with that action rather than slavishly following the text. This is a canonical example of a crucial, identity-forming theological decision that is reflective of an open, flexible, and contextual way of thinking. I believe that the church today should practice theology in a manner consistent with this canonical example.

The contributors to this volume have been asked to interact with three biblical texts or sets of texts that are indicative of particular challenges to the notion of inerrancy and to show how certain conceptions of Scripture influence the reading of texts and are likewise tested by the texts. I will conclude with an examination of these texts and challenges.

Historical Accuracy (Josh. 6)

One of the long-standing questions related to inerrancy is that of historical accuracy. One such challenge concerns the fall of Jericho. The sixth chapter of Joshua tells us that because of the advance of the Israelites, the gates of Jericho were securely barred and no one went in or out. In response to this situation, the Lord tells Joshua that the city and its inhabitants will be delivered into his hands, and instructs Joshua to have his army march around the city once a day for six days. On the seventh day, Joshua is told to march around the city seven times, with the priests blowing trumpets. When they blow a long blast on the trumpets, the whole army is to give a loud shout, after which the wall will collapse and the army will be able to go in and conquer the city. Joshua did as he was instructed, and according to the text, "when the trumpets sounded, the army shouted, and at the sound of the trumpet, when the men gave a loud shout, the wall collapsed; so everyone charged straight in, and they took the city" (Josh. 6:20).

The problem concerns the historical accuracy of the text from the standpoint of widely held archaeological assumptions concerning Jericho. Many archaeologists have concluded that during the relevant time frame of these events, "the famed battle of Jericho cannot have happened, as no city with walls existed at that time; they were destroyed several centuries earlier."[15] If this is the case, then the story in Joshua cannot be accurate, thus posing a problem for conceptions of inerrancy such as that contained in the Chicago statement.

Various responses have been offered to this challenge. Some have naturally contended that the archaeological assumptions of the majority are wrong and that Jericho was a larger settlement with walls. In fact, there is some evidence of a walled city that would be of a size appropriate to the biblical story. However, the belief among most archaeologists is that the dating of these remains is not within the plausible time frame of the Joshua story. Others have suggested that while the data may not appear to fully support the Joshua story, neither do they render it entirely impossible. They also maintain that since all evidence is subject to revision based on future findings and fresh interpretation, it remains possible that the Joshua story will yet be validated, and they point to past incidents in which this type of revision has occurred in support of the biblical narratives.

Nevertheless, the dominant view among archaeologists remains that the Jericho described in the text did not exist at the time of its reported conquest in the book of Joshua. In response to the hegemony of this view, other scholars have simply been content to acknowledge the essential historicity of the Hebrew narratives, such as that contained in Joshua, while acknowledging that this essential history can be communicated using the "mythic" language common among the peoples of ancient Near Eastern culture.[16] Such an approach would seem to expand the concept of inerrancy in directions that are more open to the exaggerations and one-sidedness of propaganda rather than a mere recitation of historical occurrence.

This willingness of some scholars to employ the language of myth while still maintaining the position of inerrancy points to the challenges posed by external evidence and a particular set of assumptions about the trustworthiness of the biblical texts. However, when all is said and done, the reality remains that we simply have no way of

---

15. Douglas A. Knight and Amy-Jill Levine, *The Meaning of the Bible: What the Jewish Scriptures and Christian Old Testament Can Teach Us* (New York: HarperOne, 2011), 20.

16. Two prominent examples of this usage of myth can be found in the following works: James K. Hoffmeier, *Israel in Egypt: The Evidence for the Authenticity of the Exodus Tradition* (New York: Oxford Univ. Press, 1996) and Kenneth Kitchen, *On the Reliability of the Old Testament* (Grand Rapids, Mich.: Eerdmans, 2003).

verifying or falsifying the explicit details contained in the story of the fall of Jericho. From my perspective, this does not pose a problem for the truthfulness of Scripture. Its ultimate purpose is not to provide precise, literal details of history but to form a covenantal community called to be a blessing to the world in keeping with the mission of God. In this context, it is a mistake to tie the authority of Scripture to an approach that cannot be verified and faces serious external challenges. To argue that the authority of Scripture is fatally compromised if it cannot sustain these challenges is to leave it vulnerable to the fickle nature of ever-changing historical contingencies and circumstances.

It also means committing to a thoroughly discredited program of classical foundationalism as a means of securing Scripture's authority. Contrary to the intentions of those who embark on this strategy, the Bible will be viewed by many as less reliable, because of this all-or-nothing approach. Either the Bible is absolutely inerrant in all matters on which it touches, or its authority as the Word of God is called into question. The result of this has been that its authority is called into question, because it was not intended to sustain such a defense.

A helpful metaphorical shift concerning biblical authority would be to think of it as part of a web of interconnected beliefs rather than as the foundation on which all other beliefs are established and built. In the web model, new evidence, fresh interpretation, and alternative viewpoints are continually assessed and incorporated as needed into the existing network of beliefs. All beliefs are subjected to critical scrutiny and may be reconstructed, replaced, or relinquished if necessary. This is in keeping with the fallibilism that is part of all epistemology in the aftermath of classic foundationalism. Inerrancy set in a nonfoundationalist or modest foundationalist framework can accommodate the generally accepted conclusions of external evidence, propose alternative paradigms, or simply defer judgment. Each of these strategies could be consistent with an approach to inerrancy understood as applying primarily to the Christotelic formation of a missional community.

Intracanonical Accuracy (Acts 9:7; 22:9)

Another type of challenge is posed by questions of intracanonical accuracy. How might potential conflicts be handled that arise from within the texts themselves? As an example of this dilemma, we are presented with two accounts of Saul's encounter with Jesus on the road to Damascus. In the description that Acts 9 offers of this encounter, Jesus identifies himself to Saul and tells him to go into the city, where he will be told what to do. In verse 7, we are told that the men traveling with Saul are speechless and that, while they hear the voice, they do not see anyone. Later, in Acts 22, Paul recounts this episode to a hostile crowd after his arrest and, according to verse 9, says that his companions saw the light but did not hear the voice of the one speaking to him.

This is sometimes cited as evidence of a contradiction, because of the differences in the two accounts. In the first, Saul's companions heard the voice but did not see anyone, while in the second, they saw the light but did not hear the voice. From the standpoint of a CSBI view of inerrancy, this is the sort of issue that must be addressed. However, the response would seem to be fairly straightforward. The harmonization of what Saul's companions saw is not terribly problematic, since Scripture records several instances when a voice is heard but no person is seen. The question as to what they heard is a bit more challenging, because the text presents a formal contradiction. In the first case, they heard the voice; in the second, they did not. Readers and commentators have often noted this difference.

In order to ease this situation, some translations have inferred that in the second text, Saul's companions did not hear with comprehension. That is to say, they heard something but did not understand it; hence, they did not hear what was being said, even though they heard something. We experience this phenomenon when we hear someone speak but do not understand what they say, and so we say, "I didn't hear you." The reply indicates an awareness of hearing sound but a lack of understanding of what was said. This is certainly a possible conclusion, although not a necessary one. Another possible response to the apparent contradiction between the two biblical accounts would be to say that in the first, the narrator tells us what really happened, while in the second, Paul tells the story from his perspective, and he is wrong. Since he is being quoted, a Chicago statement notion of inerrancy would demand that he be quoted with relative accuracy, even if his perspective does not accord with what actually occurred. It may also be that Saul's companions had different experiences, and the text is providing alternative perspectives. Indeed, we can imagine any number of possible responses that could make sense of these two accounts in such a way that they would not need to be viewed as contradictory or mutually exclusive. But it is interesting to ask why some interpreters feel the need to harmonize these accounts.

Part of the reason concerns the way the Bible has come to be read as though it is a single book, containing a single divine perspective, albeit one communicated through a diversity of authors. This notion has led to extremely artificial and precisionist assumptions about the nature of inspiration and the use of language in the Bible. These assumptions have produced a sense that the relatively banal difference observed here might somehow be problematic for a belief that the Bible is true and trustworthy. This has produced a determination to demonstrate the ways in which such textual variations and differences can be harmonized and shown to be entirely consistent with one another. The difficulty with this is that the canon is filled with examples like the one discussed here, many of which are much more challenging to harmonize. We have two creation accounts, multiple law codes, alternative genealogies, competing histories, and four gospels. The various attempts at harmonization are rooted in the apologetic concern to demonstrate the inerrancy of Scripture as the basis on which to defend the truthfulness of Christian faith. The result of this process has been increasing cultural skepticism about the Bible as well as an artificial approach to interpretation that often disables readers from seeing what the texts actually say.

Viewing inerrancy from the perspective of plurality enables readers to better appreciate the distinct contribution that each of the canonical texts makes to the whole. It also reminds us that the Christian community has been and will continue to be characterized by theological, ecclesial, and practical diversity. That these two particular texts are cited as a concern for biblical authority is indicative of a particular understanding of inspiration and inerrancy that does not do justice to the phenomena of Scripture. From my perspective, this supposed contradiction is relatively insignificant; indeed, I had never really noticed it or given it any thought until agreeing to write this essay. I also strain to see its interpretive significance. Not every detail of the Bible is pregnant with meaning simply because it is a form of the Word of God. I do not regard the challenge posed by this comparison as particularly significant with respect to the purpose of Scripture to form missional communities.

Theological Plurality (Deut. 20:16 - 17; Matt. 5:43 - 48)

In this pair of texts, we confront a difficult question relating to plurality. In Deuteronomy 20:16–17, the people of Israel are told to launch a military campaign and to completely destroy their enemies. This is in stark contrast to the words of Jesus, who, in Matthew 5:43–48, tells his followers to love their enemies and pray for those who persecute them, so that they may truly be children of the God who causes the sun to rise on the evil and the good and sends rain on the righteous and the unrighteous. The contrast presented here could hardly be more direct. In Deuteronomy, God commands hostility and death to the enemies of Israel, while in the book of Matthew, Jesus instructs his followers to love their enemies and pray for them.

Given what I have said about plurality, one possible direction to take in addressing this tension is to acknowledge that these are both legitimate perspectives. There is some truth here. For instance, it is important to make a perspectival distinction between the instruction of God to a nation and that to individuals. It is also important to observe the differences between the prescribed treatment of foreigners in Israel and the rules of war. Exodus 23:9 contains the exhortation "Do not oppress a foreigner; you yourselves know how it feels to be foreigners, because you were foreigners in Egypt." Deuteronomy 10:18–19 says that God "defends the cause of the fatherless and the widow, and loves the foreigner residing among you, giving them food and clothing. And you are to love those who are foreigners, for you yourselves were foreigners in Egypt." Hence, while the Old Testament contains harsh passages concerning violence and warfare, it also displays concern for the marginalized and disenfranchised. I believe these are indications of divine accommodation to the culture of the ancient Mediterranean world as well as the loving character of God reflected in the teaching of Jesus in Matthew 5.

Incidentally, I should add that I am an advocate of the Christian just war theory, which maintains that tragically, in a broken, distorted, and sinful world, it is sometimes appropriate and necessary for the sake of loving our neighbors to put ourselves in danger by engaging in violent acts to achieve a just end. From my perspective, two pertinent examples of such justified violence are World War II and black resistance to the societally accepted and legalized horror of the lynching tree. I appreciate that people in the pacifist tradition will have some ethical difficulties here that I do not share.

Having said this, I cannot simply leave the matter here, because of the ways in which texts such as this one in Deuteronomy and many others in the Old Testament have been used by Christians throughout history to justify conquest, colonization, enslavement, and extermination.[17] To my mind, one of the intractable difficulties with tying the inerrancy of the Bible to notions of timeless, universal, and absolute truth is precisely the manner in which this allows for the possibility of reading the ancient Hebrew texts in such a way as to justify these activities in the present. The Old Testament is a contextual accommodation to the militaristic culture of the ancient Near East. This accounts for the regular depictions of God that use the terminology of a warrior fighting on behalf of his people. This is exactly what we should expect, given the setting of the Hebrew Bible.

An alternative to this approach is to read the Bible as a plural collection of microtruths that function together under the guidance of the Holy Spirit in an eschatological and Christotelic fashion. This means that the ultimate truth and inerrancy of the Bible are finally contained not in the particular narratives and teachings of individual texts but rather in relation to its intended purpose and function in the economy of God. Scripture is the inspired instrument of the Holy Spirit, who speaks in and through the texts as a means of bearing witness to Jesus Christ for the purpose of forming a community that lives out God's love in the world as a sign and foretaste of the consummation of all things in Christ.

From this perspective, Jesus' teaching in Matthew 5 functions in a deconstructive fashion that calls into question prior assumptions and practices such as those found in Deuteronomy 20: "You have heard that it was said, 'Love your neighbor and hate your enemy.' But I tell you, love your enemies and pray for those who persecute you, that you

---

17. For example, see Stephen R. Haynes, *Noah's Curse: The Biblical Justification of American Slavery* (New York: Oxford Univ. Press, 2007).

may be children of your Father in heaven" (Matt. 5:43–45). In this teaching, Jesus is inviting a radical openness to the other in a way that revises and overturns the instruction in Deuteronomy. While we still live in the tension of the already and the not-yet of the kingdom of God, Jesus here reminds us that God's economy is not that of this world. In this way, he affirms the ongoing event of the Word of God over the traditions of reflection that have formed around that event. Even our allegiance to the Bible can draw us away from God's intentions when we read it in a static and absolutist fashion. It is the event itself, the very presence of God, to which Scripture bears witness. In the divine economy, Scripture is always an instrument in the process of that event, not its end.

R. ALBERT MOHLER JR.

John Franke has "always had mixed feelings about inerrancy" (p. 259). Actually, his feelings and thoughts about inerrancy do not appear, at least to me, to be very mixed at all. In the end, Franke goes far beyond the affirmation of inerrancy as problematic and proposes a fundamental transformation in the way evangelicals conceive of truth itself.

This radical approach is not surprising but fully in keeping with Franke's literary trajectory, especially when read in light of his 2009 book, *Manifold Witness: The Plurality of Truth*.[18] In that volume, Franke argued for evangelicals to embrace a notion of plural truth and to abandon philosophical foundationalism, even when that foundation is Holy Scripture.[19] He continues that line of argument in his essay here.

Franke's proposal would lead to a total reconceptualization of evangelical theology and the Christian truth claim—the claim that the Bible gives us revealed and objective truth. He would have us abandon the Bible as epistemic authority for evangelical theology in favor of the church as the authority, the community of faith, hearing, receiving, and negotiating a plurality of theologies drawn from an inherently diverse revelation. In one key sentence, Franke defines Holy Scripture as "the inspired instrument of the Holy Spirit, who speaks in and through the texts as a means of bearing witness to Jesus Christ for the purpose of forming a community that lives out God's love in the world as a sign and foretaste of the consummation of all things in Christ" (p. 286). The Bible is not to be read, he warns, "in a static and absolutist fashion" (p. 287). The Bible is not divine revelation, but a witness to it: "It is the event itself, the very presence of God, to which

18. John R. Franke, *Manifold Witness: The Plurality of Truth* (Nashville: Abingdon, 2009).

19. I was privileged to participate in a panel that explored Franke's theological project and proposals at the 2010 annual meeting of the Evangelical Theological Society in Atlanta, Georgia.

Scripture bears witness. In the divine economy, Scripture is always an instrument in the process of that event, not its end" (p. 287).

Clearly, John Franke's project is very different—perhaps even totally different—than that of the framers of the Chicago Statement on Biblical Inerrancy. Franke fully recognizes this difference when he categorizes the Chicago statement as "reflective of a particular form of epistemology known as classic or strong foundationalism" (p. 261). For him, the Chicago statement's "approach to knowledge seeks to overcome the uncertainty generated by the tendency of fallible human beings to error, by discovering a universal and indubitable basis for human knowledge" (p. 261).

The problem, Franke alleges, is that foundationalism "has been thoroughly discredited in philosophical and theological circles" (p. 262). Well, that is a rather stunning overstatement, but there is truth in it. Franke would have been much closer to the truth if he had claimed that foundationalism has been thoroughly discredited *in the circles within which it has been thoroughly discredited.*

There can be no doubt that the understanding of truth and knowledge foundational to the Chicago statement has been thoroughly critiqued and rejected by those who champion non-foundationalist epistemologies and theories of knowledge. But the retreat from philosophical foundationalism is not what it once was, even within the postmodern academy. Postmodernism has itself been eclipsed by subsequent intellectual movements and fashions in the context of late modernity. While strong forms of foundationalism remain out of fashion in many circles, softer forms are growing in influence. Even anti-foundationalists must operate on the basis of some truth claims or assumptions that are foundational, even to their own anti-foundationalist thought.

Furthermore, even if the larger academy had abandoned all forms of foundationalism *en masse*, that does not necessarily lead to the conclusion that the church and its theologians must do the same. As a matter of fact, I would argue that some form of foundationalism is basic, not only to the project of evangelical theology, but also to the Christian faith. In this age, this may represent one aspect of the intellectual scandal that Christianity always represents to the non-Christian mind.

As we might expect, Franke rejects inerrancy as conceived and defined within the Chicago statement. But he rejects the statement's understanding of inerrancy more as a whole than in its several parts by pulling the epistemological rug out from underneath it. Instead of a foundationalist inerrancy, Franke proposes what he calls a "fallibilist perspective" on inerrancy.

Franke asks this question: "But must we view Scripture as a foundation for human knowledge?" (p. 264). The framers of the Chicago statement, joined by most evangelical Christians, would no doubt suspect that they had misheard Franke's question. Scripture itself claims to be not only *a particular* foundation for human knowledge, but *the ultimate* and divinely-revealed foundation for all knowledge. Franke does not want to redefine inerrancy; he wants to use the term to mean something categorically different. In his fallibilist perspective, inerrancy means that the Bible, as a diverse collection of writings and theologies offering multiple and (seemingly) contradictory truths, "stands in a central position in the practice of the faith in that the Christian community reads the biblical text as Scripture and looks to it as the focal point for shaping the narrative world it inhabits" (p. 272).

In framing his argument, Franke opines that we do not have and should not seek a Bible that is an inerrant foundation for human thought. He points to John Calvin's notion of divine accommodation, but takes it far beyond the Reformer's thinking. In Franke's view, accommodation means that Scripture bears all the marks of human limitation. "These limitations," he asserts, "extend not only to the cognitive and imaginative faculties but also to the very mediums by which revelation is communicated to us" (p. 267).

In other words, the Bible is marked by the fact that human beings are fallible and that everything we touch is marked by our fallibility. Interestingly, he points us to the christological formulation adopted at the Council of Chalcedon, highlighting the council's judgment that the two natures of Christ remain distinct, even in the reality of the incarnation. That is true, of course, but the council certainly did not ascribe error to the human nature of Christ, who was without sin. "Language," he argues, "like the human nature of Jesus, remains subject to the historical, social, and cultural limitations and contingencies inherent in its creaturely character, without compromising its suitability as a medium for the Word of God" (p. 268).

This is an astounding claim, as much related to Christology as to our understanding of Scripture. Jesus was indeed socially located within language, history, and culture. But can a fully orthodox and biblical Christology argue that Christ was always "subject" to these limitations? I think not.

The radical nature of Franke's project is revealed in his discussion of God himself, including his definition of God as "being-in-act" (p. 265). Such a definition would seem to call for a rejection of a once-for-all deposit of divine revelation, even as his definition of God as "plurality-in-unity and unity-in plurality" would argue against a unified and singular conception of truth (p. 276).

As his discussion of the three specific biblical texts reveals, Franke is untroubled by plural claims to truth within and without the Bible, so he is not really concerned about the historicity of the conquest of Jericho or the historical details about Paul's Damascus Road vision. "Not every detail of the Bible is pregnant with meaning simply because it is a form of the Word of God," Franke strikingly insists (p. 284).

The conquest of the Canaanites demonstrates, Franke says, "one of the intractable difficulties with tying the inerrancy of the Bible to notions of timeless, universal, and absolute truth" (p. 286). The Sermon on the Mount, Franke argues, "functions in a deconstructive fashion" to correct the impression left by Deuteronomy 20. To speak of the Sermon on the Mount as a corrective to Deuteronomy 20 is to ignore what Jesus said as he introduced the sermon: "Do not think that I have come to abolish the Law or the Prophets; I have not come to abolish them but to fulfill them. For truly, I say to you, until heaven and earth pass away, not an iota, not a dot, will pass from the Law until all is accomplished" (Matt. 5:17–18). The total truthfulness and trustworthiness of the Bible is undermined when any Scripture text is said to function "in a deconstructive fashion" with respect to any other text. Jesus points us to progressive revelation as *fulfillment*, not correction or deconstruction.

John Franke is a brilliant and creative thinker whose theological project has taken him far beyond any real connection to the theology basic to the Chicago statement. His trajectory is headed far beyond the boundaries of evangelicalism. In his own very powerful and honest way, he has revealed the destiny of evangelical theology if it surrenders the inerrancy of the Bible.

RESPONSE TO JOHN R. FRANKE

PETER ENNS

Along with historical challenges, the diverse theological voices that we hear in Scripture present the two most pressing challenges to inerrancy that, I feel, cannot be overcome while retaining the term as it has been used in American evangelicalism. Franke, however, wishes not to pit the two against each other but to reconfigure inerrancy to embrace theological diversity as a fundamental property of Scripture. A doctrine of *biblical* inerrancy, therefore, has no choice but to account positively for the property of diversity rather than marginalizing it or explaining it away as incompatible with a text inspired by God. A defense of inerrancy that feels pressured to harmonize this diversity is, in other words, operating out of a low view of Scripture rather than bowing to its authority. Common evangelical articulations of inerrancy do not take such a stance on Scripture's diversity, and so Franke's approach is, as he puts it, an experiment in "postconservative or progressive evangelical theology" (p. 260).

One of the strengths of Franke's essay, which echoes parts of Bird's, is his focus on the ethics of inerrancy, i.e., how it has been "wielded by dominant groups as a means of asserting power and control" (p. 259). I appreciate Vanhoozer's caution not to evaluate inerrancy on the basis of its abusers, but the function of inerrancy in the fundamentalist and evangelical subculture has had a disturbing and immoral partnership with power and abuse. I do not think we can responsibly discuss inerrancy as a principle or an idea at a safe academic distance from these outcomes. The culture of anger and fear surrounding inerrancy must also be part of the discussion.

Concerning the Chicago statement, Franke (as does Bird) debunks the "meme" that inerrancy—as it is defined and used in contemporary evangelicalism—has always been the church's doctrine of Scripture. He also points out the document's commitment to "strong founda-

292

tionalism," despite the intentions of its framers or the protestations of those adherents who see themselves as modest foundationalists. Another important observation is that inerrancy is a "second-order theological construction" rather than a "direct assertion" of Scripture (p. 263). Of course, this does not in and of itself nullify inerrancy, for second-order constructions abound in Christian theology (e.g., the Trinity). But claiming that inerrancy is what Scripture "teaches about itself" is wrong. It may be inferred (hence, "second-order"), but it is not self-evident. How and whether the inference is justified is largely what the present volume is about.

For Franke, the Word of God cannot be the foundation for human knowledge, since God is infinite and must accommodate to our limitations (citing 2 Peter 3:8). Franke's understanding of God as "being-in-act" (p. 265) means that God is known covenantally, i.e., through his actions, rooted in love and mission. That God is Trinitarian (plurality-in-unity and unity-in-plurality) implies for Franke that "the love of God is not an assimilating love. It does not seek to make that which is different the same; rather it lives in harmonious fellowship with the other through the active relations of self-sacrificing, self-giving love" (p. 266). God's truth, in other words, is "relational and life-giving, rather than simply a matter of right cognition or a proper conception and expression of facts and propositions" (p. 274). Scripture's normativity, then, is a function of its plurality, a plurality seen not only in God's self but in the diverse human cultures to which God graciously accommodates in revelation.

With these parameters in place, Franke moves to his exposition of the necessity of divine accommodation in Scripture, since our finite limitations "extend not only to the cognitive and imaginative faculties but also to the very mediums by which revelation is communicated to us" (p. 267). In other words, accommodation necessitates on God's part a willingness to communicate in the medium of historically conditioned human cultures. Franke supports his view of Scripture by analogy with the incarnation of Christ. Human language, like the human nature of Christ, "remains subject to the historical, social, and cultural limitations and contingencies inherent in its creaturely character, without compromising its suitability as a medium for the Word of God" (p. 268; essentially the point I make in *Inspiration and Incarnation:*

Evangelicals and the Problem of the New Testament). The resulting paradox, inescapable in my opinion, is that "we can affirm the reality of
ultimate or transcendent truth even as we acknowledge the interpretive
character of human knowledge" (p. 269).

Furthermore, Franke locates the church's ultimate authority in
the Spirit working in and through Scripture rather than in the Spirit
being bound to Scripture (as Calvin put it). The latter "runs the risk
of collapsing the Spirit into the text and thus allowing human beings
to move from a position of epistemic dependency with respect to the
knowledge of God to one of mastery" (p. 271). I think this is well put
and speaks to the ethics of the abuse of "biblical authority" so common
in fundamentalist and evangelical contexts. Also, by saying the Spirit
"appropriates" Scripture, Franke is able to account for Scripture's self-
evident theological plurality, the midrashic handling of the Old Testament by the New Testament authors, and the diverse uses of Scripture
in the church throughout its history and at any given point in history.

Scripture's function, then, is not to protect its own interests but to
point beyond itself by calling "a new world into being" (p. 272, citing
John Goldingay). This affirmation is in my view more consistent than
is mainstream inerrantist thinking with the tectonic shift of a crucified
and risen messiah, which was neither anticipated by nor could be contained within the contours of Israel's story. My only quibble here with
Franke is that the "new world" that Jesus calls forth in the Sermon on
the Mount is not the *future* "more real" world, as he puts it. Matthew's
presentation of Jesus' eschatology is a portrait of the present, where the
heavenly and future are *already* realized in the arrival of the King. I
would have liked to have seen Franke strengthen his position by bringing to bear on his thesis the hermeneutical impact of the resurrection
of Christ and the already/not yet tension of Paul's eschatology.

Moving to our three passages, Franke's assessment of the fall of
Jericho gives due weight to the consensus position among archaeologists. He concludes that, at least at the present moment, "we simply
have no way of verifying or falsifying the explicit details contained
in the story of the fall of Jericho" (p. 281). In a sense this is correct,
since many of the specific details of the story are, and will always be,
unverifiable by archaeological means. (What exactly did Rahab say?
Did Rahab live?) But Franke also seems to step (temporarily) into the

same ditch as the other authors. What is really at stake here is not "explicit details" of the story but its broad outlines, which leave historical footprints and therefore *are* open to verification or falsification, such as the period in which Jericho might have been occupied, whether it had walls at the time, and whether the walls were razed. The current battle waged within evangelicalism is whether the evidence at present demands falsification or allows for verification of those larger questions. At the end, Franke is noncommittal about the historicity of Jericho but counsels that, in view of the serious challenges it faces, the authority of Scripture should not be tied to defending its historicity. I would have liked Franke to plot out in more detail what that type of biblical authority looks like.

Franke is not terribly bothered with the contradiction between Acts 9 and 22, seeing that Scripture elsewhere provides conflicting multiple accounts (creation, law codes, genealogies, histories, Gospels). This is true, though, as I remarked in my essay, these other instances are between different authors, not one author as in Acts. Like Vanhoozer, Franke quickly dismisses the harmonizing misreading of 22:9 ("did not *understand* the voice" rather than the correct "hear"). Franke sees here a "formal contradiction" and so a real problem for the CSBI. For Franke, however, not every detail of Scripture is "pregnant with meaning," and this contradiction is "relatively insignificant" with no "interpretive significance" for the "purpose of Scripture to form missional communities" (p. 284). I agree this is nothing to lose sleep over (unless one is a strong foundationalist literalist inerrantist), but these sort of details *are* "pregnant with meaning" with respect to grasping the author's theological purposes for composing his narrative. Here I remain more confident that the line of interpretation Vanhoozer and I explore in our essays is fruitful. But where Vanhoozer and I would agree with Franke is that these details are not pregnant with *doctrinal* meaning.

Franke sees Deuteronomy 20:16–17 and Matthew 5:43–48 as an expression of theological plurality and therefore a genuine tension for typical inerrantist thinking. He sees, however, an important distinction between these two passages that may ease the tension a bit: the former pertains to Israel as a nation and the latter to individuals. There may be some truth to this, but I would contend that the Sermon on the

Mount is also very much a "national" declaration, where Jesus, the new Moses, is instructing the Jewish hearers below on an alternate vision of the kingdom of God, one that does not accommodate common Jewish expectations of national independence from Rome.

The closest Franke comes to offering an explicit explanation for why these two passages coexist in Scripture is a passing comment: "The Old Testament is a contextual accommodation to the militaristic culture of the ancient Near East" (p. 000). I agree, but since this functionally relegates the former to a theologically subordinate status, I would have liked Franke to explore a bit more how this type of plurality can reflect Scripture's normativity. But in keeping with his main theme of tying Scripture to the mission of God, Franke chooses to focus on how passages like Deuteronomy 20:16–17 have been used to condone violence in Christian history. Such usage, though not "caused" by inerrancy, is certainly supported by a doctrine of Scripture that expects from it "timeless, universal, and absolute truth" (p. 286). Drawing out the ethics of doctrine, as Bird does, is a strength of Franke's essay, as is his embrace of Scripture's self-evident theological plurality.

RESPONSE TO JOHN R. FRANKE

MICHAEL F. BIRD

I'm grateful to be able to respond to John Franke, and I'm glad that his voice is in this conversation. Franke is continuing the project begun by the late (and much missed) Stanley Grenz of trying to indigenize evangelical theology in a postmodern context. Such a project means enabling theologians to be "in" postmodernity while not being "of" postmodernity. While their execution of that task is open to evaluation, the legitimacy of their objective is not. Thus, Franke's progressive or postconservative approach is a welcome addition to the collection, especially his goal to move inerrancy away from a static biblicism and recast it in terms of a dynamic model rooted in God's character and which works itself out in the practices of a Christotelic and missional community.

Franke makes a number of arguments that I wish to endorse and affirm: (1) that the American inerrancy tradition (AIT) should not be regarded as a panacea for resolving complex questions, nor should it be employed as a device for exercising theological and tribal power (p. 259); (2) that ancient Christian authors all affirmed the truthfulness of Scripture, but without necessarily freighting their affirmations with the same theological and philosophical baggage of the AIT (p. 261); (3) that Scripture is true in the context of divine accommodation and within the contingencies of the human situation in which Scripture is given and received (p. 267); (4) that there is a close correlation between Word and Spirit, an affirmation that is incredibly important, though sadly forgotten in some schemes of evangelical theology (p. 270);[20] (5) that Scripture not only reveals a divine word but creates a divine world in the Christ-centered and missional community of the church

---

20. Cf. Westminster Confession of Faith and London Baptist Confession (arts. I.10) both affirm that the supreme judge by which all controversies are to be solved is based on the authority of "the Holy Spirit speaking in the Scripture."

(p. 272), an idea for which Franke provides a stimulating exposition; (6) that Scripture and its interpretation involves an irreducible plurality of perspectives, albeit united in a canonical unity and a christological community (p. 266), a laudable claim, though it is open to grievous misunderstanding; and, (7) Franke's *pièce de résistance*, that the doctrine of Scripture and the practice of Scripture should incorporate perspectives from every tribe, nation, ethnicity, and culture and not rest in the hegemony of any single group (p. 279).

That said, Franke's approach leaves me dissatisfied on several fronts. First, in many ways Franke is very similar to the AIT in that an a priori conception of God drives his conception of revelation and veracity. Whereas the AIT argues that a *perfect* God means a *perfect* Bible (with culturally laden notions as to what perfection is and how it works), Franke argues that a *relational* God means a *relational* Bible (with culturally laden notions of relationality as a value and a process; p. 265). There are two problems here: (1) the divine attributes regarded as paradigmatic for God in both cases seem highly selective and geared towards a predetermined end, and (2) both schemes can end up having to mess with the *phenemona of Scripture* in order to make Scripture fit their doctrine of God. I would say that we need a fully orbed doctrine of the triune God to be a prolegomena for our doctrine of revelation. And we need a doctrine of revelation that is robust enough to engage the full breadth and depth of the phenomena of Scripture. Now I'm no Barthian, but after reading Mohler and Franke, I'm starting to think that Karl Barth's "revelational trinitarianism,"[21] where revelation is rooted in the self-disclosure of the triune God, might be a better place to start.[22]

Second, and identical to my critique of Enns, I remain concerned and confused by the attempt to explain divine accommodation to human language in terms of an incarnational model (which is polite talk for, "Are you out of your bloody mind?"). Franke says that "we can posit that what is true of the human nature of Jesus Christ with respect to divinization is also true of the words of the prophets and the apostles in Scripture" (p. 268). We should not, even for all the iced tea in Ken-

---

21. A term coined by Stanley J. Grenz, *The Social God and the Relational Self* (Louisville: Westminster John Knox, 2001), 34.

22. Cf. Karl Barth, *Church Dogmatics*, I/1.

tucky, explain the mysterious divine-human interface in Scripture with a model of revelation used to explain the miracle of the incarnation. That is because (1) it will lessen the uniqueness of the incarnation (let us remember that the incarnation is a mode of special revelation that transcends all other special revelations of God in either history or Scripture, on account of the incarnation's unique manifestation of the fullness and beauty of God enfleshed); (2) it adopts a view of inscripturated revelation that has more in common with Islamic accounts of the Qu'ran than with classic views of Christian Scripture; and (3) it risks turning bibliology into bibliolatry when the Bible becomes a mode of God's incarnational revelation of himself as revealer and redeemer. Whatever heuristic advantages such a model may have, it ultimately runs the risk of heterodox disadvantages.

Third, Franke claims that the creator-creature distinction, the contextual language of Scripture, and the analogical nature of biblical language to describe God's being mean that we should discriminate between God's *Truth* (i.e., truth as God knows it with a capital *T*) and God's *truth* (i.e., truth as God reveals it in the fallibility of human language with a lowercase *t*). I think this point is true in the sense that human language is finite, culturally contingent, and therefore analogical rather than univocal in its description of God. However, if such a distinction is pressed too far, we will be left wondering whether God's *immanent truth* (i.e., the truth about who God is in himself) is in fact radically different from God's *economic truth* (i.e., the truth as God reveals himself to be). We may grant the fallible nature of human language, but if God's revelation of himself in Scripture is to be a genuine unveiling of his transcendent and mysterious person in human words, then there must be a genuine connectivity between God's truth-in-himself and God's truth-as-he-reveals-himself. If not, then divine revelation has not occurred; what has occurred, rather, is a divine impression molded into human language. Franke is quite correct about the analogical nature of biblical language, but his "God's Truth/God's truth" model risks rendering biblical language in effect equivocal.[23]

---

23. On the distinction between biblical language as univocal, equivocal, and analogical, see Millard J. Erickson, *Christian Theology* (2nd ed.; Grand Rapids, Mich.: Baker, 2001), 205–6.

Fourth, while I appreciate Franke's critique of the foundationalist approach, I remain unsure as to where he himself sits on the truth-theory spectrum. Franke sounds like a coherentist (i.e., the Bible is true because it all hangs together so well) when he says that Scripture has the "purpose of creating a socially constructed world that finds its coherence in Jesus Christ" (p. 274), "the Christian community bears witness to the truth of the gospel of Jesus Christ through the construction of a social linguistic world that finds its coherence in Christ" (p. 274), and biblical authority resides in a "web of interconnected beliefs [rather than a] ... foundation on which all other beliefs are established and built" (p. 282). But in another sense, Franke sounds like a pragmatist (i.e., the Bible is true because it works) when he suggests that biblical doctrine functions primarily towards the formation of a Christotelic and missional community (p. 282). The problem here, as with postliberal theologies of Scripture in general, is that Scripture simply provides an internally consistent lexicon for God talk without referring to any reality outside of the community that speaks the scriptural language. And again, how does the utility of Scripture for cultivating a Christotelic and missional community depend on the truth/reality/accuracy of the claims made in Scripture about, say, the fall, the exodus, the virgin conception, or the resurrection of Jesus? Evidently Franke believes in God's acts in history, but I'm not convinced that he has sufficiently mapped that conviction to a postfoundationalist epistemology.

In tandem with that, Franke's coherentist/pragmatist notion of truth means that truth is "relational and life-giving rather than simply a matter of right cognition or a proper conception and expression of facts and propositions" (p. 274). I respond by noting that while biblical truth is more than propositions—enabling us as it does to act out the divine drama that we participate in—even so, biblical truth is no less than propositional. In fact, I would say that believing the proposition "Jesus is Lord" is the key criterion for the *coherence* of any truth claim and the *pragmatic presupposition* for living a missional life. The fact is that we do not have to choose between revelation as being either propositional or personal, for it is both.[24]

---

24. Cf. Benjamin Myers, "*Theologia Evangelii*: Peter Jensen's Theological Method," *Churchman* 118 (2004): 27–45.

In the end, Franke's postfoundationalist approach yields a fairly weak definition of inerrancy. Though committed to "the whole of Scripture [a]s truthful and trustworthy" (p. 277), inerrancy's primary function is to ensure that "no portion of the biblical narrative can properly be disregarded or eclipsed" (p. 276). That is useful insofar as it will prevent us from becoming (1) Buffet Baptists who pick and choose parts of the Bible we want to believe in, or (2) Procrustean Presbyterians who force the biblical story onto a bed of dogma. Even so, inerrancy (or infallibility or veracity or whatever) needs to do more than to merely affirm the theological equality within the biblical canon; it needs to affirm in some way the tangible connection between God's revelation of himself in Scripture and the reality to which the revelation attests.

Franke brings a wealth of insights into the discussion about inerrancy, especially about the perils of foundationalism and how divine revelation communicates truth and creates a community centered around Christ. I remain concerned, however, with Franke's reliance on selective a priori conceptions of God for determining the character of the biblical revelation, his employment of an incarnational model to describe biblical revelation, a potential rupture between God's truth as he knows it and God's truth as he reveals it, and the specific application of a postfoundationalist approach to developing a robust definition of inerrancy. In any case, we are certainly led to some forthright and Franke exchange of ideas.

I've wondered for years how John Franke would unpack the notion of inerrancy in light of his post-foundationalist epistemology and pluralist conception of truth; now I know, at least in part, through an essay dimly.

Franke acknowledges that he is "conflicted" about inerrancy, largely because of the way it has been used in biblical interpretation and theology. In particular, he bemoans the use of inerrancy as (1) an interpretive panacea, (2) a political instrument (e.g., a tool for excluding some from the evangelical family), and especially, (3) an epistemological theory. I share some of Franke's concerns (so does Enns). However, I wonder if he, like Enns, too quickly identifies the concept of inerrancy itself with its aberrations and abuses. "God" has also been associated with abuses, many of them violent (think "holy war"), but in this case Franke is willing to distinguish right from wrong uses. While I agree that there are problems with the way some people use the concept (as with "God"), I regret that he does not spend more time trying to sort out the genuine article of inerrancy (so to speak) from its corrupt iterations.

First theology is my term for the mutual relationship between one's doctrine of God and doctrine of Scripture. Franke's first theology is plural and missional. *Plural*: God is a unity-in-plurality, a harmonious, loving fellowship of Father, Son, and Spirit. *Missional*: the sending of Son and Spirit reflect (and project into time) the eternal, active, and relational love that is God's own life. We can understand Franke's view of inerrancy aright only if we view it against the backdrop of his first theology together with his construal of what Christianity is all about; namely, the act of Word and Spirit to create a new world or community—call it the kingdom of God—whose center and circumference is Jesus Christ. On Franke's view, this new world begins to come about when the Spirit uses language to effect its social construction. (This is the thrust of the section "Truth, Eschatological Realism, Christian Community, and Missional Plurality.")

It is only in the light of this nexus of first theological ideas that we can understand what Franke wants to say about the doctrine of Scripture. In a nutshell: the Bible is that language the Spirit appropriates and employs to effect the social construction of the Christian community. Franke's call for an "open and flexible theology" corresponds to his belief about the Spirit blowing when and where it wills, particularly in and through Scripture. This theme, implicit throughout Franke's essay, comes into explicit focus toward the end, when he says, in connection with the final biblical case study, that he understands the right use of inerrancy "in relation to [the Bible's] intended purpose and function in the economy of God" (p. 286). In short, Scripture is not a deposit of propositional truth (too static) but rather an instrument the Spirit uses linguistically to construct the community of God. What remains to be seen, however, is just what truth *is*. Is it, for example, the transformative process itself? It might have helped had Franke provided an interpretation of John 16:13: "When the Spirit of truth comes, he will guide you into all the truth." In any case, it helps to keep in mind Franke's emphasis on truth as *missional* (i.e., as an ingredient in the Spirit's project of constructing community) in order to appreciate his critique of the Chicago statement.

Franke's principal critique of the Chicago statement is that it "reflects" classical foundationalist epistemology. More pointed, CSBI is a bastard of modernity, the ugly progeny of Descartes' demand that all knowledge be based on an indubitable foundation. Moderns typically understand this foundation in either rationalist or empiricist terms (i.e., certainty can be had either on the basis of axioms of reason or deliverances of the senses). Inerrancy represents for Franke a third kind of foundation: one built on the propositional truths of divine revelation. Revelation fails to redeem foundationalism, however, because foundationalism (1) has been discredited as a theory of knowledge, (2) inadvertently encourages skepticism by implying that if there is but one crack in the foundation (i.e., one error) then the whole edifice is unstable, and (3) is unable to account for, or arbitrate between, the many different and often opposing interpretations, all of which claim to be founded on the Bible.

Franke is hardly alone declaring inerrancy guilty by association with modernity. It is always salutary to inquire whether our indoctrination by contemporary culture is affecting our understanding of Christian doctrine. Nevertheless, in order to knock down a position, you have to do more than say where it came from: not everything that came out of the 1970s was mistaken. Furthermore, it is not enough to say of a theory that it has been thoroughly discredited. That's not an argument. You have to show where or how foundationalism has gone wrong. Some discredited theories later turn out to be true.

What ambiguities and confusions that lurk in Franke's account stem from his "original sin" of failing to distinguish the original concept of inerrancy, which was about the truthfulness of Scripture, from its subsequent use as a warrant for literalist interpretations. It is nothing less than a category mistake to think that inerrancy (which is about biblical truthfulness) should be tied to *any* specific epistemology (which is about human knowledge). Inerrancy claims that whatever Scripture says is wholly true and trustworthy, but there is nothing in the concept of inerrancy that suggests our interpretations are infallible or certain. Quite the opposite! To pinpoint the basic problem: Franke conflates the Bible's truth as a *foundation* for theology with a particular way of relating to that foundation (i.e., *foundationalism* as a theory of knowledge). This distinction is worth pursuing further.

In the first place (and rather awkwardly for Franke), the Bible repeatedly employs the imagery of foundations. Jesus says the wise man digs deep and lays a foundation (*themelion*) on rock (Luke 6:48). Paul calls Christ a foundation (1 Cor. 3:11). Finally, and most telling, Paul says that the new community of God made possible by Christ is "built on the foundation of the apostles and prophets" (Eph. 2:20 ESV), which is to say upon oral (and possibly written) testimony. The salient point is that we can accept these foundations without becoming modern foundationalists.

Franke acknowledges that many inerrantists are "chastened" foundationalists (I would agree) but then moves too quickly to equate these with "fallibilists." Franke would do better to examine more closely the theories of modest foundationalists. Consider, for example, Alvin Plantinga's work on warranted belief.[25] Plantinga is a mod-

---

25. Alvin Plantinga, *Warrant and Proper Function* (Oxford: Oxford Univ. Press, 1993).

est foundationalist who argues that beliefs are properly "basic," and hence warranted and rational, when they are the product of a reliable belief-producing mechanism (e.g., memory; testimony) that is working properly in a cognitively clean environment. Whether or not Plantinga is himself an inerrantist, his theory is compatible with an original understanding of inerrancy. On this view, the Bible is a reliable belief-producing mechanism that produces true belief when read in conjunction with the Spirit's purifying work on our cognitive and cardiac environment. Biblical testimony on this view would be properly basic (i.e., foundational), but not in the manner of classical foundationalism.

Second, Franke claims that foundationalism leads inerrantists to take the statements of Scripture as "timeless axioms." I don't see why this is necessarily so. Empiricism is a form of foundationalism too, yet it typically works not with timeless axiomatic truths but with reports of temporal experience. As I understand it, inerrancy affirms that the Bible speaks truth on *whatever* topic it addresses, and there are many kinds of truth: historical, scientific, mathematical, psychological, theological, etc. Perhaps there are timeless truths in Scripture (e.g., "God is love"). It need not follow, however, that all biblical truth is timeless (e.g., "At that time Abijah the son of Jeroboam fell sick"; 1 Kings 14:1 ESV).

We move now, third, to the issue of fallibilism. Here too I believe that Franke confuses truth and knowledge: "In the framework of weak foundationalism, inerrancy could be mistaken and should be subject to critical scrutiny" (p. 263). I read this sentence several times and still don't know what it means. I think Franke means something like this: we should never accord ultimate certainty to our interpretations of Scripture but rather remember that we are fallible interpreters. I agree. But inerrancy, rightly understood, does not encourage interpreters to think they are infallible. Franke may well ask what benefit inerrancy is if it does not guarantee true interpretations. My own answer would be that the doctrine of inerrancy was never intended to guarantee true interpretations. We need clearly to distinguish the infallible word of truth from the fallibility of human interpretations of that word. Stated differently, we must never simply equate our interpretations of Scripture with the word of God itself. Rather, our interpretations must be offered prayerfully, in fear and trembling, and in the faith that the

Spirit will indeed guide the church into all truth (John 16:13). That Christians disagree about so many doctrines may challenge our faith in the Spirit's leading and the clarity of Scripture, but it need not falsify our belief that Scripture is without error. It is not the text but interpreters that are fallible.

I now turn to consider Franke's own reconstruction of inerrancy. He is right to call our attention to the multiple, partial human perspectives that make up the Bible, and to remind us that the Creator is infinitely greater than the creature. However, inerrancy does not require us to believe that we know God exhaustively. John Frame is an inerrantist in the Chicago statement's sense; he is also a multiperspectivalist who acknowledges that the Bible is made up of many different kinds of truth claims made from a variety of different perspectives. This does not prevent him from claiming that Scripture makes good on each and every claim that it makes: "When we say that the Bible is inerrant, we mean that the Bible makes good on its claims."[26] Each of the biblical witnesses tells the truth, and nothing but the truth, and the whole truth *insofar* as the witnesses know it. I wish Franke's essay had engaged Frame's multiperspectival inerrantism.

Franke goes farther than Frame in holding that inerrancy "functions within the context of language as a finite, socially constructed medium and does not transcend those limits" (p. 269) and that it "functions only within the limits of language alone" (p. 269). I'm wondering how he might unpack these claims in relation to the New Testament claim: "He is risen" (Matt. 28:6). How does one parse this claim in terms of small-t truth? What does it mean to say that this statement—arguably the heart of the gospel proclamation—is true "within the limits of language alone," or that it cannot be abstracted from its context? How can we tell people in the twenty-first century about Jesus without transcending/translating from the original context of the Gospels?

Finally, and perhaps most important, I wonder about the consequences of Franke's revisionist account of inerrancy on theology. In particular, I wonder about its effects on our understanding of what

---

26. John Frame, *The Doctrine of the Word of God* (Phillipsburg, N.J.: P&R Publishing, 2010), 174.

Paul says about "sound doctrine" in the Pastoral Epistles (1 Tim. 1:10; 6:3; Titus 1:9; 2:1), or on what John says about words that are "trustworthy and true" (Rev. 21:5; 22:6). How can words written by John and Paul be sound and trustworthy if their truth is limited to their context only? Franke would probably say that the question itself betrays a foundationalist mindset. Maybe so, but it's still a good question.

Franke makes a series of idiosyncratic claims about inerrancy toward the end of his article that I'm pretty sure will not catch on. For example, "Inerrancy means that none of the texts of Scripture should be forced into conformity with others for the sake of systematic unity" (p. 277). I agree that we let every biblical voice have its say. But this is an *implication* of inerrancy, not a definition. Alas, Franke never gives us a clear definition of what inerrancy is, only descriptions of what it supposedly does. For example, inerrancy "serves to deconstruct the idea of a single normative system of theology" (p. 277) and "serves to preserve the dynamic plurality contained in the texts of Scripture" (p. 276). How? Apparently by reminding us that the truth (small-t) of Scripture is made up of many (fallible) human perspectives.

I have an excellent idea of what kind of inerrancy Franke rejects, a good idea of what he thinks his recast concept of inerrancy *does*, but only a foggy idea of what he thinks his recast inerrancy *is*. He never explicitly tells us what truth is, though whatever it is, we know it is plural. I can't make up my mind, however, as to whether his concept of truth is pluralistically *realist*, in which case what we have in Scripture are fragmentary and partial glimpses of what is in Christ, or pluralistically *pragmatist*, in which case what we have in Scripture are fragmentary means or tools the Spirit uses to bring about certain social effects.

I am left with two questions. One I have already asked: what is the nature of "sound doctrine" on Franke's view? The other pertains to Scripture's missional efficacy. James Barr argues that the stories of Jesus can be effective instruments in cultivating faith-based communities even if the events they recount never happened. Does Franke's recast biblical inerrancy equal missional efficacy, which is to say a pneumatic pragmatism, where truth is a function of the Spirit's working to create community? I am reminded of the young heroine in Octavia Butler's novel *Parable of the Sower*.[27] It's set in a post-apocalyptic America, and it's the story of a young girl who composes her own "scripture" — "Earthseed: The Books of the Living" — complete with songs and wise sayings about God, that ends up forming a new community, thus prompting me to ask: if words do not need to be true in the traditional (i.e., correspondence) sense, then how is the Bible's truth different from myths like Earthseed?

27. Octavia Butler, *Parable of the Sower* (New York: Grand Central Publishing, 1993).

CONCLUSION: OPENING LINES OF COMMUNICATION

STEPHEN M. GARRETT WITH J. MERRICK

All of life is a dialogue, a dialogue between person and person, person and nature, person and God.

—Mikhail Bakhtin, an interview with
V. V. Kozhinov in 1992

Yes, sir! No, ma'am! No excuse, sir. Ma'am, I do not understand. These are the four stock answers to all questions given by new cadets entering West Point during the summer prior to their first academic year. Needless to say, these responses don't exactly engender dialogue or conversation, nor do they leave room for asking questions. Those of us with enquiring minds often tried to add another stock response: "Sir/Ma'am, may I ask a question?" As you might expect, we were met with a sharp rejoinder: "If the army wanted you to think, they would have issued you a brain at the central issue station!" So much for understanding. Of course, West Point has a method to its madness as it seeks to provide a strong dose of humility, believing that effective leaders must first understand what it means to follow. Moreover, these stock replies were never meant to be ends in themselves; rather they were the beginning of inculcating values that produced leaders of character.

Part and parcel to this methodology were intensive field exercises where we had the opportunity to embody the very things we were learning throughout the year. One of the key principles stressed was situational awareness, particularly on the battlefield. There are numerous ways to achieve situational awareness, but the essential element is clear, open, and honest communication. Without such communication, as the nineteenth-century Prussian general Carl von Clausewitz noted, the battlefield narrows, the friction intensifies, and the fog sets in, increasing the likelihood of misjudgment and fratricide.[1] Unfortunately, as we mentioned in the introduction, it seems that North American evangelicals are poised to "battle over the Bible" again. Only this time evangelicals are positioned against *themselves*. In order to avoid fratricide and engender fraternity, we believe it is necessary to find ways of opening lines of communication across various perspectives, all within the friendly confines of Christian virtue. Yet given the charged nature of the current debate, how do we propose to do this?

As you might recall, we considered at various points in the introduction the early 1980s debate between Robert Gundry and Norman Geisler. We chose to highlight this example for several reasons: (1) it exposed a number of doctrinal joints related to inerrancy; (2) its proximity to the drafting of the Chicago Statement on Biblical Inerrancy (CSBI) provided insight into how the CSBI was initially understood and used; and (3) it seemed to demarcate a shift inwards and towards a more argumentative tone. Each of these reasons shapes the structure and intended outcomes of this project as we seek to go beyond the stock answers and old battle lines in order to enrich and deepen evangelical faith and life. This project also attempts to map the contemporary debate in North American evangelicalism while looking to provide the impetus for a dialogue that includes voices of different, perhaps even disparate, tonalities from every tribe and nation who desire to understand what it means to say "Thy Word is Truth."

First, inerrancy as a doctrine is not a *solo* doctrine. It is in fact bound up with the compendium of Christian doctrine, as we argued in the introduction, using the Gundry-Geisler controversy to highlight several of these points. Hence, there are a number of theological decisions necessary prior to arriving at a doctrine of inerrancy. For example, the maxim, "What Scripture says, God says," is loaded with presumptions begging for clarification. Who is this God that speaks? Does he speak in *just* this book? If so, why this book, and how does divine speech relate to the human speakers in the Bible? Moreover, if God speaks in and through Holy Scripture, then it should be in some way discernible to the reader. How should readers approach Holy Scripture? Is there a proper disposition for right reading? If so, how do

---

1. Carl von Clausewitz, *On War*, edited by Michael Howard and Peter Paret (Princeton: Princeton University Press, 1976), 117–26.

readers nurture this disposition? The types of arguments, then, that move directly from, say, God's truthfulness to Scripture's truthfulness without considering these kinds of questions run roughshod over a number of important theological considerations, leading to a thin understanding of inerrancy and a malnourished evangelical theology. Thus, if discussions regarding inerrancy are going to advance, inerrancy's doctrinal location and rationale and the implications of these prior theological decisions should be taken into account. Otherwise, the doctrine of inerrancy is nothing more than Henry Flemming's "red badge of courage."

Second, in the late 1970s, the crafting of the CSBI was thought to be a landmark achievement. The Gundry-Geisler controversy demonstrated the prominence of the CSBI as then president of the Evangelical Theological Society (ETS), Louis Goldberg of Moody Bible Institute, appointed an ad hoc committee chaired by William F. Luck, also of Moody Bible Institute, at the 1983 annual ETS meeting. The committee made three proposals to deal with the controversy. One of the proposals called for the CSBI to be adopted as the official interpretation of the doctrine of inerrancy. Although all three of the proposals were rejected by ETS members at the time, the proposal that the CSBI serve as a point of reference in defining the doctrine of inerrancy reveals its significance to adjudicating the Gundry-Geisler controversy.[2] Moreover, the proposal seems to set the CSBI on a path toward further prominence when, nearly twenty years later in 2004, another controversy regarding open theism would move ETS members to pass a resolution solidifying the CSBI as its point of reference for defining inerrancy: "For the purpose of advising members regarding the intent and meaning of the reference to biblical inerrancy in the ETS Doctrinal Basis, the Society refers members to the Chicago Statement on Biblical Inerrancy (1978)."[3] Hence, many evangelicals still consider the formulation of the CSBI not only as an important moment of North American evangelical consensus but also one worthy of perpetuating

---

2. Leslie R. Keylock, "Evangelical Scholars Remove Robert Gundry for His Views on Matthew," http://www.ctlibrary.com/ct/2003/novemberweb-only/11-17-42.0.html; accessed 26 June 2013. Cf. Craig D. Allert, *A High View of Scripture? The Authority of the Bible and the Formation of the New Testament Canon* (Grand Rapids: Baker Academic, 2007), 165–71.

3. Allert, *A High View of Scripture?* 169; cf. http://www.etsjets.org/application_landing; accessed 26 June 2013.

today. Thus, if discussions regarding inerrancy are going to advance, they should respond to the framers' invitation to engage the document itself, not only its content but also its status, use, and viability. Otherwise, the doctrine of inerrancy may become historically blind, neglecting important lessons at a pivotal moment in North American evangelicalism's recent past.

Third, the Gundry-Geisler controversy seemed to demarcate a shift inwards and towards a more argumentative tone away from the intention of the CSBI framers to engage this issue "in a spirit, not of contention, but of humility and love, which we purpose by God's grace to maintain in any future dialogue arising out of what we have said."[4] The future and the death of dialogue came five short years later when Gundry was asked to resign from ETS. To be sure, how one interprets these events, whether as purificatory or punitive, depends upon a number of factors. Our point, though, is not to hail or exhale over the outcome of the Gundry-Geisler controversy but rather to draw attention to the ethics of inerrancy, namely that the manner of argumentation is just as important as the content. There is a place for well-reasoned, lucid, and spirited argumentation. Yet when such argumentation is ill-performed, Christian witness to the other suffers. Thus, if discussions regarding inerrancy are going to advance, Christian virtues like patience, humility, and charity should be fittingly performed in the manner of Christ. Otherwise, the doctrine of inerrancy, like any other doctrine, can become a fragging, swashbuckling sword.

Disposition and Dialogue: Considering the Other

In the introduction, we outlined the structure of the book and indicated several reasons why this perspectival arrangement was advantageous: (1) converging and diverging perspectives on the doctrine of inerrancy are largely dependent upon one's theological sensibilities and particular location in evangelicalism; (2) perspectives provide a fairer arrangement that maps aspects of the current landscape in evangelicalism, which allowed authors to express their position without trying to fit within some prescribed label; and (3) perspectives recognize the personal particularities of viewpoints (yes, authors are people too!) while acknowledging the complexity and difficulty of dialogue.

---

4. "Chicago Statement on Biblical Inerrancy," *JETS* 21/4 (December 1978): 289.

It is important to restate as well that the perspectival arrangement should not be viewed as a limited conversation between two persons but as an open conversation with crisscrossing lines of communication throughout all the essays, following the parameters and questions articulated at the outset. Moreover, the perspectival arrangement is not suggesting that the truth of the matter (or beauty and the good) is relative. There is objective reality. There is something to know. Yet it takes different perspectives, because of our finitude and fallenness, to attain an adequate understanding of it. Hence, this book is not an end in itself but one hoping to generate new theological conversations that considers old questions as well as new ones and encourages engagement with diverse perspectives within and without North America, all in an effort to enrich evangelical faith and life.[5]

Dialogical encounters between persons are at the heart of this arrangement. In response to the dehumanizing elements of German Idealism, the likes of Ferdinand Ebner, Martin Buber, Gabriel Marcel, and Franz Rosenzweig (a student of Hermann Cohen) independently arrived in the early twentieth century at what came to be known as the "principle of dialogue." The central aspect of this principle, the personal encounter between I and You, engages with the other as a subject, as a whole being, whereby the realization of the other brings us to a deep awareness of our self. By contrast, I-It encounters are characterized by description, analysis, detachment, and mastery.[6] To be sure, I-It kinds of relationships, better said experiences, are inevitable as they provide important useful information not unlike the objectifying *modus operandi* of science. Yet to dwell or live within this relationship as if it were primary leads to dehumanization and fragmentation, says Martin Buber, as human beings lose the power to relate and commu-

5. See D. Keith Campbell, "The American Evangelical Academy and the World: A Challenge to Practice more Globally," *JETS* 56/2 (June 2013): 337–54, for the need to shift the North American theologian's perspective from "*thinking* globally to *practicing* globally" (340). While including Michael Bird as a perspective outside of North America may not be considered diverse, his inclusion is designed to provoke the question, "What might inerrancy look like if other diverse voices outside of North America who seek to understand what it means to say 'Thy Word is Truth' were included?" Moreover, this emphasis should not preclude us from asking the same question within North America.

6. Martin Buber, *I and Thou*, trans. Walter Kaufmann (New York: Simon and Schuster, 1996), 53–85; see also Eugene Thomas Long, *Twentieth Century Western Philosophy of Religion 1900–2000* (Norwell, MA: Kluwer Academic, 2000), 215–34, for an overview of the principle of dialogue and its influence upon modern theology.

nity crumbles.[7] To dwell, though, within I-You kinds of relationships opens human persons up to love as I and You share a sense of mutuality, reciprocity, care, respect, compassion, commitment, and responsibility—those virtues that consider others before themselves. These kinds of encounters give way to a sense of something more, something that is more fulfilling than the immediate present. Buber maintains that God is wrapped up in this "more" and is thus the one who is the basis for and sustainer of all I-You relationships.[8] Yet how is God the basis for and sustainer of I-You relationships?

Franz Rosenzweig's contribution to the principle of dialogue focuses on divine revelation, for it is God's self-revelation in his address to human persons that not only calls human persons into being but also is the impetus for considering the other. It is the Creator's loving call, "Where are you?" and humanity's obedient, receptive response, "Here I am," says Rosenzweig, that reveals the love of God through the commandment, making it possible to love God and neighbor (Gen. 3; Deut. 6:5; Lev. 19:18).[9] Without God's self-revelation, humanity would be deaf, wrapped up in love of self. It is only in and through God's dialogical I-You encounter that humanity can recognize the other "not [as] a *'He-She-It', but an 'I',* ... not a travel acquaintance on a journey through time without beginning or end, but my brother, the consort of my destiny; ... my brother not in the world ... but in the Lord."[10] Hence, love of the other is predicated not on some common human nature but on God's self-revelation, his dialogical encounter with humanity.

Moreover, God's fuller self-revelation in Christ through the power of the Spirit reveals not only a more personal, dialogical encounter between God incarnate and humanity but also personal, dialogical encounters within the Godhead (e.g., John 17), namely between the Father, Son, and Holy Spirit. God's identity, then, is love—not just any kind of love but the greatest kind of love where one lays down his life for the other (John 15:13). That being said, God's love is dynamic, multifaceted, self-giving, sacrificial, and relational (1 Cor. 13). God's

7. Buber, *I and Thou*, 87–95.

8. Ibid., 123–28, 148–60.

9. Franz Rosenzweig, *The Star of Redemption*, trans. Barbara E. Galli (Madison: University of Wisconsin Press, 2005), 188–99.

10. Franz Rosenzweig, *The New Thinking*, trans. Alan Udoff and Barbara E. Galli (Syracuse: Syracuse University Press, 1999), 56.

love requires the other, not in the sense that he needs someone or something outside himself to be who he is. God's love is sufficient and is found within his triunity. Yet God's love is not self-seeking or self-promoting but self-giving. It cannot remain within himself. It must be sent. In short, God's sacrificial, self-giving love is the essence of the gospel in that he communicates himself (his self-giving love) through himself (his triunity) for the purpose of communing with us. God's love, therefore, can be understood only in and through relation, in and through dialogical encounter.

These dialogical encounters, though, are not mere events, mere occurrences, without existential import.[11] God's actions in the world matter. They affect not only human identity but also human action with deep existential and moral consequence. Ferdinand Ebner, in his journals from 1912, identified the ethical claim that extends from the divine I-You relationship, more specifically from God's act in Christ's death on the cross: "This is the most difficult problem for ethics: the recognition of the 'I' in the other, which actually constitutes the 'thou'; thus the 'thou' is posited as an ethical demand."[12] In other words, human persons come to realize their identity only in light of God's address in the person and work of Christ performed in the power of the Spirit, who gives the ethical demand to love God and neighbor. Personal identity is enveloped in God's sufficient, sacrificial, self-giving love and humanity's response to him. The realization of God's love comes by the Spirit when humanity obediently responds to Christ's demand for faith. In doing so, personal uniqueness is actualized and understood in and through fitting and faithful performances such that personal identity is not wrapped up in love of self but in love of the other, both God and neighbor (Luke 9:23).

As followers of Christ, dialogical encounters with others should manifest a particular disposition, characterized by Christian virtue and Christlike consideration of the other (Phil. 2). It's at this point that the dialogue principle is important for conversations on the doctrine of

---

11. As we indicated in the introduction, the use of the term *existential* should not be understood in a way that means the authors are committed to existentialist philosophy. Rather, the term is being used in a less technical sense to capture the way in which Christian teaching penetrates to the deepest core of one's identity and self-perception.

12. Ferdinand Ebner, *Schriften*, 3 vols. (Munich, 1963), 2.94.

inerrancy. A clear implication can be seen in the aforementioned discussion, albeit brief, regarding the ethics of inerrancy. Do conversations on this topic dwell within I-It kinds of relationships where description, analysis, detachment, and mastery are the focal point? Certainly, debate over concepts and ideas involve description, analysis, and clear reasoning. The question, though, is whether a turn toward the other, conceived in an I-You relationship, is made by seeking first to understand before being understood. In order to make this turn towards the other, performance of Christian virtues like patience, humility, and charity is necessary. In doing so, human frailties, finitude, and fallenness are acknowledged; possibilities for a fuller understanding of the matter (which would be unattainable otherwise) are opened; and true witness to the love of Christ at work in the world through the power of the Spirit is revealed.

One of the things that may not be so clear, though, regarding the implications of the dialogue principle for conversations on the doctrine of inerrancy is the relationship between form and content. As mentioned previously, God's chosen form of self-revelation comes through himself in a personal way, namely through the incarnate Christ in the Spirit. While he communicates a number of things about his identity in his personal, dialogical encounter with humanity, we noted that his self-giving, sacrificial love is the essence of the gospel. Yet understanding of this love is distorted and deformed if the trinitarian form in which God reveals himself is neglected, not to mention the personal manner in which he engages humanity through the life of Christ in the Spirit (Phil. 2:8). That being said, understanding of the content (God's self-giving love) is shaped by the manner or form (God's triunity) in which he communicates himself. The implication being that *how* we communicate content is just as important (perhaps more) as the content itself, both of which allude to the desires, thoughts, and intentions informing the action.

So when the medieval crusader raises his swashbuckling sword, looks to the heavens, and cries out saying, "Jesus is Lord!" while running the "infidel" through, his declaration that "Jesus is Lord" may be true on a *prima facie* level, but the manner in which he makes the declaration reveals his gross misunderstanding. He is in fact dead wrong, for the kingdom of God is not of this world (John 18:36)! As such, while arguments for a particular position on the doctrine of inerrancy may in fact turn out to be correct, the truth of the matter in effect is maligned and obscured when human action persists in ways that are ugly and unbecoming of Christ—in ways that fail to actualize a fitting disposition toward the other—particularly in our dialogical engagement with others. Hence, if the dialogue on the doctrine of inerrancy is to move forward, a fitting, Christlike disposition that considers the other is essential. How beautiful are the feet of those who fittingly perform the gospel (Rom. 10:15).

Situational Awareness: Lines of Continuity and Discontinuity

One of the difficulties of this project and particularly the perspectival arrangement was the danger that authors would simply talk past one another, confusing the matter even more. Keenly aware of this difficulty, we pressed authors through the editorial process to engage with the theological and biblical matters we outlined in the introduction, matters we believe expose the theological joints of the doctrine of inerrancy and are necessary to consider. As such, we asked authors to develop their position in light of the following: (1) God and his relationship to his creatures, (2) the doctrine of inspiration, (3) the nature of Scripture, and (4) the nature of truth. We also asked authors to consider the CSBI's historical contribution when developing their position and apply their perspective to three kinds of biblical texts that may pose as challenges to inerrancy. When examining the main essays and responses, keeping these parameters in mind, several lines of continuity and discontinuity emerged. While we wholeheartedly encourage readers to identify other important comparisons and contrasts, these lines are ones we believe will deepen evangelical faith and life, illumine the theological and hermeneutical decisions necessary to a doctrine of inerrancy, and hopefully advance a discussion that engenders fraternity rather than fratricide.

Each participant addressed how God relates to his creation through the notion of divine accommodation—the notion that the eternal God of the universe who is infinitely and qualitatively different from his creation reveals himself in a way that his finite creatures can understand him, albeit not exhaustively.[13] When considering the

---

13. Authors seem to have John Calvin's notion of divine accommodation in mind. See John Calvin, *Calvin: Institutes of the Christian Religion*, ed. John T. McNeil and trans. Ford Lewis Battles (Philadelphia: Westminster Press, 1960), 1.17.13, and for a secondary summation of Calvin's development of divine accommodation, see Ford Lewis Battles, "God Was Accommodating Himself to Human Capacity," *Interpretation* 31 (1977): 19–38.

doctrine of inerrancy, then, the question becomes *how* God speaks truth. Vanhoozer advocates a communicative model where God is true to the communicative action of his covenant by keeping his promises, a fittingness between word and deed. Franke contends that God descends to us through the use of human language with all of its cultural particularities and limitations such that the truth God speaks remains within those limitations. Michael Bird affirms God's accommodation of himself to the worldviews and expectations of human beings yet asserts that divine accommodation does not capitulate to error. Enns's understanding of God's accommodation to the historically situated human condition seems, though, to include such possibilities, even while God reigns amidst them. Mohler rejects such capitulation to error in God's divine accommodation, maintaining that human authors of Scripture were protected from all error by the Holy Spirit. Hence, participants converge on the notion that God graciously accommodates himself to human sensibilities, yet diverge when considering the manner, degree, and extent to which he does.

Inherent to discussing divine accommodation as it relates to biblical inerrancy is the doctrine of inspiration, the idea that God, through the Holy Spirit, enabled the human authors of Scripture to write what he desired to be written. The looming question is how God can preserve an inerrant text without supplanting human agency. Mohler argues for verbal-plenary inspiration of the Bible in that God, while respecting the particularities of human authors, has breathed out every last word of Scripture, going so far as to say that inerrancy "requires and defines verbal inspiration" (p. 37). While inerrancy for Vanhoozer does not require or define verbal inspiration, he operates from a much more nuanced understanding of it in that the Bible as verbally inspired "is an instance of dual-author (i.e., divine-human) discourse" where the biblical text is part of God's "divine triune discourse" (p. 214). Bird affirms to a certain degree of verbal inspiration, yet he emphasizes, following John Webster, God's sanctifying work that extends "to the human literary processes" and preserves "the meaning and power of God's Word to achieve the ends for which it was given" (p. 164). Similarly, Franke focuses on the Spirit's work to guide human speech-acts as they bear witness to God's divine speech-acts in and through Scripture and the church. Yet while biblical inspiration entails a proper relationship to God, the words of

Scripture are not divinized and are unable to "transcend their limitations as a finite creaturely medium" (p. 269). While Enns says little about inspiration in this essay, he makes an important point in that any notion of biblical truth must first reckon with the "energetic interplay of the Spirit of God working in and through ancient human authors" (p. 87).

From these snippets, there appears to be convergence, with the exception of Mohler, on the notion that inerrancy is a consequence of inspiration rather than a requirement of it. However, as Mohler aptly questions Vanhoozer regarding "where we are to locate the inspiration of the biblical text" (p. 240), this same question seems fitting to ask of all the authors. In doing so, divergences emerge. At what stage in the literary process does inspiration occur? Are the concepts and ideas inspired, or does inspiration extend to the very words and syntax of the text? If so, which text? Does inspiration occur at the textual locution, illocution, or perlocution? Or is the Spirit's work of union and communion present throughout the literary process? If so, how is human agency preserved?

How one parses divine inspiration as it relates to the production of the biblical text influences how one understands the nature of Scripture—namely, what kind of book are we dealing with? All participants converge on the idea that Holy Scripture is both divine and human. Yet how each understands these aspects leads to a number of differences. Operative among Enns's thought is an "incarnational" understanding of Scripture that sees God as present in the Spirit amidst the unabashed, historically conditioned textual phenomena of Scripture, which should have bearing on interpretative conclusions. Similarly, Franke ascribes to an incarnational analogy of Scripture, emphasizing the creaturely character of the biblical text without compromising it as a medium for the Word of God. Yet Franke develops the incarnational model further, noting how the Spirit speaks in and through the biblical text and uses it to call new eschatological realities into existence. This pneumatological instrumentality, Franke contends, is able to account for the plurality within Scripture as well as the plurality of Christian community. Mohler acknowledges the fruitfulness of the incarnational analogy, but he appeals to the debate regarding Christ's (im)peccability to highlight the fact that Scripture is still without error. The Bible is a divine-human book. Hence, when Scripture with all the marks of human particularity, language, and culture speaks, God speaks. Bird, while he recognizes the phenomenological and creaturely character of the biblical text, argues unequivocally that the incarnational model is based on a category mistake because it threatens the uniqueness of the Christ-event and divinizes the biblical text. Bird identifies Scripture, though, as divine and human based on the inner testimony of the Holy Spirit as a mode of God's self-communication in and through the exigent circumstances and particularities of the human authors. Finally, Vanhoozer sees Scripture as the triune God's personal communication to human beings through human language in that God speaks in and through the written discourse of the biblical authors.

To this point, the lines of continuity and discontinuity reveal the doctrinal intricacies involved when discussing inerrancy, for inerrancy is not a solo doctrine. Biblical inerrancy, though, raises another important issue, one that Pontius Pilate recognized when he asked Jesus during his trial, "What is truth?" (John 18:38). Some would argue that this is the heart of the matter and simply link the truth of Scripture directly to divine truthfulness. Such a quick move, as we indicated in the introduction, glosses over a number of doctrinal issues (foremost of which is the doctrine of God) and fails to even consider God's relationship to time. What emerges within the dialogue of the previous chapters regarding the nature of truth is an array of viewpoints, some of which overlap, others of which are implied, and some of which possess greater nuance. Yet all are anchored in their understanding of God. To be sure, this is a matter that requires further discussion and more careful consideration beyond this project.

Mohler's take on the nature of truth could be considered, in large part, as factual correspondence. In other words, the extralinguistic state of affairs in the Bible is accurately and precisely portrayed by the biblical authors. This does not mean that biblical truth is merely propositional, yet it does entail that there are "affirmations found within every text of Scripture—whatever its literary form" (p. 239). While not clearly defining what he means by affirmation, he seems to think, as evident in his response to Vanhoozer, that "affirmations are statements of fact" (p. 241). This understanding of truth leads him to conclude, whether considering the conquest narratives, the exodus, or Luke's account in Acts, that the Bible depicts these events as they actually happened. For Mohler, the truth of Scripture is anchored, then, in the *fact* that God is truth.

Enns also seems to be operating with a factual understanding of truth, though he does not state this explicitly. We draw this conclusion based upon his thinking that the Bible may be empirically false at times, which leads him to reject an understanding of inerrancy that understands truth primarily as factual (e.g., the Bible says that the walls of Jericho fell and archeological data says Jericho was a small, unwalled settlement). Yet Enns, while not developing this point, does state on a number occasions that any understanding of truth "must address as a first order of business the energetic interplay of the Spirit of God working in and through ancient human authors" (p. 87). In other words, when God speaks truth, he does so within the historical and cultural limitations of the biblical authors. And it's at this point where any discussion regarding the nature of truth should begin, particularly regarding the truth God speaks in and through Scripture. For Enns, the truth of Scripture is anchored, then, in God's willingness to be among us in the midst of our blindness, confusion, and ignorance.

Franke offers a much more nuanced understanding of truth that grapples with some of Enns's concerns. Franke presents an analogy by identifying truth as God knows and experiences it as ultimate truth, Truth with a capital *T*. Truth as we know and experience it is situated and fragmented, truth with a lowercase *t*. The link between the two, Franke contends, comes by inspiration, yet "inspiration does not enable them to transcend their limitations as a finite creaturely medium" (p. 269). The core element of Franke's understanding of truth is related to God's mission to the world, where God, in and through the Word and the Spirit, creates Christian communities of faith in particular sociolinguistic contexts that bear witness to the gospel and cohere in Christ. For Franke, the truth of Scripture is anchored, then, in the plurality and missional nature of God.

Vanhoozer also offers a nuanced understanding of truth, describing it as "covenantal correspondence." He considers the language of covenant to be "a communicative act that establishes or ratifies a personal relationship and aims at communion," where all language is in some sense "quasi-covenantal" (p. 216). As such, human language is a divinely ordained medium of communicative action designed for communion. Language, though, can be corrupted, chief of which is the lie leading not to communion but to alienation. Yet God proves himself to be "true" because there is "a faithful fit, between God's words and God's deeds" (p. 216). The nature of truth, then, as covenantal correspondence faithfully communicates what is. For Vanhoozer, the truth of Scripture is anchored in the fittingness between the words and deeds of the communicative, triune God.

The implicit notion in Bird's main essay regarding the nature of truth, which he makes more explicit in his responses, is a variant on the correspondence theory of truth, for there must be a "tangible connection between God's revelation of himself in Scripture and the reality to which the revelation attests" (p. 301). Moreover, while truth is more than but surely no less than propositional, it is also personal. Keenly aware of other theories of truth, he offers a christological sketch stating explicitly that "the proposition 'Jesus is Lord' is the key criterion for the *coherence* of any truth claim and the *pragmatic presupposition* for living a missional life" (p. 300). For Bird, the truth of Scripture is anchored, then, in the faithfulness of God to his Word.

While we don't see conversations from different perspectives as impossible, we do find them to be complex. Thus, we have endeavored to expose the various theological points of departure in a doctrine of inerrancy and have tried to sketch the contours of this debate by tracing various lines of continuity and discontinuity. There are, of course, other lines to trace. For example, the doctrine of God, God's actions in history, the nature of history, etc. In addition to the conversations generated between participants, we hope these four lines of inquiry we have outlined here begin to provide the kind of situational awareness necessary for a continued, fruitful dialogue. With the right disposition, we trust that new diverse lines of communication will open, enriching evangelical theology, faith, and life.

Opening Lines of Communication

As we stated at the outset, the doctrine of inerrancy is embedded within the compendium of Christian doctrine. More specifically, inerrancy is part of the doctrine of Scripture and is bound up at the very least with matters such as Scripture's sufficiency, perspicuity, reliability, and authority. The doctrine of Scripture, being a subset of divine revelation, also wrestles with matters of Scripture's inspiration, communication, and reception. When considering the subjective aspects of revelation's reception, the doctrine of salvation, Christ, the Holy Spirit, sin, humanity, and creation are also necessary to consider. In the end, the doctrine of revelation, including the doctrine of inerrancy, is ancillary to the doctrine of the Holy Spirit, Christology, and ultimately the triune God. This brief recap of the doctrinal nexus of inerrancy serves to remind us that inerrancy is shaped by a number of prior theological decisions. If lines of communication between various theological sensibilities are to emerge, then honesty about these intricacies should be prevalent.

After reflecting upon the entire project, the proposal we presented to the authors may in fact have been too robust to address in the limited space of this edited volume. Yet one of the chief goals of this project was not for it to be a be-all and end-all resource but rather for it to be a resource that we hope will generate new questions, new conversations that will include diverse voices about what it means to say, "Thy Word is Truth." With that being said, there are a number of fruitful lines of research not covered or fully developed in this volume that we believe should be considered when discussing the doctrine of inerrancy. What follows, then, is a sampling of the kinds of trajectories and questions that may deepen the discussion.

One of the underlying themes, pervading all the essays and responses, is the nature of history and God's actions in it, not to mention our subjective appropriation of God's revelatory acts in history. Eighteenth-century Enlightenment philosopher Gotthold Lessing leveled sharp criticisms against the historicity of Christian revelation, severing "the accidental truths of history" from the "necessary truths of reason," thereby creating an "ugly, broad ditch" between the so-called Christ of history and the Christ of faith.[14] This point is germane because much of the modern, Western church, particularly North American evangelicalism, has spent an inordinate amount of time trying to build a bridge across Lessing's ditch. But why do we even have to accept Lessing's premises? The "real distance," says Karl Barth, is "a problem of distance of quite another kind," namely between sinful

---

14. Gotthold E. Lessing, "On the Proof of the Spirit and of Power," in *Lessing's Theological Writings*, ed. Henry Chadwick (Stanford: Stanford University Press, 1956), 54–55.

humanity and a holy God.[15] Is God's self-revelation in Christ identical, then, with history? What might it mean to say that Jesus is Lord of history? Perhaps the matter rests not upon a distinction between historical contingency and the necessary truth of reason but rather upon an epistemic and existential one where knowledge of God in and through divine encounter is shaped by being conformed to Christ. We are beginning now to wade into deep theological waters, and longer, more sustained thought is needed to correlate a thicker understanding of history and God's actions in it with the truth God communicates to us in and through his written Word.

Another matter that deserves further consideration is the relationship between the truth God speaks and the various genres of Scripture. If God's Word written is utterly true and trustworthy, how do the various genres of Scripture communicate God's truth? Indeed this question is wrapped up with theological decisions regarding the doctrine of God, divine revelation and its subjective reception, divine inspiration, and the doctrine of Scripture. But there seems to be a linguistic point of which many biblical scholars are keenly aware. What does it mean to say that a poem is true? Is it the same as saying that a biblical narrative is true? What about apocalyptic writings? So when we say that the Bible is true and trustworthy, is our understanding of truth able to capture not only what the Bible says about truth (content) but also the various ways in which the Bible communicates truth in and through its various genres (form)? This seems to be one point where biblical scholars, theologians, and philosophers should be able to work together, exploring the nature and nuances of language and plunging the depths of theology. Moreover, if the truth communicated through various genres of Scripture does so in a variegated manner, what might this mean for biblical authority? It would seem that while Holy Scripture retains its primacy and remains authoritative, it does so with more texture. How, then, might this *text*ured account of truth and biblical authority affect our understanding of inerrancy?

Finally, a subset of the discussion on divine accommodation and God's relationship to his creation is the matter of the subjective reception of God's truth. Living in late modernity has brought this matter

---

15. Karl Barth, *Church Dogmatics*, IV/1, *The Doctrine of Reconciliation*, trans. G. W. Bromiley, ed. G. W. Bromiley and T. F. Torrance (Peabody, MA: Hendrickson, 2010), 290.

to the fore through postmodern reading strategies like reader-response theory, where interpreters play with a number of textual signs *ad infinitum* to construct meaning as they see fit. Despite the fact that such strategies tear at the very fabric of language and meaning, these strategies should alert us to the role that readers do have in receiving God's objective self-revelation, particularly as it relates to reading Holy Scripture. It seems on one level that readers are able to ascertain a measure of understanding through grammatical-historical interpretation. Yet when readers integrate the knowledge generated from their investigations without a deep existential and moral reordering, it begs the question of who is reading whom. Are readers seeking to master the text or be mastered by it? If readers approach the biblical text, though, with a proper measure of patience, humility, and willingness to listen and learn, readers are positioned to respond to what God is saying and doing in and through the text. How, then, might the doctrine of inerrancy be positioned within the compendium of Christian doctrine to account for the proper reception of God's truth?

Trevor Hart, in his book *Faith Thinking*, conceives of Christian theology as "faith thinking in community—the critical reflection which takes place within the community of the church."[16] This project has, in large part, been an exercise in "faith thinking" as we sought to spur a dialogue between various perspectives, albeit limited, on what it means to say that Holy Scripture is trustworthy and true. Engagement with the other, as we indicated in the previous section, necessitates an attentive ear prepared to listen and learn from the other, particularly from every tribe and nation. In doing so, this does not mean we jettison our various perspectives without due consideration but rather set out to persuade others that our perspective has a much better view of reality because it maps its various features and contours better than others. This kind of approach readily confronts us with the very real notion that we just might be persuaded ourselves, serving as a constant reminder to maintain our convictions both with humor and humility. Alas, we never intended, though, to instigate a dialogue simply for dialogue's sake. Instead, we set up the parameters of the project to foster the mutual enrichment and edification of evangelical faith and

---

16. Trevor Hart, *Faith Thinking: The Dynamics of Christian Theology* (Grand Rapids: InterVarsity, 1995), 230.

life. Most important, the dialogical nature of this project was designed to spur further dialogue, not simply with each other but with the triune God himself, whereby prayer becomes "the original research" of the theologian.[17] Hence, it is our prayer that as we engage with each other and with the living God of the Bible (Heb. 4:12) that "prayer [becomes a] dialogue, not man's monologue before God" in that "the essential thing is for us to hear God's word and discover from it how to respond to it."[18]

17. Ibid., 229. Hart has P. T. Forsyth in mind: "P. T. Forsyth sums the matter up nicely. Prayer, he informs us, is to the theologian what original research is to the scientist. It is that whereby we put ourselves in touch the reality to be known" (229).

18. Hans Urs von Balthasar, *Prayer*, trans. Graham Harrison (San Francisco: Ignatius Press, 1986), 14–15.

CONTRIBUTORS

Michael F. Bird (PhD, University of Queensland) is Lecturer in Theology at Ridley Melbourne Ministry and Mission College, and Honorary Research Associate at the University of Queensland in Australia. He is the author of *Jesus and the Origins of the Gentile Mission* and *The Saving Righteousness of God: Studies on Paul, Justification, and the New Perspective*. He is also co-moderator of the New Testament blog *Euangelion*.

Peter E. Enns (PhD. Harvard University) is a biblical scholar and teaches at Eastern University. He is author of several books including *Exodus* (NIV Application Commentary), *Inspiration and Incarnation: Evangelicals and the Problem of the Old Testament*, and *The Evolution of Adam: What the Bible Does and Doesn't Say about Human Origins*.

John R. Franke (PhD, University of Oxford) is Professor of Missional Theology at Yellowstone Theological Institute in Bozeman, Montana, and general coordinator for The Gospel and Our Culture Network in North America. He is the author of several books, including *Beyond Foundationalism: Shaping Theology in a Postmodern Context*; *The Character of Theology: An Introduction to Its Nature, Task, and Purpose*; *Barth for Armchair Theologians*; and *Manifold Witness: The Plurality of Truth*. His most recent book, *Missional Theology: Reforming Christianity for the Sake of the World*, is forthcoming from Baker Academic.

Stephen M. Garrett (PhD, Trinity Evangelical Divinity School) is an associate professor of Public Theology and the Philosophy of Religion in the Social Communications Institute at the Lithuanian University of Educational Sciences in Vilnius, Lithuania. He also serves as an academic fellow with Global Scholars. He is the author of *God's Beauty-in-Act: Participating in God's Suffering Glory*.

J. Merrick (MA, ThM, Trinity Evangelical Divinity School; PhD, University of Aberdeen) is Assistant Professor of Theology at Grand Canyon University, Phoenix, Arizona. Previously, he was Assistant Director for Theological Resources at Rutherford House, Edinburgh, Scotland.

R. Albert Mohler Jr. (PhD, Southern Baptist Theological Seminary) is president and Joseph Emerson Brown Professor of Christian Theology at The Southern Baptist Theological Seminary. He is the author of several books, including *Words from the Fire: Hearing the Voice of God in the Ten Commandments*, and is a contributor to *Is Hell for Real? Or Does Everyone Go to Heaven?*

Kevin J. Vanhoozer (PhD, Cambridge University) is Research Professor of Systematic Theology at Trinity Evangelical Divinity School. He is the author or editor of several books, including *The Drama of Doctrine* and *Remythologizing Theology: Divine Action, Passion, and Authorship.*

We want to hear from you. Please send your comments about this book to us in care of zreview@zondervan.com. Thank you.

 ZONDERVAN®